North Carolina Traveler

North Carolina Traveler

A Vacationer's
Guide to the
Mountains,
Piedmont,
and Coast

Edited by
Sunny Smith and
Ginny Turner

John F. Blair
Publisher
Winston-Salem, North
Carolina

Library of Congress Cataloging-in-Publication Data

North Carolina traveler : a vacationer's guide to the mountains,
  Piedmont, and coast / edited by Sunny Smith. — 5th ed.
      p.   cm.
  Includes index.
  ISBN 0-89587-175-0 (alk. paper)
    1. North Carolina—Guidebooks.   I. Turner, Ginny.
F252.3.N67   1997
917.5604'41—dc21   96–54234

Contents

The Piedmont 123

The Mountains 257

About the Contributors

Ginny Turner is a freelance writer whose travel articles have appeared in many national publications and major metropolitan newspapers. A Midwesterner by birth, she has lived in North Carolina for several years.

Sunny Smith is a recent graduate of the University of North Carolina at Chapel Hill. Born and bred in North Carolina, she has traveled the state extensively but has never been to Tennessee.

Edgar and Patricia Cheatham live in Charlotte and have contributed to Fodor travel guides and numerous other travel publications.

Rick Mashburn has written travel articles for *Travel and Leisure* magazine, the *New York Times*, and the *Washington Post*. He is a lifelong resident of North Carolina.

Ginger Moore, a freelance writer, contributes to a variety of publications on subjects ranging from business to travel. She has traveled from the North Carolina mountains to the coast.

Andrew Waters is a native North Carolinian currently residing in Winston-Salem. He is employed by Wake Forest University and just bought a new pickup.

Acknowledgments

The publisher gratefully acknowledges the assistance of the following individuals and groups who helped in the production of this book:

Quinn E. Capps, Dare County Tourist Bureau
Ann Thompson, Kitty Hawk Kites
Lloyd Childers, Currituck Beach Lighthouse
Cape Hatteras National Seashore
Oregon Inlet Fishing Center
Frisco Native American Museum and Natural History Center
Ann Ehringhaus
Carl Blake, Elizabeth City Chamber of Commerce
Penny Leary-Smith, Great Dismal Swamp Canal Welcome Center
Linda Jordan Eure, Historic Edenton
Nancy Nicholls, Edenton-Chowan Chamber of Commerce

Steve Allen, Historic Bath State Historic Site
Priscilla Hunter, Tryon Palace
Peter Driscoll
Lynne Scott, Craven County Convention and Visitors Bureau
Janis Williams, Carteret County Tourism Bureau
Doug Wolf, Dee Gee's in Morehead City
Neva Bridges, Rocking Chair Bookstore in Beaufort
Gary Smith, Cape Fear Coast Convention and Visitors Bureau
Cathy Myerow, Lower Cape Fear Historical Society, Inc.
Beth Hemingway, Hemingway's Books in Carolina Beach
Bridgette Del Pizzo, Pleasure Island Chamber of Commerce
Karen Sphar, Southport–Oak Island Chamber of Commerce
Mitzi York, South Brunswick Islands Chamber of Commerce
Barbara Lowell, Lowell's Bookworm in Holden Beach
Jim Lowell
Mary Davis, Little Professor Book Center on Oak Island
Bald Head Island Information Center
Sarah Goddin, Quail Ridge Books in Raleigh
Nancy Olson, Quail Ridge Books in Raleigh
Carolina Ballet
Nicole N. Galbo, Greater Raleigh Convention and Visitors
    Bureau
Betty M. Baker, Capital Area Visitor Center
Marcy Hege, International Focus, Inc.
A. Dale Coats, Duke Homestead and Tobacco Museum
Bennett Place State Historic Site
Edmund J. Purdy, Durham Convention and Visitors Bureau
Joel Harper, Chapel Hill–Carrboro Chamber of Commerce
Patricia E. Griffin, Chapel Hill–Orange County Visitors Bureau
Ken Smith, Fayetteville Area Convention and Visitors Bureau
Laurell Stanell, Pinehurst Convention and Visitors Bureau
Robert G. Stockton, Jr., Winston-Salem Chamber of Commerce
Laurie Thore, Greensboro Parks and Recreation Department
Gail Murphy, Greensboro Area Convention and Visitors Bureau
Sue Clark
Piedmont Environmental Center
Ron Stephens, High Point Convention and Visitors Bureau

Kaye Hist, Rowan Museum, Inc.
Willie Little, Museum of the New South
Gina King, Charlotte Convention and Visitors Bureau
John Barringer, Little Professor Book Center of Charlotte
Phil Noblitt, Blue Ridge Parkway
Beth Sander, Boone Convention and Visitors Bureau
Millie Barber, North Carolina High Country Host
Susan Gragg, Blowing Rock Chamber of Commerce
Judy Donaghy, Avery/Banner Elk Chamber of Commerce
Carolyn Sakowski
Linda Medford, Mitchell County Chamber of Commerce
Jo Lunsford Herron, Mountain Dance and Folk Festival, Inc.
Angie Chandler, Asheville Convention and Visitors Bureau
Jane Voorhees, Malaprop's Bookstore in Asheville
Kim Hewitt, Thomas Wolfe Memorial
Karen Baker, Henderson County Travel and Tourism
Anne Waters
Libby Freeman, Brevard Chamber of Commerce
Peggy Hansen, Highland Books in Brevard
Linda Harbuck, Franklin Area Chamber of Commerce
Nancy Gray, Great Smoky Mountains National Park
Nina Anderson, Museum of the Cherokee Indian
Charlie Sloan, Sloan's Bookstore in Waynesville
Scotty Ellis, Haywood County Tourism Development Authority
Susan Perkins, North Carolina Department of Environmental
    and Natural Resources
Anita Hudson, North Carolina Department of Transportation
North Carolina Division of Tourism, Film, and Sports
    Development
North Carolina Ski Areas Association

Photograph and Illustration Credits

John F. Blair, Publisher, gratefully acknowledges the cooperation and assistance of the North Carolina Division of Travel and Tourism for providing the photographs and illustrations used in this book and the North Carolina Department of Transportation for providing the maps.

Introduction

by Ginny Turner

North Carolina became my adopted home in 1985. Having lived in seven other states and traveled in 40 more, I have a good basis of comparison to say it's an appealing state to visit and a satisfying place to live.

This book profiles all the state's major destinations and attractions, plus a few minor ones even longtime residents may not be familiar with. And we've ferreted out just about everything interesting there is to see and do. We describe historic houses and modern art galleries, a 16th-century sailing ship, and a World War II battleship. We point out craft shops and farmers' markets and where to go for golf, fishing, hiking, surfing, and hang gliding.

Unquestionably, North Carolina has a lot to offer, and we hope this book will tempt readers to explore it.

Carolina Curiosities

The Tar Heel State has a few cultural oddities you'll soon discover as you travel. For example, people here "mash" elevator buttons and "carry" neighbors in carpools. Every year, the national media make a celebrity of the winner of the annual Hollerin' Contest down at Spiveys Corner. And if you should find yourself in the vicinity of Salisbury, you might want to sample a unique local product—a soft drink called Cheerwine.

When it comes to food, you'll hear more native lingo and lore. For instance, a barbecue is *not* a backyard cookout—it's a plate of chopped or sliced hickory-smoked pork served with coleslaw and hush puppies. And to ensure good luck for the coming year, you must have hoppin' John (black-eyed peas and rice) on New Year's Day.

One of the first things I noticed in North Carolina is that in warm weather, people spend a lot of time sitting on their porches watching the world go by. You'll see this anywhere you go in the state—even the humblest dwelling has a rocker or garden chair out front. I think it makes the people here seem friendlier. Even if you're a stranger, the locals will nod at you when they pass you walking down the street.

When my car broke down in the mountains, a 10-year-old boy entertained me with a magic show until the tow truck came. And once while I was having breakfast in a restaurant with my husband and our five-month-old son, our friendly waitress offered us a nugget of local child-rearing wisdom: "I don't know if it's an old wives' tale or not, but if you bump his behind on the back step, he won't have any trouble teething." We didn't take any chances. The baby was well bumped when we got home, and you know, that boy didn't have a bit of trouble with his teeth.

Tar Heels

Tar Heels, as the people of North Carolina are called, are proud of their state and their curious nickname. Originally, it was a derogatory term for the Southerners involved with the 17th-century export trade in pitch, turpentine, and pine tar. But a story that nails the tag on North Carolinians is related by Dr. William S. Powell, a noted North Carolina historian, in the March 1982 issue of *Tar Heel* magazine. During one Civil War battle in Virginia, only the North Carolina troops were able to hold their position. When they were asked by some Virginia soldiers who had retreated, "Any more tar down in the Old North State, boys?" they responded, "No, not a bit. Old Jeff [Confederate president Jefferson Davis] bought it all up." "What's he going to do with it?" the Virginians sneered. "He's going to put it on you'ns heels to make you stick better in the next fight." Hearing this story, General Robert E. Lee commented, "God bless the Tar Heel boys."

Now, the name Tar Heel refers to all North Carolina residents, but be sure to write it as two words, or you might get a chastising letter from the Society for the Eradication of the Spelling of Tar Heel as One Word.

How to Use This Book

North Carolina is divided into three distinct regions—the mountains, the Piedmont, and the coastal area. Each has a different economy and lifestyle. To make your traveling easier, we've divided this guidebook accordingly and put the regional listings into a logical geographical sequence. For example, the towns of the coastal plain and the attractions of the Outer Banks are listed not alphabetically but as you'd come to them when driving north to south.

A brief introduction to each destination explains how to get there and whom to contact for more information. Attractions are listed for each town. Additional information describes recreation options and side trips, giving you a complete rundown of what each destination offers.

Restaurants and Accommodations

Under every destination, you'll find restaurant and lodging recommendations. The entries are not comprehensive; they were selected to indicate a range, both in price and amenities. In researching this book, we visited them, but in no instance did we receive a complimentary meal or free lodging. To ensure this book's objectivity, we paid our own way.

We describe the location and mood of each restaurant and lodging, so you can tell if it's more suitable for romance or rambunctious kids. Because prices change rapidly, we have categorized restaurants and lodgings as *Inexpensive, Moderate, Expensive,* or *Deluxe.*

For accommodations, the breakdown is:

Inexpensive	Under $60 for a double room
Moderate	$60-95
Expensive	$95-125
Deluxe	Over $125

For restaurants, the breakdown is:

Inexpensive	Under $10 for one person's dinner
Moderate	$10-18
Expensive	Over $18

At the end of the book is an appendix that serves as a catchall for important information. For example, that's where you'll find information on the cost of fishing licenses and on where to write for bicycle touring maps.

From beginning to end, *North Carolina Traveler* is designed to be the most useful book available for exploring the many natural and man-made wonders of this state. We hope it will whet your appetite for some adventures of your own in North Carolina.

Courtesy of N.C. Department of Transportation

Shipwreck at South Nags Head, North Carolina
Photograph by William Russ
Courtesy of N.C. Travel and Tourism Division

The Coast

The eastern third of North Carolina—encompassing 39 of the state's counties—is made up of the coastal plain and the string of barrier islands known as the Outer Banks. The first English colony in the New World was established here, on Roanoke Island, and man's first powered flight lasted 12 seconds over the windy dunes of Kill Devil Hills. The area is probably best known as one of the most unspoiled regions on the Atlantic coast. With its miles upon miles of white-sand beaches—many of which are protected by the National Park Service as Cape Hatteras National Seashore—this national treasure offers fabulous recreational opportunities for those who like to swim, sun, surf, sail, and chase big fish.

Once the bottom of a prehistoric inland ocean, the coastal plain rises to an elevation of only 500 feet from its coastal estuaries through the swampy tidewater area to its flat, relatively treeless savanna.

The region's greatest resource—the coast itself—remained pristine for many years. Tourism began slowly because access to the barrier islands was limited; the first paved roads to the Outer Banks and down the smaller islands weren't built until 1930. But from the 1950s on, development has brought a great infusion of money to the area. Hotels, condominiums, and beach houses have sprung up as the coastal region's economic base has shifted to tourism.

Historic preservation became fashionable in the 1960s and 1970s, and many town officials learned that preserved history brought visitors. Several coastal towns that had fallen off the growth curve in the last century began major restoration efforts. As a result, the coastal plain is graced with beautiful historic districts in Bath, Edenton, New Bern, and Wilmington. These have become significant attractions in themselves. The state's best examples of historic houses from colonial times through the Victorian period are in this area.

As a counterpoint, the Outer Banks offer a great diversity of activities—swimming, shelling, camping, and dining on delicious fresh fish. Little wonder it exerts such a powerful magnetism.

To appreciate the variety of the state, your sojourn should include a visit to some part of the 300 miles of North Carolina's seacoast. Getting there from the inland area is not a very interesting drive—the scenery consists mostly of scrub trees, flat, marshy areas, some small farms, and very small towns with little to distinguish them. But once you're there, the coastal plain has much to offer—from strolling through New Bern's Tryon Palace to chugging out onto the Atlantic for deep-sea fishing.

The Outer Banks

Northern Banks and Beaches
Roanoke Island
Bodie Island
Hatteras Island
Ocracoke Island

by Ginger Moore

Visiting the Outer Banks means climbing sand dunes to fly a kite or to spot distant ships at sea. It means strolling through a quaint fishing village, hiking through a wildlife refuge, or casting a line in the surf to reel in mackerel. It means joining summer crowds on white-sand beaches or waiting in line to get your fill of fresh local seafood. A visit here is what you make it, and thousands of people make it every summer.

The beaches themselves—the biggest attraction—are considered by many to be the East Coast's finest. The Banks offer miles of pristine beaches protected from development as part of Cape Lookout and Cape Hatteras National Seashores. Travelers can also visit more populated beach areas, such as Nags Head.

Wind and waves are steadily altering the topography of the 130-mile string of sandy islands that make up the Outer Banks. Inlets have opened and closed; wide beaches have washed away. Bridges have been built to link the coastal plain with the barrier islands that protect it from the worst Atlantic weather. And that weather is no joke—the raging sea has claimed hundreds of ships off the Carolina coast in the last few centuries. So many ships have been destroyed—including the Civil War ironclad *Monitor*—that the Outer Banks have acquired the nickname "Graveyard of the Atlantic."

However, most bad weather is limited to the autumn hurricane season and the winter nor'easters. Spring and summer weather is usually much less dramatic. It can be fickle, though—showers often blow in quickly from the sea, but the sun can reappear quickly, too.

Because many Outer Banks residents—known as "Bankers"—have come from Virginia, we'll follow their north-to-south route to explore this region. The Banks are easily divided into four areas: the northern banks and beaches, including Nags Head and Kitty Hawk; Roanoke Island; Bodie and Hatteras Islands; and Ocracoke Island.

The longest stretch of undeveloped seashore on the East Coast, Cape Hatteras National Seashore extends 72 miles across three islands: the southern part of Bodie Island and all of Hatteras and Ocracoke Islands. Had it not been designated a national park in 1935 (the first park of its kind), the area certainly would have been developed the same way Nags Head was. Anyone who's seen and enjoyed the national seashore's beaches, wildlife, and natural vegetation has good reason to be thankful.

From Currituck to Ocracoke, you'll find the geography of the islands similar, but each area has its own personality. While driving the Banks in one day is possible, it won't allow you time to stop and see the highlights.

The surf remains warm enough for swimming for at least half the year, although the water temperature in May and September can be a nippy 60 degrees. The average water temperature during the summer is usually in the mid- to high 70s.

The Banks are also popular with surfers, particularly in late September, when offshore storms and hurricanes produce high waves.

Shell collectors will find a plethora of clam, scallop, and delicate butterfly shells, as well as some sand dollars and starfish.

The "season" along the Banks depends upon the weather, but Memorial Day through Labor Day normally defines the area's prime vacation time. With the warm Gulf Stream only 30 or so miles offshore, however, the season easily lasts through Thanksgiving and begins again around Easter.

Winter months along the Banks can be cold and stormy, although beach communities operate year-round.

A wide variety of accommodations can be found here, from a few resort hotels to family motels to campgrounds. As with most ocean communities, it is good advice to plan ahead. But the best advice is to come prepared to take life a little slower, to enjoy the surf, sand, and seafood—to get in touch with nature.

ACCESS:

Coming by land from the north, cross Currituck Sound on U.S. 158 via the Wright Memorial Bridge. To reach the northern communities of Duck, Sanderling, and Southern Shores, turn left onto N.C. 12. To reach the southern communities of Kitty Hawk, Kill Devil Hills, and Nags Head, turn right onto either U.S. 158 (Croatan Highway) or N.C. 12 (Virginia Dare Trail, also called the Beach Road).

Coming by land from the south, you can board either the Swan Quarter ferry or the Cedar Island ferry for Ocracoke Island. Both rides take about two and a half hours. Reservations are required in summer and are advised year-round. From the Ocracoke ferry dock, follow N.C. 12 all the way up the Outer Banks, interrupted only by a 40-minute ferry ride from Ocracoke to Hatteras.

Traveling from central North Carolina, take U.S. 64 east to Roanoke Island.

Special Note: Along U.S. 158 and N.C. 12, directions are noted by mileposts (e.g., Milepost 8), measured southward from the Wright Memorial Bridge. In the following pages, these will be used in describing locations. Rather than attempting to read addresses, you'll find this an easier way to locate everything. Even most locals use mileposts instead of street addresses.

The Dare County Regional Airport is located on S.R. 116 (Airport Road) in Manteo. It has runways of 3,290 feet and 4,300 feet. Fuel and services are offered. Call 252-473-2600.

The airport is also a hub for Southeast Airlines, which offers charter flights to and from other cities. Rental cars and limousine services are available at the airport. Kill Devil Hills, Hatteras Island, and Ocracoke Island have paved landing strips but no services.

While taxi and limousine services are available in the area, you'll need either a car or a bicycle to get around most of the Outer Banks.

VISITOR INFORMATION:

The Aycock Brown Welcome Center, located on U.S. 158 at Milepost 1.5, just over the Wright Memorial Bridge, is open from 8:30 A.M. to 5 P.M.; it offers later hours in the summer. A visitor center is open from 10 A.M. to 6 P.M. from mid-March through November on the north end of Roanoke Island, while a visitor center at the entrance to Cape Hatteras National Seashore at Whalebone Junction is open daily from 9 A.M. to 5 P.M. from mid-March through November. The centers provide information about activities, lodging, rental property, and visitor attractions. While planning your trip, contact the Dare County Tourist Bureau, P.O. Box 399, 704 U.S. 64/264, Manteo, N.C. 27954 (252-473-2138 or 800-446-6262).

Northern Banks and Beaches ....

On most maps, the road doesn't continue past Corolla. Actually, there is a direct road from Corolla to Corova, but it is only passable with four-wheel-drive vehicles. Between Corolla and the Virginia border, there are a few rural farms and tiny villages linked by dirt roads and narrow paved roads, plus a handful of roadside shops. Development has been avoided for now, and you won't find anyone in this area complaining. Hunting and fishing camps are the attraction here, where people work as decoy carvers and hunting guides.

It's hard to hold back "progress," though. Eager developers are buying up some of the last pristine beaches on the East Coast. Large beach homes have been built on the sand, and numerous ocean-to-sound communities have been developed, stirring mixed emotions among longtime residents.

Driving south through Sanderling, Duck, and Southern Shores is almost like watching a time exposure. You can practically see developments unfolding and boutiques, gift shops, and water-sports areas filling in the empty spaces. The town of Duck was once known for duck hunting (what else?) but is now noted for its pricey planned communities with solar-heated swimming pools and sailing docks, which attract those who can afford this rare piece of land as a vacation home. South of Southern Shores, commerce really picks up in Kitty Hawk and Kill Devil Hills and is moving at full bore in Nags Head.

Years ago, Kitty Hawk (called Chickahauk by the native Indians) was a small fishing village. Orville and Wilbur Wright sought out the wide-open spaces here to test their gliders. Actually, they set up camp farther south at Kill Devil Hills. There, they later piloted the first power-driven aircraft. The largest sand dune, Big Kill Devil Hill, is now the site of the Wright Brothers National Memorial.

Today, Kitty Hawk is no longer that remote site that attracted the Wright brothers. Bridges link the area to the mainland, and real-estate values are high. But despite the commercial and residential development, Kitty Hawk and Kill Devil Hills still provide a beach-town environment for vacationers and year-round residents.

Nags Head, just seven miles down the road, was the first area along the Outer Banks to be developed. According to legend, Nags Head earned its name in the late 18th century when Bankers hung lanterns around the necks of their horses to confuse merchant skippers into thinking they were heading into a safe harbor. When their ships ran aground on the shoals, Bankers pillaged their cargoes.

Two hundred years later, Nags Head is hardly a tranquil summer retreat. Some of those who spent the summers of their youth here say it hurts to see Nags Head now—crowded with motels, condominiums, restaurants, and shops.

Still, it isn't as developed as Myrtle Beach. Nags Head has retained a little rusticity and boasts its share of quality attractions. For a place that became a resort around 1838, Nags Head has been popular with beachgoers for a long time.

Attractions

Tours

Historically Speaking's Outer Banks Tours offers step-on or complete tours for motor-coach groups; call 252-473-5783.

Kitty Hawk Aero Tours (252-441-4460) and **Southeast Air Tours** (252-473-3222) offer scenic aerial tours of the Outer Banks and Roanoke Island.

Historic Places

The **Wright Brothers National Memorial**, at Milepost 8 on U.S. 158 in Kill Devil Hills, commemorates one of America's favorite moments in history, when two ordinary men took the first step into a new technological age. Although the Wright brothers' claim has been persistently challenged by some aeronautical historians who believe a Connecticut pilot beat them to it, North Carolinians, whose license plates boast "First in Flight," aren't likely to forfeit the distinction to New England.

Before Wilbur and Orville Wright flew their heavier-than-air flying machine, the two bicycle repairmen from Ohio spent three summers studying aerodynamics at Kitty Hawk and Kill Devil Hills. They made more than 1,000 flights in gliders, taking off into the wind and landing in the soft sand. Once they discovered how to control the glider, they went home to Dayton to make a powered flying machine. Back on the Carolina dunes in December 1903, Orville climbed aboard the Wright Flyer. Facing a 27-mile-per-hour wind, Orville—with the aid of sturdy helpers from the Kill Devil Hills Lifesaving Station—lifted off and was airborne for a momentous 12 seconds. The Wright brothers made three more flights that day, taking turns at the controls. But when a gust of wind overturned the plane on the

The Wright Brothers National Memorial
Photograph by William Russ
Courtesy of N.C. Travel and Tourism Division

ground, they were finished for the season.

The visitor center at the memorial, administered by the National Park Service, features displays on flight principles and the evolution of the Wrights' plane. Particularly striking are the full-scale reproductions of one of their gliders and the Wright Flyer. There's a good bookstore and a seating area decorated with paintings of aviation pioneers, where park-service personnel give talks about the first flight. Outside are two sheds that reproduce the Wrights' living quarters and workshop. Markers on the grounds indicate the length of the first four flights. You can walk them easily—the first flight was only 120 feet. The granite monument—60 feet high atop the 90-foot Big Kill Devil Hill—is floodlit at night. If you walk around it, you can see bronze busts of the brothers. The visitor center is open every day except Christmas. Summer hours are from 9 A.M. to 6 P.M. and winter hours from 9 A.M. to 5 P.M. Admission is $2 per person or $4 per car.

The National Park Service is planning several special events over the next few years to honor the 100th anniversary of the first flight, culminating in a celebration on December 17, 2003. Call the memorial at 252-441-7430 for more details.

Colington Island, accessible by a road just south of the Wright Brothers National Memorial, is a small island named for Sir John Colington. This was the site of the first permanent settlement on the Outer Banks. The scenic five-mile ride passes campgrounds and seafood shops and offers nice photo opportunities.

Currituck Beach Lighthouse in Corolla, completed in 1875, still flashes its 50,000-candlepower beam toward the sea today. The 162-foot red-brick structure with its 214 steps is the northernmost of the four lighthouses on the Outer Banks. Park your car nearby and follow the path to the lighthouse to get a closer look or climb to the top. The lighthouse is open to the public daily from 10 A.M. to 6 P.M. from April to November. Admission is $4 per person. Call 252-453-4939.

The keeper's house, located nearby, is undergoing a phased restoration. Built in 1876, the house fell into disrepair after the lighthouse went to an automated system. The exterior restoration of the house is nearly complete, but much of the interior is still undergoing renovation, but visitors may walk the grounds to get a sense of what it was like to tend to a lighthouse. North of the keeper's house is a smaller dwelling probably used as another keeper's house. Today, it serves as a museum shop. Books, lighthouse models, and information on the wild horses of Corolla are available here. The

The Currituck Beach Lighthouse
Photograph by William Russ
Courtesy of N.C. Travel and Tourism Division

hours are the same as those of the lighthouse.

Museums/Science Centers

Coastal Engineering Research Center, on the beach in Duck, is an 1,800-foot research pier managed by the United States Army Corps of Engineers. Center personnel monitor waves, tides, wind, and currents—in other words, what's happening to the beaches. Tours are offered Monday through Friday at 10 A.M. from mid-June to August.

Cultural Offerings

While the cultural scope of this area doesn't include much in the way of theater or concerts, the visual arts are well represented in a number of art galleries from Duck to Nags Head. Perhaps the best known of them is **Glenn Eure's Ghost Fleet Gallery** (252-441-6584), located at Milepost 10.5 on Gallery Row in Nags Head. The unofficial center for cultural events on the Banks, the gallery hosts poetry readings, art shows, and lectures. It also has a unique printmaking workshop. **Lighthouse Gallery and Gifts** (800-579-2827), at 301 East Driftwood Street in Nags Head, has been constructed using original U.S. Lighthouse Service plans. The structure offers an interesting glimpse at turn-of-the-century coastal life, and the shop features original works of art. **Seaside Art**

Gallery (252-**441**-**5418**), at Milepost 11 on Beach Road in Nags Head, enjoys a reputation as one of the South's most outstanding galleries, featuring original works of art by Chagall, Dali, Picasso, and Whistler. **Morales Art Gallery** has two locations, one at Milepost 10.5, 207 East Gallery Row in Nags Head (252-441-6484) and the other at Scarborough Faire in Duck (252-261-7190 or 800-635-6035). Both locations have a main art gallery featuring original art and a print gallery with limited-edition prints. Both locations also feature pottery, sculpture, and duck-stamp prints. **Greenleaf Gallery** (252-261-2009), located in Duck, offers contemporary fine art, featuring works by nationally recognized artists in many media.

Recreation

Recreational opportunities abound along the northern beaches, a favorite spot for fishing, water-skiing, surfing, hang gliding, and plain old swimming. Not all the beach areas have lifeguards, however, so remember always to swim with a partner. Currents are strong, and those magnificent waves can quickly carry you farther out than you'd like to go.

Jockey's Ridge State Park, at Milepost 12 on U.S. 158, is a giant sand dune beckoning to be climbed. The park, covering over 420 acres, features the East Coast's highest sand-dune formation—a large, isolated hill of sand and a smaller one. The elements are slowly moving the dunes in a southwesterly direction; you can see a corona of blowing sand on windy days. If you've ever wondered what it feels like to traverse the Sahara, tackle this on a warm afternoon. Shifting sands make the climb seem like a walk in another dimension. Once at the top, you may encounter some brave hang gliders and champion kite fliers. Rangers offer natural-history programs during the summer. The parking lot is north of the park. Even if you're unwilling to climb the dunes, you'll enjoy watching the kite fliers and hang gliders on the new wheelchair-accessible boardwalk. A new interpretive center opened in 1997

Hang gliding at Jockey's Ridge State Park
Photograph by T&T
Courtesy of N.C. Travel and Tourism Division

and includes a museum. Hours are seasonal, so you may want to call ahead. Admission is free. Call 252-441-7132.

If you've ever entertained the idea of hang gliding, this is the place to give it a try. **Kitty Hawk Kites** and Jockey's Ridge are the center for this sport. Kitty Hawk Kites offers several packages with hang-gliding lessons. Beginner lessons are usually three hours long (five flights) and cost about $75. A package entitled "Taste of Flight" includes the three-hour beginner lessons in Nags Head and a subsequent flight 50 minutes north in Currituck. An airplane takes a tandem glider to an altitude of 1,500 or 2,000 feet and there releases the beginner and an instructor; the beginner is then allowed to command the glider until the point of landing. Prices range from $95 for 1,500 feet to $105 for 2,000 feet. Kitty Hawk Kites also has a 21-foot artificial climbing wall for those who want to attempt that sport. It rents roller blades and, of course, sells a wide array of kites. Call 252-441-4124 or 800-334-4777.

Windsurfing and surfing are more popular on Hatteras Island, but boards and equipment are also plentiful here. **Kitty Hawk Sports** has several locations along the Outer Banks, with two of the stores offering equipment rental. The Nags Head location, at Milepost 13 opposite Jockey's Ridge State Park, offers windsurfing and kayaking equipment; call 252-441-6800. The **Kitty Hawk Sports Sailing Center** is located at Milepost 16, near Windmill Point Restaurant. It offers windsurfing and sailing lessons and rents catamarans, kayaks, and other sailing and windsurfing equipment. It also serves as a test center for some of the major brands of windsurfing equipment, so you can try out the latest; call 252-441-2756. **The Waterworks**, located at Milepost 17 on U.S. 158 in Nags Head, provides Jet Skis, day sailers, kayaks, and more; call 252-441-8875.

Grass putting courses have become the rage among golfers on the Outer Banks. There are two courses in Kitty Hawk. **Bermuda Greens** (252-261-0101) is located at the intersection of U.S. 158 and N.C. 12. It offers golf and a video-game center. **The Promenade** (252-261-4900) is located at Milepost 1 on U.S. 158. Golfing in its various forms is the focus here; the facilities include miniature golf, a grass putting course, and a driving range. You can also rent Jet Skis, sailboats, and powerboats.

Fishing from the piers is good here, particularly for such inshore favorites as bluefish, flounder, spot, king mackerel, cobia, and speckled trout. **Kitty Hawk Pier** is lighted and privately owned and offers a restaurant open at 6 A.M. for those wanting to grab a quick breakfast. It is open year-round; call 252-261-2772. **Avalon Fishing Pier** is also lighted; call 252-441-7494. **Nags Head Fishing Pier**, also privately owned, has similar features and a game room to entertain the children or the fishermen when the fish aren't cooperating. Open 24 hours, it'll even cook the fish you catch. Call 252-441-5141. You can try your luck at **Outer Banks Fishing Pier** 24 hours a day from early spring to late fall. Call 252-441-5740. All the piers charge admission, usually around $5 a day; weekly and seasonal passes are available. If you're a spectator, expect to part with a dollar for the privilege.

Golf and tennis are available throughout the area. Some resorts and hotels have private tennis courts. **Pine Island Indoor Racquet Club** offers indoor tennis and racquetball courts and frequently hosts major tournaments; call 252-453-8525. There are three golf courses open to the public: **Sea Scape Golf Club** (252-261-2158), **Nags Head Golf Links** (252-441-8073), and **Ocean Edge Golf Course** (252-995-4100) on Hatteras Island. Reservations are necessary.

If camping appeals to you, there are a few facilities to choose from: **Colington Park Campground** (252-441-6128) and **Joe and Kay's Campground** (252-441-5468) are both located on Colington Island, while **Andy's Travel Park** (252-441-5251) is located at Milepost 15.5 on U.S. 158 in Nags Head.

Seasonal Events

Seasonal events center around fishing tournaments (usually from May to November), hang gliding, windsurfing, and kite festivals. The **Annual Hang-Gliding Spectacular** is the oldest continuously held hang-gliding event in the country. It takes place in early May. The **Annual Wright Kite Festival** is held at Wright Brothers National Memorial every July. Call 252-441-4124. The **Wacky Watermelon Weekend and Windsurfing Regatta**, held in August, is a weekend filled with crazy watermelon games, a visit from the Watermelon Queen, and a windsurfing regatta. Call 252-441-6800.

The anniversary of the first flight is celebrated at Wright Brothers National Memorial each December. For information, contact the First Flight Society at 252-441-7430.

Accommodations

The worst thing about accommodations in this area may be narrowing down the long list of choices. Despite the abundance of places to stay, you'll need to make reservations in advance for high season, particularly for weekends. Your choices range from resort hotels with ocean views, pools, and on-site dining to 1950s-style small motels that cater to fishermen needing only a comfortable bed and families seeking a friendly place that won't empty their wallets before they get to the area's eateries. Most hotels are air-conditioned, and many provide in-room refrigerators. A minimum stay may be required for weekends. If you're traveling off-season, be sure to inquire about special rates.

The Sanderling Inn. *Expensive/Deluxe*. 1461 Duck Road, Duck (252-261-4111 or 800-701-4111). This definitely qualifies as resort material in quiet surroundings. The rooms and spacious suites are tastefully decorated. All rooms boast either a kitchenette or a wet bar, a microwave, private porches, and other first-class amenities. A welcome bag and wine await you, along with a staff trained to make you feel like a very important person. Indoor and outdoor pools, a health club with saunas, a sun deck, tennis courts, and a private beach complete the picture. The inn serves a complimentary buffet breakfast and afternoon tea.

Quality Inn—John Yancey Motor Hotel. *Moderate/Expensive*. Milepost 10, Kill Devil Hills (252-441-7141 or 800-592-6239). This has long been a Banks favorite for families. Regular rooms, efficiencies, and family units all come with color cable TV and refrigerators; many are oceanfront and offer patios or balconies. Rooms with hot tubs are available. A pool and a playground are offered. Children under 12 stay free.

Surf Side Motel. *Moderate/Expensive*. Milepost 16, Nags Head (252-441-2105). You'll find spacious, tastefully decorated rooms with ocean or sound views, private balconies, phones, cable TV, and complimentary continental breakfast here. Loft suites and a honeymoon suite with a Jacuzzi are also available. A wine-and-cheese hour brings guests together in the evening. An outdoor pool and a heated indoor pool are offered.

Quality Inn—Sea Oatel. *Moderate/Expensive*. Milepost 16.5, Nags Head (252-441-7191 or 800-440-4FUN). This motel features 111 units, many with balconies on the oceanfront. Its clean, comfortable rooms include phones and cable TV with HBO. It also offers an outdoor pool.

Comfort Inn North Oceanfront. *Moderate/Expensive*. Milepost 8, 401 Virginia Dare Trail, Kill Devil Hills (252-480-2600 or 800-854-5286). This inn offers an oceanfront location within view of Wright Brothers National Memorial. All rooms have color cable TV with HBO. The oceanfront rooms have a microwave, a refrigerator, and a work area with a sleeper sofa. The inn offers an oceanfront swimming pool.

Holiday Inn Express—Kitty Hawk Beach. *Moderate/Expensive*. Near Milepost 4.5, 3919 North Croatan Highway, Kitty Hawk (252-261-4888 or 800-836-2753). This two-story brick motel has 98 comfortable rooms featuring phones and cable TV with HBO. It also offers an outdoor pool. There is no charge for children under 17.

Quality Inn Sea Ranch Hotel. *Moderate*. Milepost 7, Kill Devil Hills (252-441-7126 or 800-228-5151). This was one of the Banks' first resort hotels, and its amenities (heated pool, cable TV, golf privileges, health club, and beauty salon) still make it a popular choice. All units have mini-refrigerators and microwaves. The condominium section features 28 two-bedroom suites. The restaurant is open for breakfast and dinner, and the lounge offers entertainment and dancing.

Tanya's Ocean House. *Moderate*. Milepost 9.5, Kill Devil Hills (252-441-2900). Tanya's qualifies as one of the area's surprise accommodations. From the outside, the motel resembles many others, with a courtyard arrangement around the pool, single-level brick units, and the lobby at the front. But once inside, you'll find that each individually decorated room has a special name, such as Outer Banks Unicorn, Waterlily (yes, there's a waterbed), and Wright Brothers' Camp. The rooms all have refrigerators and cable TV with HBO, and the oceanfront rooms offer a microwave. Tanya's is closed during the off-season.

Budget Host Inn. *Moderate*. Milepost 9, Kill Devil Hills (252-441-8602 or 800-BUD-HOST). This inn's reasonable rates and 40 clean rooms with king-size beds or two double beds make it a good choice.

Restaurants

The Nags Head area hardly lacks places to eat. During the high season, however, be prepared to wait in line. Some restaurants take reservations, but usually only for large groups. Seafood is the bestseller. Many restaurants also offer pasta, salads, beef, and chicken. In general, food is fried, though more restaurants are offering broiled and grilled entrées. Whatever your selection, you won't eat cheaply unless you take advantage of daily or early-bird specials. These beach towns now serve liquor by the drink, unlike Roanoke Island and points south, where only beer and wine are served.

Sanderling Inn Restaurant. *Moderate/Expensive.* Next to the Sanderling Inn in Duck (252-449-6654). Housed in the restored Caffey's Inlet Lifesaving Station and decorated with its memorabilia, this inviting restaurant offers Southern cuisine in a casual setting. All meals are accompanied by freshly baked bread and pastries. Selections include such specialties as shrimp-salad croissants, Oregon Inlet tuna, and triple chocolate mousse cake. The Sanderling also makes its own ice cream. The bar offers ocean and sound views and an outside deck. Reservations for dinner are strongly suggested. A breakfast buffet, lunch, dinner, and Sunday brunch are served.

Port O' Call. *Moderate/Expensive.* Milepost 8.5, Kill Devil Hills (252-441-7484). Port O' Call is really something to behold, particularly among the more casual establishments along Beach Road. Gourmet tastes are catered to here with candlelight and elegant table settings and furnishings. If you like Victorian style, you'll enjoy a drink or live entertainment in the Gaslight Saloon. An extensive menu includes scallops St. Jacques, Wiener schnitzel, veal Marsala, salmon, crabmeat, and prime rib. Save room for the homemade desserts and special-blend coffee. Dinner is served daily from March to January.

Etheridge. *Moderate/Expensive.* Milepost 9.5, Kill Devil Hills (252-441-2645). Etheridge guarantees fresh seafood, since the family owns the fish company by the same name in Wanchese. To keep the family atmosphere, all the menu selections are named after family members and people who work here. Try "Mama's Famous Fish Cakes" or "Galley Cook Stella's Lasagna." A children's menu is available. The restaurant also offers a full bar. Lunch and dinner are served daily from April to December.

Kelly's Outer Banks Restaurant and Tavern. *Moderate/Expensive.* Milepost 10.5, U.S. 158 in Nags Head (252-441-4116). Kelly's is decorated with mounted fish and wildlife, as well as bright brass fixtures and stained-glass windows in the raw bar. Mike Kelly likes to make the rounds to greet his guests. Selections include seafood, pasta, beef, chicken, and the chef's evening selection. The restaurant offers a full bar. Kelly's is open daily for dinner.

Elizabeth's Cafe & Winery *Moderate/Expe*nsive. Scarborough Faire in Duck (252-261-6145). This highly acclaimed, award-winning restaurant serves food cooked French-bistro style. Its wine list was cited in *Wine Merchant* as one of the 245 best restaurant wine lists in the world. The restaurant has style and charm but retains the casual atmosphere of the beach. Live jazz is performed in the courtyard when weather permits. Lunch is served Wednesday through Saturday, and dinner is offered nightly.

Penguin Isle Soundside Grill. *Moderate*. Milepost 16, U.S. 158 in Nags Head (252-441-2637). Almost all the tables in this restaurant offer a view of the sunset over Roanoke Sound. The specialties here are nouvelle seafood and island cuisine. Dinner is served nightly.

The Blue Point Bar and Grill. *Moderate*. Waterfront Shops in Duck (252-261-8090). The Blue Point serves an eclectic menu featuring contemporary Southern cooking (crab cakes, jambalaya, seasonal fish and game) in a space decorated to resemble a 1950s-style diner. Lunch and dinner are served daily.

Quagmire's. Moderate. Milepost 7.5, U.S. 12 (252-441-7232). Located in the historic Old Croatan Inn, this restaurant features gourmet Mexican and Carribean dishes which rely heavily on seafood ingredients. It also serves great Margaritas. In the summer, the sand volleyball court on the adjoining beach is in constant use. Lunch and dinner are served daily.

Black Pelican Seafood Company. *Moderate*. Milepost 4, U.S. 12 in Kitty Hawk (252-261-3171). Several years ago, new owners restored and revitalized this oceanfront standard. This restaurant offers deck-side dining in a cafe-style setting. A wood-fired pizza oven produces gourmet pizza. The fresh seafood and the raw bar are also popular. Lunch and dinner are served daily.

Goombay's Grille and Raw Bar. *Moderate*. Milepost 7.5, U.S. 158 in Kill Devil Hills (252-441-6001). This restaurant provides a cheery, colorful setting and specializes in fresh local seafood with a Caribbean flair. It also offers a raw bar and great sandwiches. Lunch and dinner are served daily year-round.

RV's. *Moderate*. Manteo–Nags Head Causeway at the end of the bypass (252-441-4963). RV's provides a casual setting with screened decks for eating outside in pleasant weather. The menu features everything from nachos to sautéed crabmeat to mesquite-grilled fish to beef dishes. The lounge is a favorite nightspot. A full bar is offered. Lunch and dinner are served daily.

Sam & Omie's. *Inexpensive/Moderate*. Milepost 16.5, Nags Head (252-441-7366). This restaurant has been a Banks tradition for 40 years. In many ways, this is the Outer Banks—the "put on you cutoffs and kick back" side of the Banks. Here, you'll meet some locals, many fishermen, and beachcombers with tales to tell. The restaurant is centered around a full-service bar, where guests can sit in booths or at small tables. The pool-table area also draws a crowd, and things can get noisy. The staff is friendly, the food good, and the prices fair. You can take home a souvenir T-shirt with Sam & Omie's motto: "Everyone should believe in something . . . I believe I'll go fishing." Breakfast, lunch, and dinner are served daily year-round.

Awful Arthur's. *Inexpensive/Moderate*. Milepost 6, U.S. 12 in Kill Devil Hills (252-441-5955). Awful Arthur's is another local hang-out. It offers a full menu of beef and seafood. If you want a cold beer, a dozen oysters, or steamed shrimp in a casual atmosphere, this is the place. Lunch and dinner are served year-round.

Roanoke Island

Lying between the barrier islands and the mainland of North Carolina, Roanoke Island has been the site of several important historic events—including the founding of the first British colony in the New World, 20 years before Jamestown and 43 years before Plymouth Rock. The settlement, now known as the Lost Colony, did not survive. Fort Raleigh, a re-creation of an earthwork fort most likely constructed by a military party established at the site prior to the Lost Colony, can be seen here today.

In the Battle of Roanoke Island in 1862, the United States Navy attacked Roanoke Island, scoring a victory for Federal forces led by Ambrose Burnside. Much of coastal North Carolina remained occupied by the Union army during the remaining years of the Civil War, and many Union sympathizers lived on the Banks and elsewhere in the state.

The largest town on Roanoke Island is Manteo, named for one of the two Roanoke Indians who returned to England with the early English explorers. The 400th anniversary celebration of the explorations sponsored by Sir Walter Raleigh brought attention and many improvements to this area. The *Elizabeth II*, a replica of a 16th-century sailing vessel, is docked at Manteo's harbor. Manteo maintains a small-town friendliness while boasting many historic sites and a blossoming downtown waterfront area.

Wanchese, named for the other Roanoke Indian who went to England, is a small fishing village on the southern end of Roanoke Island. More than 20 million pounds of fish are harvested here each year, some of them shipped to Northern markets and the rest sold to area residents and restaurants. The people are friendly and don't seem to mind if passersby stop to watch them at the docks.

Roanoke Island is primarily the jumping-off point for Banks-bound beachgoers, but many people think it has its own appeal. If you leave the main highway and drive to the end of N.C. 345, you will find Mill Landing. It is the home port for trawlers and a few companies engaged in the original business of the Outer Banks—fishing. For many people, Mill Landing is an artist's and photographer's dream.

ACCESS:

Roanoke Island can be reached via U.S. 64/264 from the mainland by crossing the William B. Umstead Memorial Bridge or from the Nags Head/Cape Hatteras area on U.S. 64/264 (Manteo–Nags Head Causeway) by crossing the Washington Baum Bridge.

The Dare County Regional Airport in Manteo is located on S.R. 116 (Airport Road). It has two runways measuring 3,290 feet and 4,300 feet. Fuel and services are offered. Call 252-473-2600.

The airport is also a hub for Southeast Airlines (252-473-3222), which offers charter flights to and from other cities. Fuel and service, rental cars, limousine service, and concessions are available. Charter and tour services are offered.

VISITOR INFORMATION:

Contact the Dare County Tourist Bureau, P.O. Box 399, 704 U.S. 64, Manteo, N.C. 27954 (252-473-2138 or 800-446-6262)

Attractions

Historic Places

Fort Raleigh National Historic Site, on the north end of Roanoke Island, is where aspiring colonists attempted to establish a settlement in 1585. As a result of Sir Walter Raleigh's propaganda campaign, his cousin Richard Grenville led a group of 600 men to found a colony here.

Grenville left Ralph Lane and a small force to build fortifications and explore the area while he returned to England. But relations with nearby natives deteriorated, and Lane and his men opted to return to England with Sir Francis Drake when he dropped by after destroying the Spanish settlement at St. Augustine, Florida.

Shortly afterward, Grenville returned with a small contingent, supplies for two years, and instructions to build Fort Raleigh and to hold the country in the name of Queen Elizabeth—no small assignment. He arranged for 15 men to stay behind while he again returned to England. Recent archaeological investigation on the site suggests that the fort was built by these soldiers.

When John White, appointed governor of the new colony, returned with more colonists in 1587, he found none of the soldiers—only a single skeleton.

In an attempt to make the colony permanent, White's colonists were complete families. It was White's daughter who gave birth to Virginia Dare, the first English child born in the New World. In spite of their efforts, the colonists were unable to live entirely off the land, and White was forced to return to England for provisions.

Threatening actions by the Spanish Armada prevented his return to the colony until 1590. To his dismay, he found that this settlement, too, had disappeared. Even the little houses inside the palisade had been dismantled. At the entrance to the palisade, White discovered the word *CROATOAN* carved on a post, but there was no cross—the prearranged distress signal. He planned to search a nearby island but was forced to leave before he could explore the area. No further clue to the fate of the colonists was found. The mystery of the Lost Colony has never been solved.

Fort Raleigh, named a National Historic Site in 1941, was explored archaeologically and then restored in 1950. The earthen embankments remain just as they were in the 1500s. The summer guided tours by National Park Service rangers help visitors imagine what life was like for the beleaguered colonists. The Lindsay Warren Visitor Center has exhibits of Indian artifacts and relics, pictures, charts, books about the early development of this area, and a 17-minute video on the settlement attempts. The site is open daily from 9 A.M. to 7:30 P.M. from June to the end of August; it is open from 9 A.M. to 5 P.M. the rest of the year. Admission to the site is free. Call 252-473-5772.

Roanoke Island Festival Park, located across from Manteo's waterfront area, is an 8,500-square-foot interactive theme park that explores the evolution of the island from its turbulent beginnings over 400 years ago to the present day. It features the *Elizabeth II*, a handsome reproduction of a 16th-century English vessel, the type of wooden ship used in the voyages to Roanoke Island organized by Sir Walter Raleigh. It was built to commemorate the New World's quadricentennial, and every detail in its 69-foot length is as authentic as possible. You can tour the ship after stopping at the visitor center to see exhibits explaining exploration,

The *Elizabeth II*
Photograph by Clay Nolen
Courtesy of N.C. Travel and Tourism Division

shipboard life (it was not a pleasure cruise to the New World by any stretch of the imagination!), and *The Legend of Two Path*, a 45-minute film on the Native Americans of the island.

During the summer, costumed guides portray mariners and colonists. There's also a gift shop and an art gallery. On special days, the acclaimed North Carolina School of the Arts holds concerts and plays at the park. The site is open daily from 9 A.M. to 6 P.M. Admission is $4 for adults and $2 for students; children age five and under are free. Call 252-475-1506.

Museums/Science Centers

North Carolina Aquarium on Roanoke Island, three miles north of Manteo off U.S. 64 on Airport Road, is one of three such facilities along the coast operated by the state. Live fish, turtles, alligators, and other specimens indigenous to area waters are presented in vivid displays. Children especially enjoy the touch tank filled with crabs, starfish, sea urchins, and other sea creatures that they can pick up and examine. Visitors can also get an intimate look at North Carolina sharks and their relatives at the 3,000-gallon shark gallery. There is a well-stocked gift shop. The aquarium is open daily from 9 A.M. to 7 P.M. Admission is $3 for adults, $2 for senior citizens and active military personnel, and $1 for children six to 17. Call 252-473-3494.

Gardens

The **Elizabethan Gardens**, located at Fort Raleigh National Historic Site on U.S. 64, are a delight for gardeners, history buffs, and anyone who enjoys beauty. At their best in April (azaleas, wisteria, and dogwoods), May (hydrangea and rhododendron), July (gardenias, roses, magnolias, and summer annuals), and September (impatiens, hibiscus, and camellias), the gardens are open year-round. The tranquil setting features an herb garden, a sunken garden, a wildflower garden, and a rose garden. Designed by landscape architects M. Umberto Innocenti and Richard Webel and maintained by the Garden Club of North Carolina, the gardens are a memorial to the English colonists who came here in 1585 and 1587 and disappeared.

Bricks used here predate the Revolutionary War. The Virginia Dare statue was sculpted after the popular Indian legend that the first English child born in the New World grew to be a beautiful woman in a local tribe. The gardens are open daily from 9 A.M. to 7 P.M. during the summer months but offer shorter hours during the off-season, so call ahead. Admission is $3 for adults and $1 for children 12-17; children under 12 are admitted free. Call 252-473-3234.

Special Shopping

The Island Art Gallery, at the Christmas Shop in Manteo (252-473-2838), has been in business over a quarter of a century and was one of the first retail shops in the area. It offers an excellent collection of paintings, pottery, baskets, jewelry, sculpture, and photographs by local and national artists.

Manteo Booksellers, at 105 Sir Walter Raleigh Street, is one of eastern North Carolina's most complete bookstores. It offers thousands of titles, from local history to children's books, cookbooks, and literature. The relaxed atmosphere is perfect for browsing. Call 252-473-1221.

Recreation

Seasonal Events

Since its first performance in 1937, *The Lost Colony* has been a star attraction. Written by North Carolina native and Pulitzer Prize winner Paul Green, the nation's first outdoor symphonic drama portrays Sir Walter Raleigh's attempt to establish an English colony on Roanoke Island in the 16th century. You won't learn the fate of the Lost Colony, but you'll have an opinion when you leave. Performed in the Waterside Theatre at Fort Raleigh National Historic Site, the play brings the poignant story to life for the audience. The Indian fights are exciting and the Elizabethan court costumes stunning. Roanoke Island part-time resident Andy Griffith once played the role of Sir Walter Raleigh.

The Lost Colony *outdoor drama*
Photograph by T&T
Courtesy of N.C. Travel and Tourism Division

Shows are held nightly except Saturday at 8:30 P.M. from mid-June to late August. Tickets are $14 for adults, $7 for children under 12 (children are admitted half-price on Sundays with a parent), and $13 for seniors ($12 on

Fridays). Group discounts are available, and reservations are recommended. Visitors should note that performances aren't cancelled until the last minute when it rains, and that the mosquitoes know about these outdoor performances—bug repellant is sold at the concession stand. Contact *The Lost Colony*, 1409 U.S. 64/264, Manteo, N.C. 27954 (252-473-3414 or 800-488-5012).

New World Festival of the Arts is held in mid-August right on the Manteo waterfront overlooking Shallowbag Bay. A variety of artists display their paintings, pottery, baskets, jewelry, and other arts and crafts.

The Wanchese Seafood Festival and Blessing of the Fleet, held each year on the last Saturday in June, features games, musical entertainment, educational exhibits, and seafood platters of fresh local fish, shrimp, clams, and steamed crabs as the fishing fleet is blessed at the waterfront. Contact the Wanchese Seafood Festival, P.O. Box 1757, Kill Devil Hills, N.C. 27948 (252-441-8144).

Accommodations

Elizabethan Inn. *Inexpensive/Moderate*. U.S. 64/264, P.O. Box 549, Manteo (252-473-2101). This Tudor-style motel offers a variety of rooms and prices. All guests may use the fitness center, indoor and outdoor pools, whirlpool, and sauna; racquetball facilities are available for a fee. There's a picnic area, and the restaurant is open for all meals. Children staying in the room with parents are free.

Duke of Dare Motor Lodge. *Inexpensive/Moderate*. U.S. 64/264, Manteo (252-473-2175). This motor lodge, run by the same family for over 20 years, provides economical lodging for families. The rooms, with predictable 1950s-style furnishings, have televisions and phones. A pool and friendly management are added features.

Inns and Bed-and-Breakfast Guest Houses

Tranquil House Inn. *Expensive/Deluxe*. Manteo waterfront (252-473-1404). Tranquil House is a reproduction of a turn-of-the-century inn, complete with rocking chairs, an upstairs porch, and 25 individually decorated rooms. Many rooms have a view of Shallowbag Bay, and several suites provide a sitting area. The inn is named for the original Tranquil House of old Manteo.

The White Doe Inn. *Deluxe*. Uppowoc Street, one block off U.S. 64/264 (252-473-9851 or 800-473-6091). This inn is located in a beautiful Queen Anne–style Victorian home which is one of the oldest on the island. Each of the five rooms has a private bath and a fireplace. A full Southern-style breakfast is provided.

C. W. Pugh's. *Moderate*. Old Wharf Road, Wanchese (252-473-5466). Located next to Queen Anne's Revenge restaurant, this bed-and-breakfast inn is the white clapboard home of a former lighthouse keeper. It offers three guest rooms in a serene, historic setting. A full breakfast is served. C. W. Pugh's is open from March to October.

Scarborough Inn. *Inexpensive/Moderate*. U.S. 64/264 not far from the Manteo–Nags Head Causeway (252-473-3979). Here, you'll find the charm and personal touches of a bed-and-breakfast inn combined with the amenities of a motel. The guest rooms in this reproduction of a 19th-century inn have televisions, phones, private baths, in-room coffee, and antique furnishings (with a story behind most of them). The wraparound porches invite you to mingle with other guests or rock awhile.

Roanoke Island Inn. *Moderate/Expensive*. 305 Fernando Street, Manteo waterfront (877-473-5511). This house overlooking Shallowbag Bay was built for the innkeeper's great-great-grandmother in the 1860s. Over the years, it has been enlarged and renovated, but always in keeping with traditional island architecture. There are eight guest rooms, a homey living room, and a second-floor porch with rocking chairs. Continental breakfast is provided, along with a variety of snacks and beverages during the day. Bikes are available for exploring the island.

Restaurants

Again, seafood is the byword here, and you'll find quite a variety to tempt you. You're only a few minutes' drive from all the restaurants in Nags Head, too.

1587. *Expensive*. At the Tranquil House Inn on the Manteo waterfront (252-473-1587). This elegant restaurant rates as one of the finest eating establishments on the island. Diners can enjoy a view of the *Elizabeth II* and Shallowbag Bay while they eat. Open daily for dinner from spring to fall.

Queen Anne's Revenge. *Moderate/Expensive*. Old Wharf Road, Wanchese (252-473-5466). Surrounded by island pines and a flowering garden, this restaurant serves fresh-off-the-boat seafood, bouillabaisse, and steaks. The clam chowder, she-crab soup, and homemade desserts are specialties. A children's menu is available, as are beer and wine. Dinner is served year-round, but call for off-season hours.

Clara's Seafood Grill and Steam Bar. *Moderate*. On the Manteo waterfront (252-473-1727). This popular restaurant serves excellent seafood dishes and has a great view of Shallowbag Bay. The marinated grilled tuna melts in your mouth. Open daily for lunch and dinner from March through December.

The Weeping Radish. *Moderate*. Next door to the Christmas Shop complex, U.S. 64, Manteo (252-473-1157). The Weeping Radish features authentic German food and atmosphere, including an in-house Bavarian brewery. Brewery tours are offered daily, but call about the schedule. The first beer brewed in America was made on Roanoke Island, so this really isn't such an unusual choice for the area. Lunch and dinner are served daily year-round.

Fisherman's Wharf. *Inexpensive/Moderate*. Wanchese Harbor (252-473-5205). Fisherman's Wharf guarantees fresh seafood—just sit by the windows and watch the fishing fleet come in. The daily specials are agreeable to the wallet. Seafood, steaks, chicken dishes, home-made desserts, and a children's menu are offered. Lunch and dinner are served from Easter to Thanksgiving.

Bodie Island

Driving south from Nags Head at Whalebone Junction, where the Manteo–Nags Head Causeway intersects U.S. 158, you'll come to Bodie Island. First, Bodie is pronounced "Body," and second, it's not really an island. As with much of this area, the sea and weather are constantly redefining boundaries, but the names stay the same. Port Ferdinando, once an inlet through Bodie Island, was used on a 1584 expedition by Philip Amadas and Arthur Barlow, who landed at Roanoke Island. The inlet closed in the early 1800s.

Although tourism has brought steady development to the Nags Head area to the north, Bodie Island has remained rather sparsely populated. With comparatively few attractions, it seems content to usher people quickly across Oregon Inlet at its southern tip to Hatteras Island, so it can maintain its relative peace and privacy.

Attractions

Historic Places

Bodie Island Lighthouse, one of the Outer Banks' famous four, is just off N.C. 12 about a mile beyond the Coquina Beach area. Built in 1872, the structure is identified by its horizontal black and white stripes. Two other structures preceded this one on the site; the first was improperly built, and the second was destroyed by the Confederates to confuse Federal ships.

After several painstaking years, the restoration of the double keeper's quarters at the lighthouse is complete. The structure now houses a book shop. The lighthouse has not been restored, so you cannot climb to the top. However, it is a twin of the Currituck Beach Lighthouse in Corolla, which can be climbed. Recently, volunteers have opened the

Bodie Island Lighthouse
Photograph by David M. Hampton

base of the lighthouse for tourists. Check with the visitor center for hours; call 252-441-5711.

The *Laura A. Barnes*, located at Coquina Beach, was one of the last schooners built in America; it dates from 1918. Only three years after its construction, the ship ran into a nor'easter that forced it onto the beach. Fortunately, the crew survived with the help of heroic men from the nearby lifesaving station. In 1973, the remains of the wreck were moved by the National Park Service to their present location.

Recreation

Coquina Beach, eight miles south of Whalebone Junction, is considered one of the best swimming beaches on the Outer Banks. This beautiful white-sand beach takes its name from the tiny shells you'll find underfoot everywhere. Unfortunately, no lifeguard is on duty, but the beach is still used. Surf fishing is also popular here. Whenever the "blues" (bluefish) are running, you can feel the excitement all over the beach.

The first Nazi U-boat sunk by Americans in World War II lies 15 miles offshore. Its destruction in 1942 was a tremendous morale booster for the United States Navy, whose outmoded fleet was being decimated so rapidly that the area was called "Torpedo Junction."

Oregon Inlet Fishing Center is worth a stop even if you're not a fisherman. (If you are, you've probably found the place on your own.) As a center of sportfishing on the Outer Banks, Oregon Inlet is home port to more than 30 charter boats. Because the area is leased from the National Park Service, all boats charge the same prices. Headboats that can accommodate up to 125 people are available for catching spot, bluefish, mullet, sea bass, and other fish. There's also a tackle shop, facilities for fish cleaning, and boat ramps. Check out the display of mounted deep-sea fish. If you're at Oregon Inlet Fishing Center around 4 or 5 P.M. in season, you may see some potential trophy winners being brought in. Call 252-441-6301 or 800-272-5199.

The only place to stay on Bodie Island is **Oregon Inlet Campground**, one of four National Park Service campgrounds on the Outer Banks. There are no utility connections or shade trees at the 120 sites. Toilets, picnic tables, cold showers, and grills are provided. The basic fee is $12. The campground is open from April to late September. Reservations are not accepted—availability is on a first-come, first-served basis. Call 252-473-2111.

Hatteras Island

Continuing south past the Oregon Inlet Fishing Center on Bodie Island, you'll cross Oregon Inlet via the Herbert C. Bonner Bridge, built in 1964 to connect Bodie and Hatteras Islands. Actually, there wasn't an inlet until 1846, when a major storm opened one. The first ship to travel through the new inlet was the *Oregon*, giving the inlet its name. Today, this is the principal passage into and out of Pamlico Sound.

The Bonner Bridge has been the subject of controversy for many years. The bridge impedes some of the tidal flow through the inlet, and constant dredging is required to keep the inlet open. Building a jetty would keep the channel open but would be expensive and could also threaten the already-eroding beach areas. One thing is sure: the stability of this three-mile bridge is important.

With most of its 50 or so miles included in Cape Hatteras National Seashore, Hatteras is probably the most undeveloped island of the Outer Banks. Although "progress" is moving in quickly, much of the land is protected by the National Park Service. Restaurants, shops, motels, and other establishments are centered around the island's seven villages: Rodanthe, Waves, Salvo, Avon, Buxton, Frisco, and Hatteras. Between the villages are fishing and swimming areas, as well as miles of natural scenery along N.C. 12.

Avon, once a center for hunting and fishing, is growing into a bustling community. One reason for its popularity is its international reputation for windsurfing. Avon has become home to the windsurfing crowd because of its consistent wind, especially in the spring and fall, and the calm, shallow waters of Pamlico Sound.

Buxton, located south of Avon, is the home of the famous Cape Hatteras Lighthouse at Cape Point. It is also a mecca for the windsurfing crowd. Canadian Hole, located one mile north of Buxton, has become one of the most popular windsurfing sites on the island. There is a paved parking area, along with bathroom facilities. Even if you aren't a windsurfer, the brilliant colors of the sails on dozens of boards make for a spectacular sight.

Frisco is the site of Billy Mitchell Air Field, a 3,000-foot paved landing strip named for the controversial army aviator who directed some bombing tests here.

The southernmost stop is Hatteras village, the Outer Banks'

second-largest commercial fishing center, after Wanchese. The prestigious, invitation-only Hatteras Marlin Tournament, held here in June, plays host to many well-known business people and politicians.

VISITOR INFORMATION:
Contact the Dare County Tourist Bureau, P.O. Box 399, 704 U.S. 64/264, Manteo, N.C. 27954 (252-473-2138 or 800-446-6262).

Attractions

Historic Places

Chicamacomico Lifesaving Station in Rodanthe was once one of the Outer Banks' most famous lifesaving stations.

The town of Rodanthe was once known as Chicamacomico, but in 1874, the postal service insisted the name be changed to something easier to spell. Unfortunately, part of the Hatteras Island's Indian heritage was lost with the town's original name.

The surfmen who stood guard along the North Carolina coast had to be extremely strong and brave to endure the ocean's storms—ships didn't usually founder on calm, sunny days. When a ship was sinking, the surfmen fired a line with a Lyle gun and pulled it to shore, or rowed or swam out to rescue the crew. The most famous rescue at the Chicamacomico Lifesaving Station took place in 1918, when Captain John Allen Midgett, Jr., and his crew saved 42 men from the burning English tanker *Mirlo* after it was torpedoed by the Germans.

The station was closed in 1954 but has been restored. On Thursday afternoons during the summer at 2 P.M., the National Park Service performs a simulated lifesaving drill. Dressed in uniforms similar to the ones worn in the early part of the century, the performers demonstrate what it was like to rescue people from a shipwreck during that time. They shoot Lyle gun projectiles and demonstrate other lifesaving equipment.

The lifesaving station and the nearby stable have been converted into a museum which houses lifesaving memorabilia, artifacts from shipwrecks, and souvenirs. It is open Tuesday, Thursday, and Saturday from 11 A.M. to 5 P.M. Admission is free. Contact the

Chicamacomico Lifesaving Station, P.O. Box 140, Rodanthe, N.C. 27968 (252-987-1552).

Little Kinnakeet Lifesaving Station in Avon was another of the lifesaving stations built along the Banks to guide ships through this treacherous area. The station was decommissioned in 1953 and moved to its present site because of beach erosion. It is currently undergoing restoration. It will be several years before it is open to the public. You can, however, walk around the outside of the buildings.

Cape Hatteras Lighthouse at Cape Point near Buxton is one stop everyone should make. Not only is Cape Point a favorite spot for surfing, swimming, and surf fishing, it's also the home of the famous black-and-white, barber-pole-striped lighthouse. The tallest structure of its kind in the United States, the 208-foot lighthouse warns passing ships of the dangerous Diamond Shoals.

Cape Hatteras Lighthouse
Courtesy of N.C. Travel and Tourism Division

The first lighthouse here, built in 1802, was destroyed. In 1869–70, the present lighthouse was placed 1,000 yards from the shore, its foundation sunk eight feet into the sand. Despite efforts to prevent further erosion, the relentless sea is threatening this North Carolina landmark; it's now less than 200 feet from the water's edge. After much controversy, the lighthouse was moved further inland in early 1999. Once lit by whale oil, the lighthouse now flashes an 800,000-candlepower beam every 7½ seconds. It can be seen 20 miles out at sea.

While the lighthouse was moved, a temporary visitor center was opened for visitors daily from Easter weekend to Columbus Day weekend. The hours vary during this time. Call the visitor center to learn the current status of the lighthouse. Tours are available weather permitting and based upon volunteer guide availability. Only 75 people are allowed inside at one time, so you may have to wait. You can climb to the top and walk around the catwalk for a great view of the area. Call the Hatteras Island Visitor Center (252-995-4474) for more information.

The **Hatteras Island Visitor Center** is located nearby in a two-story house built in 1854 that was formerly the light keeper's home. Run by the National Park Service, the center houses a museum devoted to island history and the men who served at the lighthouse. A bookstore and gift shop are on-site, and information is available about the various summer activities offered by the National Park Service. Because of budget cutbacks, it is always advisable to check operating hours and available facilities for all National Park Service sites. The center is open daily. Admission is free.

The **Buxton Woods Nature Trail** is a marked 0.75-mile walk explaining the ecosystem of the area.

Museums

Frisco Native American Museum and Natural History Center is the result of a labor of love by Joyce and Carl Bornfriend. It features authentic collections of ancient Indian artifacts gathered over the course of 50 years. Be sure you beat the sacred Hopi kiva drum and make a wish. The museum is open daily except Monday from 11 A.M. to 5 P.M. year-round. Mondays are reserved for group tours by appointment. Admission is $2 per adult, $1.50 per senior citizen, and $5 per family. Contact the museum at P.O. Box 399, Frisco, N.C. 27936 (252-995-4440).

Special Shopping

Browning Artworks, on N.C. 12 in Frisco, is an oasis of North Carolina arts and crafts featuring the works of almost 200 artisans. Pottery, baskets, carvings, weavings, jewelry, and art glass are for sale. Hours vary with the season, and the gallery is closed from January through the first few weeks of March. Call 252-995-5538.

Recreation

Activities center around the beaches, of course. In addition to exploring the nature trail mentioned above, you can enjoy surf fishing, surfing, windsurfing, and swimming. Be especially careful of the strong currents, particularly since there are no lifeguards.

If you wish to try surfing or windsurfing, there are several establishments that will accommodate your needs. **Hatteras Island Surf Shop** (252-987-2296) is located in Waves. **Fox Watersports** (252-995-4102) is in Buxton. Avon offers **Windsurfing Hatteras** (252-995-4970), **Kitty Hawk Sports** (252-441-9200), and **Avon Windsurf Company** (252-995-5441).

The **Avon Fishing Pier** (252-995-5480) offers tackle, bait, ice, a snack bar, and a lighted 930-foot pier; it is open from April to November. The **Hatteras Island Fishing Pier** (252-987-2323) in Rodanthe is 875 feet long and offers the same services. **Frisco Pier** (252-986-2533) in Frisco features a snack bar and fishing services. The **Hatteras Fishing Center** in Hatteras village, the island's largest marina, is home to several charter boats for Gulf Stream fishing. The *Miss Hatteras* also offers an evening sightseeing cruise. Call 252-986-2365.

If you'd like to see the Outer Banks from the air, **Hatteras Flying Service** offers both a northerly and a southerly trip over the area. Call 252-995-6671.

Ocean Edge Golf Course is a nine-hole executive course open to the public year-round. Call 252-995-4100.

Wildlife Sanctuary

Pea Island National Wildlife Refuge, located south of the Bonner Bridge at the north end of the island, is a resting and wintering ground for geese, ducks, swans, and other birds. Over 20 species of ducks and a variety of shorebirds winter here, including most of North America's snow geese. Managed by the United States Fish and Wildlife Service, the refuge was developed in the 1930s, when the Civilian Conservation Corps worked to stabilize the dunes and create freshwater ponds. It has been spectacularly successful in attracting birds—over 260 species have been spotted here. You'll see bird watchers trying to add new sightings to their lifetime totals. Beach-access parking is available at the refuge headquarters building. You'll also find a nature trail. Observation platforms are located throughout the area. The refuge is open during daylight hours from November to August; the visitors center is open weekdays from 9 A.M. to 4 P.M. but is closed on weekends. Admission is free. Call 252-987-2394.

Seasonal Events

The **East Coast Surfing Association Championships** are held in early September. The event began in the early 1970s after word got out about the excellent surfing in the lighthouse area. While only members can compete, hundreds of spectators watch surfers tackle the waves, which sometimes swell to eight feet in the fall (two to three feet is the summer average). Contact ECSAC, P.O. Box 400 AD, Buxton, N.C. 27920 (252-995-5785).

Accommodations

Many of the island's motels were built in the 1950s, but they provide adequate rooms with functional furniture. Recently, new motels have sprung up, and older motels have updated their facilities to meet the competition. Many of the motels are geared toward fishermen and families on a budget.

Rental listings are available from the chamber of commerce.

The Castaways Oceanfront Inn. *Expensive.* Avon (252-995-4444 or 800-845-6070 outside N.C.). This is definitely one of the most luxurious spots on the island. You won't have trouble spotting it, because this high-rise hotel stands in contradiction to most of the island's architecture. All rooms are oceanfront and have private balconies, a wet bar, a refrigerator, and cable TV. A pool and a Jacuzzi are also offered. A full-service restaurant is open for breakfast and dinner except during the winter.

Holiday Inn Express. *Expensive/Moderate.* Next to the ferry landing in Hatteras (252-986-1110 or 800-HOLIDAY). With its convenient location, this new hotel puts you in the middle of Hatteras's seashore activity. Each of the 40 rooms and 32 suites has a microwave and refrigerator. A complimentary continental breakfast is provided.

Hatteras Island Resort. *Moderate/Expensive.* Rodanthe (252-987-2345 or 800-331-6541). Located on 25 acres, this oceanfront complex includes 34 rooms, eight efficiencies, 36 cottages, a large swimming pool, a patio, and a cafe open for all meals. The cottages and efficiencies are stocked with dishes and linens. Hatteras Island Resort is open from April to December.

Cape Hatteras Motel. *Moderate.* Buxton (252-995-5611). This motel offers standard rooms with refrigerators and microwaves, along with efficiencies and duplex cottages, all with access to a pool and a

Jacuzzi. Windsurfers know this as the closest place to Canadian Hole; the store adjacent to the motel sells boogie boards and beach gear. Special touches include fish-cleaning stations, beach umbrellas, and in-room coffee.

Comfort Inn-Hatteras Island. *Moderate*. Buxton (252-995-6100 or 800-432-1441). This motel has 60 rooms featuring refrigerators, microwaves, and cable TV. The inn also offers a free continental breakfast.

Hatteras Marlin Motel. *Inexpensive/Moderate*. Hatteras (252-986-2141). Owned by the Midgett family, this motel is close to the harbor and within walking distance of shops and restaurants. Most of the rooms have double beds and cable TV. Children under six stay free. Efficiencies and cottages are available. A pool and a sun deck are also offered.

Sea Gull Motel. *Inexpensive/Moderate*. N.C. 12, Hatteras (252-986-2550). This motel features 45 oceanside units (it's a walk, though) grouped around a courtyard pool. The paneled rooms with pine furnishings are comfortable, and the efficiencies are well equipped. The motel is open from March to December.

Cape Pines Motel. *Inexpensive/Moderate*. Buxton (252-995-5666). The 19 rooms offer color TV; refrigerators and microwaves are available in the seven mini-efficiency units. Three apartments are also available. There is a swimming pool for guests, along with picnic tables with barbecues.

Restaurants

No one expects you to dress up around here. The service is friendly and the seafood's fresh.

The Breakwater Restaurant. *Moderate/Expensive*. Oden's Dock, Hatteras (252-986-2733). Overlooking Pamlico Sound, this spot specializes in seafood with a northern Italian flair. The restaurant makes its own salad dressings, and the bread is baked fresh daily. Dinner is served.

The Quarterdeck. *Moderate*. N.C. 12, Frisco (252-986-2425). This family-run restaurant has been providing good food in an informal setting for decades. In addition to fresh seafood, look for the Italian specialties, the homemade soups and desserts, and the early-bird specials. Beer and wine are offered, and brown-bagging is permitted. Lunch and dinner are served.

The Froggy Dog. *Moderate*. N.C. 12, Avon (252-995-4106). This is one of those cozy wood-and-greenery restaurants that encourages conversation. Lunch and dinner offer everything from sandwiches to seafood to liver and onions. There is live entertainment most nights and weekends. Beer and wine are offered. The restaurant is closed on Tuesdays.

Channel Bass Restaurant. *Moderate*. N.C. 12, Hatteras (252-986-2250). This restaurant is known for its locally caught, fresh seafood, large seafood platters, hush puppies, and crab Imperial. Dinner is served.

Bubba's Bar-B-Q. *Inexpensive*. N.C. 12, Frisco (252-995-5421). Bubba's will satisfy anyone's hankering for barbecue. You know it's fresh—you can watch it cooking over the hickory-wood pit fire, then enjoy generous portions of chicken, pork, or ribs with salad and fries. Save room for some homemade pie. Lunch and dinner are served daily.

The Gingerbread House. *Inexpensive*. N.C. 12, Frisco (252-995-5204). This small establishment serves wonderful baked goods beginning at 7 A.M. It is also open for dinner from Tuesday through Saturday beginning at 4:30 P.M., serving whole-wheat pizza and baked goods.

Ocracoke Island

Of all the islands along the coast, Ocracoke is the favorite of many people. Maybe it's the romance of having to take a ferry to get there. Maybe it's the beauty of 15 miles of pristine beaches, the small village built around Silver Lake, or the congeniality of the people who live there.

If you don't mind leaving nightspots, condominiums, and shopping malls behind, and if you like spending quiet evenings by the water or in cozy restaurants, you'll like Ocracoke.

Ocracoke has an intriguing history. Historians surmise that the first European explorers stumbled upon Ocracoke when Sir Richard Grenville was on his way to colonize Roanoke Island in 1585. Grenville may have left behind some souvenirs. The famous Ocracoke ponies are believed to be descendants of Spanish horses he may have purchased in the West Indies. For many years, these horses roamed wild, but their numbers have dwindled; they're now protected by the National Park Service.

In the early 1700s, shipwrecked sailors began to colonize the island, and in 1715, Ocracoke was established as a port.

Ocracoke's most infamous resident was Edward Teach, better known as Blackbeard. Safe among the hidden coves of Ocracoke, Blackbeard planned his attacks on unsuspecting ships. And as fate would have it, it was off these same shores that the dread pirate met his end in 1718. Lieutenant Robert Maynard, under orders from Governor Spotswood of Virginia, finally caught, killed, and beheaded the treacherous buccaneer in an area now called Teach's Hole, then sailed to Hampton Roads, Virginia, with Blackbeard's head. You have as good a chance as anyone of finding some of Blackbeard's treasure, supposedly still buried nearby.

The Spanish took possession of Ocracoke in 1747, blocking trade for the British. During the American Revolution, Ocracoke became a link in the supply route for George Washington's army. But during the Civil War, occupation by Federal troops disrupted all island activities, and for years afterward, only fishermen, boat pilots, and lifesaving crews inhabited the area.

During World War II, German submarines sank merchant ships and tankers off the coast, earning this area the nickname "Torpedo Junction." The war also brought communication with the outside world; no roads, electricity, or telephones had existed here until the navy built a small base on the island.

After the war, tourism developed slowly because of Ocracoke's isolation—it is still accessible only by ferry or small plane—and unassuming lifestyle. A five-story hotel seems like a skyscraper here, and most people prefer to walk or bike through the village rather than drive.

And all those miles of beach are covered only by sand, sea oats, and contented souls—not a water slide in sight.

ACCESS:

From the north, Ocracoke can be reached by ferry from Hatteras Island. The Hatteras ferry is free and leaves every 30 minutes in the summer. No reservations are permitted.

From the mainland, Ocracoke is reached by toll ferries from Cedar Island and Swan Quarter. Reservations are required during summer and are strongly recommended at other times.

Contact the Cedar Island ferry at 252-225-3551 or the Swan Quarter ferry at 252-926-1111. To listen to the ferry schedule, call 1-800-BY-FERRY.

VISITOR INFORMATION:

Contact the Dare County Tourist Bureau, P.O. Box 399, 704 U.S. 64/264, Manteo, N.C. 27954 (252-473-2138 or 800-446-6262).

Attractions

Ocracoke Visitor Center, located in the village near the drop-off point for the Cedar Island and Swan Quarter ferries, should be one of your first stops. Operated by the National Park Service, the center provides an impressive account of Ocracoke's history, as well as a fine collection of photographs documenting the island's growth. Books on local history, nature, and folklore are offered in the book shop.

If you plan to use the docks, this is also the place to check in. No reservations are taken. Dockage fees vary according to the season. During the winter, the fee is 25 cents per boat foot per day, and the fee is doubled for the summer season. Tie-up facilities are available on the lake; power hookups are offered for a fee.

As with most places on Ocracoke, the center's hours vary with the season, so call ahead. The number is 252-928-4531.

Ocracoke Coast Guard Station is nearby; you can see it from the ferry landing. However, the facility is not open to the public. Ocracoke boasts the southernmost Coast Guard station along the Outer Banks.

Village of Ocracoke
Photograph by Clay Nolen
Courtesy of N.C. Travel and Tourism Division

Ocracoke village, at the west end of N.C. 12 and wrapped around Silver Lake, is the quintessential fishing village. Walking and biking are the best ways to see everything. You'll probably want to stop by a few small shops. If you want to find out what's going on, check the post-office bulletin board. Stroll down Howard Street—one of the few streets that is marked—with its old homes, some featuring detached kitchens and cisterns for collecting water. The Methodist church displays a wooden cross carved from a sunken freighter.

Closer to the center of the village, stop in the **Community Store**, an old country store that sells everything from screwdrivers to sherbet. There is a community bulletin board out front, along with benches for sitting and chatting. On N.C. 12, you'll find the **Ocracoke Variety Store**, which offers everything from groceries and fresh meats to souvenirs and hardware. Other village shops offer an assortment of clothing, crafts, antiques, shells, and jewelry.

Ocracoke Pony Pen, located about six miles from the Hatteras ferry landing, is the home of the island's wild ponies. The ponies are the descendants of Spanish mustangs, as determined by counting the vertebrae and ribs. At one time, as many as 1,000 may have inhabited the island, but they were eventually sold off, except for the remaining two dozen. Signs direct you to the observation deck. Note that the ponies aren't always accommodating, so don't get the kids all fired up about seeing them.

Historic Places

Ocracoke Lighthouse is the oldest lighthouse on the Outer Banks and, at 75 feet, the smallest. Built in 1823 to warn passing ships of the treacherous waters around the inlet and island, the sturdy white structure is the nation's second-oldest continuously operating lighthouse. A ranger lives in the original keeper's house next door. The lighthouse is operated by the Coast Guard. The structure is occasionally open for viewing. Check with the visitor center to see if it will be open while you are on the island.

The **British Cemetery**, about two blocks from Silver Lake, is marked by the British flag. It is a memorial to four British sailors washed ashore from the *Bedfordshire*, a trawler in a fleet of antisubmarine ships loaned to the United States in 1942. It was torpedoed off Cape Lookout by a German U-boat, and four victims were buried here. The cemetery is maintained by the Coast Guard.

Recreation

On Ocracoke, recreation means communing with nature. In addition to the miles of beaches, which are part of Cape Hatteras National Seashore, you can enjoy fishing and hunting. **O'Neal's Dockside** (252-928-1111) and **Anchorage Marina** (252-928-6661) are the headquarters for chartering offshore fishing boats. Duck-hunting guides are available in season.

Ocracoke Campground, operated by the National Park Service, has 136 oceanside campsites. Drinking water, flush toilets, grills, and cold showers are available. The sites are $13 per night. Reservations are required from May to August. Due to budget cuts, the campground may be open only from May to Labor Day. Call Mistix at 800-365-CAMP for reservations.

You may also want to visit **Portsmouth Island**, once the site of the largest town on the Banks, but now an uninhabited island. Harsh weather eventually drove the 600 residents of once-bustling Portsmouth village to the other growing coastal ports. Today, you can get there only by private boat or charter boat. **Austin's Boat Tours** (252-928-5431) runs boats to the island for $15 per adult and $10 for each child 12 and under. Be forewarned—uninhabited islands are not sprayed for insects, so bring your repellant.

Accommodations

For its size, Ocracoke offers a good choice of accommodations. Most places have a limited number of rooms, however, so make reservations. Few places operate in the winter. Most are open throughout "the warm months," which usually means Easter through September. Cottages tucked among the trees around Silver Lake are also for rent.

Anchorage Inn & Marina. *Moderate*. On the harbor (252-928-1101). This five-story "skyscraper" doesn't add much to the village landscape, but it offers 35 rooms and several efficiencies. The amenities include phones, TVs, a pool, air conditioning, and continental breakfast. A boat ramp and docks with fueling facilities are available.

Boyette House. *Moderate*. N.C. 12 (800-928-4261). This attractive motel has rocking chairs on the porch, a sun deck to help your tan along, and a comfortable lobby with books. A recent expansion has

Ocracoke Lighthouse
Photograph by William Russ
Courtesy of N.C. Travel and Tourism Division

added lovely rooms with porches. Some rooms with steam baths and Jacuzzis are available. A hot tub on the deck is available to all adult guests.

Blackbeard's Lodge. *Moderate.* Off N.C. 12 (252-928-3421). This is reminiscent of one of the old family lodges popular several decades ago. Families return here yearly, even if this isn't resort material. The rooms are comfortable, with private baths and cable TV. The front desk was designed from the prow of a boat; it invites you to linger and visit with other guests or enjoy a magazine. Children enjoy the pool, and adults like to relax on the second-floor sun deck.

Inns and Bed-and-Breakfast Guest Houses

Berkley Manor Inn. *Expensive/Deluxe*. On the harbor (252-928-5911). You'll spot this beautifully restored estate from the Silver Lake ferry landing. The gable-roofed wooden structure is now run as a bed-and-breakfast inn. Its spacious rooms are decorated with traditional furniture and local artworks. Many rooms have a sitting area and a private bath. A full breakfast is included and is served in the den.

Oscar's House. *Moderate*. N.C. 12 (252-928-1311). This wonderfully quaint bed-and-breakfast house was built in 1940 by Joseph Burrus (Oscar's father), the last Ocracoke lighthouse keeper. Oscar later lived here while working as a fisherman and hunting guide. The guest rooms with shared baths are cozy and restful. The full breakfasts served here can accommodate special diets and feature fresh fruits and vegetables. This inn rents by the week during the summer.

Island Inn. *Moderate*. N.C. 12 (252-928-4351). This structure served as a school, an Odd Fellows lodge, and officers' quarters before it was restored and opened as a 35-room inn in the 1940s. Since then, there have been additions, so some sections are older and more rustic than others. The Island Inn Dining Room also enjoys a good reputation. The inn is not far from the ocean; you can also enjoy the pool.

Restaurants

Like the island itself—only 15 miles long—most of the eateries are small and quaint, but the menu selections offer variety. Your only problem will be choosing a spot. One thing to keep in mind: Ocracoke still depends on supply boats to deliver chicken, steak, and even beer. Consequently, menu offerings may not always be available. Go with the flow and order something else. It's the way of life here.

The Island Inn Dining Room. *Moderate*. At the Island Inn (252-928-7821). This restaurant offers a nice selection of entrées, all centered around reliable Southern family recipes. The crab cakes are famous and the desserts sure to entice. Beer and wine are offered. Breakfast and dinner are served daily, and lunch is available Monday through Friday.

The Back Porch Restaurant. *Moderate*. Off N.C. 12 (252-928-6401). A gourmet delight awaits you here. Tucked under shady trees, The Back Porch is a pleasant surprise on this laid-back island. It specializes in fresh food, including homemade bread and desserts, unique seafood dishes, and freshly ground coffee. Fried food is not the norm here; baked and broiled selections with a touch of France and a dash of creativity make this a popular spot. Beer and wine are offered. Dinner is served daily.

Cafe Atlantic. *Inexpensive/Moderate*. N.C. 12 (252-928-4861). The cafe serves a variety of burgers, seafood, pasta, and salad dishes for lunch. Dinner offerings include grilled seafood (crab cakes are a specialty), sautéed entrées, and homemade desserts. Beer and wine are available.

Pony Island Restaurant. *Inexpensive/Moderate*. At the Pony Motel off N.C. 12 (252-928-5701). This island favorite enjoys a good reputation, especially for steamed shrimp, homemade pastries, and nightly specials. Beer and wine are offered. Breakfast and dinner are served.

Howard's Pub. *Inexpensive/Moderate*. On N.C. 12 at the edge of the village just before the national seashore (252-928-4441). This cozy restaurant offers raw and cooked seafood dishes and an eclectic beer selection. It also has darts and other games and frequently offers live music by local musicians as well as off-island groups. This is a good spot for the whole family to eat and have fun. Open for lunch and dinner throughout the year.

The Coastal Plain

Albemarle Region
Neuse River Region
Cape Fear Coast
Southport/Brunswick Islands

by Ginger Moore

North Carolina's coastal plain stretches across nearly one-third of the state. The many appealing destinations here are well worth the trip on narrow country roads winding through flat, sometimes monotonous farmland. For a break, stop at one of the great produce stands along the way.

Most coastal-plain residents make their living from fishing, manufacturing, forestry, or farming. Harvests of corn, soybeans, and tobacco, tall pines, wildflowers, sand dunes, and sea oats predominate here. Let your mind and mood slow down and join the local pace—you'll be glad you came to visit.

Vacationers can explore the coastal plain by land or by water. Boaters will enjoy the rivers, sounds, bays, and canals sheltered by the Outer Banks, part of the chain of barrier islands extending from Florida to Chesapeake Bay. Along the Intracoastal Waterway, there are plenty of fueling and supply facilities, as well as marinas offering short-term anchorage for those who want to continue their sightseeing on terra firma.

To guide you on your travels, this book divides the coastal plain into four geographic sections—the Albemarle region, the Neuse River region, the Cape Fear coast, and Southport/Brunswick Islands—based on the primary bodies of water within them. Each region has a unique history and focus of its own.

The northeastern coastal section is known to residents as the

Albemarle region. The Pasquotank, Perquimans, Pungo, and Pamlico Rivers all have small towns perched on their banks, and all of them provide access to the sounds and the ocean. For the colonists, the waterways were transportation. For today's townspeople, the rivers and sounds provide a living and a way of life.

Emptying into Pamlico Sound, the broad estuary of the Neuse River anchors another region. Thanks to its parks, its beaches (known as the "Crystal Coast"), its national forest, its picturesque villages such as Beaufort and Oriental, and its stately, historic town of New Bern, the Neuse River region offers great diversity—elegant, historic accommodations in some places and a blue-jeans atmosphere in others.

Farther south, the Cape Fear region, steeped in history, is dominated by the deepwater port of Wilmington. The largest and fastest-growing city on the coast, Wilmington offers outstanding recreational and cultural opportunities. Between the river and the ocean lie Wrightsville Beach and Pleasure Island, located on two barrier islands. The ever-popular Carolina and Kure Beaches are found here.

The Brunswick County area—particularly the fishing town of Southport and the Brunswick Islands—has launched an intensive tourism campaign in recent years. For many natives and summer residents, this isn't all good news. These islands offer North Carolina's warmest climate and least-crowded beaches. Most development has taken place since 1954, when Hurricane Hazel destroyed many of the existing homes. Motels are sparse; cottages and condominiums have become the norm, but development still lags far behind that on the Outer Banks around Nags Head. Although Southport recently gained recognition as a movie location, there's no fast lane here. As for the islands, those who have visited the area for years hesitate to say too much—they don't want their wonderful, quiet beaches to change.

The coastal plain has figured prominently in North Carolina history. The area originally was regarded as part of Virginia. Major colonization began in 1663, when King Charles II deeded much of this land to eight Lords Proprietors—loyal monarchists and shrewd businessmen.

As settlers were attracted by generous offers of land and personal-property rights, the population of the coastal plain grew slowly. The town of Bath was chartered in 1705, but Edenton, founded 17 years later, emerged as the center of commerce and communication. In 1729, the Lords Proprietors sold their land shares back to the Crown, and Carolina became a Royal colony. However, patriots along the Carolina coast were among the first to oppose taxation by the British; in fact, the women of Edenton led a tea-party protest in 1774 that foreshadowed the later one in Boston.

During the Civil War, much of the coastal area was occupied by Federal troops, although Confederates controlled the port of Wilmington until a few weeks before the end of the war.

In the 20th century, the coastal-plain towns have returned to the business of farming and fishing.

Overall, the area is neither densely populated nor heavily traveled. But industry is beginning to revitalize the coastal plain. New bridges and highways provide links to the interstate network. And tourism continues to play a vital role in the region's economy.

When you travel this area, you'll know you're welcome.

Albemarle Region ....

Encompassing the northeastern corner of the state, the Albemarle region has a rich heritage and boasts a number of North Carolina firsts: the first church building, near Edenton; the first school; and the first capital, Edenton.

The small towns that dot this area bear curious names—Waterlily, Stonewall, Stumpy Point, Frying Pan Landing. Most are off the beaten track, but if you're interested in the history and charm of North Carolina and don't mind country roads, the trip is worthwhile.

Elizabeth City

With a population of 17,500, Elizabeth City is the economic and commercial hub of the Albemarle region and the home of a Coast Guard air station. While not exactly a tourist town, it has a growing tourism industry and is considered the gateway to the historic Albemarle region.

Settled in the 1650s, this small coastal town saw its beginnings when shipbuilders from Bermuda migrated here. When the Dismal Swamp Canal was dug in 1790, trade with the West Indies transformed the area into a vital freshwater harbor on the Pasquotank River, with access to the ocean. Elizabeth City then quickly replaced Edenton as the area's major port. The canal, the oldest still in service in the United States, provides an alternative to the Intracoastal Waterway route from Norfolk, Virginia, to the Pasquotank.

Once abuzz with important seagoing activity, the waterfront lost much of its luster for a time but is now being rejuvenated. There are small shops and good views of the harbor here. You'll find most of the historic sites in the downtown area, where private residences are being restored. The downtown district still has many private and commercial buildings dating from the 18th and 19th centuries. The Old Brick House, Hall's Creek Church, Christ Episcopal Church, and the Bayside Home are notable historic structures.

Most festivities—from the Moth Boat Regatta to the RiverSpree festival—center around the historic downtown and the nearby harbor district. Try to find a spot to dine in the harbor area in order to get a good look at the recreational boats and waterfront activities otherwise blocked from view.

ACCESS:

Elizabeth City is located where U.S. 17 and U.S. 158 meet. It is within 25 miles of the Virginia border and an hour from the Outer Banks.

Boaters can reach the area via the Intracoastal Waterway. Deepwater docking is complimentary for 48 hours.

The Elizabeth City/Pasquotank County Regional Airport, at 1028 Consolidated Road, has a 7,200-foot runway and can handle jets. Call 252-335-5634. The local Coast Guard station shares the airport.

The Trailways bus station is at 118 Hughes Boulevard; call 252-335-5183.

VISITOR INFORMATION:

Contact the Elizabeth City Chamber of Commerce, 502 East Ehringhaus Street, P.O. Box 426, Elizabeth City, N.C. 27907 (252-335-4365).

Attractions

Tours

The **Historic District Walking/Driving Tour** features a select number of private and commercial antebellum buildings in the 30-block historic district. Highlights are the Victorian courthouse, the stained-glass windows at Christ Episcopal Church, and the Neoclassic-style Federal Building. A map is available from the chamber of commerce. The tour is free. Call 252-335-4365.

Museums

Museum of the Albemarle, located on U.S. 17 southwest of town, is the place to go for literature and an orientation on the historic Albemarle area. Exhibits cover aspects of the life and work of people in 10 northeastern North Carolina counties. Adults can study the exhibit of decoys while the children enjoy the antique fire engines. Lectures and slide programs are offered by reservation only. The museum is open Tuesday through Saturday from 9 A.M. to 5 P.M. and Sunday from 2 to 5 P.M. It is closed state holidays. Admission is free. Call 252-335-1453.

Recreation

Seasonal Events

Festival of Lights and Lighted Boat Parade is held in November on the waterfront. Call 252-338-4104 for more information.

Moth Boat Regatta is held in September on the Pasquotank River. Call the Museum of the Albemarle for specific dates; the number is 252-335-1453.

Side Trips

The **Great Dismal Swamp**, stretching north from Elizabeth City across 210,000 acres into Virginia, is one of the last wooded wetlands of the region. More than 107,000 undeveloped acres are preserved as a wildlife refuge. The Great Dismal is the only live peat bog on the continent. It's home to 209 species of birds and many species of reptiles, along with rare butterflies and plants. Fed by deep springs, Lake Drummond, located across the border in Virginia, is hidden in the heart of the swamp—on sunny days, its surface reflects like a mirror. To reach this deepest interior, you must travel by boat via the Dismal Swamp Canal and Feeder Ditch.

There is a welcome center for the swamp at the rest area 15 miles north of Elizabeth City on U.S. 17. The center is open daily from June through October and Tuesday through Saturday from November to May; the hours are 9 A.M. to 5 P.M. The center offers free overnight docking for small boats. A grill and picnic areas are available. Near the center is a place to launch canoes and small boats. Nature lovers and canoeists should be alert for water moccasins and other native poisonous snakes. The launching area is open from sunrise to sunset. Call 252-771-8333.

Historic Murfreesboro, about 45 miles west of Elizabeth City, is a good choice if you're still hungry to see more colonial architecture. This early river port, founded in 1747, boasts more than 90 original 18th- and 19th-century brick and frame buildings. Located in the center of a farming area, Murfreesboro is very proud of its 12 blocks of historic buildings. Restoration is going on almost continuously, and several buildings on a walking tour are open to the public. Admission to buildings on the tour is $5 for adults and $1 for students; there is no charge for children under six. You can get a walking-tour map at the Roberts-Vaughan Village Center, at 116 East Main Street; look for the white frame house with five chimneys. The village center houses the town library, the chamber of commerce, and the historical association. The historical association arranges tours Monday through Friday from 8 A.M. to 5 P.M.; for more information, call 252-398-5922.

Newbold-White House is located on S.R. 1336 about 1.5 miles southeast of U.S. 17 Bypass in Hertford, which is 15 miles southwest of Elizabeth City. This site boasts quite a history—it was the home of Joseph Scott, one of the first Quakers to settle in the state, the meeting center of the proprietary government in the 1690s, and the location of the state's oldest brick house, built around 1730. Quakers still gather here once a year for festivities. A slide presentation, a small museum shop, and a personal tour are offered. The house is open Monday through Saturday from 10 A.M. to 4:30 P.M. from March 1 to Thanksgiving, or by appointment. Admission is $2 for adults and $1 for students and children. Call 252-426-7567.

Accommodations

Although Elizabeth City doesn't offer a wide selection, there are several reliable motels in town.

Holiday Inn. *Inexpensive/Moderate.* U.S. 17A at Halstead Boulevard (252-338-3951 or 800-HOLIDAY). This two-story motel has 160 rooms with TVs and some oversized beds. Room service, a coin laundry, and an outdoor pool are available. The cafe is open for breakfast and dinner. Children under 16 stay free, and senior citizens' rates are offered.

Vicki Villa. *Inexpensive.* 1161 North Road Street, a half-mile north of the city limit (252-335-2994). Here, you'll find 42 clean rooms with TVs, plus an outdoor pool.

Inns and Bed-and-Breakfast Guest Houses

The Culpepper Inn. *Moderate/Expensive.* 609 West Main Street (252-335-1993). This inn occupies one of the city's most impressive Colonial Revival houses. There are 11 individually decorated rooms, some with king-size beds and fireplaces. There is also a swimming pool. Rates include an "evening social" and a full breakfast.

Elizabeth City Bed and Breakfast. *Moderate.* 108 East Fearing Street (252-338-2177). This inn is located in downtown Elizabeth

City right on the Historic District Walking Tour and only a short walk from shops, restaurants, and the Pasquotank River. Each of the four rooms has a private bath. Breakfast is offered.

Restaurants

Traveling along U.S. 17, you'll encounter plenty of fast-fare offerings. If you continue toward the river, you can find seafood restaurants and delicatessens.

Mulligan's. *Moderate.* 400 South Water Street (252-331-2431). This restaurant resembles many of the wood-and-greenery chains that have proved so popular around the country. Guests can enjoy outdoor dining and occasional live music on the deck. Mulligan's serves seafood, pasta, and veal dishes. It also has a large full-service bar. Lunch and dinner are served seven days a week.

Marina. *Inexpensive/Moderate.* Camden Causeway (U.S. 158 East) right over the bridge (252-335-7307). This restaurant offers home-style seafood, ham, and liver and onions. An enclosed deck has recently been added; it offers diners a beautiful view of the Pasquotank River. A children's menu is offered, as is a full bar. The restaurant is open for lunch on Sunday and dinner Tuesday through Sunday.

Thumper's. *Inexpensive/Moderate.* 200 North Poindexter Street (252-333-1775). One of Elizabeth City's newest restaurants, Thumper's features a sports-bar atmosphere and excellent Cajun food. Lunch is offered Monday through Friday and dinner daily.

The Sandwich Market. *Inexpensive.* 706 West Ehringhaus Street (252-338-8181). This is a friendly, informal delicatessen featuring fresh salads, meats, and cheeses. You can eat in the cafe or have a picnic along the waterfront. Wine and imported and domestic beer are offered. Lunch is served daily.

Edenton

One of North Carolina's oldest and most charming communities, Edenton beckons you to get out of your car and stroll. Due in large part to the residents' commitment to preserving the town's history and to the success of Historic Edenton, this community is aptly called one of the South's prettiest towns. The National Register of Historic Places describes Edenton as having "an idyllic atmosphere that includes not only the fabric and scale of the past, but also much of its leisurely charm."

Established around 1685 and incorporated in 1722, Edenton was a prosperous port, shipping turpentine, pitch, corn, and tobacco to England. Even during the Revolutionary War, enterprising exporters slipped supplies for George Washington's army through the British blockade. Many Edenton citizens played important roles in the Revolution and in the formation of the republic.

Edenton's favorite sons include Joseph Hewes, a signer of the Declaration of Independence; Samuel Johnston, a patriot, North Carolina governor, and United States senator; and James Iredell, North Carolina's attorney general during the Revolution and an associate justice of the first United States Supreme Court.

Edenton's women also had a hand in the political action. In 1774, more than 50 local women signed a declaration stating they would support the provincial assembly's decision not to drink any more tea or wear English clothing. A bronze teapot on the village green commemorates their protest and serves as a symbol of Edenton.

In the early 1800s, large ships began to find the port hazardous. And with the completion of the Dismal Swamp Canal connecting the Pasquotank River to Chesapeake Bay, Edenton's influence diminished, as Elizabeth City and Norfolk, Virginia, became important centers for commerce. But happily, Edenton, like other towns which have fallen outside the spiral of modern development, is enjoying a reincarnation as a living memorial to our colonial heritage.

Today, the narrow residential streets shaded by giant magnolias, oaks, and pecan trees are lined with the state's largest collection of 18th-century buildings. Your first stop should be the Historic Edenton Visitor Center. There, you can join a guided tour or buy your own self-guided tour map.

Be sure to walk along the waterfront. It's a tranquil setting where visitors and locals enjoy the courthouse green, fish from Edenton Bay pier, picnic in the park, or simply enjoy a view complete with cypress trees rooted in the bottom of Albemarle Sound.

The walking tour encompasses about a five-block area, and all the historic buildings are close together. You won't be bored or disappointed, as every structure has a story behind it. And the mixture of Georgian, Federal, and Victorian architecture provides a visual feast. How nice, also, that most of these homes, some predating the Civil War, are occupied and lovingly cared for. In fact, many present-day owners are descendants of the original owners or builders. Flower gardens, climbing roses, and huge crape myrtles bloom from March through September, adding vibrant color to the well-kept residential neighborhoods.

In the business district, which is located within walking distance, you'll find small shops staffed with warm, friendly people. Cozy restaurants are conveniently nestled among the boutiques for a quick respite from touring and shopping.

ACCESS:

Edenton is located at the junction of U.S. 17 and N.C. 32 about 90 miles east of I-95.

Northeastern Regional Airport in Edenton has a 5,500-foot paved runway; call 252-482-4664. The nearest commercial airport is in Norfolk, 79 miles to the north.

Trailways buses make stops at the Edenton Bus Station at 810 Broad Street; call 252-482-2424.

VISITOR INFORMATION:

Contact Historic Edenton, P.O. Box 474, Edenton, N.C. 27932 (252-482-2637) for visitor information, or the Edenton-Chowan Chamber of Commerce, P.O. Box 245, Edenton, N.C. 27932 (252-482-3400 or 800-775-0111) for residential and commercial information.

The *Chowan Herald*, published weekly, is housed in an attractive restored building on Broad Street.

Attractions

The **Historic Edenton Visitor Center**, at 108 North Broad Street, is a must even if you're not inclined to take the walking tour. Friendly guides welcome you and invite you to watch a 14-minute slide show and browse the center. The gift shop offers a nice selection of history-oriented coloring books for children, books on state folklore, crafts, postcards, and gift items. The center is open Monday through Saturday from 9 A.M. to 5 P.M. and Sunday from 1 to 5 P.M.

from April to October. It is open Tuesday through Saturday from 10 A.M. to 4 P.M. and Sunday from 1 to 4 P.M. from November to March. Call 252-482-2637.

Tours

A self-guided tour map featuring 36 historic sites is available from the Historic Edenton Visitor Center for 50 cents. If you choose to take one of the **Guided Walking Tours**, you can purchase your ticket at the visitor center. The price depends upon which of the three tours you decide to take. The options are a one-hour tour of two historic sites, a 1½-hour tour through two sites, and a two-hour tour of five sites. Guided tours are conducted Monday through Saturday at 9:30 A.M., 10 A.M., 11 A.M., 1 P.M., 2 P.M., and 2:30 P.M. and Sunday at 1 P.M., 2 P.M., and 2:30 P.M. from April to October; the hours change from November to March. One stop on your tour might be **St. Paul's Episcopal Church** (1736-60), at Broad and Church Streets. A prime example of a colonial village church, St. Paul's has the oldest charter and is the second-oldest church building in the state. Partially burned in 1949, it was restored and still has an active congregation. **The Cupola House** (1758), at 408 South Broad Street, is a splendid example of mid-18th-century Jacobean architecture. **The Barker House** (c. 1782), was the home of Thomas and Penelope Barker. Thomas Barker was the London agent for the colony, and tradition holds that Penelope organized the Edenton Tea Party on October 25, 1774. **The Chowan County Courthouse** (1767), on East King Street is considered the finest Georgian courthouse in the South and is also the oldest courthouse in continuous use in the state. **The James Iredell House** (c. 1800–1827), at 105 East Church Street, was the home of a United States Supreme Court justice. The home and grounds represent a typical

The Cupola House
Photograph by William Russ
Courtesy of N.C. Travel and
Tourism Division

upper-middle-class homestead and offer a glimpse of the lifestyle of late-18th- and early-19th-century village dwellers.

Recreation

For those who prefer fishing to browsing through historic buildings and antique shops, Edenton offers many opportunities. The sounds, lakes, and coastal river have been stocked with striped bass by the Edenton National Fish Hatchery; there are bream, rockfish, crappie, and white perch as well.

Merchants Millpond State Park, reached by traveling 25 miles north on N.C. 32 and five miles west on U.S. 158, features 2,500 acres of cypress swamp. A major stopover for migrating waterfowl, the park offers pond fishing, canoeing (rentals are available), nature trails, picnicking, and nature programs. The park's camping facilities range from primitive to developed. Contact the Superintendent, Route 1, Box 141A, Gatesville, N.C. 27938 (252-357-1191).

Seasonal Events

The biennial **Edenton Pilgrimage** is held in April during odd-numbered years. Cosponsored by the Edenton Woman's Club and Historic Edenton, this event affords an opportunity to tour homes and buildings not usually open to the public. Call 252-482-2637.

The Peanut Festival, held the first Saturday in October, celebrates the annual peanut crop with a parade, band competitions, arts and crafts, and barbecue and other refreshments. The festival takes place at John A. Holmes High School on Broad Street. Call 252-482-2637.

Christmas festivities include the **Iredell House Groaning Board**, the **Cupola House Wassail Bowl**, and the **Candlelight Tour**—an evening tour of private residences—all held on the second Friday and Saturday in December. Call 252-482-2637.

Side Trips

Hope Plantation, about 20 miles west in Windsor, was the home of North Carolina governor and United States senator David Stone. Built in 1803, the yellow, two-story plantation house is an example of the Georgian and Federal styles. Also on the property is the 1763 King-Bazemore House, constructed of handmade brick. Its covered porch and main floor were built a half-story above the ground to catch all available breezes. The plantation is open Monday through Saturday from 10 A.M. to 5 P.M. and Sunday from 2 to 5 P.M. from January 3 to December 20 (except Thanksgiving). Admission is $6.50 for adults, $6 for senior citizens, $3 for students, and $2 for children ages six and under. Hope Plantation is located on N.C. 308 about four miles west of U.S. 13 Bypass in Windsor. Call 252-794-3140.

Somerset Place State Historic Site, 45 minutes south of Edenton near Creswell, is considered the best existing example of plantation life in the slave-supported economy of the antebellum South. Josiah Collins III, grandson of the original owner, was one of only four planters in this area with more than 300 slaves. The Collins mansion, the gardens, and several outbuildings have been beautifully preserved. A carriage drive lined by huge cypress trees leads to the front entrance of the mansion alongside Somerset Canal, which was dug to its 20-foot width by slaves in the 1780s. The site is open Monday through Saturday from 9 A.M. to 5 P.M. and Sunday from 1 to 5 P.M. (last tour at 4 P.M.) from April to October. It is also open Tuesday through Saturday from 10 A.M. to 4 P.M. and Sunday from 1 to 4 P.M. from November to April. Admission is free. Somerset Place is seven miles south of Creswell on U.S. 64; it's located near Lake Phelps and Pettigrew State Park, a nice spot for a picnic lunch. Call 252-797-4560.

Accommodations

Most visitors to Edenton prefer the ambiance of the town's charming, historic bed-and-breakfast inns. (Some accept children, but be sure to inquire about age restrictions and rate changes.) However, if inns aren't your style or cost more than you care to spend, several motels in town have surprisingly low rates.

Travel Host. *Inexpensive.* U.S. 17/32 Bypass (252-482-2017). This motel has 66 comfortable rooms and a small pool that's open in summer.

Coach House Inn. *Inexpensive.* 919 North Broad Street (252-482-2107). This inn is nothing fancy, but its 38 rooms are clean and offer cable TV.

Inns and Bed-and-Breakfast Guest Houses

The Lords Proprietors' Inn. *Expensive/Deluxe.* 300 North Broad

Street (252-482-3641). This inn is actually three historic buildings and a restored tobacco barn combined. It includes 20 guest rooms, three charming parlors, and a library—all furnished with antiques or antique reproductions. Afternoon tea and a full breakfast are provided. Supper is served to guests Tuesday through Saturday.

Dram Tree Inn. *Moderate*. 110 and 112 Water Street (252-482-4038). This is the only waterfront inn in Historic Edenton. It is close to antique shops, the waterfront, and the park. It offers two-bedroom suites with private baths.

Governor Eden Inn. *Moderate*. 304 North Broad Street (252-482-2072). This spacious Neoclassical white home accented with Ionic columns and beveled glass has four guest rooms and offers a full breakfast.

Granville Queen Inn. *Moderate*. 108 South Granville Street (252-482-5296). Each of this inn's nine guest rooms is unique and theme-designed. A five-course breakfast is served on the porch. A wine-tasting is offered on the weekends.

Trestle House Inn. *Moderate*. Soundside Road off N.C. 32 south of Edenton (252-482-2282). The Trestle House was formerly part of the Crisanti Ranch. Built from redwood railroad trestles, it has a warm, cozy air. Though Trestle House is located several miles from the historic area, it's worth the drive to enjoy the wildlife refuge located just behind the inn and the 20-acre lake that surrounds it on three sides. Canoeing, birding, and fishing are all available to adventurous guests. The inn has five guest rooms, each with a private bath, and offers a full gourmet breakfast.

Restaurants

Dram Tree Restaurant. *Moderate*. 110 and 112 Water Street (252-482-4038). You can enjoy your choice of atmosphere here; the West Indies Room offers elegant dining, while the Garden Room is light and casual. The lounge features Edenton's largest fireplace. Beer, wine, mixed beverages, and setups are available. Lunch is served Tuesday through Sunday and dinner Monday through Saturday.

Mario's Pizza. *Inexpensive*. Gaslight Square (252-482-7656). This Italian restaurant specializes in pizzas but also offers other tempting fare such as pasta and wings for fabulous prices. Lunch and dinner are served daily except on Mondays.

Bath

The state's oldest incorporated town, Bath is tucked away on a peninsula just off the Pamlico River. Chartered in 1705, it was named for the earl of Bath, one of the eight Lords Proprietors of Carolina.

Because it was the colony's first official port of entry, Bath was a meeting place for the colonial assembly.

Preachers, politicians, and pirates—including Edward Teach, the notorious Blackbeard—tended to their respective interests in the thriving trade center of Bath. The effect of pirates on the town's prosperity shouldn't be underestimated. Blackbeard's decision to settle in Bath was for a time an economic windfall, because he and his crew spent their ill-gotten wealth here. Rumors still circulate that part of Blackbeard's treasure is hidden around Bath, but no one has ever reported finding a single doubloon.

In the late 18th century, Bath declined in influence, as merchant shippers sought other ports. It's been a quiet little town ever since.

Today, Bath is located almost entirely within the boundaries of the original town plan, measuring three blocks long and two blocks wide. Part of the area is the Historic Bath State Historic Site, which has several preserved properties open to public viewing. If you don't take the tour, be sure to follow Main and Front Streets to Bonner Point to the picnic area and a view of the river.

The residents take pride in their community's heritage, welcoming visitors at the Historic Bath Visitor Center and sharing bits of history with strolling tourists. Local building codes restrict the style of new construction in order to preserve the town's uniform country appearance. While only four antebellum homes remain, you can see ballast stones taken from Bath Creek 200 years ago in the walls and foundations of some structures. Main Street has a number of late-19th- and early-20th-century homes and commercial buildings.

Don't look for McDonald's or your favorite service station (though there is Ye Olde ABC Package Store). Bath residents prefer the quiet life of fishing and boating along the Pamlico River.

ACCESS:
Bath is located on N.C. 92 about 15 miles east of Washington, North Carolina. It is also accessible by boat from the Pamlico River.

VISITOR INFORMATION:
Contact the Historic Bath State Historic Site, P.O. Box 148, Bath, N.C. 27808 (252-923-3971).

Attractions

Historic Bath Visitor Center, on N.C. 92 as you drive into town, is an important stopping place. Its 15-minute orientation film, *Bath–The First Town*, is educational as well as entertaining. You can also join a guided tour or pick up a map for a self-guided tour. The center is open Monday through Saturday from 9 A.M. to 5 P.M. and Sunday from 1 to 5 P.M. from April to October. It is also open Tuesday through Saturday from 10 A.M. to 4 P.M. and Sunday from 1 to 4 P.M. from November to March. Call 252-923-3971.

Tours

If you opt for the guided **Historic Bath Tour**, allow 90 minutes. Departing from the visitor center, you'll see the Bonner House (1830); the Palmer-Marsh House (1751), which boasts a gabled roof, a double chimney, and 18th-century appointments and has the distinction of being both the oldest house in Bath and the home where Edna Ferber stayed while researching *Showboat*; and the Van der Veer House (1790), which contains exhibits reflecting Bath's history. Admission for the Bonner and Palmer-Marsh Houses is $2 for adults and $1 for students. Call 252-923-3971.

Historic Places

St. Thomas Episcopal Church, on Craven Street, is the oldest church in the state. Built in 1734 and later restored, the church is a simple, rectangular brick building with no steeple. Visitors are welcome.

Side Trips

Aurora Fossil Museum, 12 miles south of Bath across the Pamlico River on Main Street in Aurora, is a small museum exhibiting fish fossils from the Pliocene period (5 million years ago). You'll learn about the geologic forces that created the coastal plain; you can even search for specimens in a mound across the street. To get to the museum, ride the free ferry across the Pamlico River, then take N.C. 306 into Aurora. The museum is open Tuesday through Friday from 9 A.M. to 4:30 P.M. and Saturday from 9 A.M. to 2 P.M. from June to August, or by appointment. Admission is free. Call 252-322-4238.

Accommodations

Inns and Bed-and-Breakfast Guest Houses

Bath is a very small town. Many visitors drive from Washington or Greenville, making Bath a day trip.

River Forest Manor. *Moderate*. 738 East Main Street, Belhaven (252-943-2151). This stately Georgian mansion serves as an inn and has its own marina on the Pungo River section of the inland waterway. Decorated in Victorian style, the manor has 11 fireplaces and 12 guest rooms. Boaters often dock here to enjoy River Forest's 56-dish evening buffet or Sunday brunch.

Neuse River Region ....

Of all the coastal regions, the area around the Neuse River offers the most diversity. After winding snakelike for nearly 50 miles, the Neuse River (pronounced "Noose," and named for the Neusiok Indians, who once inhabited its shores) spreads into an estuary that empties into Pamlico Sound. The Neuse's fingers reach into Craven, Pamlico, and Carteret Counties, where you'll find picturesque fishing villages such as Beaufort and Oriental, historic New Bern (the home of Tryon Palace), and miles of beach, national forest, and recreation areas.

Along one shore, Croatan National Forest surrounds the Cherry Point Marine Air Station. Along another, back roads lead to summer camps and small towns unspoiled by flashy commercial development. You can reach Minnesott Beach by car or free ferry across the Neuse from Cherry Branch. Farther upriver at Kinston, you can visit the remains of the CSS *Neuse*, the last ironclad ship built during the Civil War.

If you're game for hiking a dozen miles through forest and swamp, pick up the Neusiok Trail near Cherry Point. Indians, Huguenots, Quakers, and other early inhabitants found fertile land and good hunting and fishing in this area. You can do the same.

New Bern

With a beautiful historic district, interesting shops and galleries, and a variety of restaurants and pleasant accommodations, New Bern is an ideal place to step back in time while enjoying the amenities of the present.

Settled in 1710, New Bern is North Carolina's second-oldest town. Its location between the Neuse and Trent Rivers appealed to Swiss and German Protestants seeking to establish a colony free from religious persecution. As New Bern grew more and more prosperous from shipping tar, pitch, and turpentine to New England, England, and the West Indies, it eventually superseded then-capital Edenton in economic importance.

When the colonial assembly was held in 1766, Royal Governor William Tryon selected New Bern as the site for a permanent capital of the colony. Tryon Palace, North Carolina's first capitol building, was completed in 1770, and New Bern became the political center of the colony. As the seat of government, it was a focal point for the events leading to the Revolution, and even after the capital was moved to Raleigh in 1794, New Bern maintained its influence on state politics and economics.

The town continued to grow in wealth and stature until the Civil War, when Federal forces captured it early in 1862. But during Reconstruction, New Bern recovered relatively quickly because of its prosperous lumbermills and seafood industry.

Have you heard that Pepsi-Cola is the "Pride of the Carolinas"? In the 1890s, C. D. Bradham, a New Bern pharmacist, invented "Brad's Drink" and sold it in his drugstore. Today, we know that drink as Pepsi-Cola. Unfortunately, Bradham went bankrupt during the sugar shortage of World War I. A small amount of syrup had been stockpiled, however, and new distributors revived the drink. A Pepsi-Cola memorabilia store opened its doors in 1998 on Middle and Pollock Streets to commemorate the 100th anniversary of the creation of the soft drink.

Since World War II, the New Bern area has grown to its current population of 22,000. Tourism increased dramatically after Tryon Palace was reconstructed in the 1950s. A historic district was created. New Bern soon saw proof of its new appeal when bed-and-breakfast inns began to open.

Don't leave New Bern without spending time in its historic district, with its many houses and public buildings of Georgian, Federal, Victorian, and Classical Revival architecture. The post–Revolutionary War period stimulated architectural innovation here. Many of those buildings have been carefully restored and maintained and most are occupied by residents of the town.

The downtown district is a pleasant blend of old and new. The city is second only to Charleston, South Carolina, in the number of places on the National Historic Register. There are shops offering antiques, nautical gifts, clothing, imports, dolls, and novelties. You'll also find genuine 1950s lunch counters and small restaurants.

While you're touring the town, you'll undoubtedly notice a recurring theme on plaques and statues—the black bear. New Bern shares this symbol with its sister city, Berne, Switzerland. A framed bear banner from Berne, presented in 1896 by the Swiss ambassador to the United States, hangs in city hall. Cast-iron black bears, also gifts from Berne, look down from above the entrances. You'll find another at the Fireman's Museum. Challenge the children—have them count all the black bears around town.

ACCESS:

New Bern can be reached via U.S. 70 or U.S. 17. Located at the confluence of the Neuse and Trent Rivers, the city is also accessible via the Intracoastal Waterway. Marinas are available for private boaters.

The Trailways bus station is located at 504 Guion Street; call 252-633-3100.

USAirways commuter planes fly into Craven County Regional Airport. Its runways are 4,000 and 6,000 feet. Carolina Air, Inc., is a fixed-base operation offering fueling and maintenance. Call 252-638-8591.

VISITOR INFORMATION:

Contact the Craven County Convention and Visitors Bureau, P.O. Box 1413, New Bern, N.C. 28563 (252-637-9400 or 800-437-5767).

New Bern's daily newspaper is the *Sun Journal.*

Attractions

Tours

Self-Guided Walking Tour maps are available from the visitors bureau, located at 314 South Front Street. If you choose to cover the entire area, plan to walk about eight blocks. The tour takes at least an hour, depending on how long you want to linger. Another alternative is to drive to the concentrated areas—the palace, Johnson Street, Pollock Street—and then walk. You'll see many attractive historic homes and commercial buildings, along with a few shops and eateries. Much of the tour is on quiet residential streets well shaded by tall trees.

The downtown area is tranquil by most urban dwellers' standards. Crossing Broad Street (U.S. 70/17) is the biggest challenge. Along the tour, you'll see a variety of stately brick and frame homes of Victorian, Federal, and Neoclassic Revival architecture. Most of the churches of historic note are open during the week. A taped narration of the walking tour is available at the visitors bureau.

New Bern Tours offers a comprehensive trolley tour of downtown New Bern focusing on the city's architectural beauty. For rates and times, call 252-637-7316 or 800-849-7316.

Tryon Palace
Photograph by William Russ
Courtesy of N.C. Travel and Tourism
Division

Historic Places

Tryon Palace and Gardens is located at 610 Pollock Street, one block south of U.S. 17 and U.S. 70 Business. The complex covers more than 13 acres in the historic district. It includes the palace and outbuildings, the gardens, the John Wright Stanly House, the Dixon-Stevenson House, and the New Bern Academy Museum. When completed in 1770, the palace was declared the most beautiful building in the colonial Americas by Europeans and colonial visitors alike. It's just as impressive today.

When William Tryon became governor of the colony in 1765, he commissioned English architect John Hawks to design and supervise the construction of the government house. In 1770, Tryon and his family moved into Tryon Palace. When Tryon's successor, Josiah Martin, moved in, he contracted with Hawks to build a smokehouse, a poultry house, and a pigeon house. New Bern was eventually designated the capital of the new state, and in 1777 the first legislative assembly convened there.

The main building was destroyed by fire in 1798, but by then New Bern and Tryon Palace had lost some of their political significance, as Raleigh had replaced New Bern as the state capital. Palace lots were sold and other buildings erected, until only the west wing remained. Many attempts were made through the years to restore the palace. Schoolchildren saved their pennies, and proceeds from historical pageants were donated. In 1939, researchers turned up the original Tryon Palace plans in New York, and a restoration trust fund was established by Mrs. Maude Moore Latham, a native of New Bern. Ultimately, she donated a large sum to the fund and inspired others to do so as well.

Mrs. Latham died in 1951, before any substantial work had been done on the project; it was completed by a state commission headed by her daughter, Mrs. John A. Kellenberger. Historians and archaeologists meticulously researched the project, one of the most ambitious historical reconstructions ever attempted. On April 8, 1959, Tryon Palace was officially opened to the public and has been one of the state's major attractions ever since.

As you approach the palace, the branches of giant oaks arch over the allée. A colonnade joins the main building with the reconstructed east wing and the west wing, the only remaining part of the original building. This wing serves as a stable, granary, and carriage house.

Tours begin in the visitor center with a 20-minute film. In the palace, a gracious guide in period costume then leads visitors through the elegant quarters. The entrance hall, with its floor of Italian white marble and Belgian black marble, is very striking, and the rest of the palace is no less impressive. It's furnished with 18th-century English and American art and antiques—including English cut-glass chandeliers—that reflect the look and style of the palace at the time of the Tryon governorship.

On the tour, you'll learn about North Carolina history and historical restoration. For example, the library is filled with 400 books known to have been owned by the Tryons. The parlor features a walnut spinet made in the 1720s by Thomas Hitchcock. On the tables in the council chamber are beeswax candles, quill pens, and reproductions of documents to help you visualize Governor Tryon dealing with the crises of his day. For inspiration, he could look up at the full-length portraits of King George III and Queen Charlotte.

Climb the broad staircase of mahogany and pegged walnut, illuminated by a skylight dome in the roof. There, in the private quarters, you'll see beautiful canopy beds, draperies of rich silk and damask, and delicate furniture upholstered in red velvet and needlework. Margaret Tryon's bedroom is resplendent in shades of pink, with doll furniture duplicating the full-scale furnishings. The second-floor drawing room and supper room contain beautiful silver and china.

The Tryons owed their gracious lifestyle to a large complement of servants. In the servants' quarters, people in period dress reenact the typical daily activities of the palace: cooking, spinning, weaving, and laundering. Pleasant aromas drift from the open hearth, where food is prepared.

At the end of the tour, you're free to wander through the palace gardens. You may meet a variety of historical character actors, from

Mr. and Mrs. Tryon to Mr. and Mrs. Dixon to sailors and servants. There's a "green garden" with small trees and crape myrtles, designed to be viewed from the house; a kitchen garden for herbs and foodstuffs; the bright and colorful Maude Moore Latham Memorial Garden; and the Kellenberger Garden. You're likely to spot some palace gardeners at work. From the south lawn, you can see the Trent River. Originally, the grounds extended to the river, where English ships used to dock.

One of the outbuildings serves as a crafts and garden shop, where visitors can purchase plants grown on the grounds and other garden-related items, such as herbal vinegar. There's a museum shop on the corner of Eden and Pollock Streets.

Allow at least three hours for your visit. Tryon Palace is open Monday through Saturday from 9 A.M. to 5 P.M. and Sunday from 1 to 5 P.M. and offers extended summer hours between Memorial Day and Labor Day. It is closed Thanksgiving, December 24 through December 26, and New Year's Day. Admission to the palace complex and gardens is $12 for adults and $6 for students through high school. Admission to the gardens, kitchen office, and academy only is $7 for adults and $3 for students. Call 252-514-4900 or 800-767-1560. The ticket price includes admission to the Dixon-Stevenson House, the John Wright Stanley House, and the New Bern Academy Museum.

The **Dixon-Stevenson House** was built around 1830 for a middle class merchant of New Bern. The furnishings are in the Empire and Federal styles. You'll see original hand-carved woodwork and rope and cable molding throughout the house.

The **John Wright Stanly House**, built in the 1780s, was the home of this Revolutionary War patriot. Inside the architecturally outstanding Georgian-style house are 18th-century antiques. And yes, George Washington slept here, during his 1791 tour of the South. The house also served as temporary headquarters for Union general Ambrose Burnside, who captured New Bern in 1862.

The **New Bern Academy Museum** focuses on New Bern's architecture and early education and the city's occupation by Union forces during the Civil War. The New Bern Academy was founded in 1764, making it one of the oldest secondary schools in America. The museum is located in an 1809 building once used by the school. It is open daily from 1 to 5 P.M. Admission is included with the ticket to

Tryon Palace or can be obtained separately at a cost of $3 for adults and $1 for students.

Another house museum that's a must-see is the **Attmore-Oliver House**, at 511 Broad Street (entrance located at 510 Pollock Street). Built in 1790, the home is furnished with 18th- and 19th-century antiques and features a Civil War museum room and a doll collection. It is open Tuesday through Saturday from 1 to 4:30 P.M. from April to early December, or by appointment. There is no charge for admission, but donations are accepted. Call 252-638-8558.

Christ Episcopal Church (1715), at Middle and Pollock Streets, and **First Presbyterian Church** (1819–22), at New Street near Middle Street, are handsome edifices usually open to the public. Gifts from King George II, including a silver communion service, are still used at Christ Church. First Presbyterian was one of many buildings used as hospitals during the Civil War.

Museums

The Fireman's Museum, at 408 Hancock Street, is a rather unique and off beat way to learn about the history of the town. New Bern seems a good setting for such a museum, since it boasts two of the oldest continuously operating fire companies in the country: the Atlantic Fire Engine Company, begun in 1845, and the Button Company, started in 1865. Museum guides offer stories of famous fires as they show visitors steam pumpers and an extensive collection of firefighting equipment, Civil War relics, and pictures. Though they are not allowed on the trucks, children will enjoy hearing about an old firehorse named Fred, whose mounted head hangs near equipment he used to pull. The museum is open Monday through Saturday from 10 A.M. to 4:30 P.M. and Sunday from 1 to 5 P.M. It is closed Thanksgiving, Christmas, and New Year's Day. Admission is $2 for adults and $1 for students. Call 252-636-4087 for more information.

Cultural Offerings

Bank of Arts, at 317 Middle Street, is the home of the Craven Arts Council and Gallery. It is a cultural and architectural treat. Situated in a 1912 Neoclassic bank building, the gallery displays artwork including pottery, paintings, sculpture, and photography. All exhibits change every six weeks. The 30-foot ceilings provide excellent acoustics for concerts, and the ornate plaster and Beaux-Arts style are a visual plus. During the summer months, the arts council offers music-in-the-park concerts. The gallery is open Monday through Saturday from 10 A.M. to 5 P.M.; it is closed some holidays. Admission is free. Call 252-638-2577.

The New Bern Civic Theatre stages performances at the Saax Bradbury Playhouse, located at 414 Pollock Street. Visiting professionals and local players act in a variety of Broadway musicals and plays. Call 252-633-0567.

Recreation

Croatan National Forest, immediately southwest of New Bern via U.S. 17/70, includes more than 159,000 acres of coastal forest, waterways, and estuaries. The wooded expanse is a favorite of nature lovers; it's also the northernmost home of the alligator. Even if you don't want to look for alligators, you'll enjoy finding the many dwarf and insect-eating plants, particularly the Venus's-flytraps; the best place to look for them is on the pocosins (Indian for "swamp on a hill"). Camping, swimming, boating, picnicking, and fishing are available; hunters pursue deer, turkeys, quail, and ducks. Contact the District Ranger, 141 East Fisher Avenue, New Bern, N.C. 28560 (252-638-5629).

Minnesott Beach, located near the ferry across the Neuse on U.S. 306, offers clean river beaches and a golf course. A free ferry leaves Cherry Branch at frequent intervals between 5:45 and 12:45 A.M. and returns from Minnesott Beach at intervals between 6:15 and 1:15 A.M. Crossing time is 20 minutes.

The **Neuse River Recreation Area**, on U.S. 70 about 11 miles southeast of New Bern, offers camping, fishing, swimming, and hiking facilities. Call 252-638-5628.

Seasonal Events

Spring Historic Homes and Garden Tour is held every April, when the azaleas and dogwoods are usually at their best. At least 10 private historic homes are open to the public. Cosponsored by the New Bern Historical Society and the New Bern Preservation Foundation, the tour also features churches and other historically significant buildings. It's a delight for anyone who has admired the exteriors of these houses and is dying to see the inside. Tickets are $13.50 in advance and $15 the day of the tour. Contact Spring Historic Homes and Garden Tour, P.O. Box 207, New Bern, N.C. 28563 (252-633-6448 or 252-638-8558).

Rotary Cup Sailing Regatta is an exciting sailboat race held on the Neuse River near Fairfield Harbor during Labor Day weekend. The festivities, spread over the course of Friday and Saturday, include a concert at the farmers' market and a five-kilometer road race. The event is sponsored by the Rotary Club of New Bern.

Rotary Cup Sailing Regatta
Courtesy of N.C. Travel and
Tourism Division

During the **Chrysanthemum Festival** in mid-October, downtown comes alive. There's street dancing, antique and craft shows, food, and entertainment. Contact the Mum Festival Events Office at 252-638-5781.

The Annual Christmas Celebration of Tryon Palace runs from the day after Thanksgiving through mid-December. Tryon Palace and five historic homes are authentically decorated and open to the public. The admission fee is the same as that for touring the palace and the historic homes the rest of the year. Candlelight tours are offered on Friday and Saturday from 5 to 9 P.M. at the same cost. Call 252-514-4900 or 800-767-1560.

Side Trips

Oriental, about 25 miles east of New Bern, is one of those tranquil harbor towns that people like to keep secret. If you find Oriental a place to take off your shoes and stay awhile, you won't be the first person to have been captivated by its unpretentious charm. In the several gift and antique shops, you'll run into people who will be glad to tell you about their hometown. There's affluence here, too; you'll see some attractive houses situated along the waterfront.

Located at the gateway to Pamlico Sound, Oriental is considered a sailing capital of the East Coast. Many boat owners who live inland keep their vessels here. The Oriental Sailing School enjoys a fine reputation, its students coming from many states to gain experience. Charters are available, as are excellent fishing and diving.

To get to Oriental, take U.S. 17 east from New Bern, then follow N.C. 55.

If you decide to stay, you have a choice of accommodations:

The Cartwright House. *Moderate/Expensive*. One block from the Neuse River (252-249-1337). This inn features a lovely garden and is located just a short walk from shops, restaurants, and the river.

The Inn at Oriental. *Moderate*. 508 Church Street (252-249-1078). A friendly English-style bed-and-breakfast built in 1899, the inn has eight guest rooms with private baths. It serves a full breakfast.

Oriental Marina Motel. *Inexpensive/Moderate*. On the harbor (252-249-1818). Here, you can dock the boat and take a dip in the pool. Try the crab cakes in the motel's restaurant for dinner, and then wake up to a full breakfast delivered to your room in the morning.

Oriental is a nautical town, a theme that carries through to its casual restaurants. **The Trawl Door**, a Silver Spoon Award winner (it could have been the carrot cake), is located in a former hardware store; the locals rave about the specials.

CSS *Neuse* State Historic Site and the **Richard Caswell Memorial** are located within Kinston's city limits. The memorial commemorates North Carolina's first governor with an audiovisual program and a statue. Outside under a shelter are the remains of the ironclad *Neuse*. The last ironclad built by the Confederacy, it was finished too late to help the faltering South. As it was steaming down the Neuse River to New Bern in 1865, a party of Union soldiers prepared to attack it. Rather than risk capture by the enemy, the crew sank the vessel. It remained embedded in the mud for nearly a century and was finally pulled out in 1963. It was then partially restored and put on display. The sites are open Monday through Saturday from 9 A.M. to 5 P.M. and Sunday from 1 to 5 P.M. from April to October. They are also open Tuesday through Saturday from 10 A.M. to 4 P.M. and Sunday from 1 to 4 P.M. from November to March. Admission is free. Call 252-522-2091.

Accommodations

For its size, New Bern offers a wide choice of accommodations, ranging from upscale hotels with marinas to quaint bed-and-breakfast inns whose rooms hold their own history. Even with the selection, however, it's wise to make reservations. Inquire about children; there may be an extra charge. If you are traveling off-season, ask about special rates.

Sheraton Grand New Bern. *Moderate/Expensive*. On the waterfront at Middle and Craven Streets (252-638-3585 or 800-326-3745). The Sheraton provides the amenities of a leisure and business hotel plus 156 slips for docking. At least half of the hotel rooms and suites have a view of the Trent and Neuse Rivers. The restaurant overlooks the marina and the pool area. Lower rates are offered off-season. Ask about the senior-citizen discount.

Comfort Suites Riverfront Park. *Moderate*. 218 East Front Street (252-636-0022 or 800-228-5150). This motel is situated on the Neuse River next to Union Point Park. It features a refrigerator and microwave in every suite and an outdoor pool with a waterfront courtyard. Jacuzzi suites are also available. A complimentary continental breakfast is included.

Days Inn. *Moderate*. 925 Broad Street (252-636-0150 or 800-329-7466). This motel offers 110 rooms, cable TV, and a swimming pool.

Hampton Inn. *Moderate*. U.S. 17/70 Bypass (252-637-2111 or 800-448-8288). This chain motel offers an exercise room, a swimming pool, HBO, and golf packages.

Ramada Inn Waterfront & Marina. *Moderate*. 101 Howell Road at the junction of U.S. 70 and U.S. 70E Bypass (252-636-3637 or 800-272-6232). This motel has 112 rooms and four suites, all with a river view. It offers a complimentary newspaper, cable TV, and a restaurant, along with senior-citizen, business, and military rates.

Inns and Bed-and-Breakfast Guest Houses

Harmony House Inn. *Moderate/Expensive*. 215 Pollock Street (252-636-3810 or 800-636-3113). Built in the 1850s and added onto as its owner's family grew, Harmony House is an interesting Greek Revival home with a wide front porch. The present owners have furnished the entire inn with antiques and reproductions, many made by local craftsmen. The inn offers eight guest rooms with private (and spacious) baths and two suites. A full breakfast is served.

The Aerie. *Moderate*. 509 Pollock Street (252-636-5553 or 800-849-5553). This two-story Victorian home, built in 1870, is only one block from Tryon Palace. Each of its seven individually decorated guest rooms has a private bath. A full breakfast is served in the attractive dining room.

Kings Arms. *Moderate*. 212 Pollock Street (252-638-4409 or 800-872-9306 or www.bbhost.com/kingsarmsinn). Constructed in 1847, Kings Arms has gone through many changes over the years. Named after an old tavern said to have been a favorite spot of members of the First Provincial Congress, the Colonial-style inn has eight spacious guest rooms with fireplaces and private baths and one suite. A full breakfast is served in your room with the morning paper.

New Berne House. *Moderate*. 709 Broad Street (252-636-2250 or 800-842-7688). Hospitality abounds in this stately Colonial-style home. Guests can enjoy a variety of complimentary refreshments during the day. Fine antiques and traditional furnishings are featured in the seven guest rooms, each of which has a private bath. A full breakfast is served. Call and ask about the monthly Mystery Weekends, sure to keep you entertained your entire stay.

Restaurants

New Bern offers a variety of dining options ranging from gourmet to casual chic to dependable. Prices are comparable to those in larger cities, but in most cases, so is the quality of the food.

Henderson House. *Expensive*. 216 Pollock Street (252-637-4784). This restaurant has been winning awards since 1973. Housed in an elegant brick Federal home included on the National Register of Historic Places, it has a touch of elegance that enhances the gourmet offerings. Delicacies include cold plum and apricot soup and coquilles St. Jacques. The desserts are equally appealing. Dinner is served Wednesday through Sunday.

The Harvey Mansion Restaurant & Lounge. *Moderate/Expensive*. 221 South Front Street (252-638-3205). This landmark, listed on the National Register of Historic Places, is a well-known dining spot overlooking the Trent River. The gold-medal-winning chef offers exciting international cuisine. The house has six formal dining rooms and a lounge in the cellar and often offers live entertainment.

Open daily for dinner.

The Flame. *Moderate/Expensive*. 2303 Neuse Boulevard (252-633-0262). In this restaurant's unique Victorian atmosphere, guests enjoy steak, lobster, fabulous stuffed baked potatoes, and a gourmet salad bar. Dinner is served Tuesday through Saturday.

Fred and Claire's Restaurant. *Moderate*. 247 Craven Street (252-638-5426). Tucked under a cheery awning downtown, Fred and Claire's serves a variety of unusual dishes, including quiches, omelets, and specialty sandwiches. Credit cards are not accepted. The restaurant is open Monday through Saturday from 11 A.M. to 7 P.M.

Pollock Street Delicatessen & Restaurant. *Inexpensive/Moderate*. 208 Pollock Street (252-637-2480). This New York–style deli serves a variety of fresh salads, generous sandwiches, a creative selection of entrées that changes daily, and homemade desserts. Credit cards are accepted. Breakfast, lunch, and dinner are served daily.

Morehead City

The mention of Morehead City conjures up images of fishing boats and fresh seafood. This port, located across the Intracoastal Waterway from Beaufort and linked to the Atlantic Beach area, plays host to ocean freighters and charter boats alike. The largest town in Carteret County, Morehead City attracts many visitors who know that, for eight months of the year, Gulf Stream fishing brings in marlin, amberjack, dolphin, mackerel, tarpon, and bluefish.

During the 1850s, John Motley Morehead, a former North Carolina governor, purchased land in this area, brought in the railroad, and dreamed of developing a commercial center on Bogue Sound. The Civil War disrupted his plans, but by the turn of the century, Morehead City had become a summer resort, attracting wealthy vacationers to its hotels and cottages.

The fishing industry continued to grow, and in 1952, a deepwater port was established. The Morehead City State Port continues to be a shipping center for several industries. Its two 115-ton gantry cranes give the port one of the largest lifting capacities in the South.

Today, Morehead City is an interesting mixture of the old and the new. The waterfront area, with its charter fleets, gift and antique shops, fish markets, and restaurants, is especially appealing.

Attractions

Museums

Carteret County Museum of History is located at 100 Wallace Drive, near the Crystal Coast Civic Center. This small museum provides a look into the county's past, offering displays of quilts, seashells, Indian artifacts, and furniture built or used in the area. There's also a small art gallery. Owned by the historical society, the museum is open Tuesday through Saturday in the afternoons. Admission is free. Call 252-247-7533.

Recreation

Fishing is unquestionably the number-one game in town. Onshore and offshore fishing trips are available, as are charter rigs. Marlin, cobia, amberjack, dolphin, mackerel, and bluefish are brought to the docks daily, and tournaments are held throughout the year—this is your chance to join the pros! Bring your own boat or rent a boat and gear at the waterfront. You can test your scuba-diving skills at **Olympus Dive**; call 252-726-9432. A list of charters and headboats is available from the Carteret County Tourism Bureau; call 800-786-6962 or look it up on the Web at www.sunnync.com.

Seasonal Events

Big Rock Blue Marlin Tournament, held the second week in June, attracts blue-marlin fishermen from far and near. Cash prizes total over $1 million (the winner takes home nearly $500,000). This is touted as the largest billfish tournament on the East Coast and is a part of the World Billfish Series. For information, call 252-247-3575. For a listing of all fishing tournaments, call the Marine Fisheries Department at 252-726-7021.

The North Carolina Seafood Festival is held the first weekend in October. The festival takes place on the Morehead City waterfront. Of course, the main attraction is fresh local seafood, but there are also bands, crafts, and more. For information, call 252-726-6273.

The Bald Is Beautiful Convention and Contest has acquired quite a reputation. Bald men's clubs from various locales compete in categories such as "Most Kissable" and "Shiniest Head." The public is welcome to attend, but if you're bald just on top, don't expect to take home any prizes. For more information, call 252-726-1855 or contact The Bald Is Beautiful Convention at 102 Bald Drive, Morehead City, N.C. 28557 or via the Web at www.members.aol.com/baldusa.

Accommodations

Morehead City offers rates that are generally less expensive than those at Beaufort and Atlantic Beach. It is so close to both that it may be worthwhile to stay here. Rates change with the season.

Hampton Inn on Bogue Sound. *Moderate/Expensive*. 4035 Arendell Street (252-240-2300 or 800-538-6338). This is one of the few places in Morehead City where you can book a room with a view of the sound. The hotel offers free continental breakfast, free in-room movies, an exercise room, and an outdoor pool overlooking Bogue Sound. There are also two-room suites with a separate living area, a microwave, a wet bar, and a refrigerator.

Comfort Inn. *Moderate*. 3100 Arendell Street, (252-247-3434 or 800-422-5404). Comfort Inn provides one king-size or two double beds in comfortable rooms with cable TV. Free continental breakfast is served each morning, and guests receive a complimentary newspaper. A pool, golf packages, and a fitness room are offered. Nonsmoking rooms are available.

Econo Lodge. *Moderate.* 3410 Bridges Street (252-247-2940 or 800-533-7556). This motor inn has a colonial theme; each unit is decorated differently. Packages are available for golf and fishing. The inn offers a free continental breakfast, cable TV, and a pool.

Best Western Buccaneer Motor Inn. *Moderate.* 2806 Arendell Street (252-726-3115 or 800-682-4982). The amenities here include free hot breakfast, a complimentary newspaper, cable TV, golf packages, and a pool. Rooms with a king-size bed and a Jacuzzi are also available.

Restaurants

You've probably caught on by now—the accent here is on fresh seafood. The problem is making a decision once you hit the waterfront area. The seafood is fresh no matter where you go; if you're not a seafood lover, other menu selections are available. Most places welcome casual attire.

Nikola's. *Expensive.* Fourth and Bridges Streets (252-726-6060). Nikola's provides an elegant atmosphere with attractively appointed tables and serves specialties such as veal Marsala, shrimp scampi, and broiled rack of lamb. These come with an appetizer, pasta, salad, vegetables, hot homemade bread, dessert, and a beverage. An extensive wine list is offered. Reservations are suggested. Dinner is served Tuesday through Saturday.

Sanitary Fish Market & Restaurant. *Moderate.* 501 Evans Street (252-247-3111). The locals still call it Tony's, but even with its changed name, this restaurant offers a tremendous variety of seafood, served in a casual atmosphere. Operated since 1938, it has a reputation to uphold. It's large—Tony's started with 12 stools and now seats 600. The restaurant is open daily for lunch and dinner; it is closed during December and January.

Captain Bill's Waterfront. *Moderate.* 701 Evans Street (252-726-2166). This establishment has offered informal family dining since the early 1940s. Seafood, chicken, and nightly specials are the favorites, along with homemade desserts. Captain Bill's lemon pie is famous. You can take home some homemade fudge, too. The restaurant is open for lunch and dinner daily except during February.

Mrs. Willis' Restaurant. *Moderate*. Bridges Street behind Morehead Plaza (252-726-3741). Mrs. Willis' is a tradition around here. Ma Willis started cooking barbecue, chicken, and pies for take-out in 1949, moved her operation to the garage in 1956, and then went on to the big time. This restaurant is still family-run and a favorite of the locals. The barbecue is especially good. Lunch and dinner are served daily.

The Charter. *Moderate*. 400 Evans Street (252-726-9036). This waterfront seafood restaurant offers weeknight specials that change daily. The salad bar is popular, and you can have your seafood broiled rather than fried. There's also a back deck overlooking the sound. Dinner is served daily.

Rockefellers. *Moderate*. 405 Arendell Street (252-808-2292 or 252-808-3280). This newly renovated restaurant has the best water view in town, with two outdoor decks overlooking the Intracoastal Waterway. The dining room includes an oyster bar, while the cafe offers lighter fare. Lunch and dinner are served daily in the cafe, while dinner is offered daily in the dining room.

Raps Grill and Bar. *Inexpensive/Moderate*. 715 Arendell Street (252-240-1213). Look for the distinctive green awning to find this unique restaurant. Raps is housed in a renovated 1912 building and includes a 35-foot solid-oak bar. Seafood, pasta, chicken, burritos, quiche, and burgers fill the menu. You can also get Maryland-style steamed hard-shell crabs. Lunch is served Monday through Saturday and dinner seven days a week.

Bogue Banks

A 25-mile-long barrier island, Bogue Banks is partially sheltered by Cape Lookout. In the past 15 years, native wildlife has been supplanted by the beach lovers who swarm here each summer. With its wide beaches, shelling, swimming (beware of the strong currents!), and fishing, Bogue Banks is one of the state's most popular beach areas.

Until 1970, Bogue Banks was a sleepy fishing area with one state park. Then came a building boom that created traffic jams and disrupted commercial fishing. The maritime forest began to disappear as the Bogue Banks landscape took on high-rise condominiums, motels, and beach cottages. Unfortunately, little attention was paid to the environmental consequences; some protective dunes were removed to provide a better ocean view, creating erosion and narrowing the beaches. But most new developers have shown respect for the ecological value of the dunes.

Along the coast, hotels are spaced well apart and provide plenty of beach—even a modicum of privacy. You're far enough from the road so that only the sounds of surf, sunbathers' radios, laughing children, and the snapping of pop-tops reach your ears.

The western part of the island, Emerald Isle, where cottages and low-rise condominiums are the norm, offers more beachfront and less congestion than Atlantic Beach, located at the eastern end. Though the boom continues, the beaches are still beautiful, and the attraction of Bogue Banks isn't diminishing.

To enhance the area's image, the local chamber of commerce sought an appealing nickname and found a gem—the Crystal Coast.

ACCESS:
Bogue Banks may be reached via U.S. 70 and the Morehead City–Atlantic Beach bridge or via N.C. 58 and the B. Cameron Langston Bridge from Cape Carteret to Emerald Isle.

VISITOR INFORMATION:
Contact the Carteret County Tourism Bureau, P.O. Box 1406, Morehead City, N.C. 28557 (252-726-8148 or 800-786-6962).

Atlantic Beach

Three miles south across the bridge from Morehead City, Atlantic Beach is located at the east end of Bogue Banks. It provides the typical resort atmosphere—sand and surf, summer crowds, and nightlife. This is where you'll see most of the tourist-oriented development on Bogue Banks. Farther west in Salter Path and Pine Knoll Shores, family cottages are the rule. Past Indian Beach on N.C. 58, Emerald Isle is a quiet but steadily growing community where you'll see fewer buildings over two stories in height but more family cottages.

Theodore Roosevelt State Natural Area and the North Carolina Aquarium at Pine Knoll Shores are part of the 322 acres—including 2,700 feet of beachfront—donated by the Roosevelt family and protected by the state.

Attractions

Museums/Science Centers

North Carolina Aquarium at Pine Knoll Shores, located on Roosevelt Drive five miles west of Atlantic Beach, displays marine and coastal plants and animals in touch tanks, aquariums, and a variety of exhibits. One of three such facilities along the state's coast, the aquarium houses one of the largest indoor saltwater systems anywhere. You'll have an opportunity to view a loggerhead turtle and an octopus eyeball to eyeball. Programs and field trips are offered throughout the year; check with the aquarium for special programs and events which may require advance registration because of limited space. A bookstore is on the premises. The aquarium is open from 9 A.M. to 7 P.M. daily from Memorial Day through Labor Day; hours from September to May are 9 A.M. to 5 P.M. daily. Admission is $3 for adults, $2 for senior citizens and active military personnel, and $1 for children over age six. Call 252-247-4003.

Recreation

Fort Macon State Park, two miles east off N.C. 58, has the distinction of being one of the 10 most-visited state parks in the country. It includes a 385-acre park and the historic brick Fort Macon, built in 1834. It's sometimes so crowded that a ranger has to direct traffic into the parking lot. In summer, the park offers a public swimming area with lifeguards and concessions, along with bathhouses that are open from 10 A.M. to 6 P.M. The boardwalk, picnic grounds, and fishing jetties are open all year. Park rangers conduct nature programs and free guided tours of the fort in summer at 11 A.M., 1 P.M., and 3 P.M. The park is open from 8 A.M. until dark. No surfing or beach vehicles are allowed.

Fort Macon was named for United States senator Nathaniel Macon, who helped procure funds for its construction. Initially occupied by Confederates during the Civil War, it was heavily bombarded by Union forces. Once the fort fell, Union troops were in control of much of the North Carolina coast. Fort Macon was garrisoned again during the Spanish-American War and World War II.

A self-guided tour with audiovisual displays provides historical background for all ages. A museum exhibits tools, weapons, and artifacts, as well as offering a short slide presentation; the bookstore has a wide selection of historical material. The museum is open daily except Christmas from 9 A.M. to 5 P.M. Admission is free. Call 252-726-3775.

Theodore Roosevelt State Natural Area, between Atlantic Beach and Pine Knoll Shores, is more suitable for naturalists and researchers than for a family on an outing. The 250-acre area is set aside for the study and preservation of coastal plant and animal life; there are no camping or recreational facilities. Call 252-247-4003.

Atlantic Beach offers a good selection of camping facilities. Try **Holiday Trav-L-Park** (252-354-2250), a five-star beachfront facility. **Salter Path Family Campground** (252-247-3525) and **Arrowhead Campground** (252-247-3838) provide waterfront campsites with full facilities. A complete list is available through the Carteret County Tourism Bureau.

For fishing, a good bet is **Bogue Inlet Pier**, just two miles east of the bridge to Emerald Isle. For information on fishing tournaments, call the Marine Fisheries Department at 252-726-7021.

Seasonal Events

Worthy Is the Lamb, an inspirational musical drama of the last days of Christ, is performed at the Crystal Coast Amphitheatre, located on the mainland three miles north of the bridge to Emerald Isle. First shown in 1988, the production is the only fully orchestrated passion play in existence. It features period costumes, ships, horses, and chariots against the natural backdrop of the White Oak River, which serves as the Sea of Galilee. The set represents a part of Jerusalem. Performances are given Thursday through Saturday at 8:30 P.M. from mid-June to the beginning of September; the schedule is then cut back to Friday and Saturday performances until mid-September. Admission is $13 for adults, $11 for senior citizens, and $6 for children ages seven to 12; children six and under are free if held. Contact the Crystal Coast Amphitheatre, P.O. Box 1004, Swansboro, N.C. 28584 (252-393-8373 or 800-662-5960).

The Emerald Isle Beach Music Festival, held in May at the Holiday Trav-L-Park on Coast Guard Road, features live bands playing old soft-rock favorites. The festival provides the perfect occasion for dancing what seems to be the state dance, the shag, which is similar to the jitterbug but without acrobatics. Call 252-354-2872.

One of the most prestigious fishing tournaments in the region is held annually in Atlantic Beach. The **Hardee's King Mackerel Tournament** takes place in September and often draws quite a crowd. Call 252-247-2334 for more information.

Side Trips

Once you hit the sand, you may not want to take any side trips—but you have to leave the beach sometime. Just a few miles over the Emerald Isle bridge to Cape Carteret is **Swansboro**, a small, historic fishing village on the White Oak River. Merchants are redoing the storefronts and filling their shops with delightful wares. You can see a number of historic homes—and even dine in a few that have been renovated into restaurants and cafes.

During the summer, you may want to visit **Hammocks Beach State Park**. A passenger ferry leaves from Hammocks Beach Road (S.R. 1511), located off N.C. 24. From Memorial Day to Labor Day, it runs every hour from 9:30 A.M. to 5:30 P.M. Monday and Tuesday and every half-hour Wednesday through Sunday; in April and October, the ferry is available hourly from 9:30 A.M. to 4:30 P.M. Friday through Sunday; and in May and September, it operates hourly Wednesday through Sunday from 9:30 A.M. to 4:30 P.M. The ferry fee is $2 for ages 13 and up and $1 for children four to 12; call 910-326-4881. At Hammocks Beach, you can enjoy primitive camping, picnicking, channel and surf fishing, shelling, and nature programs.

Accommodations

Visitors can find a variety of accommodations, most in big hotels and motels. They are spread well apart, and many have their own beach areas. Real-estate agencies on Bogue Banks handle cottage rentals, usually available by the week or month; the Carteret County Tourism Bureau can provide agency numbers. Easter weekend marks the beginning of the summer season, when rates go up and reservations are strongly recommended. The places mentioned here are only a sampling of what's offered.

Sands Resort/A Place at the Beach. *Expensive*. Salter Path Road, Atlantic Beach (252-247-2636 or 800-334-2667). This resort has sparkling-clean one-, two-, and three-bedroom units. Situated on the ocean, it offers surf fishing, golf packages, two pools, lighted tennis courts, and children's programs in summer.

Sheraton Atlantic Beach Resort. *Expensive*. Salter Path Road, Atlantic Beach (252-240-1155 or 800-624-8875). This resort offers ocean-view suites with king-size beds, Jacuzzis, and in-room movies. Indoor and outdoor pools, an exercise room, a restaurant, and a nightclub are among the amenities.

Holiday Inn. *Moderate/Expensive*. Salter Path Road, Atlantic Beach (252-726-2544 or 800-HOLIDAY). The rooms here are spacious and attractively furnished, and children sleep free in the room with their parents. There's also a theme park nearby. A pool, a wading pool, and tennis and golf privileges are offered.

Ramada Oceanfront Inn. *Moderate/Expensive*. Salter Path Road, Atlantic Beach (252-247-4155 or 800-338-1533). All the rooms here have private balconies overlooking the ocean. There's also a pool, cable TV, and 300 feet of private beach. Golf and tennis privileges are offered.

Days Inn. *Moderate/Expensive*. 602 Fort Macon Road, Atlantic Beach (252-247-6400 or 800-972-DAYS). Located on the sound, this hotel has 90 rooms with refrigerators and balconies. An outdoor pool and a boat ramp are available to guests.

Oceanana. *Moderate*. Fort Macon Road, Atlantic Beach (252-726-4111). This 130-unit hotel offers such features as a playground, a pool, and a lifeguard on duty at the private beach during the summer. The staff will even freeze the fish the kids catch. Bikes, lawn games, a grill, and free poolside breakfast are offered. Kitchen units are available at a higher rate.

Royal Pavillion. *Moderate*. 125 Salter Path Road, Pine Knoll Shores (252-726-5188 or 800-533-3700). Royal Pavilion enjoys 1,100 feet of private beach and a reliable reputation. This fully decked hotel has two outdoor pools and two walkways to the beach as well. A full service restaurant and a lounge are also available to guests. Suites are available.

Bogue Shores Motel Condominiums. *Moderate*. Salter Path Road, Atlantic Beach (252-726-7071). It may not have all the amenities, but this motel look-alike does offer sound-front location, a boat dock, and a pool. Guests can walk to the beach. Since these units are furnished by individual owners, check to see what you're getting. Many have kitchen facilities, including microwave ovens. Linens are provided.

Restaurants

Everything from seafood and steaks to sandwiches and barbecue is offered along the Crystal Coast. Prices can be steep, particularly during the summer months. For lower prices and greater selection, Morehead City is the alternative.

Channel Marker. *Moderate/Expensive*. Morehead City–Atlantic Beach Causeway (252-247-2344). This restaurant enjoys a view of the waterfront and a reputation for steaks and seafood. An atrium lounge features hot hors d'oeuvres Monday through Thursday. Dinner is offered daily.

Frank and Clara's. *Moderate/Expensive*. Salter Path Road, Indian Beach (252-247-2788). Set back from the road under giant oaks in an unusual stucco building, Frank and Clara's offers Western beef and fresh seafood. Candlelit but casual, the restaurant has a lounge where live entertainment is offered on weekends. Dinner is served Tuesday through Sunday.

Rucker John's Restaurant. *Moderate*. Emerald Isle Plantation Shopping Center, Emerald Isle (252-354-2413). A welcome addition at the west end of the island, Rucker John's features salads, sandwiches, beef, chicken, and homemade desserts. Lunch and dinner are served Monday through Saturday.

New York Deli. *Inexpensive*. Crow's Nest Shopping Center, Morehead City–Atlantic Beach Causeway (252-726-0111). This deli really does make New York–style sandwiches, including subs and stadium dogs. Meats, cheeses, and imported beers are also available as take-out items for your own beach party. The deli is open Monday through Sunday from 9:30 A.M. to 5:30 P.M.

Beaufort

Envision a charming village with a picturesque waterfront, a historic district of century-old homes, small shops, and snug restaurants—then open your eyes and you're in Beaufort (pronounced Bo-furt; Byew-furt is in South Carolina).

The third-oldest town in North Carolina, Beaufort was the third-largest port in the state at the time of the American Revolution. The area remained undefended during the war; the British didn't come into town until after General Cornwallis's surrender at Yorktown.

Beaufort served as an important military port during the War of 1812, a time when much privateering occurred here. One of the most famous of those who harassed British shipping was Captain Otway Burns, who remained after the war and became a successful merchant and politician in Beaufort.

After enjoying a period of relative calm when agriculture and commerce prospered, Beaufort again played a military role during the Civil War—this time as a center for blockade runners supplying the Confederate army. However, after General Ambrose Burnside captured New Bern, Beaufort was occupied by Federal troops.

After the Civil War, Beaufort became a fishing center. Catching and

North Carolina Maritime Museum
Photograph by William Russ
Courtesy of N.C. Travel and
Tourism Division

processing menhaden, used for fish meal and industrial oils, became the principal business. There was some resort trade during the summer, but the economy was unstable for many years until an effort was made in the 1970s to restore the town and its waterfront.

That effort was well worth it, for Beaufort now enjoys prosperity as a destination for vacationers and sportfishermen. And it hasn't lost its ambiance. The wide boardwalk along the waterfront is ideal for strolling, enjoying an ice-cream cone, and watching yachts and fishing boats come and go.

The late Michael J. Smith, pilot of the space shuttle *Challenger*, was from Beaufort. A small granite monument next to the boardwalk honors him and his crew.

ACCESS:

Beaufort is located on U.S. 70 just over the Grayden Paul Bridge from Morehead City. The historic area and waterfront are three blocks from the highway.

Michael J. Smith Airport is a county-maintained field with three runways up to 4,250 feet long; call 252-728-1928. USAirways service is available at New Bern's Craven County Regional Airport; call 252-638-8591.

The Trailways bus station is located at 105 North 13th Street in Morehead City; call 252-726-3029.

Slips are available for docking at the Beaufort waterfront (252-728-2503) and Town Creek Marina (252-728-6111).

VISITOR INFORMATION:

Contact the Carteret County Tourism Bureau, P.O. Box 1406, Morehead City, N.C. 28577 (800-786-6962).

Coaster magazine, a free publication available in many locations, provides visitor information.

Attractions

Tours

English Double-Decker Bus Tours originate at the Beaufort Historical Association, located at 138 Turner Street. This is an excellent way to find out about the history and folklore of the area. Children especially enjoy riding on the upper level of the bus. The tour runs 45 minutes to an hour. Tours are offered Monday, Wednesday, and Friday at 11 A.M. and 1:30 P.M. and Saturday at 11 A.M. The cost is $6 per adult and $4 per child.

For a slightly different boat tour, try **Lookout Cruises**. This company takes passengers out to Cape Lookout on a 42-passenger catamaran and offers a morning dolphin-watch cruise and a sunset cruise. Tours depart from the Beaufort waterfront. For information, call 252-504-SAIL.

The *Crystal Queen* is a replica of an old paddle wheeler. It offers cruises around the Beaufort–Morehead City waterfront, Shackleford Banks, and Fort Macon. The cruises leave from the Beaufort waterfront and are offered at 11:30 A.M., 2 P.M., 4:30 P.M., and 7 P.M. daily. These cruises generally run 1½ hours and cost $8 per adult and $4 per child ages six to 12. Dinner and D.J. cruises are available on the weekends, but the times vary, so call ahead. Reservations are required for the dinner cruises, and the cost is $25 per adult. For more information, call the Crystal Queen office at 252-728-2527 or the dock at 252-728-3329.

Historic Places

Old Town Beaufort Historic Site, operated by the Beaufort Historical Association, encompasses a full block of historic houses, many built before 1830. Begin at the Beaufort Historic Site Welcome Center, located at 130 Turner Street, where you can take a guided tour of buildings on the historic site. An hour-long walking tour is offered Monday through Saturday at 10 A.M., 11:30 A.M., 1 P.M., and 3 P.M. If you're not in the mood for walking, bus tours are available Monday, Wednesday, and Friday at 11 a.m. and 1:30 p.m. and Saturday at 1:30 p.m. The price for both tours is $6 for adults and $4 for children ages six to 12. Call 252-728-5225 or 800-575-7483.

The Old Burying Ground, located on Ann Street, was deeded to the town in 1731. There are intriguing stories connected with many of the gravestones. One story maintains there's a girl buried in a keg of rum—she died while at sea and was preserved until she could receive a proper burial. Lots more stories await you. Visitors often look surprised when natives or friends want to take them to see "the Cemetery." Tours are offered on Tuesday, Wednesday, and Thursday at 2:30 P.M. and cost $5. Check at the Old Town Beaufort Historic Site for more information on tours.

Museums/Science Centers

North Carolina Maritime Museum, at 315 Front Street, evolved from rented storefront buildings into a $2.2-million complex that welcomes thousands of visitors annually. It's easy to understand why.

A wealth of knowledge about the sea and coastal habitats is presented in exhibits, aquariums, photographs, films, and special programs, all in a visually appealing way. Guided field trips are offered year-round for those interested in shelling, fossil hunting, salt-marsh exploring, and bird-watching. There's a well-stocked bookstore and, for serious study, an inviting research library. Across the street is the Harvey W. Smith Watercraft Center—part of the maritime-museum complex— where traditional boatbuilding is still practiced. You can watch the craftsmen as they build and restore wooden boats and make models. The museum is open Monday through Friday from 9 A.M. to 5 P.M., Saturday from 10 A.M. to 5 P.M., and Sunday from 1 to 5 P.M. Admission is free. Call 252-728-7317.

Recreation

Whether you want to learn to scuba dive or snorkel or whether you're an experienced diver who wants to check out some of the local wrecks, **Discovery Diving Company** can probably fix you up. If you are an experienced diver and want to join an all-day charter, they'll hook you up with other people who want to go on a similar expedition. Call for rates; the number is 252-728-2265.

Seasonal Events

The Old Homes Tour and Antique Show, sponsored by the Beaufort Historical Association, is a popular drawing card. Held the last weekend in June, the event features guided tours of the Old Burying Ground, historic homes—many of which are not otherwise open to the public—gardens, and churches. The antique show is held in the Crystal Coast Civic Center in nearby Morehead City. Double-decker bus tours are conducted all weekend, and special entertainment is provided. For ticket information, contact the Beaufort Historical Association, P.O. Box 1709, Beaufort, N.C. 28516 (252-728-5225 or 800-575-7483).

Each year during the week of Thanksgiving, the Old Town Beaufort Historic Site offers its **Traditional Thanksgiving Feast**. For information (and a menu), call 252-728-5225.

The Traditional Wooden Boat Show, usually held in May at the North Carolina Maritime Museum, welcomes an assortment of wooden boats to the waterfront. Proud builders enjoy swapping stories. A regatta, rowing races, and workshops are held. Call 252-728-7317.

Side Trips

Cape Lookout National Seashore is the famous Atlantic headland located off Beaufort Inlet. Extending over 55 miles of barrier islands, the national seashore is not only a protected loggerhead turtle breeding ground but an excellent fishing and shelling spot as well. During the summer, daily ranger-led programs are offered for all ages.

Cape Lookout Lighthouse, built in 1859, is still blinking. Although you can't go in the lighthouse, you can see the renovated keeper's quarters and summer kitchen. For ferry information, contact the National Park Service at Harkers Island at 252-728-2250.

Carrot Island/Rachel Carson Estuarine Sanctuary is located just across Taylor Creek from the Beaufort waterfront. The island's name is a corruption of Cart Island, so called because fishermen could once take their carts there. The island is part of the estuarine sanctuary, which serves as a habitat for shorebirds and the famous wild Banks horses. The sanctuary is accessible by boat, and two ferrys run from Front Street as well. Swimming, shelling, clamming, and bird- and pony-watching are some of the favorite activities there.

The **Inner Islands** around the marsh and sound are dominated by Cedar Island, the ferry link to Ocracoke Island. **Cedar Island National Wildlife Refuge** provides feeding grounds for migratory waterfowl. Harkers Island is famous for its tradition of boatbuilding; the Core Sound "sharpie," a shallow-draft boat with sails on either side, is still made here. This entire area is often called "down East." Many of its residents are descendants of original 18th-century settlers.

Accommodations

Inns and Bed-and-Breakfast Guest Houses

Accommodations in Beaufort are like the town itself—quaint and charming and leaning toward the historical. Bed-and-breakfast inns reign here. Prices during the spring and summer are higher than at other times of year.

Beaufort Inn. *Expensive*. 101 Ann Street (252-728-2600 or 800-726-0321). The Beaufort Inn serves breakfast in its comfortable living room. The rooms are tastefully furnished and have private baths. Many have balconies overlooking the harbor.

Inlet Inn. *Expensive*. 601 Front Street (252-728-3600). Each of this inn's harbor-front rooms has a seating area, a bar, a refrigerator, a ceiling fan, and cable TV. Many rooms have French doors that open onto private porches with rocking chairs. Others have fireplaces or window seats with vistas of Cape Lookout. Guests receive a continental breakfast.

Langdon House. *Expensive*. 135 Craven Street (252-728-5499). This home has a wonderful double-decker front porch, a meticulously restored interior, and one of the most hospitable hosts in town. Each of the four guest rooms has a private bath and is furnished in the style of the 18th century. Nothing fancy or pretentious here—just a step back in time. A full breakfast is included. Children under 12 are not allowed.

The Cedars. *Expensive*. 305 Front Street (252-728-7036). The Cedars provides an elegant setting with a view of the waterfront. Each of its six guest rooms has a private bath. Children are allowed here, but with all the antiques and Oriental knickknacks, they should be well behaved. A full breakfast is provided.

Pecan Tree Inn. *Moderate/Expensive*. 116 Queen Street (252-728-6733). The seven air-conditioned rooms here have private baths. There is also a suite with two connecting guest rooms, and two other suites have Jacuzzis and king-size canopy beds. The 5,500-square-foot English flower and herb garden is a pleasure to walk through. An expanded continental breakfast is served.

Delamar Inn. *Moderate/Expensive*. 217 Turner Street (252-728-4300). Built in 1866, this inn offers three guest rooms furnished with antiques; each room has a private bath. The innkeepers will loan you a bicycle or a beach chair, then greet you with soft drinks and cookies for a relaxing time on the upper porch after your busy day.

Captain's Quarters. *Moderate/Expensive*. 315 Ann Street (252-728-7711). This lovely Victorian house has friendly hosts and a large parlor to welcome you. The three guest rooms, each with its own unique decor, have private baths. Join other guests on the wrap-around front porch in the evening for a salute to the sunset. The full European breakfast features fresh fruit and homemade biscuits. Children under 12 are not allowed.

Restaurants

For a town this size, Beaufort offers a good number of choices. You're at the coast, so oysters, shrimp, scallops, and crab are natural choices. Key lime pie seems to be a favorite dessert offering. You'd have to spend several days here to hit all the eateries. The rustic and nautical decor fits well with the town, and like everyone else you will meet in Beaufort, the staffs are friendly. Opening and closing times depend on the season and the crowds, so it's wise to call ahead for hours and seating availability.

Spouter Inn. *Moderate/Expensive.* 218 Front Street (252-728-5190). Lunch here features creative sandwiches and homemade soups and chowders. The dinner menu changes with the availability of fresh seafood. The banana-cream crepe and the chocolate peanut-butter pie are worth leaving a little room for at the end. Lunch and dinner are served.

The Veranda. *Moderate/Expensive.* 300 Front Street (252-728-5352). This is a nice place to enjoy a meal overlooking the water. The menu features salads, pasta, steaks, and seafood. Lunch and dinner are served daily with the exception of lunch on Sunday (and Saturday during the off-season).

Beaufort Grocery Company Restaurant. *Inexpensive/Moderate.* 117 Queen Street (252-728-3899). This restaurant has a great reputation with the locals. After the deli closes in the afternoon, the menu changes to feature regional nightly specials. The restaurant does all its own baking. The chef is a graduate of the Culinary Institute of America, so the specials are a treat. Reservations are recommended for dinner. Lunch, dinner, and Sunday brunch are served.

Loughry's Landing. *Inexpensive/Moderate.* 510 Front Street (252-728-7541). This may be your choice when you want to enjoy waterfront dining and a good meal at a good price. The nautical decor accents the seafood entrées, voted the best non-fried seafood around. Be sure to try the steamed crab legs accompanied with a wine from their award-winning selection. Lunch and dinner are served daily.

Clawson's 1905 Restaurant. *Inexpensive/Moderate.* 429 Front Street (252-728-2133). This restaurant takes you back to 1905, when Mr. Clawson ran his waterfront grocery store here. Photographs and memorabilia hang on the walls. You can enjoy Buffalo wings, ribs, seafood salads, and sandwiches. The atmosphere is casual. Lunch and dinner are served daily.

The Net House. *Inexpensive/Moderate.* 133 Turner Street (252-728-2002). The Net House enjoys a fine reputation with locals and visitors alike. The she-crab soup and the Key lime pie are house specialties. Be prepared to wait on busy summer weekends. Dinner is served daily.

The Dockhouse. *Inexpensive*. 500 Front Street (252-728-4506). This is a great spot for watching the myriad sailboats and yachts docked at the marina and enjoying subs, pita sandwiches, and Mexican specialties in a relaxed environment. Musicians entertain nightly during peak season. Lunch and dinner are served daily.

The Royal James Cafe. *Inexpensive*. 117 Turner Street (252-728-4573). This is the place to go if you want to enjoy some local color without the yachting crowd. The oldest continuing business in Beaufort, the cafe can thank local trawler captains, sailors, and marine-lab students for its success. Here, you can find hamburgers served with a secret sauce. The cafe also features 45-year-old regulation pool tables. It is open Monday through Saturday from 9 A.M. to 11 P.M.

Cape Fear Coast

The Cape Fear coast, the southernmost promontory on North Carolina's coastline, includes some of the East Coast's best beaches—Carolina, Kure, and Wrightsville. Topsail Beach, which is technically not part of the Cape Fear coast, is also within easy driving distance of Wilmington. The centerpiece of the region is the deepwater port city of Wilmington, which is emerging as one of the state's leading metropolitan areas. With the completion of I-40, Wilmington is now easily accessible to highway traffic along the eastern seaboard.

Of all the coastal regions, the Cape Fear area is the one best suited to year-round tourism. In summer, Wrightsville Beach and Pleasure Island contribute greatly to the flourishing coastal economy. In the cooler months, Wilmington takes the spotlight with its various seasonal festivals, including the city's biggest and splashiest event, the North Carolina Azalea Festival in April.

The enduring appeal of the historic district and the battleship *North Carolina* has helped Wilmington and the surrounding region broaden its scope; you'll find a delightful variety of accommodations in the Cape Fear area.

Wilmington

If you bypass Wilmington on your way to the beach, you'll be missing out on one of North Carolina's most inviting cities. Today, Wilmington has one of the largest districts listed in the National Register of Historic Places—it covers 200 blocks. Situated along the riverfront—Wilmington's most attractive area—the district is a strong tourist attraction and the setting for cultural and gastronomic activities.

Walk by the river. Get to know the city's friendly residents. Visit Riverfront Park, the historic homes, and the intriguing shops in restored buildings. This old-and-new city has much to offer.

Wilmington is taking its place in the state as a cultural center, and its downtown revitalization is the envy of many American cities.

Settled in 1732, Wilmington soon eclipsed other Cape Fear River

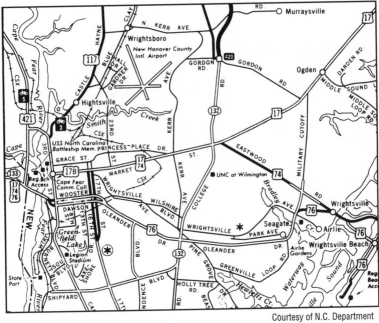

Courtesy of N.C. Department
of Transportation

towns commercially and culturally. The colonists who moved into the area bought large tracts of land cheaply to develop indigo and rice plantations. One of these, Orton Plantation, is still maintained as a tourist attraction.

Colonial Wilmingtonians were among the first to rebel against British taxation. In 1765—eight years before the Boston Tea Party—a group of armed citizens protesting the hated Stamp Act demanded that the stamp master resign.

In 1776, during the American Revolution, area patriots faced Tory forces at Moores Creek Bridge, 20 miles northwest. After a three-minute "battle," the Tories were driven back. The British returned to the Wilmington area in 1781 under General Cornwallis and occupied the town for several weeks before marching to Virginia and eventually surrendering at Yorktown.

After the Revolution, merchants exported naval stores (tar, rosin, pitch, and turpentine) on a large scale, gaining wealth and political power. Wilmington became the naval-stores capital of the world. The Wilmington & Weldon Railroad, linking the area to Virginia, reinforced this position from the time of its completion in 1840.

Because of its connection to the Confederate capital of Richmond,

Wilmington was a prime target during the Civil War. However, because of its location upriver from the mouth of the Cape Fear, it was more protected than other Southern ports. Fort Fisher, at the river's mouth, kept Union ships at bay, and brave blockade runners managed to export cotton and import guns and supplies for Confederate troops. By 1864, Wilmington, the only Confederate port still open, handled nearly all the munitions and supplies for the defense of Richmond. Finally, in 1865, Federal forces launched a massive naval bombardment against Fort Fisher. When resistance collapsed, Wilmington quickly fell. Within weeks, the war ended.

Wilmington bounced back afterward, with cotton replacing naval stores as the primary export commodity. Later, during the world wars, shipbuilding became important. But Wilmington nevertheless went into a decline in the 1940s. The rail system faltered because of the growing popularity of automobile travel. However, the port modernized and kept the economy going.

In the late 1960s, Wilmington was "rediscovered." New highways increased its accessibility, and interest in historic preservation flowered. A convention center, a luxury waterfront inn, a park, and a marina area were established in the historic district.

As the state's leading deepwater port, Wilmington has a secure economic base, especially with the boost it's received in the last two decades from tourism. It's not surprising that Wilmington is one of the fastest-growing areas of the state.

ACCESS:

Wilmington can be reached by U.S. 421 from the north, U.S. 74/76 from the west, U.S. 17 from the south, and I-40 from the northwest.

Wilmington International Airport is served by US Airways, United Express, Midway Corporate Airlines, and A.S.A.-Atlantic Southeast, the Delta connection; call 910-341-4333.

The Trailways bus station is at 201 Harnett Street; call 910-762-6625. The Wilmington Transit Authority provides local bus service; call 910-343-0106.

VISITOR INFORMATION:

Contact the Cape Fear Coast Convention and Visitors Bureau, 24 North Third Street, Wilmington, N.C. 28401 (910-341-4030 or 800-222-4757 in the U.S., 800-457-8912 in Canada). Their Web site can be accessed at www.cape-fear.nc.us. The bureau is located in the 19th-century courthouse.

The local newspaper is the *Wilmington Morning Star.* Free *Encore* and *Scene* magazines have up-to-date event listings.

Attractions

Tours

A **Self-Guided Walking Tour** introduces visitors to some of the attractive historic district. You can pick up a map at the Cape Fear Coast Convention and Visitors Bureau. You can tour some landmark buildings and enjoy, from the outside, restoration efforts on other private Victorian, Queen Anne, and Georgian houses. Many have plaques identifying the person who built or is primarily associated with the house; orange plaques mean the house is at least 75 years old, and black ones mean it is 100 years old or more.

Thalian Hall, at 310 Chestnut Street, was completed in 1858 as the city hall. It has been extensively renovated. Bright white and built in the Italianate style with massive Corinthian columns, the east wing is a beautiful opera house with two balconies and an ornate proscenium framing the stage. It originally seated 950 people (in the days when Wilmington had only 10,000 citizens) and hosted such talents as Lillian Russell, Buffalo Bill Cody, and John Philip Sousa. In 1986, when the National Opera Company presented Sousa's *El Capitan* at Thalian Hall, the composer's grandson, John Philip Sousa III, opened the performance.

The **Burgwin-Wright House**, at 224 Market Street, is a three-level gentleman's townhouse built in 1770 by John Burgwin, treasurer of the North Carolina colony. The white frame Georgian home with double piazzas held in place by Ionic columns is now an attractive house museum furnished with 18th-century antiques and reproductions. Among its unique features are the fresh-air areas, which allow ventilation; closets, rarely found in houses of that era; and a separate three-story kitchen. General Cornwallis and his staff occupied this house before their defeat at Yorktown, during which time the cellar was used as a dungeon for prisoners (though many escaped through an underground tunnel to the river). Today, the house also serves as headquarters for the North Carolina Society of Colonial Dames, who restored and maintain it. You can tour the house Tuesday through Saturday from 10 A.M. to 4 P.M. Admission is $5 for adults and $2 for full-time students. Call 910-762-0570.

Another outstanding building you can tour is the **Zebulon Latimer House**, at 126 South Third Street, an ornate, four-story Italian Revival residence that reflects the opulent lifestyle of many 19th-century Wilmingtonians. Built in 1852 by a wealthy dry-goods merchant, this was the first home in town to have electricity. You'll find Empire and Victorian furnishings and appointments—many original to the house—which the Latimers collected during European visits. A lovely piazza with a canopied roof leads to an appealing Victorian garden, the site of exclusive garden parties even today. The Latimer family occupied the house until 1963, when it was

Zebulon Latimer House
Courtesy of N.C. Travel and
Tourism Division

purchased and restored by the Lower Cape Fear Historical Society, which has its headquarters here. The home is open Monday through Friday from 10 A.M. to 3:30 P.M. and Saturday and Sunday from noon to 5 P.M. A $5 admission fee is charged for adults; $2 is charged for students. Call 910-762-0492.

Be sure to round out your tour of historic sites by visiting the **Bellamy Mansion Museum**, located at 503 Market Street. The mansion was built in 1859 on the eve of the Civil War, and the family lived there only a short time until it was displaced by Union forces. The Bellamys regained their stately home after the war, however, and held it in the family until 1946, when it came under the stewardship of Preservation North Carolina. Now, visitors can walk throughout the 22-room mansion museum and learn about the history of the house and the people who lived here. The restored Victorian gardens are also available for enjoyment, and restoration is under way to open the slave quarters and a reconstruction of the carriage house in the near future. Tours are offered Wednesday through Saturday from 10 A.M. to 5 P.M. and Sunday from 1 to 5 P.M. Admission is $6 for adults and $3 for students. There is no charge for children five and under. Call 910-251-3700.

A special discount ticket is available to tour all three of these historic museums and homes. It offers a 20 percent discount on the admission fee to all the sites and is available at any of the three.

Wilmington Adventure Walking Tours start at the foot of Market Street at the riverfront and take visitors on a trip back in time. Tour guides share historical events, architectural details, and unusual stories from Wilmington's past. (Did you know that Madame Chiang Kai-shek's father was ordained in Fifth Street Methodist Church here in the 1890s?) This is an excellent orientation tour if your time is limited, or it can set the scene for the rest of your stay. Custom tours are available if you have a special interest. Tours are given Monday through Saturday at 10 A.M. and 2 P.M. from April to November. During the off-season, tours can be made by appointment. The fee is $10 for adults and $5 for children six to 12. Call 910-763-1785.

Riverboat cruises, originating at the riverfront, are a nice way to rest your weary feet and enjoy some historic scenery. The *Henrietta II*, named for the first steam paddleboat in North Carolina, offers a tour of the waterfront and river. The narrated cruises last 90 minutes and are offered Tuesday through Sunday at 11:30 A.M. and 2:30 P.M. during June, July, and August; the 11:30 cruise is not offered during the rest of the year. Snacks and drinks are available on board. The fee is $10 for adults and $4 for children ages two to 12. A dinner cruise is offered from April through December; times vary, so call ahead for scheduling information. Call 910-343-1611 or 800-676-0162.

You can also rent **horse-drawn carriages** or ride on a **horse-drawn trolley** for a narrated tour of the historic district. The tours operate Tuesday through Sunday from 10 A.M. to 10 P.M. from April to October. They operate on Friday from 7 to 10 P.M., Saturday from 11 A.M. to 10 P.M. and Sunday from 11 A.M. to 4 P.M. during November, December, and March. The price is $8 for adults and $4 for children 12 and under. Call 910-251-8889.

Historic Places

The Battleship *North Carolina*, at Eagles Island, is a major state attraction. The 36,600-ton ship with 18-inch armor and nine 16-inch guns was considered the world's greatest sea weapon during World War II. It earned 15 battle stars and participated in every major naval offensive in the Pacific. When the *North Carolina* was undergoing sea trials in 1941, she was seen entering and leaving New York's harbor so often that columnist Walter Winchell dubbed her "The Showboat," a nickname her crew became proud of during her stellar wartime career.

After the war, she was retired to the mothball fleet and was decommissioned in 1960. North Carolina's citizens wanted her, however, and raised $330,000—much of it in coins from schoolchildren—to bring her to Wilmington a year later. It was no small engineering feat to maneuver the 728-foot battleship up the Cape Fear River and negotiate a 90-degree turn into a berth. Now, she sits serenely across the river from Wilmington and can be seen from almost anyplace downtown.

Especially popular among children, the battleship is quite interesting—even to those who don't usually care about such things—because of the way it's displayed. The self-guided tour allows you to see every aspect of shipboard life—kitchens, cobbler's and machine shops, radio and radar rooms, admiral's cabin, post office, even showers. The engine room is an astonishing three-story

Battleship *North Carolina*
Photograph by William Russ
Courtesy of N.C. Travel and
Tourism Division

fantasy of wires, pipes, gauges, and tubing. Color-coded signs indicate shorter and longer versions of the tour. You can push buttons at intervals to hear explanations of where you are. In the gun turret, for example, you'll be able to hear the sounds of the ship's massive guns firing.

The visitor center includes information on the ship and a gift shop. You can have a picnic lunch outside on the lawn and enjoy a lovely view of Wilmington.

The battleship memorial is open daily from 8 A.M. to 8 P.M. from mid-May to mid-September and from 8 A.M. to 5 P.M. during the rest of the year. Admission is $8 for adults, $7 for senior citizens and active-duty military personnel, and $4 for children six to 11. For those who don't want to drive over the bridge to see the battleship, a river taxi departs from the bottom of Market Street for a five-minute crossing to the memorial grounds. It runs at half-hour intervals (except for 11:30 A.M. and 3:30 P.M.) from 10 A.M. to 5 P.M. from Memorial Day to Labor Day. The fee is $2 round-trip. Call 910-251-5797.

Museums

Cape Fear Museum, at 814 Market Street, is a good place to start learning about the social and natural history of the lower Cape Fear area. Founded in 1898 by the United Daughters of the Confederacy, the museum features exhibits and photographs tracing Wilmington's history and includes a scale model of the town in 1863. Also displayed are mementos of notable Wilmingtonians such as basketball star Michael Jordan, football player Roman Gabriel, and musician Charlie Daniels. The museum is open Tuesday through Saturday from 9 A.M. to 5 P.M. and Sunday from 2 to 5 P.M.; it is closed Thanksgiving and Christmas. Admission is $2 for adults and $1 for students and senior citizens; there is no charge for children five and under. Call 910-341-4350.

St. John's Museum of Art, at 114 Orange Street, fills a three-building complex that includes the former St. Nicholas Greek Orthodox Church. The museum features permanent and temporary exhibits of the work of artists of many eras. The permanent collection includes Mary Cassatt prints. The Hughes Gallery, which is housed in the church, showcases the works of North Carolina artists. Enthusiastic docents conduct tours; lectures and films are also offered. The museum is open Tuesday through Saturday from 10 A.M. to 5 P.M. and Sunday from noon to 4 P.M. except holidays. Admission is $5 for families, $2 for adults, and $1 for students ages five to 18. The museum may be toured free of charge on the first Sunday of each month. Call 910-763-0281.

The Wilmington Railroad Museum, at the corner of Red Cross and Water Streets, is a tribute to the days when the railroad was the king of transportation. Volunteers staff the small museum, which is packed with memorabilia—equipment, insignias, buttons, timetables—from the 1840 Wilmington & Weldon Railroad to the present Amtrak system. Model trains run continuously. One section of the museum is a re-created waiting room complete with sound effects. When you see the brick building with a caboose out front, you'll know you're there. The museum is open Monday, Tuesday, and Thursday through Saturday from 10 A.M. to 5 P.M. and Sunday from 1 to 5 P.M. year-round. Admission is $3 for adults, $2 for seniors and active military, and $1.50 for children ages five to 17. Call 910-763-2634.

Gardens

Greenfield Gardens, on Carolina Beach Road (U.S. 421 South), is a municipal garden that is especially beautiful in the spring. If you're weary of sightseeing, this is a perfect place to picnic, fish, or stroll around a 180-acre cypress-studded lake and feed the ducks. Tots love the playground and the paddleboats. A path for biking and walking leads visitors around trees and well-tended flower beds. In the summer, musical entertainment is featured in the amphitheater. Admission is free. Call 910-341-7855.

Special Shopping

The Cotton Exchange, in the 300 block of North Front Street, is a complex of specialty shops and restaurants in turn-of-the-century brick buildings, some of which were originally cotton warehouses. As you browse, you'll find art, antiques, clocks, and potpourri, among other things. Most of the shops are open Monday through Saturday from 10 A.M. to 5:30 P.M.; some are open Sunday from 1 to 5 P.M. Free parking is available.

Chandler's Wharf, on the riverfront at the corner of Water and Ann Streets, offers shopping and dining in a cluster of small historic buildings, including the former harbor master's house. Most of the shops are open Monday through Saturday from 10 A.M. to 5:30 P.M. Free parking is available.

Cultural Offerings

Thalian Hall Center for the Performing Arts, at 310 Chestnut Street, takes its name from the Thalian Association, a community theater group tracing its roots to 1799. Built in the 1850s and expanded and modernized in 1989, the center is a nonprofit, city-funded agency. Maurice Barrymore and John Philip Sousa were among the early performers in the proscenium theater. Now, more than two dozen arts groups produce or present work in the multipurpose facility. For tickets or information on scheduled events, call 910-343-3664.

Opera House Theatre Company, at 2011 Carolina Beach Road, is a nonprofit organization that presents professional theater featuring guest artists. Revivals of old favorites can be seen as individual shows or as part of a series subscription. One-act plays and lesser-known works are also performed. Call 910-762-4234.

Recreation

The beaches and fishing piers along Wrightsville, Carolina, and Kure Beaches provide enough recreational opportunities to keep everyone in the family happy. All the local beaches have public access, marked by signs along the roadside—but make sure you heed the

Dangerous Current signs. Parking is available in small lots or on side streets. Pier-fishing fees are normally $4 to $5, or you can try surf fishing. Surfing is particularly popular here; it's restricted to certain areas, also clearly marked by signs.

Several major fishing tournaments attract big-catch hopefuls. The **Wrightsville Beach King Mackerel Tournament** in September and the **U.S. Open King Mackerel Tournament** at Southport in late September or early October are two of the most popular. The Marine Fisheries Department can provide a complete list; call 910-395-3900.

Golfers have some attractive courses to choose from, a few fashioned from former plantation land. You might try **Echo Farms Golf and Country Club** (910-791-9318), **Belvedere Plantation Golf & Racquet Club** (910-270-2703), or **The Cape Golf and Racquet Club** (910-799-3110). You can also inquire at the Cape Fear Coast Convention and Visitors Bureau about golf packages.

Seasonal Events

The North Carolina Jazz Festival, held each February, brings nationally known artists to Wilmington for several days of concerts. Call 910-341-4030.

North Carolina Azalea Festival, held in April, is Wilmington's most famous annual event. Gardens in the city and environs are at their most beautiful. Garden tours, workshops, a horse show, beauty pageants, a parade, and celebrity visits fill the week's calendar. If you haven't seen Wilmington when the azaleas and dogwoods are blooming, make it a point to do so. Call 910-763-0905.

Wilmington also hosts the **Cape Fear Blues Festival** in July. Call 910-341-4030.

Riverfest, held in October, draws everyone's attention to Riverfront Park. Arts and crafts, trolley and horse-drawn-carriage rides, boat races, and a raft regatta are among the attractions. Music and dancing make this a festive occasion. Call 910-452-6862.

Old Wilmington by Candlelight Home Tour is a Christmas tradition sponsored by the Lower Cape Fear Historical Society on the first weekend in December. You can visit restored private homes not usually open to the public. Some especially pretty homes attract long lines. Tickets cost $15 for two nights' worth of tours and are available at the Zebulon Latimer House, at 126 South Third Street. Call 910-762-0492.

Side Trips

Fort Fisher National Historic Site—See *Pleasure Island: Historic Places*

North Carolina Aquarium at Fort Fisher—See *Pleasure Island: Museums/Science Centers*

Orton Plantation
Photograph by William Russ
Courtesy of N.C. Travel and
Tourism Division

Orton Plantation Gardens, 18 miles south of Wilmington on N.C. 133, were planted in 1910 by the Sprunt family. The gardens bloom from March through August, though the exact blooming dates of the azaleas, camellias, magnolias, tulips, and various annuals depend on the weather. The gardens are located on a former rice plantation, where beautiful, ancient live oaks arch over the paths. The antebellum Orton home isn't open to the public, but you can go inside a small white chapel nearby. The gardens are open daily from 8 A.M. to 6 P.M. from March to August and from 10 A.M. to 5 P.M. from September to November. Admission is $8 for adults, $7 for seniors, and $3 for children ages six to 12. Call 910-371-6851.

Brunswick Town State Historic Site, 18 miles south of Wilmington on N.C. 133, commemorates the first settlement in the Cape Fear area. Abandoned by 1830, most of the town is gone, but excavated foundations are maintained as archaeological displays. The visitor center offers a slide show and exhibits. Stay for a picnic on the grounds if you like. The site is open Monday through Saturday from 9 A.M. to 5 P.M. and Sunday from 1 to 5 P.M. from April to October; it is also open Tuesday through Saturday from 10 A.M. to 4 P.M. and Sunday from 1 to 4 P.M. from November to March. Admission is free. Call 910-371-6613.

Poplar Grove Historic Plantation, nine miles northeast of Wilmington on U.S. 17, was one of the first peanut-producing plantations in the state. The 16-acre grounds are studded with huge oak, sycamore, magnolia, and poplar trees. The centerpiece is the three-level Greek Revival manor house, built around 1850 by Joseph Foy, a humanitarian as well as a pioneer in the peanut industry.

Costumed guides conduct a tour through the main house; you can also visit the barn, the smokehouse, the tenant house, and the separate kitchen. The Planter's Inn Restaurant, located on the grounds, serves lunch and dinner. A small country store features crafts and collectibles. Admission for the house tour is $7 for adults, $6 for senior citizens and military personnel, and $3 for children ages six to 16; children under six are free. The plantation is open Monday through Saturday from 9 A.M. to 5 P.M. and Sunday from noon to 5 P.M. No house tours are offered in January. Call 910-686-9518.

Moores Creek National Battlefield, 20 miles northwest of Wilmington on N.C. 210 in Currie, is the site of the battle often called "the South's Lexington and Concord," where British hopes of an early Southern invasion were dashed. As a result, North Carolina became the first colony to instruct its delegates to vote for independence at the Continental Congress. A visitor center offers displays and an audiovisual presentation about the battle. Self-guided trails feature picnic facilities. The battlefield is open daily except for Christmas and New Year's from 9 A.M. to 5 P.M. Admission is free. Call 910-283-5591.

Duplin Wine Cellars, 40 miles north of Wilmington on U.S. 117 in Rose Hill, is a small, family-run business offering an orientation film, a walking tour through the winery, and samples of North Carolina wine. Using recipes and methods passed down from the Germans and Swiss who settled in North Carolina in the early 1700s, Duplin Wine Cellars has received awards for its magnolia and scuppernong wines. The winery produces more than 120,000 gallons per season. Tours and tastings are offered Monday through Saturday from 9 A.M. to 5 P.M. except on major holidays. Contact Duplin Wine Cellars, P.O. Box 756, Rose Hill, N.C. 28458 (910-289-3888).

Topsail Island is about a 45-minute drive north from Wilmington on U.S. 17. When pirates lurked in these waters, they would hide behind the dunes and wait to attack passing ships. Looking for topsails became important—thus the name Topsail Island. For the most part, the island is covered with sandy beaches, family cottages, and a smattering of motels and restaurants. The northern half is privately owned, though there's some development. Around Topsail Beach, it's busier.

If you'd like to stay, accommodations are available:

St. Regis Resort. *Expensive/Deluxe* (910-328-0778). A two-night minimum is required at this ultrachic resort located on the northern end of the island at Snead's Ferry.

Jolly Roger Motel. *Inexpensive/Moderate*. Topsail Beach (910-328-4616). The Jolly Roger is an oceanfront motel, restaurant, and pier complex.

For more information, contact the Topsail Island Chamber of Commerce, P.O. Box 2486, Surf City, N.C. 28445 (910-328-4722).

Accommodations

Wilmington offers a number of places to stay, ranging from bed-and-breakfast inns in historic homes to a nine-story convention hotel on the waterfront. Rates generally go up after Memorial Day, and rooms fill quickly during the Azalea Festival.

The Inn at St. Thomas Court. *Expensive/Deluxe*. 101 South Second Street (910-343-1800 or 800-525-0909). This inn combines modern amenities and business facilities with a historic setting. The one- and two-bedroom suites, all individually decorated in period design, feature color cable TV, telephones, and wet bars; some even have fully equipped kitchens. A daily newspaper is offered.

Wilmington Hilton. *Moderate/Expensive*. 301 North Water Street (910-763-5900 or 800-662-9338). The Hilton is a quality hotel at an ideal location at Riverfront Park, directly across the river from the battleship. An outdoor pool, a gift shop, a fitness center, and free airport transportation are offered. The restaurant is open for all meals, and the lounge offers nighttime entertainment. A 150-foot dock is provided for guests arriving by boat. Children stay free with parents.

Comfort Inn Executive Center. *Moderate*. 151 South College Road (910-791-4841). Located near the University of North Carolina at Wilmington, the Comfort Inn offers spacious rooms in a contemporary setting. You can enjoy a complimentary continental breakfast—complete with newspaper—in the lobby each morning and cocktail service in the evening. Wake-up calls and room-service coffee are also offered. The inn features an outdoor pool and complimentary passes to a Nautilus facility located within walking distance.

Hampton Inn. *Inexpensive*. 5107 Market Street (910-395-5045 or 800-HAMPTON). The Hampton Inn caters to families and business travelers, offering contemporary rooms, a hospitality suite, an outdoor pool, free HBO and local calls, and a free continental breakfast in the lobby. The hotel is three miles from downtown. Children 18 and under stay free with a parent.

Inns and Bed-and-Breakfast Guest Houses

The Taylor House Inn. *Expensive.* 14 North Seventh Street (910-763-7581 or 800-382-9982). Built in 1908, this five-star inn is a fine example of Neoclassic architecture. Located in the historic district, the house features large guest rooms with private baths, antique furnishings, ceiling fans, and fireplaces. Guests enjoy a full breakfast in the dining room.

Catherine's Inn Bed and Breakfast. *Expensive.* 410 South Front Street (910-251-0863 or 800-476-0723). Housed in a restored 1875 home, this inn features guest rooms with fireplaces, telephones, air conditioning, and private baths. Breakfast is included.

The Wine House Bed and Breakfast. *Expensive.* 311 Cottage Lane (910-763-0511). Here, you can enjoy a brick-walled courtyard and the privacy of separate guest-house accommodations. Each suite features a queen-size bed, a fireplace, a ceiling fan, a wet bar, a refrigerator, and a private bath.

The Worth House. *Expensive.* 412 South Third Street (910-762-8562). The Worth House is a restored Victorian home in the historic district. Furnished with antiques, each of the spacious guest rooms has a sitting area or a private porch, along with a private bath. Guests are treated to a full breakfast in the dining room or in their room. The hosts can arrange carriage rides.

Anderson Guest House. *Moderate.* 520 Orange Street (910-343-8128). This is an 1851 Italianate home with two separate guest quarters overlooking the gardens. The rooms feature antique furnishings, ceiling fans, and a fireplace. Guests enjoy refreshments on arrival and a gourmet breakfast on the porch or in the dining room. No credit cards are accepted.

Restaurants

Another indication of Wilmington's growth is the number of restaurants in the city. The choices range from fast food and barbecue to seafood and upscale fare.

Faxon's by the River. *Moderate/Expensive*. 138 Front Street (910-762-8898). This is one of the friendliest and tastiest restaurants in Wilmington. Everything in this eatery is fresh and made to order. Among the Southern-style dishes offered here are hoppin' john, cornmeal-fried catfish, shrimp and grits, and homemade potato salad. Lunch is served Monday through Friday, dinner is served Monday through Saturday, and brunch is available on Sunday.

Harvest Moon. *Moderate/Expensive*. 5710 Oleander Drive (910-792-0172). Located between downtown Wilmington and Wrightsville Beach, this new establishment has quickly emerged as one of the area's most popular restaurants. It specializes in "New Southern" cuisine, a large portion of which is prepared in a wood-burning oven. Open for dinner Monday through Saturday.

Paleo Sun Cafe. *Moderate/Expensive*. 35 North Front Street (910-762-7700). This addition to the downtown restaurant scene has earned a following for its full-flavored nouvelle cuisine. The desert-toned interior is obliquely lit and has Art Deco features that nicely offset the primitive decorations. The menu offers a large selection of unique seafood dishes. The beef and chicken dishes are a little less imaginative but still good. Dinner is served Thursday through Sunday.

Pilot House. *Moderate*. Chandler's Wharf, 2 Ann Street (910-343-0200). The riverfront setting, the nautical artwork, and the airy atmosphere enhance the candlelight dining here. The menu features local seafood, veal, special salads, and desserts meriting gourmet praise. There is also an outdoor deck overlooking the river. A full bar is offered. The restaurant serves lunch and dinner daily, along with Sunday brunch.

Elijah's. *Inexpensive/Moderate*. Chandler's Wharf, 2 Ann Street (910-343-1448). Elijah's has won awards for its chowder, so you know the menu features serious seafood, all of it freshly prepared. Other options include grilled chicken and meal-size salads. The oyster bar is a popular gathering spot—and the view is great. A full bar is offered. Lunch and dinner are served daily.

Roy's Riverboat Landing. *Inexpensive/Moderate*. 2 Market Street (910-763-7227). Here, you'll find a neighborhood-pub atmosphere as well as a good selection of seafood and pasta. On weekends, you can go upstairs to enjoy jazz, a nightclub act, or dancing. A full bar is offered. Lunch is served Tuesday through Sunday and dinner daily.

Szechuan 130 and **Szechuan 132**. *Inexpensive/Moderate*. 130 North Front Street (910-762-5782) and 419 South College Road

(910-799-1426). There is not much decor at these two locations, but the food has made them the most popular Chinese places in town. The College Road location serves the students at UNC-Wilmington and vacationers at Wrightsville Beach, while the North Front Street location serves the folks downtown. Open daily for lunch and dinner.

Wrightsville Beach

As with any beach area, the time of year you choose to visit Wrightsville Beach will determine the atmosphere you find. Fall and winter, the quiet times, may favor you with Indian-summer temperatures and excellent surf fishing or chill you with gusty winds and choppy waters. Summertime fills the cottages with vacationers enjoying the easy life at the beach.

While this is a popular summer resort area, Wrightsville Beach is also a year-round home for about 1,800 people, as witnessed by the new planned communities centering around marinas and golf courses. These people are here to stay. Some are retirees, others former summer residents who have decided to come home to nest in a favorite spot.

Once known as "the Banks," Wrightsville Beach was at one time accessible only by small boat. Then along came some enterprising businessmen who built a small clubhouse along the strand. In 1853, this facility became known as the Carolina Yacht Club, one of the earliest organizations of its kind in the country. When the Sea Coast Railroad connected the area to Wilmington, Wrightsville Beach's tourist appeal blossomed. Moonlight excursions, complete with musicians, took passengers to the beach for turtle-egg hunting, along with other nature activities that might come to mind on a dark, secluded beach. Eventually, summer cottages and a few resort hotels began to spring up.

By the turn of the century, the beach railway line was electrified, opening up the area to more visitors and residents. The Lumina was one of the most famous structures to be built on Wrightsville Beach, and one that fills many locals with nostalgia even today. A resort of sorts, it had a pavilion and bathing facilities that attracted sunseekers during the day. At night, thousands of electric lights illuminated the resort's exterior as couples danced to an orchestra in the ballroom. Outside, silent movies were projected on a large screen for the audience on the sand. (Now, how can a video-game parlor match that for fun?) Wilmingtonians took the trolley to the Lumina for the evening, where they were joined by visitors from all over the South.

In later years, the complex fell into disrepair. It was destroyed in 1934 by a fire that swept the island. Although residents rebuilt many of the damaged structures, the Lumina was never reconstructed. And the trolley line was replaced by a paved highway with a bridge connecting Wrightsville Beach to the mainland.

Today, thanks to its proximity to Wilmington, Wrightsville Beach offers both the advantages of an island beach escape and the amenities of a lively city.

ACCESS:
Wrightsville Beach is about six miles east of Wilmington on U.S. 74/76. A small drawbridge separates the island from the mainland.

VISITOR INFORMATION:
Contact the Cape Fear Coast Convention and Visitors Bureau, 24 North Third Street, Wilmington, N.C. 28401 (910-341-4030 or 800-222-4757 in the U.S., 800-457-8912 in Canada).

Recreation

This area has one of the largest recreational fishing fleets north of Florida. Numerous boats offer private charters, and others take out larger fishing parties. Charter boats are usually limited to six people and specialize in Gulf Stream fishing and offshore sportfishing. Bait and gear are furnished. Try **Batson's Charter Boats** (910-458-8671). For sailboat charters, call **WaterWays Sailing** (910-256-4282).

For golf or tennis, consider **The Cape Golf and Racquet Club** (910-799-3110) or **Belvedere Plantation Golf & Racquet Club** (910-270-2703).

Seasonal Events

Regattas and fishing tournaments are held throughout the year. Two favorites are **The Cape Fear Open Marlin Tournament** (910-256-6666) and the **Wrightsville Beach King Mackerel Tournament** (910-256-3581). For additional information, call the

Marine Fisheries Department at 910-395-3900.

Accommodations

Lodgings here range from small motels to high-rise condo/hotel/ resort complexes to beachfront cottages. The Cape Fear Coast Convention and Visitors Bureau can provide a list of rental agencies.

Blockade Runner Resort Hotel. *Expensive*. 275 Waynick Boulevard (910-256-2251 or 800-541-1161). A touch of elegance at Wrightsville Beach, this hotel and conference center features harborfront and oceanfront rooms, an indoor health club, bike rentals, and an outdoor pool. The restaurant, open for all three meals, draws local residents for its seafood specialties. The sailing center has rentals and charters. Children under 12 stay free with parents. Seasonal rates are offered.

The Surf Suites. *Expensive*. 711 South Lumina Avenue (910-256-2275). Here, you'll find oceanfront suites with contemporary furnishings. Each suite has a private balcony, a kitchenette, and cable TV. An outdoor pool provides an alternative to the spacious beachfront area. Located next to a pier, this motel is popular among families that like to fish.

One South Lumina. *Moderate/Expensive*. 1 South Lumina Avenue (910-256-9100). **A Summer Place**. *Moderate/Expensive*. 1102 North Lumina Avenue (910-256-3764). Both of these complexes offer one-bedroom luxury suites with fully equipped kitchens, washers and dryers, private balconies, cable TV, and accommodations for six. One South Lumina is oceanfront, while A Summer Place is just a short walk from the ocean and Johnny Mercer's Pier. Weekly and monthly rates are offered.

Restaurants

After spending a day on the beach, a lot of people don't want to dress up to go out, and there are plenty of restaurants here to cater to them. Then again, maybe you'll want a change of pace—you'll find that, too.

Oceanic Restaurant Bar & Grill. *Moderate/Expensive*. 703 South Lumina Avenue (910-256-5551). This restaurant offers panoramic ocean views from dining rooms on three levels. It specializes in fresh local seafood, including broiled and fried seafood platters. There is an oyster bar, as well as outdoor dining on a 700-foot pier. Lunch and dinner are served daily.

The Bridge Tender. *Moderate/Expensive.* Airlie Road (910-256-4519). This is definitely a popular place, serving a wide selection of beef and seafood entrées. The decor is casually elegant and the view nautical, even if you don't get a window seat overlooking the marina. A full bar is offered. The restaurant serves lunch Monday through Friday and dinner daily.

Carolina's. *Moderate.* 1610 Pavilion Place (910-256-5008). Located near the bridge, this family-owned restaurant serves great sandwiches for lunch and pasta and fresh seafood dishes for dinner. The desserts are homemade. Lunch and dinner are served daily.

David's Deli. *Inexpensive.* Plaza East Shopping Center (910-256-9070). If you're looking for a friendly neighborhood pub minus the wild crowd roaming in off the streets, David's is a good choice. This comfortable eatery offers a wide selection of salads, sandwiches, pasta, seafood, and even bagels. Ask about the nightly seafood specials and specialty drinks. A full bar is offered. Lunch and dinner are served daily.

Middle of the Island Restaurant. *Inexpensive.* 216 Causeway Drive (910-256-4277). Known affectionately among locals as "The M.O.I.," this tiny restaurant isn't a place to take folks to impress them—unless they like an amiable waitress, good country-style cooking (the breakfast will stick to your ribs), and a small-town atmosphere. Breakfast, lunch, and dinner are served daily.

Causeway Cafe. *Inexpensive.* 114 Causeway Drive (910-256-3730). The Causeway Cafe rivals Middle of the Island in popularity, especially for its home-cooked breakfasts. The food isn't exotic, but it sure is good. Breakfast and lunch are served Tuesday through Sunday.

Pleasure Island

Getting to the beaches of Pleasure Island is not the most scenic of drives, but the trip is well worth it. Don't be discouraged by all the motels, restaurants, and commercial trappings you'll see as you drive down U.S. 421. Sometimes, it's even hard to find the ocean, particularly around Carolina Beach. Poke between the hotels and condominiums—public beach accesses are marked. Then you'll find the white-sand beaches with gentle breezes and refreshing surf that have appealed to ocean lovers for decades. Even the most modest motel has enough beachfront to allow you to throw down a towel and stay awhile. Indeed, the farther south you go, the more the population and development thin out and the more nature takes over.

Pleasure Island came into its own as a resort area around the turn of the century, when Wilmingtonians built summer homes here, hoping to develop the area as access improved. It wasn't until good roadways came along, though, that the area really began to grow. Despite the threat of overdevelopment—much of this area has been rebuilt since the last major hurricane hit in 1984—Pleasure Island draws its loyal fans with the simple rewards of the beach: swimming, sunning, and socializing.

You'll also find a fleet of charter fishing and pleasure boats waiting to take you out to sea, along with several large fishing piers along the beaches. An air of quiet congeniality still exists here. And that is why many find it a pleasure to visit.

ACCESS:
Pleasure Island is located 12 miles south of Wilmington on U.S. 421. It can also be reached via the Southport–Fort Fisher toll ferry.

VISITOR INFORMATION:
Contact the Pleasure Island Chamber of Commerce by mail at 1140-B North Lake Boulevard, Carolina Beach, N.C. 28428 (910-458-8434) or via the Web at http://www.caro-kure.wilmington.net.

Attractions

Historic Places

Fort Fisher State Historic Site, at Kure Beach, marks the site that withstood the heaviest naval bombardment in history until the 20th century. In January 1865, it took an assault of 10,000 Federal troops and hundreds of thousands of pounds of projectiles to capture the largest earthwork fortification in the Confederacy. The port of Wilmington capitulated soon after, and with its main supply route cut, the Confederacy was forced to surrender within weeks. Only the fort's breastworks remain. From a trail around the mound, you can see the Cape Fear River. Occasionally, groups reenact Confederate encampments under the trees nearby.

The visitor center features a slide show and displays of artifacts, tools, etchings, models, and dioramas that illustrate Fort Fisher's history and the role of blockade runners. By 1864, some 32 Union ships were blockading the Cape Fear River's mouth, but it was so lucrative to bring supplies into Wilmington that hundreds of specially modified blockade-running ships played what was known as "the deadly game." Scores of them were sunk.

With grounds that include a picnic area and plenty of room to roam, this is a nice place to give the children a history lesson and get the kinks out at the same time. This is also the state headquarters for underwater archaeology. The site is open Monday through Saturday from 9 A.M. to 5 P.M. and Sunday from 1 to 5 P.M. from April to October; it is also open Tuesday through Saturday from 10 A.M. to 4 P.M. and Sunday from 1 to 4 P.M. from November to March. It is closed Christmas and New Year's Day. Admission is free. Call 910-458-5538 for more information.

Museums/Science Centers

North Carolina Aquarium at Fort Fisher, across the road from Fort Fisher State Historic Site, is one of the three state marine-resource centers along the coast. Serving as a center for information, marine education, and research, the facility provides a wonderful opportunity to view live sharks, sea turtles, and other marine animals. The touch tank is a favorite for children of all ages; there's also a special children's corner. Educational programs are offered throughout the year. The aquarium is open daily from 9 A.M. to 7 P.M. Admission is $3 for adults, $2 for seniors and active military, and $1 for children ages six to 17. Call 910-458-8257.

Recreation

Carolina Beach State Park, 10 miles south of Wilmington on U.S. 421, encompasses 712 acres near Carolina Beach. Located inland on the Intracoastal Waterway, the park has more than 80 tent and trailer campsites. Picnicking, fishing, hiking, summer nature-study programs, and a marina are offered. Call 910-458-8206.

Carolina Beach Family Campground, 1½ miles from the beach, offers full hookups, a swimming pool, and laundry facilities. The campground is open from Memorial Day to Labor Day. Call 910-392-3322.

Accommodations

Supposedly, there are more motels and hotels on Pleasure Island than in any other barrier-island community except Nags Head. Rates are seasonal and are at their highest from June to Labor Day. The following lodgings are only a few suggestions—the selection is overwhelming. The chamber of commerce can provide a list of rental agencies if you prefer staying in a cottage or condominium.

Darlings by the Sea. *Expensive/Deluxe.* 329 Atlantic Avenue, Kure Beach (910-458-8887). This lighthouse inn features five fabulously appointed oceanfront whirlpool suites that are a sure bet for a romantic getaway. The amenities include king-size beds with goose-down comforters, private terraces overlooking the ocean, an ocean-front fitness center, and a lush courtyard. The "Getaway Together" long- weekend package enables guests to check in at noon on Friday and check out at 4 P.M. on Sunday. A gourmet breakfast is stocked in guests' wet bars each night.

Atlantic Towers. *Moderate/Expensive.* 1615 South Lake Park Boulevard, Carolina Beach (910-458-8313). While this is one of those high-rises casting shadows on Carolina Beach, Atlantic Towers is an attractive complex. The 11-story oceanfront hotel-condo-minium complex features 137 tastefully decorated units with 24-hour security, cable TV, a pool, a laundry, and meeting and banquet facilities. Suites sleep up to six. Weekly and monthly rates are available.

Cabana DeMar. *Moderate/Expensive.* 31 Carolina Avenue North, Carolina Beach (910-458-4456). This oceanfront motel-condo-minium complex features one- and two-bedroom suites with com-plete kitchens, dining and living rooms, balconies, and cable TV. A covered park, a pool, a laundry, and meeting rooms are available. Golf and marina facilities are nearby. Weekly rates are offered.

Seven Seas Inn. *Moderate/Expensive.* Kure Beach (910-458-8122). Located on the beach, this hotel offers rooms and efficiencies and a variety of amenities including a fish-cleaning facility. Golf and fishing packages are available, and it's just a short walk to the pier and dining. The kids will love the two oceanfront pools.

King's Motel. *Moderate/Expensive*. 318 Carolina Beach Avenue North, Carolina Beach (910-458-5594). You'll find a friendly atmosphere at this family-run oceanfront motel, which offers standard rooms and one- and two-bedroom efficiencies, all attractively furnished. There's a solar-heated pool, a guaranteed respite from the ocean waves. The motel is just a block from the boardwalk and the fishing fleet. Weekly rates are offered.

Admiral's Quarters. *Moderate*. U.S. 421, Kure Beach (910-458-5050). This oceanfront motel offers both standard rooms and fully equipped efficiencies. Guests enjoy the two pools, the second-floor sun deck, and the beach complete with lifeguards. The motel is just a half-block from the pier and restaurants. Midweek specials are offered during spring and fall.

The Docksider Inn. *Inexpensive/Moderate*. U.S. 421, Kure Beach (910-458-4200). This attractive motel will catch your eye, since it's designed a little differently from most of the small motels along the strip. It's described as "lovingly crafted by a master builder," and that fits. The Docksider's rooms and efficiencies have a nautical theme. Guests can enjoy Sunday mornings at poolside with coffee, juice, and doughnuts. The Sunketch, a rooftop sun deck, is open to all. A two-night minimum is required on weekends. The inn boasts a AAA rating of Two Diamonds and a Mobil rating of Two Stars.

Restaurants

On any of these beaches, restaurants range from hot-dog stands to tablecloth-and-candlelight spots. In fact, picking a place to eat can be difficult unless you've decided to rent a cottage and cook some fresh seafood yourself. Keep in mind, too, that many people enjoy going into Wilmington for dinner.

Big Daddy's Seafood Restaurant. *Moderate*. Kure Beach (910-458-8622). This beach dining tradition since 1968 claims to serve "seafood at its best." You'll find that a lot of people endorse that opinion. Steaks and prime rib are also favorites. Children's and senior citizens' menus are offered as is a full bar. Dinner is served nightly from March to November.

The Marina's Edge. *Moderate*. 300 North Lake Park Boulevard, Carolina Beach (910-458-6001). Diners can pick a live lobster out of the lobster tank, enjoy the raw bar, or select one of the fresh local seafood entrées. There are also plenty of steak and chicken entrées for landlubbers. Open for lunch on Saturday and Sunday and for dinner seven days a week.

Stella Mae's Cafe. *Inexpensive/Moderate*. 6-C North Lake Park Boulevard, Carolina Beach (910-458-3778). If you're looking for some down-home cooking, you're looking for Stella Mae's. This place offers some of the best family-style cooking in the area. You can feast on chicken and dumplings or porkchops. Or if you're in a really upper-crust kind of mood, the prime rib is sure to please. Lunch and dinner are served daily except for Monday.

Mama Mia's Italian Restaurant. *Inexpensive/Moderate*. 6 South Lake Park Boulevard, Carolina Beach (910-458-9228). Now, this is Italian, and a nice alternative to the fried-seafood and burger eateries. You can enjoy anything from pizza to a full pasta dinner in a friendly, unpretentious atmosphere. Free delivery is offered on the island. Dinner is served daily, and lunch is offered on Saturday.

Southport/Brunswick Islands

Whether you take the ferry from Fort Fisher or the highway south along the river, you'll end up in Southport. Situated at the southeastern tip of North Carolina, Southport is "where the pine trees meet the palms."

This historic fishing village is at the mouth of the Cape Fear River on the west bank. While it's a quiet, small Southern town, Southport is also an important crossroads. Located midway between New York and Miami on the Intracoastal Waterway, it is a favorite place to stop among boaters. Fishing is good here, too.

Southport is one of the larger towns in the area. Beach residents can shop at a well-stocked grocery store, have some seafood at a local restaurant, or stroll among the town's famous oak trees.

The ferry to Bald Head Island—now a semiprivate resort and preserve—originates here. The Southport–Fort Fisher ferry also boards here, saving about an hour's worth of driving back to the Wilmington area—besides, it's more fun to take the ferry.

Southport has some majestic old homes, a feature that hasn't gone unnoticed by Hollywood. In recent years, Southport and its environs have served as backdrops for several major motion pictures. Several blocks of early-20th-century homes are listed on the National Register of Historic Places. With this growing popularity have come more shops and conveniences, but Southport still retains the image of a quiet Southern seaport.

Oak Island, linked to the mainland by a high-rise bridge, includes Long Beach, Yaupon Beach, and Caswell Beach. More heavily wooded than most barrier islands, Oak Island offers beaches that remain comfortably uncrowded. Some motels are located here, but most summer visitors rent cottages by the week. Restaurants, though small, are family-run and reliable. Nightlife—beach music and a dance floor—can be found in Long Beach.

A scenic walkway spanning Davis Creek in Long Beach gives visitors a closeup view of indigenous wildlife and vegetation. Visitors can also get a view of the Oak Island Lighthouse and Fort Caswell, both dating from the 19th century. The lighthouse is owned by the Coast Guard and the fort by the North Carolina Baptist Assembly. Neither is open to the public.

You'll find plenty of parking and public beach access at the ends of side roads. Shelling along the beaches is good or even excellent, depending on the drift of the tides. And if you're dreaming about catching your meal, the waters are filled with mackerel.

The South Brunswick Islands can guarantee a peaceful atmosphere, white-sand beaches, and over 200 days of sunshine a year. Because these beaches are marketed as "North Carolina's Best-Kept Secret," many who have already discovered Holden Beach, Ocean Isle Beach, and Sunset Beach want them to remain relatively unknown.

While Holden Beach has a high-rise bridge and some new, big cottages at its eastern and western ends, life remains low-key. You'll have to go over the bridge to get to the water slide and the miniature golf course. That's about it, except for plenty of beach space and opportunities for surf fishing, crabbing, shrimping, biking, clamming, and talking with your family or whomever you meet on the beach.

Ocean Isle Beach has a number of condominiums and homes that are making it more crowded than it used to be. Yet the island's atmosphere is still tranquil.

Sunset Beach is the smallest and least developed of these islands. Life is slower here, since the only access is a one-lane bridge. Most people don't mind a bit. If you're too impatient to wait, you've probably come to the wrong place.

ACCESS:
Southport, about 25 miles south of Wilmington, is accessible via N.C. 133 and N.C. 87. It can also be reached from Pleasure Island on the Southport–Fort Fisher ferry. Oak Island is reached via N.C. 133. The three South Brunswick Islands are connected to U.S. 17 by small state roads.

VISITOR INFORMATION:
Contact the Southport–Oak Island Chamber of Commerce, 4841 Long Beach Road SE, Southport, N.C. 28461 (800-457-6964). For Holden, Ocean Isle, and Sunset Beaches, contact the South Brunswick Islands Chamber of Commerce, P.O. Box 1380, Shallotte, N.C. 28459 (910-754-6644 or 800-426-6644).

Attractions

Museums

Southport Maritime Museum, located at 116 North Howe Street, houses an interesting collection of memorabilia pertaining to the nautical history of the Lower Cape Fear area. There is a self-guided tour which takes you through 12 designated stations. The museum is open Tuesday through Saturday from 10 A.M. to 4 P.M. Admission is $2 for adults and $1 for seniors. Call 910-457-0003.

Museum of Coastal Carolina at 21 East Second Street in Ocean Isle Beach, is a hands-on interactive museum that invites the exploration of the natural history and heritage of the Carolina's coastal wildlife. The Reef Room features a "walk under the sea" that allows kids of all ages to discover what really lurks in the deep-blue waters off the Carolina coast. Native American, maritime, and Civil War artifacts are on display, and the swamp and waterfowl dioramas are quite interesting and educational. From Memorial Day through Labor Day, the museum is open from 9 A.M. to 5 P.M. on Tuesday, Wednesday, Friday, and Saturday, from 9 A.M. to 9 P.M. on Monday and Thursday, and from 1 to 5 P.M. on Sunday. The rest of the year, it is open from 9 A.M. to 5 P.M. on Friday and Saturday and from 1 to 5 P.M. on Sunday. Admission is $3 for adults and $1 for children under 12. Call 910-579-1016.

Cultural Offerings

Franklin Square Art Gallery, in Southport's Franklin Square Park, features exhibits by local artists working in a variety of media from clay to oils. One of the state's few youth galleries is here, too. The building was erected in 1904 as a school. It later became the city hall, then a library. While you're here, visit the hand-pump well on the grounds. Town lore says that those who drink from the well are destined to return to Southport. So if you like the place, help yourself.

Recreation

Of course, there's the standard beach activity on the barrier islands. If you're interested in charter-boat fishing, it's available right at Southport's docks. Or try free pier fishing at **Southport Municipal Pier**, located near the foot of Howe Street on the Cape Fear River.

Boiling Spring Lakes, a recreational and residential community less than 10 miles from Southport, offers a number of picnic and swimming areas. A municipal park nearby features fishing and motorless boats.

Southport is becoming a mecca for antique shoppers. There are over 15 shops and 75 dealers involved in the sale of antiques and collectibles in this community.

The area is also becoming known for its excellent golf courses. Many of Brunswick County's 27 golf clubs—some of which have more than one course—are open daily to the public and offer championship play. Several courses host prestigious golf tournaments each year. Among the courses are **Brick Landing Plantation** (800-438-3006) at Ocean Isle; **Marsh Harbour Golf Links** (800-552-2660) in Calabash; **Ocean Harbour Golf Links** (910-579-3588) in Calabash; **Pearl Golf Links** (910-579-8132) in Calabash; **Sea Trail Plantation** (800-624-6601) in Calabash; and **Oyster Bay Golf Links** (800-697-8372) at Sunset Beach. For a complete list of golf courses in the area, contact the Southport–Oak Island Chamber of Commerce.

Seasonal Events

The **North Carolina Fourth of July Festival** in Southport enjoys quite a reputation, attracting over 30,000 people each year. Children's events, food, crafts, music, and the traditional parade and fireworks provide family fun. No alcoholic beverages are allowed.

U.S. Open King Mackerel Tournament, held in late September or early October, has become one of the state's most popular tournaments. More than 500 boats usually enter in pursuit of a $100,000 purse. Call the Southport–Oak Island Chamber of Commerece at 800-457-6964 or the Marine Fisheries Department at 910-395-3900. The **South Brunswick Islands King Mackerel Classic** is held Labor Day weekend. This tournament also offers over $100,000 in prizes. Call 800-426-6644.

The **Christmas by the Sea Festival**, held in December, finds all types of festively decorated vessels making their way from the marina to the waterfront park in Southport. There are home tours and musical concerts as well. Call 800-457-6964.

The **North Carolina Oyster Festival** is held in mid-October in Shallotte. What began as a small oyster roast in 1979 has now grown into the official oyster festival of North Carolina. Along with a road race and musical entertainment, there is, of course, fresh seafood—especially oysters. The highlight of the festival is the North Carolina Oyster Shucking Championship. The winner of the oyster-shucking contest is judged on precision, neatness of final tray presentation, and time. Call 910-754-6644.

The **North Carolina Festival by the Sea** is held in Holden Beach on the last full weekend in October. Over 150 arts-and-crafts vendors display their wares, and the selection of cuisine spans the globe. Other festivities include dances, music, a parade, and a 5K run. Favorite events at the festival are the sandcastle and kite-flying contests. For information, contact the Greater Holden Beach Merchant Association at 910-842-3828.

Side Trips

Orton Plantation Gardens—See *Wilmington: Side Trips*
Brunswick Town State Historic Site—See *Wilmington: Side Trips*
If you take the ferry to **Bald Head Island** during the summer months, you may be lucky enough to spot a loggerhead turtle. While it's best to look at night, you can observe some activity during the day. The loggerheads are an endangered species, and part of the island has been set aside as a nature preserve. Once on the island, you will need to rent a golf cart or a bicycle or use your legs to get around, because cars aren't allowed. You can rent golf carts and bicycles at the store at the island's ferry terminal.

There are several package tours of the island which include lunch or dinner. You can stay on the island, but there are no economy deals. Call Bald Head Management at 910-457-5000.

You can also visit Bald Head Island Lighthouse, which is open from 7 A.M. to 8 P.M. year-round. This lighthouse, affectionately known as "Old Baldy," was built in 1817 and is the oldest lighthouse in North Carolina. There is no fee for admission, but only six people at a time are allowed to enter the lighthouse.

Just before you drive into South Carolina, you'll find **Calabash**, a small town peppered with seafood restaurants, all claiming to serve "the original Calabash seafood." Calabash cooking simply means that the

Bald Head Island Lighthouse
Photograph by William Russ
Courtesy of N.C. Travel and Tourism Division

seafood is dipped in a light batter, then quickly fried. This place can get very crowded in the summer, since it attracts people from up and down the coast, including the Myrtle Beach, South Carolina, area. Choosing from the more than 30 restaurants can be a bit overwhelming. Be patient—the lines are usually long and the restaurants bustling. Most people who frequent Calabash don't really recommend one restaurant over another.

Accommodations

Because of its small size, Southport has few accommodations. Most visitors choose the beach areas, but there are some options. For rentals on the South Brunswick Islands, check with the chamber of commerce; call 910-754-6644 or 800-426-6644. For rentals in Southport and Oak Island, call the Southport–Oak Island Chamber of Commerce at 800-457-6964.

The Islander Inn. *Expensive/Deluxe*. 57 West First Street, Ocean Isle Beach (910-575-7000 or 888-325-4753). This oceanfront family resort offers an extended list of amenities, including in-room wet bars with refrigerators, 25-inch color TVs with HBO, data-port telephones with voice mail, and daily maid service. A heated indoor pool, hot tub, an oceanfront outdoor pool, and a sun deck are also available. An expanded continental breakfast is included in the room rate. Golf packages are available.

Ocean Isle Inn. *Moderate/Expensive*. 37 West First Street, Ocean Isle Beach (910-579-0750 or 800-352-5988). The oceanfront rooms here are slightly more expensive than those with views of the sound. There is an outdoor pool, as well as a heated indoor pool and a hot tub. Golf packages are also available.

The Winds Clarion Inn. *Moderate/Expensive*. 310 East First Street, Ocean Isle Beach (910-579-6275 or 800-334-3581). This hotel features oceanfront rooms and one- to four-bedroom suites with kitchens. There is a heated pool which is enclosed in winter. Bicycles, beach umbrellas, and chairs may be rented during the summer. Tennis and golf packages are also available.

Sea Captain Motor Lodge. *Inexpensive/Moderate*. 608 West Street, Southport (910-457-5263). This motor lodge has double, queen, and efficiency rooms. Conveniently located next to the marina, it is a favorite among boaters and fishermen. It offers a large pool, a full-service restaurant, and a lounge.

Inns and Bed-and-Breakfast Guest Houses

Theodosia's. *Deluxe.* Harbour Village on Bald Head Island (910-457-6563, 800-656-1812 or www.southport.net/theodosia.html). This is one of only two nonprivate accommodations on Bald Head Island. The rates are high, but it's very exclusive. There are ten individually decorated rooms with private baths and cable television. Golf carts and bikes are complimentary with each room.

Restaurants

This is definitely seafood country, and you can count on its being fresh. Many of the restaurants around here are small and family-run—not a bad combination. If you like fried seafood, you might take a trip to Calabash, but there are lots of alternatives.

The Italian Fisherman Restaurant. *Moderate.* On the water at Sunset Beach (910-579-2929). This restaurant can satisfy those groups that include both seafood lovers and diners who favor other fare. Seafood and steaks are on the menu, but so are traditional Italian dishes. Dinner is served Thursday through Tuesday.

Jones' Seafood House. *Inexpensive/Moderate.* 6404 East Oak Island Drive, Long Beach (910-278-5231). This family-owned restaurant is a local favorite. It specializes in Calabash-style seafood and offers a full-service bar. Open daily for dinner.

Ship's Chandler. *Inexpensive/Moderate.* 101 West Bay Street, Southport (910-457-6595). Not only does this friendly restaurant offer an enviable view of the Cape Fear River out to Bald Head Island, but it also boasts outstanding seafood and some of the best hush puppies around. Beer and wine are offered. Lunch and dinner are served daily.

Port Charlie's Waterway Restaurant. *Inexpensive/Moderate.* 317 West Bay Street, Southport (910-457-0801). This inviting spot also enjoys a view of the river and Bald Head Island; diners get a front-row look at the boats heading into and out of the marina. Docking facilities are available for guests. Seafood and steaks reign here. Dinner is served Monday through Saturday.

Archibald's Delicatessen & Rotisserie. *Inexpensive.* 138-A East Brunswick Avenue, Holden Beach (910-842-6888). This is a real New York–style deli featuring freshly baked pastries and croissants. Open for lunch Monday through Saturday and for dinner Friday and Saturday.

Courtesy of N.C. Department of Transportation

Skyline of Raleigh, the state capital
Courtesy of Greater Raleigh
Convention and Visitors Bureau

The Piedmont

North Carolina's central region, stretching over 44 of the state's 100 counties, is an area of low, rolling hills thickly covered with oak, elm, and loblolly pine trees. Called the Piedmont because it lies at the foot of the Appalachian Mountains, it has rocky, red-clay soil that has long provided good farmland for tobacco.

The Piedmont—which includes Charlotte, Raleigh, Durham, Chapel Hill, Winston-Salem, High Point, and Greensboro—is the most prosperous and the most populous area of North Carolina. It's a thriving center for industries ranging from textiles to high technology.

Although Raleigh is the capital, Charlotte is the state's largest city, and the two have been engaged in a rivalry for status for many years. Charlotte has emerged as a major Southern financial center. Raleigh, Durham, and Chapel Hill form the Triangle area, surrounding Research Triangle Park, a campus-style setting for research and light-manufacturing facilities. The largest and most successful venture of its kind in the country, the park has been the catalyst for shifting the state's economy from one primarily dependent on agriculture to one increasingly oriented toward research, medicine, and technology.

The Triangle's transformation has fueled development in other parts of the Piedmont as well, notably the Triad area—Greensboro, Winston-Salem, and High Point—which has traditionally been an important textile and tobacco center. High Point is the hub of another prime North Carolina industry—furniture. It is home to over 100 furniture-manufacturing facilities, including 15 of the largest in the world.

Four of the finest universities in North Carolina are in the Piedmont: Duke University, North Carolina State University, the University of North Carolina at Chapel Hill, and Wake Forest University. These schools also happen to be fierce Atlantic Coast Conference basketball foes.

The area features some top-ranked attractions as well. North Carolina Zoological Park in Asheboro rates among the country's most sophisticated zoos. The American Dance Festival brings international attention to Durham each summer. And any serious golfer will admit a yearning to play the renowned courses at Pinehurst.

Driving through the Piedmont is pleasant, although you won't find great geographical diversity or striking views. In the gently undulating countryside, you'll see farms with fat dairy cattle or healthy crops of corn, soybeans, and tobacco in small fields. Sometimes, you can see farmers taking loads of cured tobacco leaves to auction houses. Once you get off the interstate highways, you'll travel two-lane roads cut through red earth; stands of tall pines drop carpets of needles, especially in the Sandhills region. These pleasant landscapes make traveling to see the museums, gardens, historic sites, and great basketball games of North Carolina's Piedmont a memorable experience.

The Triangle

Raleigh
Durham
Chapel Hill
Research Triangle Park

by Ginny Turner

Three distinct communities form North Carolina's Triangle—the capital city of Raleigh, the research and medical city of Durham, and the university town of Chapel Hill. Each has its special character and is fiercely loyal to its college basketball team: the Wolfpack at North Carolina State University in Raleigh, the Blue Devils at Duke University in Durham, and the Tar Heels at the University of North Carolina at Chapel Hill. Fan devotion is nontransferable.

Although longstanding sports rivalries and other differences have polarized these cities in the past, they are now linked in cooperative efforts for the future development of the region. Once dependent upon tobacco processing, the area's economy now looks to other enterprises, most notably Research Triangle Park (RTP). Conceived in the mid-1950s, RTP has been an enormous success; its firms now employ about 40,000 area residents, and the emphasis is steadily shifting to medical and biomedical technology.

The Triangle is a region to be reckoned with. Not only are its cities benefiting from the infusion of money and new jobs, but so are many small towns around the Triangle's periphery. Lifestyles are changing. New restaurants and shops appear frequently. The Triangle is increasingly urban, its residents in general well educated.

But all this economic and social upgrading hasn't destroyed the area's natural attributes and traditions. Although a new interstate highway connects the three major Triangle communities, buffering stands of pine and acres of small farms remain. You can find exotic foods in the Triangle's gourmet specialty stores, but you can also enjoy hickory-smoked pork at frequent community pig pickings. The area's political spectrum is equally broad, ranging from a strong local Democratic party to Senator Jesse Helms and the conservative Republican Congressional Club.

Perhaps the Triangle's greatest appeal is its wide range of offerings for the traveler. You can stay in urban Raleigh, the growing community of Durham, or the sylvan town of Chapel Hill and still be within easy striking distance of the other two.

Raleigh

Raleigh is difficult to characterize. It doesn't have a distinctive symbol, such as a Space Needle or a Corn Palace, or a nationally known festival or sporting event. A longtime *Raleigh News and Observer* columnist once admitted, "It's a tough nut to crack—it has no unifying theme."

Raleigh is the seat of state government, the home of numerous colleges, and the city where most newcomers arriving to work in the Research Triangle choose to live. As a result, there are three different "worlds" in Raleigh, deriving from the three major industries—government, education, and high technology. There's a definite geographic division as well—the city's encircling freeway, referred to as "the Beltline." Inside its circle, the work of government goes on, and residents live in established neighborhoods of old Victorian houses. Outside it, North Raleigh seems to be erupting with contemporary-style housing developments and retail centers, and Southern accents are rare.

Raleigh is a planned state capital. Edenton was the provincial capital and New Bern the colonial capital, but the General Assembly Convention of 1788 directed that a new site for the state capital be chosen. The commissioners settled on a site and named it for Sir Walter Raleigh, who tried to establish the first English settlement in the New World on North Carolina's Outer Banks.

Today, the heart of the city still reflects the one-square-mile grid laid out by the first surveyor. At the center stands the State Capitol, and on the surrounding blocks are city, county, and state government buildings. It's relatively quiet here—no rushing traffic or canyons of tall buildings.

It took many years before the population spilled over the limits of that original square mile. By 1840, Raleigh had only 2,244 residents, but after the railroad reached town and new factories opened, it took only 10 years to double that figure.

Before the Civil War, North Carolinians were sharply divided on the issue of secession. They remained so even after the legislature voted to join the Confederacy on May 20, 1861, making North Carolina the second-to-last Southern state to secede. Apart from troop-mustering activity, Raleigh remained out of the range of action.

But in April 1865, Union general William Sherman, whose army had just devastated Georgia and South Carolina, approached the city with 60,000 soldiers. Because Raleigh's mayor rode out to meet him and surrender the city, Sherman spared it from looting and destruction. Later that month, Sherman accepted the surrender of Confederate general Joseph Johnston at Bennett Place in Durham, ending the war in the Carolinas, Georgia, and Florida.

The years after the Civil War saw steady development in Raleigh, as cotton mills and other manufacturing operations started up. Affluent citizens built ever more elaborate homes in the shady neighborhood now known as Historic Oakwood, which is filled with two- and three-story frame houses with turrets, domes, decorative chimneys, fancy railings, columns, and bay windows.

During that time, the second "world" of Raleigh was developing, as the town's colleges began to attract students. Two of the schools— St. Augustine's College and Shaw University—were among the nation's first colleges for African-Americans, and two others—Meredith and Peace Colleges—are well-regarded women's schools. But the educational heavyweight is North Carolina State University, which has evolved into one of the top engineering schools in the nation. Later, St. Mary's College (now a women's college-prep school), Wake Technical Community College, and Southeastern Baptist Theological Seminary joined the roster.

Raleigh's third "world" dates from 1956, when Governor Luther Hodges led the development of a long-range plan that would alter the future of the city and the state—the plan for Research Triangle Park. As the tenant list for the park lengthened through the 1970s, Raleigh enjoyed new growth and status.

Today, it seems that Raleigh natives are outnumbered by newcomers working for medical and high-technology research firms. The original one-square-mile city now sprawls over 80 square miles and has a population of over 267,000.

It's easy to sample all three of Raleigh's "worlds" in one day: you can visit the State Capitol, the Executive Mansion, and the Legislative Building downtown; dine at one of the fine restaurants or nightspots outside the Beltline; and enjoy a performance by a touring ballet company or a frenzied basketball game at N.C. State. Then you'll understand Raleigh.

ACCESS:

Unlike many major cities, Raleigh isn't located at the intersection of interstate highways. To get there by car from the north-south routes, take U.S. 70 South from I-85 in Durham, or exit I-95 at Rocky Mount and take U.S. 64 West. I-40 runs east-west, linking Raleigh with Chapel Hill and Hillsborough, where it feeds into I-85. Eastbound, I-40 goes all the way to the coast, ending in Wilmington.

Raleigh-Durham International Airport, a 15-minute drive from the center of the city, is served by 13 major passenger airlines. Several taxi and limousine services are available.

Amtrak's Carolinian connects Raleigh to Washington, D.C., Philadelphia, and New York. The Amtrak station is at 320 West Cabarrus Street; call 919-833-7594 or 800-872-7245.

The Trailways bus station is at 314 West Jones Street; call 919-833-3601.

VISITOR INFORMATION:

For sightseeing in the immediate downtown area, contact the Capital Area Visitor Center (919-733-3456), located at 301 North Blount Street. The visitor center is open Monday through Friday from 8 A.M. to 5 P.M., Saturday from 9 A.M. to 5 P.M., and Sunday from 1 to 5 P.M.

For information about the greater Raleigh area, contact the Greater Raleigh Convention and Visitors Bureau, P.O. Box 1879, One Hanover Square, Fayetteville Street Mall, Suite 1505, Raleigh, N.C. 27602 (919-834-5900 or 800-849-8499). You can also access their Web site at www.raleighcvb.org.

Raleigh's morning paper, the *News and Observer*, is the premier newspaper in eastern North Carolina. Event listings appear in the Friday "What's Up" section. The weekly *Spectator* and *The Independent*, both free publications, also list events.

Historic Places

The **North Carolina Executive Mansion**, at 200 North Blount Street, is a striking example of Victorian architecture; it's also regarded as having the most beautiful interior of any American governor's residence.

Considering that North Carolina was one of the original 13 colonies, this is a very recent home for the

The Executive Mansion
Courtesy of N.C. Division of Tourism, Film, and Sports Development

state's chief executive. When New Bern was the capital city, the governor lived at Tryon Palace. After the capital was moved to Raleigh in 1794, there were two successive governor's mansions, the second of which was so badly damaged during the Federal occupation in the Civil War years that subsequent governors lived in hotels or in their own homes.

The North Carolina General Assembly of 1883 voted the munificent sum of $25,000 to build an appropriate mansion. Money went a lot farther in those days, but even though prison labor was used in the mansion's construction, it took more time and funds than anticipated. When it was finally completed in 1891, it was a showcase of North Carolina materials and craftsmanship. The bricks were made of Wake County clay, the steps of Cherokee County marble, and the elaborately carved, highly polished interior woodwork of native hardwoods.

The governor and his family live in the Executive Mansion year-round, but limited tours are offered throughout the year. The electric gate swings open, and as you walk up the brick carriage drive, you can see the designs in the slate roof, the many gables, the dormer windows, and the decorative spindles supporting the porch roofs.

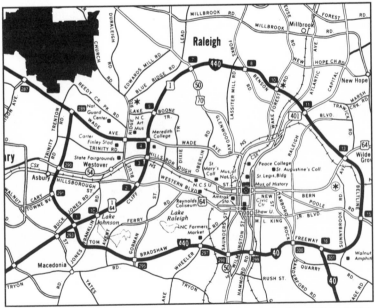

Courtesy of N.C. Department
of Transportation

The Grand Hall is just that, with gleaming chandeliers, huge gilt mirrors, and portraits of former governors on the walls. Volunteers in each of the downstairs rooms tell stories about events there, such as Franklin Roosevelt's visit, and point out special items, such as the state silver, which is engraved with longleaf pine, dogwood blossoms, and the state seal.

The tour lasts about 30 minutes. Tour hours vary; call the Capital Area Visitor Center (919-733-3456) for hours of operation and reservations. The Capital Area Visitor Center is located across the street from the mansion.

Historic Oakwood District, off North Person Street between Jones and Boundary, is a serene, oak-shaded neighborhood adjacent to the Executive Mansion. It contains more than 400 private homes dating from the 19th century, most restored to their original appearance. Architectural styles represented include Greek Revival, Queen Anne, "Shotgun," and Victorian. The area went into decline after World War I because residents preferred living farther from downtown. In the 1970s, however, a neighborhood revitalization effort culminated in the formation of the Society for the Preservation of Historic Oakwood, a nonprofit corporation designed to protect the area from urban development.

Today, Historic Oakwood is an attraction, and prices of individual houses have risen dramatically. The society publishes a brochure, *Walking Tour of Historic Oakwood,* describing the history and salient features of nearly 70 houses. The brochure is available free at the Capital Area Visitor Center.

Mordecai Historic Park/President Andrew Johnson Birthplace, at the corner of Mimosa Street and Wake Forest Road, was built around 1785 and was once one of the largest plantations in the central Carolinas. It is named for its second owner, Moses Mordecai. The two-story frame plantation house, with pillars at the front door and a second-story porch above, was a country estate until 1907, when Raleigh expanded its city limits to include the property. It was occupied by a family member until 1968, when it was purchased by the city as a historic park. Visitors can tour the house and see the family's Victorian furniture, as well as the original library of 19th-century books.

Also on the Mordecai Historic Park property are the Ellen Mordecai Garden, two 19th-century outbuildings, and a gift shop. Along a wide path are three other historic buildings relocated here from other parts of the city, including an 1810 office building and St. Mark's Chapel (1847). Even older is a tiny (12-by-18 foot) 1795 house with a barn-shaped gambrel roof; this structure was the birthplace of President Andrew Johnson. It has been restored to its probable original appearance and contains period furnishings.

Visitors may walk around the buildings during daylight hours. The houses are open to the public Monday and Wednesday through Saturday from 10 A.M. to 3 P.M. and Sunday from 1 to 3 P.M. year-round except major holidays. Tour time is approximately one hour, with the last tour given promptly at 3 P.M. A small admission fee is charged. Call 919-834-4844.

Wakefield, or the **Joel Lane House**, is located at Hargett and St. Mary's Streets. Built in 1760, it is the oldest home in Raleigh. It was named for Margaret Wake, wife of Royal Governor William Tryon.

Colonel Joel Lane, the other person for whom the home is named, is regarded as the "Father of Raleigh." Lane sold the state 1,000 acres in 1792 to be developed into its permanent capital. The fact that the general-assembly commissioners stayed at Wakefield for nearly two weeks prior to selecting the site may have had something to do with their decision.

The one-and-a-half story white frame building has been moved slightly from its original location. It is open Tuesday through Friday from 10 A.M. to 2 P.M. from March to mid-December and the first and third Saturday of each month from 1 to 4 P.M. It is also open by special request. There is a small admission fee. Call 919-833-3431.

Government Buildings

The administration of North Carolina's affairs takes place in buildings within walking distance of one another. March through May, you'll often see classes of students on field trips, getting their civics lessons first-

State Capitol
Courtesy of N.C. Division of Tourism, Film, and Sports Development

hand. You can arrange to join a tour at the Capital Area Visitor Center, or you can pick up brochures there and go on your own.

The **State Capitol**, on Capitol Square, was completed in 1840 and has since been restored to its original appearance. Its copper dome rises 97.5 feet over the cross-shaped building. The body of Confederate president Jefferson Davis lay in state under the rotunda in 1893. Now, a replica of an Antonio Canova statue of George Washington stands in the very center of the area. Until the 1880s, the building housed all the functions of state government, but in 1888, the state supreme court and the state library moved to a new structure, and in 1963, the legislature got its own building. You can see the old Senate and House of Representatives chambers, both of which have been beautifully restored. You may wonder how they all got along sitting so close together. Occasionally, the governor's office is open to the public.

On the grounds are a number of statues and monuments to North Carolina citizens. These include *Three Presidents North Carolina Gave the Nation*, which honors Andrew Jackson, James Polk, and Andrew Johnson, and the poignant *Women of the Confederacy*. The three major statues on the grounds are the Vietnam Memorial, the Confederate Memorial, and the North Carolina Veterans' Memorial.

The State Capitol's front entrance is on Wilmington Street. The building is open Monday through Saturday from 9 A.M. to 5 P.M. and Sunday from 1 to 5 P.M. It is closed on state holidays. Admission is free.

The **Legislative Building** is located at Halifax and Jones Streets. Completed in 1963, it was the first building constructed in the United States for the sole purpose of housing a state general assembly. On the sidewalk in front of the Jones Street entrance is a 280-foot terrazzo mosaic of the state seal. Up a long, red-carpeted staircase is the visitors' gallery, which looks down on the House and Senate chambers. The legislature is in session in the spring. The building is open Monday through Friday from 8 A.M. to 5 P.M., Saturday from 9 A.M. to 5 P.M., and Sunday from 1 to 5 P.M. It is closed state holidays. Unaccompanied children are not admitted. There is no charge.

Museums

North Carolina Museum of Art, at 2110 Blue Ridge Road, is a state-funded art museum. It opened in 1952 in a renovated office building, displaying $1 million worth of art donated from the private collection of merchant Samuel Kress. The museum now occupies a $15-million building designed by Edward Durell Stone, the architect of the original Museum of Modern Art in New York. It contains an important collection of European paintings and significant 18th- and 20th-century American works. Other collections of note feature Greek and Roman sculpture, silver and pewter Jewish ceremonial art, and West African and Oceanic masks and headpieces. Lectures, workshops, films, family events, and performing-arts events are offered regularly. There's also a gift shop and a popular cafe. The museum is open Tuesday, Wednesday, Thursday, and Saturday from 9 A.M. to 5 P.M., Friday from 9 A.M. to 9 P.M., and Sunday from 11 A.M. to 6 P.M.; it is closed Monday. Admission is free. Call 919-839-6262.

North Carolina Museum of Natural Sciences, at 102 North Salisbury Street (the entrance is on Bicentennial Plaza), is especially attractive to children, thanks to its preserved mammals and fish, its live snakes, and its exhibits of earth sciences. The focus is on the natural history and environment of North Carolina, from the seacoast to the mountains. One popular exhibit is the 50-foot-long skeleton of a whale suspended from the ceiling of the mezzanine. The gift shop offers educational materials related to the exhibits. The museum is open Monday through Saturday from 9 A.M. to 5 P.M. and Sunday from 1 to 5 P.M. Admission is free. Call 919-733-7450.

North Carolina Museum of History, at 5 East Edenton Street, is a repository of thousands of artifacts—including a dugout canoe, hand-stitched quilts, and a Homestead Grays uniform—that reflect the history of North Carolina through personal stories and individual items. Visitors can see dioramas portraying the state's cultural history from the days of the Native Americans and the pioneers to the development of industry. The museum is open Tuesday through Saturday from 9 A.M. to 5 P.M. and Sunday from noon to 5 P.M. Admission is free. Call 919-715-0200.

Special Shopping

North Carolina State Farmers Market is located at 1201 Agriculture Street (Exit 297 off I-40 at Lake Wheeler Road). It is the largest produce center in the state. Visitors can shop for fresh produce, crafts, flowers, and plants in an open setting. An on-site restaurant serves country-style breakfast and lunch. Operated by the North Carolina Department of Agriculture, the market offers local truck farmers a place to sell their produce. This is a favorite Saturday-morning stop for Raleigh natives. The market is open Monday through Saturday from 5 A.M. to 6 P.M. and Sunday from noon to 6 P.M. year-round. Admission is free. Call 919-733-7417.

City Market, at the intersection of Blount and Martin Streets, is a Spanish mission–style 1914 marketplace which serves as a unique area for shopping, dining, and entertainment. Specialty shops sell antiques, pottery, gems, clothing, gourmet food, and gifts. Retail and restaurant hours for City Market vary. Call 919-828-4555.

Cultural Offerings

The North Carolina Symphony was founded in 1932, at a time when few people had money to spend on music. Area music lovers met in Chapel Hill and formed the North Carolina Symphony Society for the purpose of organizing an orchestra. Reorganized in 1940 and supported in part by state funds, the society now has over 17 chapters that raise funds for travel expenses for the symphony's public and school concert series. The symphony offers a classical and pops series often featuring guest artists; a pops series on summer weekends; and children's concerts year-round. Most performances are in Memorial Auditorium, at South Wilmington and South Streets, but a new auditorium will open in the winter of 2000 next to the old facility. For information, call 919-733-2750 or 800-292-7469. For tickets, call 919-831-6060.

Raleigh Little Theatre (RLT) has a strong tradition in the city. Founded in 1936, it presents a season of 13 productions for both adults and children, including musicals, classics, comedies, and mysteries—and they're likely to be plays you've heard of. Performances are in RLT's theater at 301 Pogue Street. For information, call 919-821-4579. For tickets, call 919-821-3111.

Theater in the Park, a well-supported community-theater group, performs a lineup of dramas, comedies, and musicals in Pullen Park, near N.C. State. The annual production of *A Christmas Carol* is a Raleigh favorite. Call 919-831-6058.

NCSU Center Stage, at N.C. State's Stewart Theatre, is the Triangle's answer to Off Broadway. It presents professional touring performances, including jazz, dance, nationally acclaimed repertory companies, children's theater, and more. Call 919-515-1100.

North Carolina Theatre brings fine productions of large-scale Broadway musicals to the area. Tony-nominated actor Terrence V. Mann is the artistic director and stars in many of the productions.

Performances are in Memorial Auditorium, at South Wilmington and South Streets. For information, call 919-831-6941. For tickets, call 919-831-6944.

Raleigh Ensemble Players specializes in contemporary Off Broadway plays, musicals, and original plays by local artists. It performs its shows at Artspace at City Market. Call 919-832-9607.

Artspace, at the corner of Blount and Davie Streets in downtown Raleigh, is a center for visual and performing artists. Galleries and working artists' studios are open for tours, demonstrations, and sales. **The Connecting Gallery** is located between Artspace and City Market and is an extension of Artspace's exhibition area. Admission is free. Artspace is open Monday to Saturday from 9 A.M. to 5 P.M. Special gallery walk-throughs are sponsored on the first Friday of each month from 9 A.M. to 9 P.M. Call 919-821-2787.

Visual Art Exchange is a private, nonprofit arts association made up of 400 members ranging from art enthusiasts to professional artists. Classes, workshops, and exhibits are offered for members and the public. The gallery is located at 325 Blake Street. Its hours are Tuesday through Saturday from 11 A.M. to 4 P.M. Call 919-828-7834.

Carolina Ballet is the Triangle's latest cultural talk of the town. This professional ballet company kicked off its inaugural season in the fall of 1998. Performances are held in Memorial Auditorium. Call 919-303-6303.

College Life

North Carolina State University is one of the three major universities in the Triangle. Created by the North Carolina General Assembly in 1887 as an agricultural and engineering college, it is now regarded as one of the top 10 engineering schools in the nation. It has also distinguished itself in many other fields, such as biotechnology and design. Nearly 28,000 students are enrolled.

Part of the University of North Carolina system, it's situated on a 623-acre downtown campus. A 1,000-acre adjunct campus is under development, and additional research farms, greenhouses, and forests are located elsewhere in the state. The 116-foot granite Memorial Tower marks the campus on Hillsborough Street, and you're free to drive through the area to see the gracefully designed brick buildings.

N.C. State leads the state in research expenditures, with an annual

*Memorial Tower at
North Carolina State University*
Courtesy of N.C. Travel and Tourism
Division

research budget of over $130 million. It was the first institution in the world to build and operate a nuclear reactor for educational purposes. It was named by *Business Week* as one of the top 12 institutions in the United States receiving industry funds for research.

Recreation

Pullen Park, adjacent to N.C. State at 520 Ashe Avenue, is by far the city's most popular park. Its 65 acres feature a train that goes around the park and a lake with pedal boats and children's boat rides. The highlight is the 1911 Denzel carousel—one of 6,000 such hand-carved carousels built in the early 1900s, and one of only 170 remaining intact. The park also includes picnic facilities, a pool, and tennis courts. Call 919-831-6468.

William B. Umstead State Park is located northwest of Raleigh, with entrances off U.S. 70 and I-40 West. It offers picnicking, camping, and hiking, including a short nature trial and an extensive hiking trail into the heart of the woods. Special trails are set aside for those who want to tour the park on horseback. For information, call 919-571-4170.

Falls Lake, northwest of Raleigh at 13304 Creedmoor Road in Wake Forest, is a reservoir with beaches, boat ramps, fishing, water-skiing, picnic areas, and campgrounds. This 12,000-acre lake is one of the largest recreation facilities in the state. Call 919-676-1027.

Lake Wheeler, located on Lake Wheeler Road just south of the city, has 650 acres of lake and parkland. Sailboat, johnboat, and canoe rentals are offered, as are private boating, water-skiing, fishing, rowing, kayaking, and picnicking. Open year-round except major holidays, the facility also holds special events ranging from open-air concerts to fishing tournaments to world-class powerboat championships. Call 919-662-5704.

There are several golf courses in the area. Among them are **Cheviot Hills Golf Course** (919-876-9920), off U.S. 1 North; **Ra-**

leigh Golf Association (919-772-9987), at 1527 Tryon Road; and **Wildwood Green Golf Club** (919-846-8376), at 3000 Balley Bunion Way, off Strickland Road. Remember, you're not far from the courses in the Pinehurst area.

For information on public tennis courts, call **919-890-3285**.

Construction on **Raleigh Entertainment and Sports Arena** began in July 1997. The facility will open its doors in the fall of 1999. The 21,000-seat venue will feature major attractions such as the N.C. State basketball team and the **Carolina Hurricanes**, a National Hockey League competitor. The arena will also play host to conventions and large meetings. Call **919-834-5900**.

Seasonal Events

Artsplosure Spring Jazz and Art Festival, held the third weekend in May, is a city-sponsored festival featuring regional and national performing artists in continuous shows on outdoor stages, plus arts-and-crafts shows in several public venues. There's no shortage of food, either. Call 919-832-8699.

National Hollerin' Contest is held at Spiveys Corner, 40 miles south of Raleigh, on a Saturday in June. Besides contestants who holler, the event features music, clogging, and a barbecue. The winning "hollerer" enjoys a brief moment of stardom, which sometimes includes appearances on national talk shows. Call 919-733-4171.

Lazy Daze is an arts-and-crafts festival held at the end of August in Cary's old downtown section. It's a good event for doing your Christmas shopping. Live bandstand entertainment is provided. Call 919-469-4061.

North Carolina State Fair, held in mid-October, features a wide range of livestock and agricultural exhibits, crafts, a Midway, rides, and entertainment. This is where the state's finest goats, heifers, lop-eared rabbits, quilts, pumpkins, and home-canned peaches compete for honors. It's crowded on weekends. The fairgrounds have an unusual Spanish mission–style entrance and are located at 1025 Blue Ridge Road. Call 919-733-2145.

Historic Oakwood Candlelight Tour, held in mid-December, offers walk-through visits to many of the beautiful Victorian homes you may have been admiring from the outside. The holiday decorations are quite stunning. The tour is a fund-raiser for the Historic

Oakwood Association. Tickets typically go on sale around Thanksgiving. Call 919-834-0887.

International Festival of Raleigh, held in early October, is a mosaic of the world's tastes, sights, and sounds. Held in the heart of the city, it features ethnic foods and a world bazaar, along with exhibits, dancing, demonstrations, continuous entertainment, and a beer garden. Over 45 ethnic groups are involved. Call 919-832-4331.

First Night is an alcohol-free New Year's Eve celebration of the arts held in various locations throughout Raleigh. It features art exhibits, music, dance, comedy, theater, and magic. The event culminates in a countdown to midnight, followed by fireworks. For information, call 919-832-8699.

Side Trips

See *Triangle Side Trips*

Accommodations

Most of Raleigh's new hotels are located around the northwestern intersections of the Beltline, which provides easy access not only to downtown but also to the airport, Durham, and Research Triangle Park. Because competition is fierce for the lucrative business trade, you can expect prompt, efficient service at most hotels.

Sheraton Raleigh Capital Center Hotel. *Expensive/Deluxe*. 421 South Salisbury Street (919-834-9900). This is where the glitz is, starting with a two-story atrium and an escalator to the registration desk. Located adjacent to the convention-center complex, this is basically a convention hotel and serves as a good meeting place for business appointments. The rooms have contemporary decor. A lounge, two restaurants, an indoor pool, and a health club are offered.

Brownestone Hotel. *Expensive*. 1707 Hillsborough Street (919-828-0811 or 800-331-7919). Within walking distance of N.C. State, this hotel provides rooms with private balconies and large, comfortable beds. It also boasts a bar and restaurant on-site.

Hilton North Raleigh. *Expensive*. 3415 Wake Forest Road (919-872-2323). The Hilton has become an important regional convention center. Its 338 spacious rooms are furnished to be relaxing. A lobby bar with a grand piano, a lounge, an indoor pool, an exercise room, and free airport transportation are offered.

The Raleigh Marriott Crabtree Valley. *Moderate/Expensive.* 4500 Marriott Drive (919-781-7000). The Raleigh Marriott's guest rooms, designed for the business traveler, offer amenities such as sophisticated fire protection, individual climate control, two telephones, and cable TV with in-room pay movies. A lounge serving complimentary breakfast and afternoon hors d'oeuvres is on the executive floor, and a bar and restaurant are available for all the guests.

The Velvet Cloak Inn. *Moderate/Expensive.* 1505 Hillsborough Street (919-828-0333). The Velvet Cloak is the only hotel in the area with a doorman in tail coat and white gloves. With outside entrances to each of its attractively decorated rooms and suites, the inn at first glance seems more like a motel, but that's before you see the lobby, with its polished marble floors and antiques, the indoor atrium, and the pool.

Holiday Inn State Capital. *Moderate.* 320 Hillsborough Street (919-832-0501). The exterior of this hotel looks like some outsize Telstar satellite, but it features attractive rooms, all with city views. Only two blocks from the State Capitol, it's convenient for visiting the downtown museums and buildings. The Top of the Tower Restaurant features dining on the 20th floor; it is open for breakfast, lunch, and dinner. Guests can enjoy live entertainment in the lounge in the evenings.

Hampton Inn Raleigh North. *Moderate.* 1001 Wake Town Drive (919-828-1813). Conveniently located near the Wake Forest Road exit off the Beltline, the Hampton Inn draws business people who want quality at a low price. Free local calls, HBO, an outdoor pool, and continental breakfast are offered.

Inns and Bed-and-Breakfast Guest Houses

The Oakwood Inn. *Expensive.* 411 North Bloodworth Street (919-832-9712). Built in 1871, this bed-and-breakfast is located in the heart of Historic Oakwood. The restored house is painted lavender and has darker gingerbread railings on the porches. Potted palms, floral wallpaper, potpourri in open bowls, and antique furniture enhance the romantic, Victorian-era ambiance. The guest rooms are individually decorated. A full breakfast is served in the dining room beneath a crystal chandelier.

The William Thomas House. *Expensive*. 530 North Blount Street (919-755-9400). Originally a residence and office of a Raleigh attorney, this bed-and-breakfast blends the spirit of Victorian times with traditional Southern hospitality. The house, built in 1881, features four guest rooms with private baths and is conveniently located within walking distance of the Executive Mansion, the State Capitol, museums, and restaurants. There's a large porch with a swing and rocking chairs and a comfortable dining room.

Restaurants

Raleigh offers a number of fine restaurants, with new ones opening regularly. Although the restaurants are scattered throughout the city, a great number of good dining options can be found in the northwest area, where U.S. 70 meets the Beltline.

Angus Barn. *Expensive*. U.S. 70 (919-787-3505). This restaurant gives new meaning to the traditional steakhouse. The rustic barn is decorated in Americana—quilts, restored farm equipment, and antiques. Prime rib, steak, lobster, and filet mignon are the most popular specialties. Located close to the airport, Angus Barn is very accommodating to travelers on a schedule. A full bar is offered. Reservations are recommended except on Saturday, when they're not accepted. Dinner is served daily.

The Melting Pot. *Expensive*. 3100 Wake Forest Road (919-878-0477). A specialty restaurant that's fun for special events, the Melting Pot is a great favorite with young people. Fondue is prepared over a burner right in front of you, and once it reaches the proper temperature, your waitperson leaves you to dip your beef, chicken, or mixed seafood. The several variations of cheese fondue come with vegetables and bread to dip. If you're not too full, the chocolate fondue is wonderful. Beer and wine are offered. Dinner is served nightly.

Winston's Grille. *Moderate/Expensive*. 6401 Falls of the Neuse Road (919-790-0700). Winston's is well recommended by locals, who enjoy its casual elegance. Sandwiches, salads, char-broiled burgers, and Cajun items comprise the lunch menu. Dinner entrées include veal Marsala, shrimp Dijon, and London broil. A full bar is offered. Lunch and dinner are served daily, and brunch is offered on Sunday.

518 West Italian Cafe. *Moderate/Expensive*. 518 West Jones Street (919-829-2518). This Italian restaurant is gaining a reputation for its freshly made pasta, as well as for its specialty pizzas and daily specials. Lunch is served Monday through Saturday; dinner is served nightly.

42nd Street Oyster Bar. *Moderate*. West Jones and West Streets (919-831-2811). This is one of Raleigh's trendiest and liveliest restaurants. Inside the Art Deco entrance, the mood is casually sophisticated, which means the walls are covered with photos, license plates, and mounted fish, but the patrons sitting at raised tables in the bar are in business suits. You can have your oysters fried, steamed, or on the half shell; six varieties are featured. Daily specials include such items as shrimp Creole, barbecued flounder, and blackened catfish. Lunch selections include shrimp fettuccine and soft-shell crab sandwiches. A full bar is offered. The restaurant is open for lunch and dinner Monday through Friday and for dinner only on Saturday and Sunday.

Cappers Restaurant and Tavern. *Moderate*. North Hills Shopping Center, Six Forks Road (919-787-8963). This establishment serves up zesty jambalaya, deep-fried eggplant brimming with shrimp and scallops, and great pasta dishes, as well as blues or jazz most nights. Lunch is served Monday through Friday, and dinner is served nightly except Sunday.

Jean Claude's Cafe. *Moderate*. 6112 Falls of the Neuse Road (919-872-6224). This popular restaurant serves up informal French-country fare, including crepes and omelets. Be sure to ask about the daily specials. Lunch and dinner are offered Monday through Saturday.

Fox and Hound. *Moderate*. MacGregor Village Shopping Center, U.S. 64 East, Cary (919-380-0080). The bar here duplicates an English pub, with its dark wood and antique accents. The dining room has plush seating and a Tudor flavor. Chutneys and conserves, an authentic "Ploughman's Lunch," and, of course, a variety of British ales and stouts are offered. Lunch is served Monday through Saturday, and dinner is offered nightly.

Irregardless Cafe. *Inexpensive/Moderate*. 901 West Morgan Street (919-833-8898). This cafe seems to be lingering in the late 1960s, with lots of hanging plants, sprouts on the sandwiches, and a casual atmosphere, but the food is very fresh and tasty. The offerings include chicken, fish, and vegetarian dishes and great homemade desserts. A full bar is offered. Lunch is offered Sunday through Friday, and dinner is offered Monday through Saturday.

Durham

Durham—thriving city of industry, education, medicine, and research—was almost called Prattville. William Pratt, however, refused to give the North Carolina Railroad right of way across his land, fearing the noise would frighten the horses of customers at his general store; that's how farsighted he was. Instead, a young doctor, Bartlett Durham, offered four acres nearby, and in 1850, the railroad named its new station Durhamville. It later became Durham's Station and eventually just Durham. A small community grew up around it, and in 1869, when it was incorporated, there were officially only 258 residents.

Eleven years later, however, the population approached 3,000, owing mostly to a significant event that took place in 1865. In April of that year, Confederate general Joseph Johnston, commander of the Army of Tennessee, met with Union general William Sherman in Durham at the Bennett family farmhouse to discuss terms of surrender. While hostilities were suspended, Federal troops raided the countryside, looting—among other things—the warehouse that stored J. R. Green's "Spanish Smoking Tobacco." The brightleaf tobacco, cured with charcoal, tasted very different from what the Yankees were used to. After returning home, scores of them wrote asking to buy more of it.

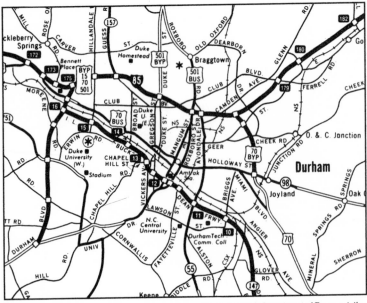

Courtesy of N.C. Department of Transportation

And here—in one of North Carolina's favorite stories—is where the famous Duke family entered the picture. Freed from a prison camp in New Bern, Washington Duke walked 135 miles home to his children and the ruins of his farm. His small store of cured tobacco had escaped "liberation." After his children packed it in hand-sewn muslin bags, he and his young son, Buck, traveled through eastern North Carolina in a cart drawn by blind mules to sell it.

Realizing that there was more money in processing tobacco than in growing it, the elder Duke built a tiny factory and began selling his own brand, becoming one of several manufacturers doing so. By 1871, a tobacco auction house opened, and the city of Durham quickly became the commercial center of North Carolina's brightleaf tobacco belt.

Son James Buchanan "Buck" Duke had little formal education but a remarkable business sense and the confidence to take big risks. He developed the family business into a major enterprise—the first to use a cigarette-manufacturing machine—and almost single-handedly created the market for cigarettes in America. W. Duke & Sons Company devoured its competition, including the brand sold as Bull Durham. Buck Duke eventually created the American Tobacco Company, a massive conglomerate that virtually monopolized the industry.

The development of tobacco as a major industry rehabilitated the state after the Civil War, but today, the social and economic position of tobacco is quite different. Demand for North Carolina brightleaf— or "leaf," as it's called in newspaper headlines—has declined, partly because of current health concerns and partly because cigarette companies are also buying imported tobacco. It seems that an obvious solution for the small farmers who grow it would be diversification, but much of the land in Piedmont North Carolina that is ideal for growing tobacco is very poor for growing anything else.

Many North Carolinians have mixed feelings about tobacco, its federal price supports, and the industry as a whole. But it was tobacco money that developed other industries in the state, such as textiles and power production, and created the great Duke University and its outstanding medical center.

Today, Durham has a population of 212,000 and has attained distinction in several fields. For example, North Carolina Mutual Life Insurance Company is the largest black-owned financial institution in America, and the state-funded North Carolina School of Science and Mathematics is the nation's foremost residential public high school.

Sometimes called "the City of Medicine," Durham is home to the highly regarded Duke University Hospital and other medical and research centers. Over 30 percent of Durham's work force is employed in health-related jobs.

As for culture and entertainment, the prestigious American Dance Festival at Duke University presents internationally known artists to sellout crowds each summer. And of course, the Durham Bulls baseball team has captured the city's heart. The 1995 season saw the Bulls finally leave the beloved Durham Athletic Park for a new state-of-the-art facility. But by all accounts, the new downtown ballpark is first-rate and ranks as one of the premier minor-league facilities in the country. The new park seats almost 10,000 and draws over 400,000 fans a season. In 1998, the park expanded in keeping with the club's new AAA classification.

Durham's downtown fell into decline in the 1960s and 1970s, but the new ballpark, the newly renovated Carolina Theatre (featuring classic, foreign, and critically acclaimed films), several new restaurants and nightclubs, and the continued success of the Durham Arts Council are all making the area a lively arts-and-entertainment district again. In conjunction with all this activity, several old office buildings and warehouses are being renovated.

Like the other Triangle communities, Durham is full of bright and interesting people and places. You'll never lack for something to do while visiting or living here.

ACCESS:

Durham, at the apex of the Triangle, is located at the intersection of I-85 and U.S. 70. I-40 skirts the western edge of the city.

Raleigh-Durham International Airport is less than 20 minutes away.

The Trailways bus station is at 820 West Morgan Street; call 919-687-4800.

VISITOR INFORMATION:

Contact the Durham Convention and Visitors Bureau, 101 East Morgan Street, Durham, N.C. 27701 (919-687-0288). You can access their Web site at http://DCVB.Durham.NC.US.

The daily newspaper is the *Herald-Sun.* It includes a special-events insert on Friday called "The Preview." The *Raleigh News and Observer* has a special Durham section every day and a "Weekend" section on Friday. You'll find listings of events and restaurants in the *Spectator* and the *Independent*—both free. For a complete listing of events, call the Durham Bullhorn at 800-772-BULL.

Attractions

Historic Places

Bennett Place State Historic Site, at 4409 Bennett Memorial Road, is one of those places where you have to use a lot of imagination to appreciate its importance. The site is a reconstruction of the small farmhouse where Confederate general Joseph Johnston twice met Union general William Sherman in April 1865 and signed the largest troop surrender of the Civil War, ending hostilities in the Carolinas, Georgia, and Florida.

In the farmhouse, furnished with little more than a table and chairs, a guide explains the fateful meeting and the two versions of the surrender that Johnston and Sherman worked out, and how their respect for each other led to a genuine friendship. In the visitor center, a 15-minute slide show traces the Civil War in North Carolina leading up to the surrender. Displays with photos, artifacts, and excerpts from letters illustrate conditions in the state during the Civil War. For example, visitors learn that calico cost $30 a yard in 1864, and that some people used ground okra seeds instead of coffee. Civil War books and souvenirs are on sale. The site is open Monday through Saturday from 9 A.M. to 5 P.M. and Sunday from 1 to 5 P.M. from April to October; it is also open Tuesday through Saturday from 10 A.M. to 4 P.M. and Sunday from 1 to 4 P.M. from November to March. Admission is free. Call 919-383-4345.

Duke Homestead State Historic Site and Tobacco Museum, at 2828 Duke Homestead Road, is the ancestral home of the Dukes, perhaps North Carolina's best-known family.

After the Civil War, Washington Duke, recognizing that money was to be made from processing tobacco, built a small factory. His son Buck Duke built the small company into a major manufacturing concern that ultimately became the American Tobacco Company, a conglomerate of firms that held a virtual monopoly on the sale of tobacco in the United States between 1890 and 1911.

Duke Homestead, owned and maintained by Duke University for 43 years, was given to the state in 1974. Now, the two-story white frame house the Dukes lived in is open to the public. Visitors can see early tobacco-manufacturing processes in a reconstruction of the first factory. The visitor center presents a 20-minute film and displays of advertisements and machinery that contributed to the story of tobacco in North Carolina. The museum is open Monday through Saturday from 9 A.M. to 5 P.M. and Sunday from 1 to 5 P.M. from April to October; it is also open Tuesday through Saturday from 10 A.M. to 4 P.M. and Sunday from 1 to 4 P.M. from November to March. Admission is free. Call 919-477-5498.

West Point on the Eno, at 5101 North Roxboro Road in northern Durham, is a 371-acre natural and historic city park that preserves part of an 18th-century mill community on the Eno River. Before or after the kids have run across the bridge on the river and looked at the water pouring over the little dam, you can look through the restored West Point Mill, which operated from 1778 to 1942, and the McCown-Mangum House (1843), now a museum with some original family furnishings. The pack house, originally used to store tobacco, became a darkroom for pioneer photographer Hugh Mangum. It now displays many of his glass negatives and some of his equipment in a small museum of photography.

The park gates are open from 8 A.M. to sundown. The historic buildings are open Saturday and Sunday from 1 to 5 P.M. from March through December. Admission is free. Call 919-471-1623.

Historic Stagville, on Old Oxford Highway, is a state-owned center for the study and teaching of the preservation of wooden buildings. It's located in the Richard Bennehan House, the manor house of a plantation established in 1787. The two-story frame house remained in the family until 1950. Liggett and Myers Tobacco Company purchased it in 1954 and later deeded it to the state to establish the center.

The original parlor of the house has some photos and a few pieces of family furniture on display; other rooms have portions of the walls and woodwork exposed to show the construction methods. Upstairs is a lecture room for classes and presentations on preservation technology.

The center also features the Great Barn, the largest agricultural building in the state when it was built by slaves in the mid-1800s, and Horton Grove, a row of slave quarters undergoing renovation.

This historic facility does an excellent job of showing the impressive contributions African-Americans have made to our culture. The center is open Monday through Friday from 9 A.M. to 4 P.M. It is closed on state holidays. Admission is free. Call 919-620-0120.

Museums

The **Museum of Life and Science**, at 433 Murray Avenue, is the premier museum for children in the Triangle. Adults won't be bored here, either. From prehistory to space exploration, the museum offers interactive, hands-on displays of science and technology that are sure to promote lively family discussion. You can view the NASA lunar lander in a dramatic two-story moonscape of *Apollo XV*'s camp, or even "pilot" a completely refurbished Apollo command mock-up.

Also popular are the weather section, which allows you to walk through a 50-foot-high tornado, the one-mile ride on the narrow-gauge Ellerbee Creek Railway, the water play area, the farmyard, and the nature preserve, which features deer, buffalo, and other North Carolina wildlife.

A major museum expansion includes the Magic Wings Butterfly House and Insectarium, an indoor botanical garden with more than 1,000 exotic butterflies in free flight.

The exhibits change periodically. The gift shop sells educational books, toys, and gifts related to museum programs. The museum is open Monday through Saturday from 10 A.M. to 6 P.M. and Sunday from 1 to 6 P.M. during the summer. From Labor Day to Memorial Day, the hours are Monday through Saturday from 10 A.M. to 5 P.M. and Sunday from noon to 5 P.M. It is closed Thanksgiving, Christmas, and New Year's Day. There is an admission fee. Call 919-220-5429.

Gardens

Sarah P. Duke Gardens, on Duke University's West Campus, are a delight to the eye and a restorative to the spirit. Established to honor Sarah Duke (the wife of Benjamin Duke) by her daughter Mary Duke Biddle, the 55 landscaped acres include a lily pond, a large gazebo covered with Chinese wisteria, and great sweeps of azaleas—all surrounded by pine forest. One area is devoted to plants native to the state. Ramps make the gardens accessible to the handicapped, but some of the paths are rather steep. The gardens are open daily from 8 A.M. to sundown. Admission is free. Guided tours can be arranged by calling 919-684-3698.

Cultural Offerings

In September 1988, the Durham Arts Council celebrated the completion of a $5-million renovation of the former Durham High School into the **Royall Center for the Arts**, a fine-arts center at 120

Morris Street that looks like a late-18th-century palace, complete with a two-story portico.

Beyond the glass-enclosed atrium lobby are two gallery areas, the smaller one for paintings and the larger one for juried exhibits of paintings, graphic art, and sculpture. The displays change often. The facility is home for 18 arts organizations, among them the Durham Symphony, the Durham Savoyards, the Young People's Performing Company, and the African-American Dance Ensemble. The building houses a theater and studio classrooms for public classes in many art media. For information on classes or performances, call 919-560-2787.

American Dance Festival is a midsummer extravaganza of presentations by some of the finest contemporary dance companies. In terms of international recognition, American Dance Festival is North Carolina's most prestigious event.

Most of the companies that participate are American, while others are Asian, African, and European—and all are widely acclaimed. Performances are held in two auditoriums at Duke University, and tickets, which sell out quickly, are available individually or by subscription. For a schedule or more information, contact American Dance Festival, P.O. Box 90772, Durham, N.C. 27708 (919-684-6402). To order tickets, call 919-684-4444.

Broadway at Duke is a series of touring-company performances of relatively new Broadway dramas and musicals at Page Auditorium on the Duke University campus. Call 919-684-4444.

Duke University Artist Series features performances in Page Auditorium by widely acclaimed music, dance, and opera artists. Call 919-684-4444.

Durham Chamber Arts Society presents various performances by touring chamber groups in Duke's Reynolds Auditorium. Call 919-684-4444.

College Life

To most people, Durham is synonymous with **Duke University**. Founded in 1924 by Buck Duke as a memorial to his father, the university was created from the Methodist-affiliated Trinity College. Washington Duke had contributed to Trinity for a number of years, and toward the end of his own life, Buck Duke, seeking to make a contribution of his own and to protect his fortune from the tax collector (and probably to ensure that Durham would never forget his family), decided to make the dream of Trinity's president, William Few, a reality: he would transform Trinity College into a world-class university.

In 1924, Duke gave $6 million for immediate physical expansion, then set aside $40 million, mostly in tobacco and power stock, in the form of a charitable trust—the Duke Endowment. Duke University was the principal beneficiary of the income, though several other colleges in North and South Carolina were also included. Through subsequent grants and codicils to his will, he bequeathed an additional $40 million to the school.

Duke University officials didn't waste the opportunity; the school now holds a scholarly reputation that ranks it among the finest universities in the country. Duke has a student population of 10,000 and is especially noted for its medical and nursing schools, but it has also earned respect for its law and divinity schools, the Fuqua School of Business—and, of course, the Blue Devils basketball team.

Because Duke's two campuses are separated by several miles, you'll need a car to get around.

The East Campus, near downtown Durham, contains the Georgian-style stone buildings of the original Trinity College. A statue of Washington Duke, seated in a fringed Victorian armchair with lion-head armrests is at one end of the quadrangle and domed Baldwin Auditorium is at the other. Near the statue is the Duke University Museum of Art, which houses a collection of American and European paintings, medieval sculpture, pre-Columbian exhibits, and a Far Eastern gallery with Chinese jade and porcelain. The museum is open Tuesday, Thursday, and Friday from 10 A.M. to 5 P.M., Wednesday from 10 A.M. until 9 P.M., Saturday from 11 A.M. to 2 P.M., and Sunday from 2 to 5 P.M. Admission is free. Call 919-684-5135.

The newer West Campus, which includes the medical center, is located in a pine forest two miles west of downtown Durham. It is built of gray stone quarried in North Carolina; in fact, once Buck Duke discovered that the stone he liked best was produced locally, he bought the quarry for the university. With room to spread out, the planners did just that, so a considerable amount of walking is required to navigate the campus, as public parking is limited.

The centerpiece of the new campus, Duke Chapel, is definitely worth a visit. Based on the design of the original Canterbury Cathedral, the elegant Gothic-style edifice has a 210-foot tower with a 50-bell carillon. Its soaring interior is lighted by 77 stained-glass windows, and the arch at the rear of the nave houses a 5,000-pipe organ. Entombed in the memorial chapel are Washington Duke and his sons James and Benjamin. The chapel is open to visitors from 8 A.M. to 10 P.M. during the school year and from 8 A.M. to 8 P.M. during the summer. Interdenominational worship services are held on Sunday at 11 A.M. Duke Chapel is also used for occasional chamber-music or choral concerts and for a steady stream of weddings in June.

For a lovely view of the campus, an elevator in the chapel

The tower of Duke Chapel
Photograph by William Russ
Courtesy of N.C. Travel and Tourism Division

takes visitors to a small viewing area at the top of the tower. The student workers who operate the elevator are not always on duty; for a schedule, call 919-684-2572 or look them up on the Web at www.chapel.duke.edu.

Visitors are also welcome at the greenhouse facilities on the West Campus, where 12,500 square feet of glass shelter 2,500 plant species from many environments. The greenhouse is open daily from 10 A.M. to 4:30 P.M.

A statue of Buck Duke stands opposite the entrance to Duke Chapel. Gazing out over the campus, cane in hand, smoking a cigar, he looks quite pleased with what he sees.

North Carolina Central University is located at Fayetteville and Lawson Streets. Founded in 1910, it was the first state-supported liberal-arts college for blacks in the nation. No longer segregated, it now has 6,000 students from all ethnic backgrounds. The 56 Georgian Revival–style buildings on the campus include a museum of art and a top-ranked law school.

Recreation

Eno River State Park is a 2,040-acre undeveloped park along the Eno River; West Point on the Eno is part of this park. It offers hiking, walking, camping (by permit only), canoeing, and rafting. The office is on Cole Mill Road Extension, off Hillsborough Road. Call 919-383-1686.

B. Everett Jordan Lake, a 47,000-acre lake that provides flood control, a water supply, and public recreation, was created when the United States Army Corps of Engineers built a dam to prevent flooding in the Cape Fear River basin. Different parts of the lake are managed by the North Carolina Division of Parks and Recreation, the Wildlife Resources Division, the Division of Forest Resources, and the Corps of Engineers. The best access to Jordan Lake is via N.C. 751 to U.S. 64, where there are several recreation areas. All of these areas provide boat-launching ramps; some offer picnic and swimming areas, tent and trailer camping facilities, showers, and marked hiking trails. Admission is $4 per car. Call 919-362-0586.

Duke Forest stretches over 7,900 acres between Durham and Chapel Hill. Managed by Duke University's Nicholas School of the Environment, it's used as an outdoor laboratory by Duke and neighboring universities. Its dirt roads are open for hiking, running, and horseback riding; some picnic sites are available. Call 919-613-8013.

Golf is pleasant year-round at **Duke University Golf Course** (919-681-2288), at N.C. 751 and Science Drive, and at **Hillandale Golf Course** (919-286-4211), at Hillandale Road. For further information, call 919-688-BULL or 800-772-BULL.

The **Durham Bulls**, class AAA affiliate of the Tampa Bay Devil Rays, play at their new ballpark located on Blackwell Street between Dillard and Mangum Streets, adjacent to Durham Freeway. Designed by the same architectural firm responsible for Camden Yards in Baltimore, the new park seats approximately 10,000 and features a grassy-knoll seating area. For schedule and ticket information, call 919-956-2855.

Seasonal Events

Festival for the Eno, held on the Fourth of July weekend, is the liveliest summer celebration in the Piedmont. More than 50 North Carolina musical groups and dancers perform continuously on three stages at West Point on the Eno. You'll hear blues, bluegrass, and gospel music, and you can even learn to clog. Folk arts and crafts are for sale. Admission is $10 for adults; children 12 and under are free. Call 919-477-4549.

Centerfest, held downtown in September, is a two-day event featuring musicians on four stages, wandering street performers, a children's area, an international food court, and over 120 artists' booths. The event is free. Call 919-687-0288.

Bull Durham Blues Festival, held in September at the old Durham Athletic Park, offers two evenings of music running from 6 P.M. to midnight. Tickets are available for one or both nights and are less expensive if purchased in advance. Call 919-683-1709.

Side Trips

See *Triangle Side Trips*

Accommodations

Most hotels and motels are located in the northern and western parts of the city to accommodate visitors to Duke University and the many medical facilities.

Washington Duke Inn & Golf Club. *Expensive/Deluxe*. 3001 Cameron Boulevard (919-490-0999). This glamorous hotel is set in a pine forest that borders Duke University Golf Course. The 10-foot-high entry door matches the scale of the expansive, elegant lobby. Washington Duke, the father of Duke University's benefactor, is honored behind the registration desk, where visitors can see his gold-headed cane mounted in a gilt frame. The hotel's color scheme is putty and mauve, beginning with the exterior paint and continuing through the 171 rooms, elegantly furnished with antique reproductions and Chinese porcelain. The lounge seems like part of a country house; a deer's head hangs over the hearth, where a fire burns. Both the lounge and the restaurant overlook the attractive golf course. Ask for a room on the golf-course side.

Durham Hilton. *Moderate/Expensive*. 3800 Hillsborough Road (919-383-8033). Located only a minute from I-85, the Durham Hilton is in a relatively secluded, parklike setting. The outdoor pool and the surrounding woods are in view from most of the 194 large rooms. There's also a health club and a sauna, if you want to continue your workout indoors.

Regal University Hotel. *Moderate/Expensive*. 2800 Campus Walk at U.S. 15/501 Bypass, Morreene Road (919-383-8575). The Regal is a beautiful property surrounded by loblolly pine trees. Inside the striking three-story entrance, a lobby bar overlooks the indoor pool. The 322 oversize rooms allow visitors to spread out and get comfortable.

Brownestone Guest House Inn. *Moderate*. 2424 Erwin Road (919-286-7761). Brownestone is a distinctive hotel located close to Duke University Hospital and other medical facilities. Its bland exterior belies the charm inside. The large, quiet rooms overlook a wooded area; a VIP floor offers extra amenities. An indoor pool and a sauna are offered.

Comfort Inn. *Inexpensive*. 3508 Mount Moriah Road (919-490-4949 or 800-228-5150). The Comfort Inn offers qualities you'd expect to find in a higher-priced hotel, but at bargain rates and in a very good location. A free newspaper and continental breakfast are offered in the large lobby, which is furnished with Queen Anne tables and chairs. The rooms are spacious and comfortably appointed.

Inns and Bed-and-Breakfast Guest Houses

Arrowhead Inn. *Expensive*. 106 Mason Road (919-477-8430). This 1775 inn is a beautiful white frame house with two-story pillars. The guest rooms in the manor house, as well as the two in the carriage house, are decorated in period styles, and many of them include whirlpools and fireplaces. A full gourmet breakfast is served in the formal dining room. The inn is several miles north of downtown Durham but is worth the extra effort it takes to get there.

Restaurants

Durham residents benefit from the demanding tastes of business people who visit Research Triangle Park. The variety and the quality of service found in Durham restaurants attract Raleigh and Chapel Hill residents as well.

Magnolia Grill. *Expensive*. 1002 Ninth Street (919-286-3609). Magnolia Grill is many locals' choice for best restaurant in the Triangle. This bistro is essentially one large room divided into different levels, but the tables aren't so close together that you feel you're dining with your neighbors. The menu, which changes daily, includes up to a dozen appetizers, such as hickory-smoked grilled quail, and half a dozen entrées, such as grilled swordfish in avocado sauce. In addition to being delicious, the food is beautifully presented. A full bar is offered. Reservations are recommended. Dinner is served Tuesday through Saturday.

Cafe Parizade. *Moderate/Expensive*. Erwin Square, 2200 West Main Street (919-286-9712). This is one of the latest creations of Durham restaurant impresario Giorgios Bakastias. The menu features Mediterranean specialties such as fettuccine with fresh salmon and black pepper dill cream. Diners can enjoy selections from the espresso bar and the excellent dessert menu. Lunch is served Monday through Friday and dinner daily.

Anotherthyme. *Moderate*. 109 North Gregson Street (919-682-5225). Anotherthyme is known for its inventive treatment of seafood and vegetarian dishes, served in a stylish atmosphere. The menu changes often, but the appetizers might include such items as asparagus salad, and the entrées might include salade niçoise with grilled tuna fillet, spinach fettuccine with sea scallops, Mexican batter-fried shrimp, and vegetable-filled burritos. A full bar is offered. Lunch is served Tuesday through Friday and dinner is served nightly.

Pop's: A Durham Trattoria. *Moderate*. 810 West Peabody Street (919-956-7677). Located in a former warehouse downtown in the Brightleaf district, Pop's has high ceilings, an open kitchen, and a wood-fired oven. This northern Italian restaurant was named one of the top new restaurants in the country by *Bon Appétit*. Open Tuesday through Sunday for dinner.

Foster's Market. *Inexpensive/Moderate*. 2694 Durham–Chapel Hill Boulevard (919-489-3944). Owned by Sara Foster, a chef and former member of Martha Stewart's catering team, this specialty and takeout food store also serves breakfast, lunch, and dinner. Tables and chairs have been set up on the porch and deck for drop-in meals. Open daily.

Fishmonger's Seafood Market Crab & Oyster House. *Inexpensive/Moderate*. 806 West Main Street (919-682-0128). This is the place for people who like fresh seafood—period. The restaurant has all the charm of a fish market, which is just what it is. The decor consists of charts of fish species and inflatable sharks hanging from the ceiling. Guests place their order by the lobster tank and wait for it at tables with vinyl cloths covered with paper—crayons are provided for the artistically inclined. The lunch selections feature sandwiches such as tuna fillet or mackerel on a sub roll. The spinach salad with scallops in bacon dressing is great. At dinner, guests can order steamed shrimp, mussels, clams, three kinds of crab, or Louisiana crawfish. Beer and wine are offered. Lunch is served every day except Monday, and dinner is served nightly.

Bullock's Bar-B-Cue. *Inexpensive.* 3330 Wortham Street (919-383-3211). This is where out-of-towners are taken when they ask about real Southern food. The wall inside the front door is covered with photos of famous visitors. But on customarily busy days, the people who wait in line for tables are locals looking to satisfy their craving for hickory-smoked chopped barbecue and hush puppies. Also on the menu are breaded fish, stuffed shrimp, and Cajun chicken, all of which come with crowder peas, turnip greens, yams, or pinto beans. The decor is unassuming but clean and pleasant, and the service is good. No alcohol is offered, and only cash is accepted. Lunch and dinner are served Tuesday through Saturday.

Chapel Hill/Carrboro ....

Many first-time visitors are surprised at how small the town of Chapel Hill seems—at first glance, it appears to be one main street bordering the University of North Carolina campus. But that belies the real size of the town, which has a population of 43,500, including the 24,000 students at the university. Franklin Street, the main artery, extends east past stone and frame sorority and fraternity houses to another business district and access to I-40. To the west is the town of Carrboro, population 14,200, which sits cheek by jowl with Chapel Hill but remains steadfastly separate.

Those who expect to find Chapel Hill a stereotypical small Southern town are mistaken. So many residents are transplants from other areas that it sometimes seems native North Carolinians are in short supply. The "immigrants" who come here to work for the university or corporations in Research Triangle Park find it a pleasant place to live. In fact, it's sometimes referred to as "the southern part of heaven." Chapel Hill has a cosmopolitan outlook not found in most towns its size—even other university towns.

Residents take pride in their historic buildings and have worked to preserve them. A number of beautiful 19th-century homes are located in the blocks along the north side of the university area. The best example is the antebellum Horace Williams House on Rosemary Street, now used for small gallery showings, a concert series, and public functions.

A less salutary result of Chapel Hill's popularity is the residential development necessary to accommodate the many people who want to live here. Retail development is characterized by an abundance of unique specialty shops and shopping centers.

The town received its name thanks to the one-room, log New Hope Chapel, which stood on a hill that was often referred to as New Hope Chapel Hill. In 1789, the North Carolina legislature chartered the nation's first state university here on donated land. Since then, the history of the university and the town have been closely intertwined.

The heart of Chapel Hill is unquestionably the University of North Carolina, generally referred to as UNC or Carolina. Even if you're not directly associated with the university, it's hard to ignore. The August day when thousands of students return is almost like a festival—they promenade up and down Franklin Street gaily greeting friends, and normal traffic patterns all but disappear.

You can't live here without loving the Tar Heels. Although the nickname applies to all the university's sports teams, it most often refers to the basketball team, which has been very successful in the Atlantic Coast Conference over many years and has captured three NCAA men's basketball championships, most recently in 1993. Basketball fever is pervasive and fierce. A favorite bumper sticker around town asks, "If God is not a Tar Heel, why is the sky Carolina Blue?"

ACCESS:

Chapel Hill is located at the intersection of U.S. 15/501 and N.C. 54. I-40 links Chapel Hill with Research Triangle Park and Raleigh to the southeast and Hillsborough and I-85 to the northwest.

The community is served by Raleigh-Durham International Airport, located a 25-minute drive away. Small private planes can be accommodated at the Horace Williams Airport, which has a 4,500-foot lighted landing strip; call 919-962-1337.

The Trailways bus station is at 311 West Franklin Street; call 919-942-3356.

VISITOR INFORMATION:

Contact the Chapel Hill–Carrboro Chamber of Commerce, 104 South Estes Drive, Chapel Hill, N.C. 27515 (919-967-7075) or the Chapel Hill–Orange County Visitors Bureau, 501 West Franklin Street, Suite 104, Chapel Hill, N.C. 27516 (888-968-2060).

The local newspapers are the *Chapel Hill Newspaper*, the *Chapel Hill Herald*, the *Daily Tar Heel*, and the *News of Orange County*. For a listing of activities, check the *Spectator* or the *Independent*, free weekly magazines. The *Raleigh News and Observer* publishes an "Orange Metro" section daily and a "What's Up" section on Friday.

Attractions

Gardens

The **North Carolina Botanical Garden**, off U.S. 15/501 Bypass just south of the N.C. 54 intersection, is a regional center for research, conservation, and interpretation of plants, especially those native to the Southeast. Classes and meetings are held in the Totten Center, which is surrounded by collections of native plants. Three habitat areas corresponding to the three geographic areas of the state—the coast, the Piedmont, and the mountains—have been established; plants found in each area are labeled. There are also special collections of ferns and carnivorous plants, along with an herb garden. The visitor area includes two miles of woodland trails. The gardens are open from 8 A.M. to 6 P.M. on weekdays year-round. They are open from 1 to 6 P.M. on Saturday and Sunday during daylight savings time but are closed on weekends most of the rest of the year.

Special Shopping

Carr Mill Mall, on the corner of Greensboro and Weaver Streets in Carrboro, is an old textile mill renovated into an attractive arcade of specialty shops and restaurants. Its handmade bricks give the exterior a mellow appearance.

A Southern Season, located in Eastgate Shopping Center, between U.S. 15/501 and East Franklin Street, is a vast emporium of gastronomic delights, among them dozens of varieties of mustard, spices, salad dressings, teas, coffees, imported chocolates and cookies, and wines. A deli offers sandwiches, pasta salads, and espresso. A Southern Season is open Monday through Saturday from 10 A.M. to 7 P.M. and Sunday from noon to 6 P.M. Call 919-929-7133.

Cultural Offerings

PlayMakers Repertory Company, in Paul Green Theatre on Country Club Road on the UNC campus, was founded in 1976. During its season, which runs September through May, PlayMakers stages six productions ranging from classic to contemporary plays. The theater is named for the UNC alumnus and Pulitzer Prize–winning playwright known as the father of outdoor drama. A member of the League of Resident Theatres, the company has achieved national recognition. For schedule and ticket information, call 919-962-PLAY.

The Arts Center, at 300-G East Main Street in Carrboro, is dedicated to the visual, literary, and performing arts. It began in 1975 as a painting class in a loft. Now a full-fledged community arts center, it offers a wide variety of classes and performances for an enthusiastic public that comes from far beyond Carrboro. More than 100 classes—in art, crafts, music, dance, theater, writing, and photography—are available for adults, youths, and children. Performances in its 375-seat theater include readings of new plays; a film series; presentations by jazz, folk, and classical musicians; and presentations by guest actors and companies. Several programs are designed especially for children. For schedule and ticket information, call 919-929-2787.

Carolina Union, located on the UNC campus, offers a variety of programs including a performing-arts series, concerts, lectures, and art exhibits. Large events are presented in the 1,600-seat Memorial Hall. Additional venues include the Cabaret and other auditoriums located in the student union. For schedule and ticket information, call 919-962-1449.

College Life

The **University of North Carolina at Chapel Hill**, chartered in 1789, was the nation's only public university to accept and graduate students in the 18th century. The doors opened formally on January 15, 1795, but it was nearly a month before the first student arrived—he walked 150 miles from Wilmington—and another two weeks before he had a classmate. Now, almost 24,000 students attend what was recently rated by college presidents as one of the top 10 public universities in the nation. It is the flagship of a university system that comprises 16 state-supported four-year schools.

Most visitors come to attend sports events and concerts or to see their children who are students. Others come just to see the attractive campus itself. Its brick paths leading across tree-shaded quads create an atmosphere so appealingly collegiate that you may wish you were college age.

A recorded historic walking tour is available at the UNC Visitors Center in the Morehead Planetarium from 10 A.M. to 4 P.M. from Monday through Friday and from 10 A.M. to 2 P.M. on Saturday. A weekly scheduled tour is given on Saturday at 11 A.M.; reservations are not required. Group guided tours can be arranged by calling 919-962-1630.

If you strike out alone, you'll find many notable features. The pillared and domed Old Well is a historic landmark and the unofficial symbol of the university. At one time the only source of water for the town, it's since been converted into a drinking fountain. It stands in front of the three-story South Building. Built of handmade bricks now faded with age, South Building was originally a dormitory; its most famous resident was a future president, James Polk, class of 1818. It now serves as the main administration building. The plaque on the side of Old East, located nearby, proclaims to be the oldest state-university building in the nation. Finished in 1795, it's also the oldest structure in Chapel Hill. It still serves as a dormitory.

The architectural highlight of the campus is the Greek Revival PlayMakers Theatre. Constructed of rust-colored stucco, it features a portico with columns topped by stalks of wheat and ears of corn. Built as a library in 1851, it now accommodates plays and commencements. The spirit of the building was seriously compromised during the Civil War, when one of General Sherman's Union cavalry units stabled horses inside. In 1925, after major interior alterations, it became the home of the Carolina PlayMakers—the campus drama group now called PlayMakers Repertory Company—which currently performs in Paul Green Theatre.

The Old Well at the University of North Carolina at Chapel Hill
Photograph by Clay Nolen
Courtesy of N.C. Travel and Tourism Division

When Union troops bivouacked on campus, they cut down most of the trees for firewood. The Davie Poplar, under which William R. Davie supposedly sat when he selected the school's site in 1792, was spared this fate thanks to the university president's wife, who—so an undocumented story goes—placed herself between the tree and the Yankee woodcutters.

The Morehead-Patterson Bell Tower is an Italian Renaissance campanile built in 1930 and dedicated to two families that produced many generations of UNC graduates. The 12 bells in the 172-foot tower chime the quarter-hour and play melodies at intervals during the day.

Coker Arboretum is named for Dr. W. C. Coker, a botanist who developed a damp pasture into a beautiful botanical laboratory planted with more than 400 species of ornamental flowers, trees, and shrubs. Laced with pathways, this parklike area is especially inviting when showy spring flowers are blooming. Its best feature is the 200-foot wisteria arbor, which blooms in April.

Morehead Planetarium, on the UNC campus off East Franklin Street, is especially popular with children when they learn that NASA astronauts have trained for space in the Star Theater. The 68-foot dome, an extremely accurate star projector, and a variety of special-effects devices re-create the night sky in planetarium shows that are entertaining as well as educational. Programs change throughout the year and are offered throughout the day, evening, and weekend. The planetarium's "Sky Rambles" treat visitors to a narrated walk through the current night sky every Friday at 3:30 and 7:30 P.M. Admission is $4 for adults and $3 for children, seniors, and students. The art galleries and science exhibits in the building are free. Call 919-962-1236.

In front of the planetarium is the Sundial Rose Garden, where hundreds of hybrid roses bloom around a 35-foot stone sundial. Poetic verses and international times are inscribed in the huge exhibit.

Battle Park, at Country Club Road and South Boundary Street, extends over a wooded slope highlighted by the Forest Theatre, a Greek-style outdoor amphitheater once used by the Carolina PlayMakers. The only facilities are a few tables for picnicking.

The Ackland Art Museum, on Columbia Street at Franklin Street, opened in 1958 and became an adjunct to the university in 1968. It boasts a collection of 14,000 items, primarily paintings, sculpture, drawings, and photographs, plus a substantial number of Greek and Roman antiquities. The museum is open Wednesday through Saturday from 10 A.M. to 5 P.M. and Sunday from 1 to 5 P.M. It is closed major holidays.

Recreation

B. Everett Jordan Lake—See *Durham: Recreation*

Golf is offered at **Finley Golf Course**, part of UNC. It's located on Finley Golf Course Road off N.C. 54 East. To reserve a tee time, call 919-962-2349.

If you are interested in playing tennis, call the Chapel Hill Parks and Recreation Department at 919-968-2784.

Seasonal Events

Apple Chill Festival, held the second or third Sunday in April, is a street fair on Franklin Street, offering arts, crafts, and various foodstuffs for sale and entertainment on two stages. **Festifall** is a similar event the first Sunday in October. Both are sponsored by the Chapel Hill Parks and Recreation Department.

Side Trips

See *Triangle Side Trips*

Accommodations

For its size, Chapel Hill has a steadily improving range of lodging choices. Now, even visitors to Research Triangle Park choose to stay here. But it's still almost impossible to find a vacancy during UNC graduation in May.

The Carolina Inn. *Expensive/Deluxe*. 211 Pittsboro Street (919-933-2001 or 800-966-8519). This Chapel Hill landmark, built in 1924 and located on the UNC campus, is the epitome of Southern charm. The large front porch invites relaxing and taking in the immense greenery of the area, and the Colonial-style furniture in the lobby begs for guests to sit and talk a spell. A major renovation was completed in 1995, and the inn now boasts one of the classiest restaurants in town.

The Siena. *Expensive*. 1505 East Franklin Street (919-929-4000 or 800-223-7379). Opened in 1987, this lovely 80-room hotel offers traditional European style; its owners were enthralled with what they found on a visit to Italy and wanted to bring its essence home. The hotel's architecture and color schemes are reminiscent of Italian hill towns. The lobby is resplendent with antique furniture and prints of Italy. The amenities include a concierge, 24-hour room service, a complimentary full breakfast, and a fitness center. Children stay free with an adult and pets are allowed as well.

Sheraton Chapel Hill. *Expensive*. 1 Europa Drive, off U.S. 15/501 (919-968-4900). This hotel features 168 comfortable rooms with contemporary furnishings, a warm, welcoming staff, and a striking mural reminiscent of Chagall in the large lobby. Among the amenities are a concierge, a gift shop, an outdoor pool, and a tennis facility.

Best Western University Inn. *Moderate*. Raleigh Road (N.C. 54), two miles east of UNC (919-932-3000). University Inn is another old standby in Chapel Hill. All 84 of its rooms face the parking lot, but they're quiet and attractively furnished. Complimentary juice and rolls are available for breakfast in the coffee room. An outdoor pool is offered.

Holiday Inn. *Moderate*. U.S. 15/501 Bypass near Eastgate Shopping Center (919-929-2171). As the company's ads say, there are no surprises at a Holiday Inn. The 135 rooms are spacious and pleasant. An outdoor pool is offered. The cafe is open for breakfast and dinner.

Hampton Inn. *Moderate*. 1740 U.S. 15/501 North (919-968-3000). Part of a chain of motor inns catering to business people, this no-frills hostelry has 122 pleasant rooms. It's an excellent value. An outdoor pool and free continental breakfast are offered.

Inns and Bed-and-Breakfast Guest Houses

The Inn at Fearrington. *Deluxe*. Fearrington Village, eight miles south of Chapel Hill on U.S. 15/501 near Pittsboro (919-542-2121). Since opening in 1986, this inn has become the centerpiece of a charming rural community that includes a restaurant, a bookstore, a garden gift shop, and a large barn full of Belted Galloway cows imported from Scotland. Each of the 31 rooms and suites is decorated with English-pine antiques and chintz fabrics. The rooms overlook a beautifully landscaped courtyard. The baths are equipped with heated brass towel racks and stocked with fragrant toiletries. A free full breakfast and afternoon tea are offered.

The Inn at Bingham School. *Moderate/Expensive*. N.C. 54 at Mebane Oaks Road (919-563-5583 or 800-566-5583). Bingham School—a prep school for men that opened in 1845—no longer exists, but its headmaster's house has been renovated into an airy and appealing inn 12 miles west of Chapel Hill. The house features its original paneling and brickwork, while added amenities such as light fixtures and private bathrooms make the five large guest rooms more modern. The rooms are individually decorated with period antiques and old quilts; four have working fireplaces. A room in the former milk house is often used as a bridal suite. A full breakfast is served in the breakfast room or dining room, each of which offers a view of the surrounding farmland.

Restaurants

Chapel Hill offers a lot more than typical college-town fare. Students and faculty frequent the dozen eateries on Franklin Street near the university, but restaurants of varying cuisine and price range can also be found elsewhere in town.

Fearrington House. *Expensive.* Fearrington Village, eight miles south of Chapel Hill on U.S. 15/501 near Pittsboro (919-542-2121). This huge, beautifully restored farmhouse makes a romantic setting for "the new cuisine of the South." A Four Diamond restaurant, it offers dishes such as salmon ravioli with shrimp sauce, sautéed soft-shell crab, braised veal, and grilled duck. Reservations are necessary. Dinner is served Tuesday through Sunday.

La Résidence. *Moderate/Expensive.* 220 West Rosemary Street (919-967-2506). French specialties are featured in this restaurant, which manages to be both cozy and elegant. The several adjoining rooms are warmly decorated and filled with candlelight. Ask to sit overlooking the front garden, with its herbs and bright flowers. The menu changes nightly but offers about six appetizers and six entrées, which often include seafood, sweetbreads, and beef. A full bar and an extensive wine list are offered. Dinner is served Tuesday through Sunday.

Il Palio. *Moderate/Expensive.* In The Siena, 1505 East Franklin Street (919-918-2545). The decor in this Four Diamond restaurant is northern Italian, and so is the cuisine. There's a polish to the service here that you won't find everywhere. A full bar is offered. Lunch and dinner are served daily.

Top of the Hill. *Moderate/Expensive.* 100 East Franklin Street, upstairs from First Union (919-929-8676). This popular new microbrewery was started by some Carolina alums, and their love of food, beer, and Chapel Hill is quite clear. The outdoor patio is a great place to relax, enjoy a beer, and people-watch on a summer night. A full bar is available. Lunch and dinner are served daily. Brunch is served on Sunday.

Crook's Corner. *Moderate/Expensive.* 610 West Franklin Street (919-929-7643). A collection of wooden folk-art animals stands on the roof of this well-known restaurant. So many people come for the North Carolina specialties that guests often have to wait for a table unless they arrive just at opening. The fare includes burgers, collards with dumplings, barbecue, hoppin' John, shrimp and grits, and black-pepper cornbread. A full bar is offered. Dinner is served daily, and brunch is offered Sunday.

Mama Dip's Country Kitchen. *Moderate*. 405 West Rosemary Street (919-942-5837). This is the kind of Southern home cooking you'd get at your grandmother's—fried chicken, broiled trout, catfish, yams, okra, and sweet potato pie. The decor is unassuming; several booths and small tables are covered by vinyl cloths. Food critics love the place for its down-home style. It even won a Bisquick Best Award as one of the nation's top 25 eateries. Breakfast, lunch, and dinner are served daily.

Ram's Head Rathskeller. *Moderate*. In an alleyway off Franklin Street near the NationsBank building (919-942-5158). This Chapel Hill tradition since the 1940s is a favorite of students and locals alike. The specialties include lasagna and "Roast Beast." Be sure to add your name and the date you ate at "the Rat" on the wall by your booth, like the several generations before you. Open daily for lunch and dinner.

Pyewacket. *Moderate*. The Courtyard, 431 West Franklin Street (919-929-0297). This restaurant features a varied menu of creative vegetarian and seafood dishes, such as shrimp and linguine primavera and curried vegetables. Daily specials and seasonal desserts are offered, as is a full bar. Lunch is served Monday through Saturday and dinner daily.

Carolina Coffee Shop. *Inexpensive/Moderate*. 138 East Franklin Street (919-942-6875). The oldest restaurant in Chapel Hill, the Carolina Coffee Shop is a place where professors and students alike come to relax and discuss philosophy, politics, and sports. The dark interior and classical music lend themselves to long discussions or curling up with a good book over dishes ranging from pasta to seafood to burgers. A full bar is offered. Open daily for breakfast, lunch, and dinner.

Sutton's Drug Store. *Inexpensive*. 159 East Franklin Street (919-942-5161). If you want to taste the flavor of Chapel Hill, this is one of the best places. You can munch on anything from chicken pot pie to veggie burgers at this little grill while taking in the numerous photos of memorable UNC students and alumni who have dined here. When things get a little too hectic, the pharmacist will even come over to take your order, though the cook hasn't been seen filling prescriptions yet. Open daily for lunch.

Research Triangle Park ....

In 1959, the area southeast of Durham was mainly scrub pines and poor farmland. But through the concerted efforts of Governor Luther Hodges and a cadre of academic and business leaders, a large parcel of this land was developed into the premier planned research center in the United States. Research Triangle Park (RTP) encompasses 6,800 acres, and its more than 50 research organizations, businesses, and government agencies now employ over 40,000 people and have combined annual payrolls estimated to exceed $1 billion. It is a private, non-profit entity owned and operated by the Research Triangle Foundation.

The site for RTP was chosen because of its proximity to research personnel and facilities at the three major universities in the Triangle—Duke University in Durham, the University of North Carolina at Chapel Hill, and North Carolina State University in Raleigh—and its easy access to Raleigh-Durham International Airport.

Since 1965, when International Business Machines moved its data-communications operation here, development has been steady. Today, park tenants include Northern Telecom, Glaxo-Wellcome Company, and Data General, among others. Driving through the rolling terrain, you'll see large, contemporary office buildings and research facilities set among tall pine trees. Several new hotels—with more to come—accommodate the influx of business travelers.

You'll have to look long and hard to find a Tar Heel opposed to RTP. Not only has the surrounding region benefited from the increased tax base, highway improvements, airport expansion, and new jobs, but the excellent reputation earned by the park has encouraged growth throughout North Carolina. This fruitful collaboration of industry, academia, and state government promises even greater rewards in the future.

ACCESS:
Research Triangle Park is located among Raleigh, Durham, and Chapel Hill on I-40 and near the intersection of N.C. 54 and N.C. 55. It's about 10 minutes from Raleigh-Durham International Airport, served by 10 major passenger airlines.

VISITOR INFORMATION:
Most people come to RTP exclusively for business, but if you finish yours and want to know what's happening in the Triangle, you can find event and restaurant listings in the *Spectator* and the *Independent*, both free. For information, contact the Durham Convention and Visitors Bureau, 101 East Morgan Street, Durham, N.C. 27701 (919-687-0288).

Accommodations

Surrounding the park are a number of hotels, all of which work hard to meet the needs of the business traveler—those expense accounts are their bread and butter. To keep the rooms occupied on weekends, many hotels offer bargain weekend rates. Locals take advantage of these special incentives to enjoy an upscale weekend away without going away.

Sheraton Imperial Hotel and Convention Center. *Expensive/ Deluxe.* I-40 (Exit 282) at Page Road (919-941-5050 or 800-325-3535). This is a top-quality property with polish, panache, and everything but intimacy. In the center of the large lobby is a fountain lit by a skylight and surrounded by full-grown ficus trees. Nearby are a complete health club and fitness center, a lobby bar, a restaurant, a lounge, and an abundance of meeting space.

Marriott Research Triangle Park. *Expensive/Deluxe.* 4700 Guardian Drive, Durham (919-941-6200 or 800-228-9290). This hotel has a bright and airy two-story entrance with a pleasant peach-and-green color scheme and an abundance of potted plants and flowers. Etched-glass panels separate the lounge from the entrance. The restaurant is open for all meals. The attractive, comfortably appointed rooms have polished wooden desks. An indoor pool and a health club are also offered.

Radisson Governors Inn. *Expensive.* Between N.C. 54 and I-40 (Exit 280) at Davis Drive (919-549-8631 or 800-333-3333 inside N.C., 800-682-1229 outside N.C.). Its exterior is unexciting, but step inside this inn and you will be dazzled by its polished marble floor, crystal chandelier, and plants in shiny brass pots. Its oversize rooms are delightful—most have an armoire instead of a closet, a polished wooden desk and chair, and a seating area with upholstered couch and chair. The hotel also has a pool, tennis courts, meeting facilities, a restaurant, and a lounge.

Red Roof Inn. *Inexpensive*. Off of I-40 (Exit 270) on Chapel Hill Boulevard (919-489-9421 or 800-843-7663). You won't find a lot of extras at this chain motel, but you will find clean, reliable rooms and a convenient location. Research Triangle Park is only one exit down the interstate; the airport and downtown Durham are about six miles away in opposite directions.

Restaurants

Here, most dining is done in the hotels—those mentioned above and others. Remember that RTP is within easy striking distance of most restaurants in Raleigh, Durham, and Chapel Hill.

Cascades. *Moderate/Expensive*. In the Sheraton Imperial (919-941-5050). The Sheraton's restaurant offers all three meals for a reasonable price. A breakfast buffet and a lunch buffet are available, or guests can dine off the menu. Dinner can range from a simple sandwich to prime rib or lamb chops with mint jelly. The Devereux Room can be rented out for private meetings or special occasions. Open daily.

The Galleria. *Moderate/Expensive*. In the Radisson Governors Inn (919-549-8631). This restaurant offers a wide variety of items for breakfast, lunch, and dinner. For breakfast, diners can go the healthy route with granola, yogurt, and fruit, or they can indulge with bacon and eggs. The lunch buffet is a Research Triangle Park favorite, but you can also order from the menu. During the week, be sure to make reservations for lunch. Dinner offers a nice mix of steaks, salads, pasta, and even pizza. Open daily.

Triangle Side Trips

A pre–Revolutionary War town, **Hillsborough** has hosted a disproportionate share of historic events for its small size. Located 12 miles north of Chapel Hill, it was the center of the Regulator movement, a protest in the 1760s against corrupt officials. During the Revolution, it was the staging area for the British army under Lord Cornwallis. In 1788, Hillsborough hosted the state convention to ratify the federal Constitution. In 1865, it served as temporary headquarters for Confederate general Joseph Johnston, who signed the final surrender of the Civil War.

Hillsborough's historic district boasts over 100 late-18th- and early-19th-century structures and is listed on the National Register of Historic Places. Small signs posted in front date them and identify the families who built them. The *Historic Hillsborough* brochure, with a map and histories of the homes, and other visitor information are available at the Hillsborough Area Chamber of Commerce, at 150 East King Street (919-732-8156).

Hillsborough Hog Day Festival is a barbecue festival held downtown the third Saturday in June. It features entertainment, an antique car show, a potbelly-pig beauty contest, and, of course, cooks competing to cook the best barbecue. Call 919-968-2060.

Hillsborough Historical Society Home and Garden Tour, held in April during odd-numbered years, combines a quilt show, arts and crafts, entertainment, and a tour of some of the area's historic homes. Call 919-968-2060.

The town offers some fine accommodations:

Hillsborough House Inn. *Moderate/Expensive.* 209 East Tryon Street (919-644-1600). Located on seven acres, this Italianate mansion features an 80-foot veranda, five bedrooms with baths, and a kitchen-house suite with a whirlpool and fireplaces.

Colonial Inn. *Inexpensive.* 153 West King Street (919-732-2461). Colonial Inn (c. 1759) is one of the oldest inns in America. Its eight rooms, most with private baths, are furnished with antiques. Specializing in Southern cooking, the inn's restaurant is open to the public for lunch and dinner except on Mondays.

Bentonville Battleground, about 35 miles south of Raleigh near Newton Grove, was the site of the largest Civil War land battle in North Carolina and the last Confederate offensive of the war. Fighting between Union general William Sherman and Confederate general Joseph Johnston lasted three days in March 1865 and claimed more than 4,000 casualties. Only a month later, Johnston joined Sherman at Bennett Place in Durham to sign a surrender of the armies of the Carolinas, Georgia, and Florida.

Bentonville Battleground is an open area with a small farmhouse—Harper House—restored to the way it looked as a field hospital for both armies. Maps and a film in the visitor center trace the battle.

During special summer living history programs, guides are costumed as Confederate soldiers. Reenactments are performed every five years; the next is scheduled for March 2000. The battlefield is open Monday through Saturday from 9 A.M. to 5 P.M. and Sunday from 1 to 5 P.M. from April through October; it is open Tuesday through Saturday from 10 A.M. to 4 P.M. and Sunday from 1 to 4 P.M. from November through March. Take N.C. 50 south to Newton Grove, then take U.S. 701 north and S.R. 1008 east. Admission is free. Groups are encouraged to make advance reservations. Call 910-594-0789.

Kerr Reservoir, 50 miles north of Durham, is part of the United States Army Corps of Engineers project that created a 50,000-acre lake extending into Virginia. There are three marinas and seven recreation areas; they vary as to facilities, but all of them offer picnicking, boat ramps, and camping with water and electric hookups. In mid-May, there is a bass-fishing tournament. Only the Satterwhite and Bullocksville areas are open all year; the others are open April to October. To reach the area, take U.S. 1 north to Henderson, then take N.C. 39 north. You'll see signs for the several recreation areas. For information and camping reservations, call **919-438-7791**.

Cedar Creek Craft Gallery, about 10 miles north of Durham, displays and sells the products of more than 200 craftspeople, most of them from the region. Not all of the craftspeople display work at the same time, but you'll always find pottery—both functional and decorative pieces—plus candles, baskets, quilts, jewelry, and woodcarvings. The gallery is open daily from 10 A.M. to 6 P.M. Drive nine miles north from Durham on I-85, take the Creedmoor exit (Exit 186A), and follow the Cedar Creek signs. Call **919-528-1041**.

The Country Doctor Museum, about 30 miles east of Raleigh in Bailey, honors the tradition of the country physician in the late 19th and early 20th centuries. Often alone, covering a large, rural practice, the country doctor was always on call. Many times, these doctors traveled great distances in severe weather to tend patients, with only the traditional bag of medicine and equipment to aid them. The museum, located in a small frame house, is a composite of two actual doctor's offices—one an apothecary, the other an 1890 examining room. The museum is open Tuesday through Saturday from 10 A.M. to 4 P.M. and Sunday from 2 to 5 P.M. Groups are welcome as long as they make an appointment. Take U.S. 64 east to Zebulon, then take

U.S. 264 (Exit 581) to Bailey. There is a small admission fee. Call 919-235-4165.

Tobacco Farm Life Museum, about 40 miles southeast of Raleigh in Kenly, is dedicated to preserving the heritage of the early tobacco farmer. Since half of the country's flue-cured tobacco is grown within 50 miles of Kenly, it seemed a good location to establish a museum offering farm tours. Visitors can see an orientation video outlining the history of tobacco culture and tobacco auctions, then stroll through exhibits of artifacts—tools and equipment of the flue-cured tobacco farmer, along with household equipment and furniture used in rural life in the early 1900s. There is also a restored farmhouse on the grounds. The museum is open Monday through Saturday from 9:30 A.M. to 5 P.M. and Sunday from 2 to 5 P.M. Admission is $2 for adults and $1 for senior citizens and children ages five to 12; children under five are free. The museum is located off I-95 at Exit 107. Call 919-284-3431.

Fayetteville ....

The city of Fayetteville is deeply tied to our country's military, both in its history and its current economy and character. During the Revolutionary War, General Cornwallis and his British troops camped near Fayetteville on their way to meet George Washington's Continental Army at Yorktown. Unbeknownst to Cornwallis, Chesapeake Bay Harbor had been blockaded by the French navy under the command of the Marquis de Lafayette, leading to the British surrender. After the war, Fayetteville became one of the many cities named in honor of Lafayette.

Fayetteville's military significance really dates from 1918, the year when Congress established a field artillery training post outside the city. The post was originally occupied by 5,000 men and was called Camp Bragg, after Confederate General Braxton Bragg. The following year, a landing field was added to the military post. The field was named after First Lieutenant Harley H. Pope, a flier whose plane crashed in the Cape Fear River. Within five years, the post became a permanent military base and was renamed Fort Bragg.

Fort Bragg expanded immensely during World War II, when it served as the training ground for all five divisions of the airborne forces. Today, it supports a population of 71,500 people (including active-duty military, dependents, and civilian employees) and is one of the largest army bases in the world. It is the home of the 18th Airborne Corps, the 82nd Airborne Division, the First Special Operations Command, and the John F. Kennedy Special Warfare Center. Pope Air Force Base supports airborne and special-operations units at Fort Bragg.

The flavor of the city has been deeply affected by its association with the military base. Many of the civilians you meet in the city have jobs at the base, and there are numerous businesses in and around the city that cater to military personnel. However, there is more to the city than just the military presence. Fayetteville is extremely proud of its history and has done a great deal in recent years to preserve its historic buildings. The city boasts 59 structures that are listed on the National Register of Historic Places.

The city is also proud of its many festivals. More than 100 festivals, fairs, and events take place in the city each year. In April, the Dogwood Festival celebrates the blooming of the dogwoods, azaleas, daffodils, and wisteria in eastern North Carolina. In September, the city hosts the International Folk Festival. The festival, the first of its kind in the state, includes a "Parade of Nations," ethnic entertainment and crafts, and a wide assortment of exotic food.

ACCESS:

Fayetteville is located just east of I-95 roughly 26 miles south of I-40. The city can also be reached via U.S. 401, U.S. 301, N.C. 24, or N.C. 87.

Fayetteville Regional Airport, served by USAirways and Atlantic Southeast Airlines, is just south of the city off I-95 Business. For information, call 910-433-1160.

The Amtrak station is located at 472 Hay Street; call 910-483-2658.

The Greyhound/Trailways bus station is located at 324 Person Street; call 910-483-2580.

VISITOR INFORMATION:

Contact the Fayetteville Area Convention and Visitors Bureau, 245 Person Street, Fayetteville, N.C. 28301-5733 (910-483-5311 or 800-255-8217).

The city's daily newspaper is the *Fayetteville Observer-Times*. *Paraglide* is the official newspaper of Fort Bragg and Pope Air Force Base. *Up and Coming* is a free weekly paper that lists upcoming events and performances.

Attractions

Tours

Fort Bragg, located on the northwest side of town off N.C. 24, is one of the largest army bases in the world, and much of it can be seen by the public. More than 500 miles of roadway traverse the base, which covers 161,000 acres. Most of these roads are open to civilians. Visitors can take a self-guided tour of the base that includes 15 stops. As you drive through the fort, you may come across live ammunition and artillery testing (if that happens, be sure to stay in the car) or, weather permitting, you might witness an airborne jump. A favorite attraction at the fort is the Golden Knights parachute team. The precision and acrobatics displayed by the Golden Knights in their free-falling routines are the reasons they have received more awards than any other parachute team in history. For information on Fort Bragg, call 910-396-5401.

There are also other attractions located inside Fort Bragg. The **John F. Kennedy Special Warfare Museum** provides a look at unconventional warfare, with an emphasis on the army's Special Forces. The museum houses a collection of unusual weapons, military art, and cultural items from all over the world. It is open Tuesday through Sunday from 11 A.M. to 4 P.M. Admission is free. Call 910-432-1533.

The **82nd Airborne Museum** houses artifacts collected by this world-famous division from World War I to Operation Desert Storm. It is open Tuesday through Saturday from 10 A.M. to 4:30 P.M. and Sunday from 11:30 A.M. to 4 P.M. Admission is free. Call 910-432-3443.

For security reasons, **Pope Air Force Base** is closed to the public. However, a limited tour of the base can be arranged in advance by calling 910-394-4183. A display of vintage aircraft open to the public is located just inside the Reilly Road gate to the base.

Historic Places

The **Market House**, located on Market Square, was built in 1832 on the site of the old State House, which was destroyed by fire in 1831. It was within the walls of the State House that North Carolina ratified the Constitution of the United States in 1789 and chartered the University of North Carolina. When General Sherman marched through the city in 1865, he is said to have spared the Market House because of its unusual Spanish-Moorish architecture. For decades, meat and produce were sold beneath the arches of the building by local farmers, while the second floor was used as the town hall. In recent years, the second floor has been used as a public library, chamber of commerce offices, and an art museum.

Heritage Square, located at 225 Dick Street, is a historic area that includes three separate buildings. The Sandford House was built in 1800 and is a fine example of Colonial Georgian architecture. Adjacent to it is the Oval Ballroom, a freestanding single room built in 1830 that is an early example of the Greek Revival style. The third building is the Baker-Haigh-Nimocks House. Constructed in 1804, it is a typical example of coastal Carolina architecture and features a unique barrel staircase. All three buildings are on the National Register of Historic Places. The buildings can be toured by appointment. There is a fee of $3 for adults and $.50 for children. Call 910-483-6009 for information.

Museums

Museum of the Cape Fear, located at 801 Arsenal Avenue, covers the history and culture of 20 counties in southeastern North Carolina and is located at the site of the original Fayetteville Arsenal. The E. A. Poe House, a restored Victorian house constructed in 1897, is a big attraction. Admission is free. The museum is open Tuesday through

Saturday from 10 A.M. to 5 P.M. and Sunday from 1 to 5 P.M. Call 910-486-1330 for information.

Recreation

Golf is a popular recreational pursuit in Fayetteville. It was here that the first golf ball was hit in this country, by a Scot named Alex MacGrainin in 1728. There are more than 40 courses scattered within a 40-mile radius of the city. You might try **Baywood Golf Club** (910-483-4330), **Cypress Lakes** (910-483-0359), **Gates Four Golf and Country Club** (910-425-2176), **Hope Mills Golf Course** (910-425-7171), or **Kings Grant Golf and Country Club** (910-630-1114).

Cape Fear Botanical Garden, at 536 North Eastern Boulevard, is an 85-acre botanical retreat that overlooks Cross Creek and the Cape Fear River. The garden features an old farmhouse, perennial gardens, wildflowers, majestic oaks, nature trails, and numerous species of native plants. It is open Monday through Saturday and Sunday afternoon. The garden is closed on Sunday from mid-December through mid-February. Admission is $2 per person; children under 12 are admitted free. Call 910-486-0221 for more information.

Seasonal Events

The **Dogwood Festival**, held at the end of April, is a 10-day celebration of the blooming of the spring flowers. Events include parades, arts and crafts displays, pageants, and concerts. One of the most popular attractions is a self-guided tour along an 18-mile pathway graced by more than 100,000 blooming dogwoods, daffodils, azaleas, and wisteria. The event even claims its own official species of dogwood tree. Call 910-323-1934.

The military presence in Fayetteville gives the city a surprisingly cosmopolitan flavor. The **International Folk Festival**, held in late September, demonstrates this fact each year. The most popular attraction at this event is the assortment of exotic food from all over the world. There are also dancing and music exhibitions, as well as the popular Parade of Nations. Call 910-483-2073.

Sunday-on-the-Square, held the first weekend in May, attracts approximately 50,000 people each year. More than 100 artists and craftspeople sell handmade creations such as pottery, baskets, and jewelry. Live entertainment includes jazz, classical, pop, country, and blues music, as well as several dance performances. Children will enjoy the magicians, mimes, jugglers, and puppeteers. Call 910-323-1776.

Contact the Fayetteville Area Convention and Visitors Bureau for information on the many other fairs and festivals each year.

Accommodations

Courtyard by Marriott. *Moderate.* 4192 Sycamore Dairy Road (800-321-2211). This hotel offers comfortable rooms at reasonable prices. The biggest draw is that it is adjacent to the Cross Creek Mall complex, the largest retail area between Washington, D.C., and Miami.

Radisson Prince Charles Hotel and Suites. *Moderate.* 450 Hay Street (910-433-4444). This beautiful hotel opened in 1924. Since then, it has been restored. The building is now on the National Register of Historic Places, and the hotel is a member of the Historic Hotels of America. Features include cable television and a fitness room.

Holiday Inn Bordeaux. *Moderate.* 1707 Owen Drive (910-323-0111 or 800-325-0211). This huge hotel features nearly 300 guest rooms and suites, as well as a large conference center, a full-service restaurant, a night club, and an outdoor pool.

Quality Inn Ambassador. *Moderate.* 2205 Gillespie Street (910-485-8135). The nicely decorated rooms and the parklike setting give this chain motel a distinctive touch. The rooms have cable television, and golf packages are available. A full-service restaurant is located next door.

Comfort Inn Cross Creek. *Inexpensive.* 1922 Skibo Road (910-867-1777 or 800-537-2268). Conveniently located near several shopping centers and Fort Bragg, this motel offers 176 rooms and has recently been renovated. A complimentary continental breakfast is provided.

Restaurants

There are a number of good, reliable, and moderately priced chain restaurants in Fayetteville, particularly near I-95. Some of the city's most distinctive independent eating establishments are listed below.

DeLafayette Restaurant. *Expensive.* 6112 Cliffdale Road (910-868-4600). Set in an old gristmill on a lovely pond, this is one of Fayetteville's most exquisite restaurants. The menu is an interesting blend of continental, Creole, and Cajun cuisine, and the wine cellar offers many excellent selections. Dinner is served Tuesday through Saturday. Reservations are suggested.

Hilltop House Restaurant. *Moderate/Expensive.* 1240 Fort Bragg Road (910-484-6699). This restaurant, located in historic Haymount, offers relaxed dining in an early-20th-century home. It serves traditional American cuisine, steaks, seafood, and Greek specialties. The restaurant features a lounge and an outdoor patio. It is open daily for lunch and dinner. Brunch is served on Sunday.

Trio Cafe. *Moderate/Expensive.* 201 South McPherson Church Road (910-868-2443). This upscale establishment has the look and feel of a busy New York restaurant. The professionally trained chefs offer up scrumptious continental cuisine. The rack of lamb, veal chops, and chocolate torte are particularly good. Open daily for dinner.

Lobster House. *Moderate/Expensive.* 448 Person Street (910-485-8866). As you might expect, the specialty at this well-known restaurant is seafood. Chicken and beef dishes are also served. Several aquariums provide the interior decoration. Open for lunch and dinner Monday through Saturday.

Chris's Open Hearth Steak House. *Moderate/Expensive.* 2620 Raeford Road (910-485-2948). This popular Fayetteville restaurant has been family owned and operated for several generations. The specialties here are steak and prime rib, but there are also some excellent chicken and seafood selections. Open daily for dinner.

Huske Hardware House Brewing Company. *Inexpensive/Moderate.* 405 Hay Street (910-437-9905). The brewpub features an American grill with fresh seafood, Angus beef, specialty wraps, and six to eight house-brewed beers. Patrons served on the mezzanine overlook historic Hay Street and the lower level of the establishment, built in 1903 by Major Benjamin R. Huske. Open for lunch and dinner Monday through Saturday. The full-service bar is open Monday through Saturday from 11 A.M. to 2 A.M.

Pinehurst and Southern Pines ....

by Ginny Turner

Pinehurst began as a dream of James W. Tufts, a Boston inventor who was accustomed to creating something out of nothing. In 1895, he paid $1 an acre for 5,000 acres of cutover timberland near the village of Southern Pines. Good only for growing tall pine trees, the land was so sandy that the region was dubbed the "Sandhills." But Tufts saw it as a good location for a winter resort where guests could enjoy the mild climate. He built a beautiful hotel and invited landscape architect Frederick Law Olmsted, known for designing New York's Central Park, to lay out the grounds and a New England–style village of shops.

Golf had only recently been imported from Scotland, and some guests used the hotel grounds to try out their new clubs. The story goes that a dairy worker reported to Tufts that guests were "hitting the cows with a little white ball." Not one to miss an opportunity, Tufts invited golf star Donald Ross to design a few courses on the property—eventually, the number grew to eight.

The combination of challenging courses and a pleasant climate quickly made Pinehurst's reputation and drew top-ranked golfers, especially after the World Open Championship was played on Pinehurst's Number Two course. Developers soon created other golf resorts in the area to capitalize on the attraction, turning the area into a golfers' mecca. Now, over 40 courses are located within 15 miles of Pinehurst and Southern Pines.

The village of Pinehurst still has a quaint atmosphere, with loblolly pines and magnolias shading the streets and brilliant spring colors featuring blooming azaleas and peach trees. The shops here offer gifts, accessories, and upscale clothing.

Southern Pines is a pleasant town four miles to the east. There, you'll find banks, drugstores—all the usual elements necessary to keep a community going—assembled in an understated way. You'll also find unique shops, galleries, and eateries along the tree-lined streets of the downtown area. Very few buildings are over two stories tall.

People who live here are quick to tell you there's a lot to do besides playing golf. For instance, there are ample opportunities for playing tennis, antiquing, touring historic homes, and attending equestrian events, concerts, and festivals. But they admit the main reason anyone comes to Pinehurst and Southern Pines is to follow that little white ball.

ACCESS:

Southern Pines is located approximately four miles south of the intersection of U.S. 1 and U.S. 15/501. Pinehurst is four miles to the west close to the intersection of N.C. 5 and N.C. 2.

Moore County Regional Airport offers commuter air service, with daily connecting flights to USAirway's Charlotte hub. Call 910-692-3212 or 800-428-4322.

Amtrak's Silver Star stops in Southern Pines; the track separates the two sides of Broad Street. Call 800-872-7245.

VISITOR INFORMATION:

Contact the Pinehurst Area Convention and Visitors Bureau, P.O. Box 2270, 1480 U.S. 15/501, Southern Pines, N.C. 28388 (910-692-3330 or 800-346-5362 or try their Web site at http://www.homeofgolf.com).

The twice-weekly newspaper in Southern Pines is the *Pilot*. The local magazine is *Pinehurst: The Magazine of the Sandhills*. For information about area events, call 910-692-1600.

Attractions

Museums

The **Tufts Archives**, located in the Given Memorial Library in Pinehurst, displays local golf memorabilia. The archive wing features scorecards, clubs, trophies, and other historic items used by golf legends on local courses. An extensive photograph collection and personal artifacts of golf-course designer Donald Ross and the Tufts family, who founded and managed Pinehurst for four generations, are also featured. Other displays document the social and cultural history of Pinehurst. Hours are 9:30 A.M. to 5 P.M. from Monday through Friday and 9:30 A.M. to 12:30 P.M. on Saturday. There is no admission fee. Open year-round. Call 910-295-3642.

The **Malcolm Blue Farm**, located on Bethesda Road in Aberdeen, is an antebellum farm that is on the National Register of Historic Places. Visitors can tour the farmhouse, barn, gristmill, and a museum with displays on the rural history of the area. The site is open Thursday through Saturday from 1 to 4 P.M. Call 910-944-3840.

Shaw House Property, at Morganton Road and Southwest Broad Street in Southern Pines, contains three historic homes. The Shaw House was built around 1840 by Charles C. Shaw. The Garner House is a simple, one-room pioneer home with a loft. The third house is the Britt-Sanders Cabin, built around 1770 and moved to the property.

The houses are open Thursday through Saturday from 1 to 4 P.M. For information, call 910-692-2051.

Gardens

Sandhills Horticultural Gardens, at Sandhills Community College on Airport Road in Pinehurst, feature Sir Walter Raleigh Garden, a 1.5-acre replica of a formally landscaped Elizabethan garden, plus the Ebersole Holly Collection, which is the largest accessible holly collection in eastern America. There's also a conifer garden, a native wetlands trail garden, and the newest addition, the Succulent Garden, which features desert plants in an open-roofed adobe building. The gardens are open during daylight hours year-round. Admission is free, and guided tours are available. Call 910-695-3882.

Weymouth Woods Nature Preserve, at 1024 Fort Bragg Road in Southern Pines, offers over 600 acres of natural area, 4.5 miles of hiking trails that wind past streams and ponds, and fields of wildflowers. A nature museum helps visitors interpret the flora and fauna of the region. The preserve is open daily from 9 A.M. to 5 P.M. Admission is free. Call 910-692-2167.

Special Shopping

Midland Crafters and **Midland Crafters Too,** on Midland Road, are galleries that display and sell the work of regional craftspeople. You'll find pottery, woodcarvings, leatherwork, woven goods, and jewelry. Demonstrations of craft techniques are scheduled almost weekly during the spring and fall. The galleries are open Monday to Saturday from 9:30 A.M. to 5:30 P.M. and Sunday from 2 to 5 P.M. Call 910-295-6156.

Sandhills Women's Exchange, on Azalea Road in Pinehurst, features handmade early-American crafts and baked goods. A tearoom serves lunch on weekdays. The exchange is open Monday through Friday from 10 A.M. to 4 P.M. and Saturday from 11 A.M. to 3 P.M. from September to May; seasonal hours may apply in the winter, however, so call ahead for hours in January and February. Call 910-295-4677.

Covering a little more than two blocks in all, the **Cameron Historic District,** about 10 miles north of Southern Pines on U.S. 1, is the heart of a farming area. Its old buildings—some dating back to the 1870s—contain over 60 antique dealers with enough goods to keep antique prowlers occupied while golfers play their games.

Cultural Offerings

Sunrise Theater, at 250 Northwest Broad Street in Southern Pines, is a multipurpose facility. The building, which dates to 1898, is used for performances by resident groups such as Sandhills Little Theatre and Community Concerts International and for many other arts-council programs and events. For schedule information, call 910-692-3611.

Recreation

Golf, golf, and more golf—it's the prime attraction. The weather gets a little brisk in the winter and a mite steamy in midsummer, but the claim of year-round golf is authentic here. There are more than 40 courses around the Pinehurst area—a new one for each day, if you stay a month. By then, you'd know which were your favorites and which you'd want to play again.

The golf resorts often have more than one course—Pinehurst Resort has eight. Most offer golf packages that include greens fees and meals, plus special seasonal rates. The hotels and motels without their own courses have courtesy tee times at area courses, so they offer golf packages, too.

Tennis is also very popular here, with nearly 100 courts available. Many resorts have their own courts. For information on public courts, call the Moore County Parks and Recreation Department at 910-947-2504.

Pinehurst Driving and Training Track is an important winter training center for Standardbred horses, as well as a setting for numerous equestrian events. You're welcome to watch workouts October to May from 7 A.M. to noon; the earlier you arrive, the more you'll see.

Seasonal Events

Southern Pines/Pinehurst House and Garden Tour, sponsored by the Southern Pines Garden Club, takes place in April, when the area is at its brightest. Many private homes and gardens are open to the public.

Tour de Moore is a 100-mile bicycle race that circles the county. Run since 1976, it attracts an international field of competitors.

On the same day as the Tour de Moore, Southern Pines hosts **Springfest**, an arts-and-crafts fair held in the downtown area. Both events are held on the last Saturday in April.

The area hosts so many golf tournaments that it would take many pages to list them. If you're interested in competing or watching, contact the Pinehurst Area Convention and Visitors Bureau.

Side Trips

North Carolina Zoological Park—See *Triad Side Trips*
Seagrove—See *Triad Side Trips*
The House in the Horseshoe State Historic Site, 10 miles north of Carthage, was once the home of Phillip Alston, a prominent Whig before the American Revolution. Situated on a horseshoe bend of the Deep River, the two-story white plantation house is furnished partly with items from the colonial era. The house's history is told by the staff during brief tours. From Sanford, take N.C. 42 west for 10 miles to Carbonton; turn left on S.R. 1644 and drive five more miles. The site is open Monday through Saturday from 9 A.M. to 5 P.M. and Sunday from 1 to 5 P.M. from April through October; from November through March, it is open Tuesday through Saturday from 10 A.M. to 4 P.M. and Sunday from 1 to 4 P.M. Admission is free. Call 910-947-2051.

Accommodations

The Pinehurst/Southern Pines area offers a variety of accommodations, but it's heavy on golf resorts. Many of the accommodation ratings for Pinehurst-area hotels reflect package rates, which generally include golf, some meals, and other amenities. Rates fluctuate widely according to the time of year, the day of the week, the length of your stay, and how much golf you play. Be sure you book the package that best suits you.

Pinehurst Resort and Country Club. *Deluxe*. Carolina Vista Drive, Pinehurst (910-295-6811 or 800-487-4653). This has been called the premier golf resort of the mid-South, with the most beautiful hotel, the loveliest grounds, the most gracious service, and the most challenging golf courses. Visitors must pay for all this, of course, but few ever dispute the value they receive. Opened in 1901, the bright white four-story edifice has a gleaming copper roof crowned with a cupola. Another signature feature is the columned wraparound porches with white rocking chairs and ceiling fans. The grass in the driveway circle looks as if it's been trimmed with manicure scissors. The hotel rooms are tastefully furnished. Four-bedroom villas and lakeside condominiums are also available. The list of facilities here is a long one, starting with eight championship golf courses, four of which were designed by Donald Ross. Number Two, renowned because of the major international tournaments it has hosted, commands higher greens fees, but many regular Pinehurst players find Number Seven equally challenging. Tennis courts are available at the upscale tennis club, host to major tournaments. In warm weather, five pools are open, plus a marina on Lake Pinehurst, that offers swimming, fishing, windsurfing, paddleboats, and canoeing. The tab for a visit here can vary considerably. The rate for a two-night package during high season (spring and fall) is around $710 per person, based on double occupancy. The fee includes golf, unlimited use of other facilities, and breakfast and dinner daily. Rates are lower at other times.

Pine Needles Resort. *Deluxe*. On N.C. 2 just off U.S. 1 in Southern Pines (910-692-7111). Pine Needles Resort is a two-story brick building overhung by loblolly pines. The lobby has a high ceiling, a large fireplace, and a cozy feel. Guests dine casually at large tables in a similar room. The rooms have wood paneling for a touch of rusticity; half of them overlook the championship golf course. Rates vary significantly through the year; special packages which include meals are available. The peak rate is $640 per person for double occupancy for three days and two nights; this includes meals and 36 holes of golf. The greens fees are $135 and include a cart.

Mid-Pines Inn and Golf Club Resort. *Expensive/Deluxe*. 1010 Midland Road, Southern Pines (910-692-2114 or 800-323-2114). This elegant three-story hotel, built in 1921, has wings that stretch out as if embracing its beautiful golf course. Its stately interior is enhanced by a crystal chandelier in the lobby, Chinese prints in the hallways, and fresh flowers on every table in the attractive dining room, which looks out over the Donald Ross–designed golf course. Many of its 112 airy rooms have carved headboards and a sofa. Again, rates vary dramatically according to the room and time of year. Package rates which include golf and all meals are available.

Residence Inn. *Moderate/Expensive*. 105 Brucewood Road, off U.S. 15/501 (910-693-3400 or 888-702-GOLF). This all-suite hotel may be the place to go if you have a large party—the rates are actually quite reasonable if you break them down per person. The golf packages include greens fees, continental breakfast, and a nightly reception. The suites include fully equipped kitchens in case you want to cook your own meals after hitting the links.

Pine Crest Inn. *Moderate*. Dogwood Road, Pinehurst (800-371-2545). Formerly owned by golf champion Donald Ross, Pine Crest Inn looks like an old New England inn—homey and slightly worn, but warm and welcoming. It's within walking distance of the village of Pinehurst and five Pinehurst Country Club courses that will accommodate guest golfers. The rooms aren't especially striking, but the friendliness of the staff has earned a high rate of repeat visitors. Rates include breakfast and dinner.

Holiday Inn. *Moderate*. U.S. 1 at Morganton Road, Southern Pines (910-692-8585). This motel offers 162 guest rooms and suites, a restaurant, a pool, tennis courts, a game room, and a fitness center. Package rates include greens fees at area courses.

Best Western/Pinehurst Motor Inn. *Inexpensive/Moderate*. U.S. 1 South, Aberdeen (910-944-2367 or 800-528-1234). This motel offers attractively decorated guest rooms, some with refrigerators. An outdoor pool, a playground, and a barbecue grill are provided; continental breakfast and a daily newspaper are included. Tee times can be made at many area courses.

Hampton Inn. *Inexpensive/Moderate*. 1675 U.S. 1 South, Southern Pines (910-692-9266 or 800-HAMPTON). This property in the heart of golf country offers comfortable rooms, complimentary breakfast, an outdoor pool, a fitness room, and a coin laundry. Package rates which include greens fees at several area courses are available.

Inns and Bed-and-Breakfast Guest Houses

Magnolia Inn. *Expensive/Deluxe*. Magnolia Road, Pinehurst (910-295-6900 or 800-526-5562). Built in 1896, this recently renovated inn is located in the heart of Pinehurst. The 11 guest rooms, each with a restored bathroom, are elegantly decorated with antique furnishings. The inn features a full-service dining room and a pub next to the outdoor swimming pool. Arrangements for golf at many area courses can be made with your room reservation.

Knollwood House. *Expensive*. 1495 West Connecticut Avenue, Southern Pines (910-692-9390). From its circular garden in front to its rear sunroom overlooking Mid-Pines Resort, this 1927 English manor–style house is reliving its heyday. It once hosted such guests as Walter Hagen and Ben Hogan. There are two guest rooms and four suites, each with a private bath and cable television. Breakfast is included. Golf packages are available.

Restaurants

The majority of dining in the area is done at the resorts, as most room packages include meals, but there is a fairly good selection of restaurants to choose from. The selection ranges from pubs to grills to ethnic eateries to national chains.

Carolina Dining Room. *Expensive.* Pinehurst Resort, Carolina Vista, Pinehurst (910-295-6811). This elegant restaurant has crystal chandeliers and tables that overlook impeccably groomed grounds. Reservations are required. A full bar is offered. The prix fixe dinner features entrées that change daily. Breakfast and lunch are also served daily.

Sleddon's Restaurant. *Expensive.* 275 South Bennett Street, Southern Pines (910-692-4480). Diners will enjoy the intimate lounge and dining rooms in this restaurant located in a 1920s home. The continental menu is highlighted by a distinctive wine list. Dinner is served Tuesday through Saturday; reservations are required.

Donald Ross Grill. *Moderate/Expensive.* Pinehurst Country Club (910-295-8433). The menu here features sandwiches and burgers for lunch and steaks, pasta, and seafood for dinner. Lunch is served daily. Dinner is served on a seasonal basis.

Henning's Restaurant. *Moderate/Expensive.* Holiday Inn, U.S. 1 at Morganton Road, Southern Pines (910-692-8585). Henning's serves a buffet for breakfast, lunch, and dinner and also offers a varied menu. A broad skylight illuminates the dining room, and windows overlook the swimming pool. A full bar is offered. The restaurant is open daily.

Longleaf Country Club. *Moderate.* 2001 Midland Road, Southern Pines (910-692-4411). The clubhouse here offers a formal dining room and a separate, cozy grillroom with a fireplace. The ambiance reflects this facility's history as a former training ground for some of the country's top thoroughbred horses. Sandwiches and grilled items are available for dinner. Lunch is served Tuesday through Sunday. Dinner is served Wednesday through Saturday.

The Squire's Pub. *Moderate.* 1720 U.S. 1 South, Southern Pines (910-695-1161). This restaurant features a casual pub atmosphere and a British and American menu. A full bar is offered. Lunch and dinner are served Monday through Saturday.

The Triad

Winston-Salem
Greensboro
High Point

by Rick Mashburn

At the geographical center of the Triad lies a town described as "the only little country crossroads with 14 video stores." Kernersville's Main Street looks as old-fashioned and homey as Andy Griffith's Mayberry, yet the traffic alone tells you that things aren't what they seem. Surrounding Main Street are shopping centers, apartment complexes, and office parks by the dozen. Kernersville is still a small country town in many ways, but its central location among Winston-Salem, Greensboro, and High Point has made it an extension of all three of those cities.

Kernersville is a fitting symbol for the Triad. It dramatically illustrates the economic growth that has fostered cooperation among Winston-Salem, Greensboro, and High Point. And Kernersville also demonstrates the Triad's thorough mix of urban and rural, which to many minds is the area's chief attraction.

"Too bucolic" is how the former president of RJR Nabisco described Winston-Salem in 1987, when he moved the company's headquarters to the less-green pastures of Atlanta. His choice of words became the subject of widespread ridicule, but not necessarily because those words were inappropriate. Cattle actually graze right in the middle of Winston-Salem; their pastures are on the property of the Methodist Children's Home, wedged between downtown and the city's most affluent residential neighborhood. Yet anyone who appreciates life in the Triad knows that one need not surrender fresh air and open land for the more sophisticated pleasures of city life.

In the Triad, visitors can dine on bouillabaisse at a French restaurant or eat a scrumptious chicken-pie supper at a country church. Good roads put the Triad's three principal cities within easy reach of each other, which means residents frequently enjoy the offerings of the other towns. Equally easy is an escape to 6,000-acre Hanging Rock State Park in the foothills of the Blue Ridge Mountains, or to the mountains themselves, since they're only a two-hour drive away, or even to the beach, only four hours away.

Greensboro, the largest of the three cities, has a population of nearly 205,000; Winston-Salem boasts almost 172,000 residents and High Point a little over 73,000. Yet the area's total population is said to be 1.1 million, making the Triad second only to the Charlotte area in North Carolina. Though unsuccessful, a recent effort to bring major-league baseball to the Triad area shows just how much the area has grown over the last several years.

The Triad's cities exhibit differences as well. Urban cows notwithstanding, Winston-Salem is widely recognized for the high quality of its visual and performing arts. With seven colleges, including a 12,000-student branch of the University of North Carolina, Greensboro boasts a youthful population that keeps in touch with the latest in popular culture—whether music, fashion, or food. Although it's the smallest Triad city, High Point contributes greatly to the cultural life of the area. As the center of the furniture industry, it is in the national spotlight twice a year during the International Home Furnishings Market. It also draws crowds to its annual North Carolina Shakespeare Festival.

The Triad's towns and countryside offer visitors a wide range of sites and activities. Old Salem, the restored Moravian village, is the chief attraction. Other frequently visited sites include the Revolutionary War battleground at Guilford Courthouse, just north of Greensboro, and North Carolina Zoological Park, to the south.

In addition, the Triad is a good place to get off the beaten path and visit a country potter or listen to a string band. Geographically, this is the heart of North Carolina, and in many ways, you'll find the state's essence here.

Winston-Salem

Let's get things straight from the beginning: the cigarettes were named for the town, not the other way around. And while the health-care industry is now the city's largest employer, Winston-Salem owes much to tobacco. When Richard Joshua Reynolds came to the city from Virginia and established what would become the nation's second-largest tobacco company, it caused Winston-Salem to grow from a tiny town into one of the state's largest metropolitan areas.

Winston and Salem were unhyphenated, politically separate municipalities until 1913, although they had merged geographically long before then. Salem was established by the Moravians in 1766. When Forsyth County was formed in 1849, Salem was the logical choice for the county seat, but the church elders didn't want their town to be sullied by the riffraff that would accompany court sessions. Hence, Salem sold the northern part of its land to the county, and a courthouse was built less than a mile from its town square. The new town was named for Colonel Joseph Winston, hero of the Battle of Kings Mountain in the Revolutionary War.

Although Salem was a prosperous community from the beginning, Winston grew much faster than its church-centered neighbor. It could easily be argued that Richard Joshua Reynolds built Winston. When he arrived in 1874, the city had 400 residents. Forty years later, R. J. Reynolds himself employed 10,000 workers in his tobacco factories. Throughout the late 19th century, both tobacco factories and textile mills lured young farm women, then their families, from the foothills and the Blue Ridge Mountains.

While R. J. Reynolds built his tobacco empire, his wife, Katharine, worked to improve the lives of his employees. In 1908, she led other prominent Winston women in creating the city's YWCA, which served as a kind of halfway house for new factory hands making the transition from life on the farm to life in Winston. She also persuaded her husband to open a cafeteria and a nursery for his workers. She built a model farm at Reynolda, the family's country home, where the latest agricultural practices and food-preservation techniques were taught to neighboring farmers.

This legacy of community involvement has remained a strong influence in Winston-Salem. Today, the patronage of the Reynolds family and its company is evident in the many streets, parks, medical facilities, educational buildings, museums, high-rises, and shopping centers bearing a variation on the Reynolds name or that of a Reynolds in-law.

The family was also behind the relocation of Wake Forest University to Winston-Salem. In 1946, a Reynolds family foundation offered Wake Forest College $250,000 a year in perpetuity if it would move from its campus near Raleigh. Later, Mary Reynolds Babcock donated land in Winston-Salem for the campus, and the foundation's financial support was doubled. Today, Winston-Salem boasts an active college scene that also includes Winston-Salem State University and Salem College.

Although the Reynolds family's largesse has served the city well, it perhaps has made the community more conservative than it might otherwise have been. For instance, one doesn't talk about the death of R. J. and Katharine's son Z. Smith Reynolds in polite company even more than 50 years after his rumored murder or suicide at a party at Reynolda. Well-mannered Winston-Salem residents try to ignore the fact that the death is to this day the subject of books, films, and television shows.

In recent decades, Winston-Salem's spirit of community involvement has focused largely on the arts—which is altogether fitting, in light of the artistic accomplishments of the city's first residents, the Moravians. In 1949, Winston-Salem patrons and artists created the nation's first arts council. In 1963, the country's first state-supported performing-arts school, the North Carolina School of the Arts, was founded in Winston-Salem. Reynolda House was transformed into a museum of American art in 1965. The city's many arts institutions—galleries, orchestras, museums—have been exceptionally well housed and supported. Even though large-scale sponsorship has decreased in recent years, Winston-Salem still has a shining reputation in the arts community.

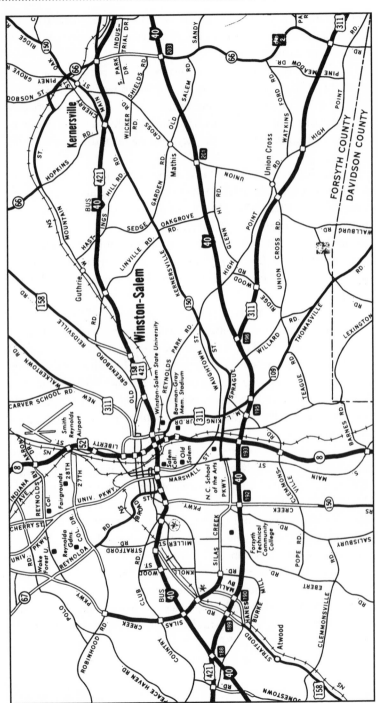

ACCESS:

Winston-Salem is located west of Greensboro at the intersection of I-40 Business and U.S. 52. I-77 passes 30 miles west of the city.

Piedmont Triad International Airport, served by eight airlines, is centrally located among Winston-Salem, Greensboro, and High Point. Some hotels offer free limousine service to and from the airport. Smith Reynolds Airport, located off Liberty Street in Winston-Salem, offers commercial commuter flights and space for private planes.

The Trailways bus station is located at 250 Greyhound Court; call 336-724-1429.

VISITOR INFORMATION:

Contact the Winston-Salem Convention and Visitors Bureau, 601 West Fourth Street, P.O. Box 1408, Winston-Salem, N.C. 27102 (336-725-2361 or 800-331-7018), or the Winston-Salem Visitors Center, 601 North Cherry Street, Winston-Salem, N.C. 27701 (336-777-3796).

The city's daily newspaper, the *Winston-Salem Journal*, lists weekend entertainment in Friday's "What's On" section.

Triad Style, a free weekly tabloid available in hotels, restaurants, and stores, also has a calendar of events.

Attractions

Historic Places

Old Salem, located on Salem Road just south of downtown, is an 18th- and 19th-century village settled by German-speaking Moravians. Within two dozen blocks are over 90 restored and reconstructed buildings, including several that are open to the public as museums. As the modern city of Winston-Salem has grown up around it, Old Salem has maintained its special character without becoming isolated from present-day influences, such as automobile traffic and a contemporary student population of young women at Salem College. The shady town square, the tidy vegetable gardens, the working craftsmen, and the inviting aroma of bread baking in a wood-fired oven help bring Salem's past to life.

Members of the early Protestant sect called the Unity of Brethren, the Moravians derived their name from their homeland, Moravia, now part of the Czech Republic. Persecuted for centuries in their own land, the Moravians emigrated to Bethlehem, Pennsylvania, in 1740. Thirteen years later, they bought a 100,000-acre tract in the Carolina wilderness and named it Wachovia, after the ancestral home of their patron. Salem, founded in 1766, became Wachovia's principal town.

Old Salem preserves the remnants of a community and a culture that were extraordinary in many ways. While most 18th-century back-country settlers were struggling in isolation to raise food for their children, Salem's residents worked together to create the South's first public waterworks. They not only created sturdy and handsome buildings, furniture, and pottery, but they also had time for music, painting, and, above all, religion.

Salem was a "congregation town," meaning that the church governed the economy and social structure of the community, in addition to being its spiritual center. The church owned all the land and controlled business operations. Marriages had to be approved by the church elders, and strict dress codes were enforced. From the age of 14, single men lived together; they shared in the preparation of meals, kept a communal garden, and worshipped together daily. Single women lived together in their own house across the town square. Even in the cemetery, God's Acre, the dead were segregated according to gender and marital status.

Despite such regulations, the Moravians' life was far from austere. Their communal practices allowed Salem residents to prosper and enjoy a comfortable life.

Tours of Old Salem usually begin at the Single Brothers House, a large, half-timbered structure built in 1769. Here, costumed crafts-men—including a joiner, a weaver, a cooper, a potter, and a tin-smith—use traditional tools and methods to reproduce Salem wares. The communal life of Salem's single men is reflected in the sparsely furnished chapel, where they gathered for vespers and singing, and in the large kitchen and dining area in the basement.

Salem's first privately owned home was the Miksch House (1771).

Old Salem
Photograph by Clay Nolen
Courtesy of N.C. Travel
and Tourism Division

This small, rather dark building was the residence of Matthew Miksch, a sickly man who eked out a living as a small-scale merchant and tobacconist while his wife baked and sold gingerbread. Behind the house is a reconstruction of Miksch's workshop, with displays of tobacco products.

Much larger and more comfortable is the Vierling House (1802), the home of Salem's most prominent early physician, who took Matthew Miksch's daughter as his second wife. In one of the front rooms is Dr. Vierling's apothecary, which contains a collection of medical instruments in use at that time. Vierling was an accomplished musician, and a pianoforte and flute similar to those he played are on display in the sitting room. The entire house is furnished according to a thorough inventory of the doctor's possessions made just after his death. The kitchen in the house and the washing and baking house behind it are used for demonstrations of early-19th-century domestic skills, in which hardy women undertake a weekly cycle of cleaning, washing, ironing, and cooking using only historically authentic techniques and materials.

The latest of Old Salem's museum houses, the John Vogler House (1819) shows how quickly the economy and the tastes of the town progressed. Vogler, a silversmith, was the first Salem resident to build a home using elements of the Federal style of architecture, which was popular at that time.

Salem Tavern, built in 1784 and now a museum, helps explain how change came to Salem. Because of its many craftsmen and merchants, Salem became a trading center. The tavern always did a brisk trade with non-Moravians who came to town on business, bringing ideas from the outside. The tavern had both an "Ordinary Room," for those dining at a fixed rate, and a "Gentlemen's Room," for those who could afford better service. Behind the tavern is a large reconstructed barn with displays of farm equipment. The Old Salem Tavern Dining Room offers meals in the Tavern Annex (1816).

Another building open to the public is the Boys School (1794), now a museum with an exceptional collection of Moravian pottery. At the Winkler Bakery (1800), bread, cookies, and distinctive Moravian sugar cakes are baked daily and offered for sale. In the Market-Fire House (1803), located on the town square, is an exhibit of firefighting equipment. And a costumed guide discusses the art of the cobbler in the Shultz Shoemaker Shop (1827). Old Salem's symbol, a 16-foot coffeepot, was built in 1858 as an advertisement for two tinsmiths.

The gardens across Academy Street from the Single Brothers House were based on a 1759 drawing from the nearby Moravian community of Bethabara; that drawing is believed to have been the earliest garden plan in America. The beds have a distinctive diagonal layout. Behind the Miksch Shop is a reconstruction of a community medicinal-herb garden, also from Bethabara drawings. Other period kitchen gardens are scattered throughout Salem; the largest concentration is along Salt Street north of the visitor center.

Several gift shops are located in restored buildings. Home Moravian Church (1800) and the Single Sisters House (1786), now part of Salem College, are other important buildings in Old Salem.

Be sure to take a stroll in God's Acre, the graveyard, where simple, flat tombstones have been laid in perfectly spaced rows.

The annual events at Old Salem include Salem Christmas, featuring tours, holiday decorations, strolling brass bands, and horse-drawn wagon rides. The Christmas Candle Tea, sponsored by Home Moravian Church and held in the Single Brothers House, draws large crowds for a candlelight "Lovefeast" of coffee, buns, and song. On the night before Easter, several brass bands wander throughout Winston-Salem, waking residents with a song in the early hours; then the bands and thousands of onlookers gather at Salem Square for more music and a walk to God's Acre for a sunrise service. On the Fourth of July, a solemn torchlight parade around Salem Square is part of a reenactment of the country's first official Independence Day celebration, held in Salem in 1783.

Don't plan to see Old Salem hastily—allow several hours for your visit. Old Salem is open Monday through Saturday from 9 A.M. to 5 P.M. and Sunday from 1 to 5 P.M. Admission to all of the museums is $15 for adults and $8 for children ages five to 16. Call 336-721-7300.

Historic Bethabara Park, at 2147 Bethabara Road, is the site of the first settlement of the Moravians in Wachovia. Here, in 1753, some 15 settlers arrived from Pennsylvania and spent their first night in a trapper's abandoned cabin. Bethabara, which means "house of passage," was never intended to be a permanent settlement. Although it thrived, most of its residents moved to Salem in 1772.

Today, the 80-acre park contains the foundations of Bethabara's buildings and the 1756 palisade fort, which has been reconstructed in accordance with archaeological findings. Still standing are the handsome Gemeinhaus (1788), furnished and open for tours, and the Potter's House (1782), containing exhibits on the pottery industry in the settlement. Bethabara also has a visitor center with exhibits and a slide presentation.

The buildings are open daily from April through November 31 and by appointment for group tours all year. The hours are Monday through Friday from 9:30 A.M. to 4:30 P.M. and Saturday and Sunday from 1:30 to 4:30 P.M. Admission is free. Call 336-924-8191.

Reynolda House Museum of American Art, on Reynolda Road just north of Coliseum Drive, is a museum in the former home of tobacco magnate R. J. Reynolds and his wife, Katharine. The superb collection is highlighted by Frederic E. Church's masterpiece, *The Andes of Ecuador*, and includes important paintings by Thomas Eakins, William Merit Chase, and Mary Cassatt. Georgia O'Keeffe, Thomas Hart Benton, and Jacob Lawrence are among the 20th-century artists represented. The works range from Jeremiah Theuss's 1755 portrait of Mrs. Thomas Lynch to recent paintings, drawings, and prints by Jasper Johns, Frank Stella, and Chuck Close.

The house, designed by Charles Barton Keen and built between 1914 and 1917, is worthy of a visit in its own right. Many of the original furnishings remain on view. In the basement are a bowling alley, a handball court, and a swimming pool added in the 1930s, while on the third floor is a collection of the Reynolds family's clothing. Surrounding the house is Reynolda Gardens, 20 acres of formal flower beds, vegetable gardens, and wooded paths. Reynolda Village, now a complex of shops, was originally the model farm Katharine Reynolds established on the estate.

The museum is open Tuesday through Saturday from 9:30 A.M. to 4:30 P.M. and Sunday from 1:30 to 4:30 P.M. Admission is $6 for adults, $5 for senior citizens, and $3 for students and children. Call 336-725-5325.

Museums/Science Centers

The Museum of Early Southern Decorative Arts, at 924 South Main Street, is an affiliate and neighbor of Old Salem that concentrates on non-Moravian decorative arts of the South. Twenty-one furnished rooms, many actually taken apart at their original locations and reassembled, demonstrate the varied styles of three regions—the Chesapeake, the Carolina low country, and the back-country settlements. The earliest room, Crisscross Hall (1640), is almost medieval

Reynolda House
Photograph by William Russ
Courtesy of N.C. Travel
and Tourism Division

in character, with its diamond-paned leaded windows and its court cupboard, the earliest existing piece of Southern furniture. By contrast, the dining room from White Hall (1820) in South Carolina is formal and very lavish, with an inlaid dining table and a magnificent silver sugar urn.

The museum is primarily a research institution; the approach here is more academic than at Old Salem. The museum is open Monday through Saturday from 9:30 A.M. to 4:30 P.M. and Sunday from 1:30 to 4:30 P.M. A guided tour of all the rooms takes about an hour and costs $10 for adults and $6 for children ages five to 16. Call 336-721-7360.

Southeastern Center for Contemporary Art (SECCA), at 750 Marguerite Drive off Reynolda Road, isn't a museum but a complex of galleries that offers 21,000 square feet of exhibition space and a 300-seat auditorium. All the artists represented are from the Southeast. In addition to the abundant visual art, SECCA has a lively educational program that offers a wide variety of performances, lectures, and films. SECCA is located on the 32-acre estate of the late industrialist James G. Hanes. Some of the galleries are housed in an addition to the estate's 1929 English-style house; the living room and library contain their original furnishings. The center's gift shop carries regional crafts, art books, and amusing things for children. SECCA is open Tuesday through Saturday from 10 A.M. to 5 P.M. and Sunday from 2 to 5 P.M. Admission is $3 for adults and $2 for students and senior citizens; children under 12 are free. Call 336-725-1904.

SciWorks, located on Museum Drive off Hanes Mill Road, is especially popular with children. Visitors can whisper into a parabolic dish and be heard distinctly by someone 40 feet away, make a shadow and walk away from it, see a coin accelerated to 100 miles an hour by gravity, and participate in many other hands-on demonstrations. SciWorks is open Monday through Saturday from 10 A.M. to 5 P.M. Admission is $7 for adults and $5 for senior citizens and students, and $3 for children ages three to five. Call 336-767-6730.

The Diggs Gallery is located on the ground floor of O'Kelly Library on the campus of Winston-Salem State University, located off Dr. Martin Luther King, Jr., Drive. It offers five traveling exhibitions a year and focuses on African-American and contemporary art, with some shows of historical interest. The gallery is open Tuesday through Saturday from 11 A.M. to 5 P.M. Admission is free. Call 336-750-2458.

R. J. Reynolds Tobacco USA, the cigarette-manufacturing component of RJR Nabisco, makes about one of every three cigarettes sold in America. At the 28-acre Whitaker Park plant on Reynolds Drive, some 450 million cigarettes are made daily. A museum on the grounds is devoted to the history of tobacco merchandising, with abundant examples of old advertisements and packaging. Souvenirs—including cigarettes—are sold in the gift shop. Admission is free. Call 336-741-5718.

Special Shopping

Reynolda Village is a complex of specialty shops, restaurants, and offices in the former farm buildings of Reynolda, the estate of R. J. and Katharine Reynolds. A remodeled dairy barn with a white silo, a cattle shed, and even a chicken house make a distinctive setting for one of the city's largest concentrations of high-end shopping. Gourmet foods, cooking supplies, linens, children's toys and clothes, health foods, and leather goods are among the offerings. The complex is located off Reynolda Road between Coliseum Drive and Silas Creek Parkway.

Piedmont Craftsmen, Inc., is an organization representing more than 350 of the Southeast's finest craftspeople. Works by many members of the organization are sold at a shop and gallery located at 1204 Reynolda Road. Piedmont Craftsmen is best known for its decidedly contemporary work in clay, wood, fiber, glass, leather, and other media, yet the shop also carries traditional items, including dulcimers and simple wood-fired pottery. Membership in the organization is open to craftspeople in the Southeast who have been accepted after a stringent jury process. The store is open Tuesday through Saturday from 10 A.M. to 6 P.M. and Sunday from 1 to 6 P.M. Call 336-725-1516.

Cultural Offerings

North Carolina School of the Arts (NCSA), at 200 Waughtown Street, was the first state-supported arts school in the nation. It contributes immeasurably to the cultural life of Winston-Salem. Faculty members and students from the School of Music comprise the majority of performers in the city's symphony. Drama teachers share their talents by directing plays for the community theater. Many graduates in all fields have stayed in Winston-Salem, writing music and plays and forming dance schools and children's-theater companies. The city's residents also benefit from what happens on campus; each year, the school sponsors as many as 200 public performances by students, faculty, and visiting artists. It also offers first-rate performances by The Actors Ensemble, a group of drama faculty. Members of the music faculty make up the Clarion Wind Quintet, which tours extensively in addition to performing at home. Concerts by the student NCSA Jazz Ensemble are especially popular, and the annual production of *The Nutcracker* has long been a citywide favorite. About 40 events a year are held in the school's opulent Stevens Center, at 405 West Fourth Street downtown. Other performances are held at Performance Place on the campus. Call 336-721-1945 for ticket information.

The Winston-Salem Piedmont Triad Symphony Orchestra's fall-through-spring season includes six programs, each performed on Saturday and Tuesday evenings and Sunday afternoon at the Stevens Center. In the summer, the symphony's "Music at Sunset" series offers outdoor concerts at Tanglewood Park. The symphony also sponsors a children's concert series. Call 336-725-1035.

Piedmont Opera Theatre presents two fully staged operas a year—one in the spring, the other in the fall—in the Stevens Center. The principal singers are usually guest artists from New York. Call 336-725-7101.

Fiddle and Bow, the Triad's traditional-music society, sponsors several concerts a year featuring acoustic music from around the country and abroad. Call 336-727-1038 for schedule information.

Piedmont Chamber Singers is a 28-voice choir whose music ranges from Renaissance to 20th-century works. The group's annual subscription series includes three concerts, a Valentine's gala, three concerts at the local arts council's downtown atrium, and free Christmas concerts in the Gemeinhaus at Historic Bethabara Park. Call 336-722-4022.

The six annual shows produced by the city's community theater group, the **Little Theatre of Winston-Salem**, include dramas, comedies, and musicals. The group has its own theater at 610 Coliseum Drive. Call 336-725-4001.

In addition to touring throughout the Southeast, the **North Carolina Black Repertory Company** produces four plays a year at different locations in its hometown. The company also produces and hosts the National Black Theatre Festival, which draws well-known African-American actresses and actors to Winston-Salem every other summer. Call 336-723-2266.

Sawtooth Building, located at 226 North Marshall Street, houses three art galleries featuring presentations by local artists, traveling exhibitions, and national juried shows. A renovated 1910 textile mill with a distinctive jagged roofline, the building is also home to the Sawtooth Center for Visual Design, which offers classes in arts and crafts. The building is open daily from 9 A.M. to 9 P.M. Call 336-725-8916.

Delta Arts Center, at 1511 East Third Street, is dedicated to the promotion of African-American arts and humanities. It is open daily from noon to 5 P.M. Call 336-722-2625.

Recreation

Tanglewood is a 1,152-acre park of exceptional beauty that offers a wide variety of facilities. It is the former estate of Mr. and Mrs. William Neal Reynolds, who bequeathed it to Forsyth County; their former home is known as Tanglewood Manor House. A campground in the park offers full hookups in some of its sites. One of the two golf courses on the premises is the home of **The Vantage Championship**, one of the largest Senior PGA tournaments. Other activities include tennis, fishing, horseback riding, picnicking, swimming, and boating. **The Tanglewood Steeplechase**, which takes place on the second Saturday in May, is one of three steeplechases in North Carolina. It attracts more than 20,000 people, who dress and feed themselves with great panache. Tanglewood is also the setting for the Winston-Salem Piedmont Triad Symphony's Sunday pops concerts in the summer, as well as a festive Fourth of July concert with fireworks. During the Christmas season, it hosts the popular Festival of Lights. The park is on U.S. 158 some 10 miles southwest of the city. Admission is $2 per car. Hours vary; call 336-778-6300.

Hanes Park, at Reynolda Road and West End Boulevard, is the largest park within the city. The emphasis is on activities, but there are also opportunities for lounging and for walking by a pleasant stream. Among the facilities are 20 clay tennis courts with lights, three ball fields, a quarter-mile track, and a large playground. Call 336-727-2137.

The 365-acre city-owned **Salem Lake** is surrounded by an 1,800-acre park. Nearly seven miles of trails circle the lake. This is usually a quiet place, though it is a popular spot for fishing, and offers rowboats and motorboats for rent. To reach the park, take Reynolds Park Road to Salem Lake Road. Call 336-650-7677.

Seasonal Events

The **Dixie Classic Fair** offers nine days of Ferris wheels, cotton candy, and blue-ribbon roosters. It's held around the first full week in October. The Midway is a mile long. Two particularly popular features are the racing pigs and the big-name entertainment, usually a country-music singer. The fairgrounds are at University Parkway and Deacon Boulevard. Call 336-727-2236.

The **Crosby National Celebrity Golf Tournament** is an amateur celebrity golf tournament held in late spring or early summer at Bermuda Run Country Club in Advance, 11 miles southwest of Winston-Salem. The four-day event, a fund-raiser for charities, is presided over by Kathryn Crosby, widow of Bing Crosby. Players from participating corporations are matched with celebrity players, usually entertainers or professional athletes (but not professional golfers). Call 336-998-8312.

The **Piedmont Crafts Fair** is held each fall on the third weekend in November in the Benton Convention Center. The over 100 exhibitors are members of the Piedmont Craftsmen organization, and their wares are for sale. Attendance at the three-day fair averages 7,000 to 10,000. Call 336-725-1516 or look the fair up on the Web at http://www.webfresco.com/pci/.

Side Trips

See *Triad Side Trips*

Accommodations

Adams Mark Winston Plaza. *Expensive/Deluxe.* 425 North Cherry Street (336-725-3500). A stylish 17-story, 605-room hotel, Adams Mark is as grand as it gets in Winston-Salem. The well-appointed public areas have abundant examples of contemporary North Carolina arts and crafts. Guests are served complimentary coffee and a newspaper with their wake-up call. An indoor pool, a sauna, a game room, and an exercise club are among the amenities. The hotel is connected by skywalk to the Benton Convention Center and is near other downtown attractions, including the Stevens Center.

Holiday Inn Select. *Moderate/Expensive.* 5790 University Parkway (336-767-9595). This hotel is located off U.S. 52 on the north side of the city. An outdoor swimming pool and sports facilities are among the amenities.

Comfort Inn-Cloverdale Place. *Moderate.* 110 Miller Street (336-721-0220). This contemporary five-story brick complex offers a variety of rooms and is convenient to Baptist Hospital. An outdoor swimming pool and a fitness center are available.

Courtyard by Marriott. *Moderate.* 3111 University Parkway (336-727-1277). This attractive Williamsburg-style inn is located one block from the Lawrence Joel Veterans Memorial Coliseum. It is less than a mile and a half from Wake Forest University and Whitaker Park.

Inns and Bed-and-Breakfast Guest Houses

The Colonel Ludlow Bed and Breakfast Inn. *Deluxe.* 434 Summit Street at West Fifth Street (336-777-1887). Most bed-and-breakfast inns in old houses have been so carefully restored that they no longer have the feel of the past. The Colonel Ludlow (1887) hasn't forsaken modern-day comforts, yet it's still evocative of the Victorian era. The parlor, dining room, and nine guest rooms are charmingly decorated with antique furniture, prints, books, and knickknacks. Each room has its own bath, and most have two-person Jacuzzis.

Henry F. Shaffner House. *Expensive/Deluxe.* 150 South Marshall

Street, just off I-40 Business (336-777-0052). Named for its original owner, a cofounder of Wachovia Loan and Trust Company, this elegant 1907 home offers nine individually decorated guest rooms with telephones and cable TV. Among the amenities are a sunroom and a library/reading room. Guests receive a breakfast complete with freshly baked pastries, as well as evening wine and cheese. The house is located within walking distance of Old Salem and downtown Winston-Salem.

Augustus T. Zevely Inn. *Expensive/Deluxe*. 803 South Main Street (336-748-9299). This historic inn is the only lodging located on the grounds of Old Salem. Accommodations range from single rooms to suites. Each room is individually decorated in the Moravian style with reproductions from the Bob Timberlake collection, and several of the rooms have working fireplaces. All rooms have a private bath, television, and telephone. Rates include breakfast and wine and cheese in the evening.

Brookstown Inn. *Expensive*. 200 Brookstown Avenue (336-725-1120). The Salem Cotton Company mill (1837) has been converted into a complex with offices, shops, a restaurant, and the 71-room Brookstown Inn. The spacious rooms are furnished with early-American antique reproductions and quilts, and some have nonworking fireplaces. A complimentary breakfast is served in the dining room, and afternoon wine and cheese are offered in the sitting room. Brookstown Inn is located only a few blocks from Old Salem.

Tanglewood Manor House Bed and Breakfast Inn. *Moderate/Expensive*. Tanglewood Park (336-778-6370). This bed-and-breakfast inn was fashioned from the former home of William Neal Reynolds, the brother of tobacco magnate R. J. Reynolds. The two-story white brick house, built in 1859, overlooks a broad, tree-shaded lawn in front and part of an arboretum in back. The guest rooms are decorated with antique reproductions, including some canopy beds. Overflow guests may stay in an 18-room strip motel, Tanglewood Lodge, which shares a parking lot with the inn. A continental breakfast for guests of the bed-and-breakfast is served in the dining room, which has a striking fieldstone fireplace.

Restaurants

Fabian's. *Expensive*. 1100 Reynolda Road (336-723-7700). This is one of the most posh restaurants in town. Reservations are required for a luxurious five-course dinner. Guests are told to plan on taking at least 2½ hours for dinner, but as good as the food and atmosphere are, you're sure to linger over the meal much longer. Upstairs is a full bar where patrons can relax with a drink with or without reservations. Dinner is by reservation only Tuesday through Saturday nights.

Staley's Charcoal Steak House. *Expensive.* 2000 Reynolda Road (336-723-8631). Steaks are grilled over hickory wood in a large fireplace in the main dining room. Staley's has old-fashioned sophistication. A full bar is offered. Dinner is served Monday through Saturday.

Ryan's Steaks, Chops and Seafood. *Expensive.* 719 Coliseum Drive (336-724-6132). From the window tables, the view of a gently rolling stream and huge oak trees sets the atmosphere for fine dining at Ryan's. Steaks, prime rib, veal, and fresh fish are among the specialties. Dinner is served Monday through Saturday.

Old Salem Tavern Dining Room. *Expensive.* 736 South Main Street (336-748-8585). A meal in the Tavern Annex makes the Old Salem experience complete. Moravian chicken pie is a favorite at lunch. For dinner, those who crave authenticity can try fried cornmeal mush, venison, and gingerbread from an early Salem recipe. A full range of more contemporary fare is also available. A full bar is offered. Reservations are suggested. Lunch is served daily and dinner Monday through Saturday.

Bernardin's. *Expensive.* Center Stage Shopping Center, 373 Jonestown Road (336-768-9365). The decor here is intimate and romantic. Dishes include curried oysters, seared scallops, roasted breast of duck, pepper shrimp, and filet mignon. Lunch is served Monday through Friday with dinner Monday through Saturday.

Noble's Grille. *Moderate/Expensive.* 380 Knollwood Street, just off I-40 Business (336-777-8477). Its architecture gives Noble's Grille an airy, California feel. Most seats allow a view of the open kitchen containing a wood-burning, open-flame grill. The food is served on colorful pottery dinnerware. Fried oysters with organic spinach salad and bacon vinaigrette is a popular offering. Different pizzas, calzones, and fish dishes are offered each day. The owner raises his own rabbits and grows many of the vegetables and herbs. A full bar is offered. Lunch and dinner are served Monday through Friday; dinner is served Monday through Saturday.

South by Southwest. *Moderate/Expensive*. 241 South Marshall Street (336-727-0800). South by Southwest offers creative southwestern food that picks up where routine Tex-Mex leaves off. Unusual appetizers such as green-chile corn fritters with pineapple-jalapeño salsa are featured. Try the enchiladas—made from blue corn—with smoked chicken. A full bar is offered. Dinner is served Monday through Saturday.

Lucky 32. *Moderate*. 109 South Stratford Road (336-777-0032). Lucky 32 has earned a reputation as one of Winston-Salem's most popular restaurants. The reason may be the extensive menu; you can get everything from burgers and gourmet pizzas to fresh seafood and pasta entrées, making this a nice choice for groups with a wide range of tastes. The wood-and-brass fixtures create an elegantly casual atmosphere. Open daily for lunch and dinner.

Bistro 900. *Moderate*. 900 South Marshall Street (336-721-1336). This restaurant serves Italian and American cuisine in a casual atmosphere. The bar area offers live jazz every Thursday through Saturday night. Dinner is served Wednesday through Saturday.

Leon's Cafe. *Moderate*. 924 South Marshall Street (336-725-9593). With advertising coming primarily by word of mouth, Leon's has always managed to draw a crowd. The menu, which changes daily, always includes beef, chicken, duck, and lamb dishes but leans most heavily on fish with unusual sauces. Beer and wine are offered. Dinner is served daily.

Royal Thai Restaurant. *Inexpensive/Moderate*. 514 South Stratford Road (336-777-1597). Royal Thai is one of the exceptions in a city that generally offers mediocre ethnic cuisine. The authentic Thai food is freshly prepared with classic ingredients like lemon grass, Thai basil, and Thai pepper. Dinner is served daily; lunch is served Sunday through Friday.

Village Tavern. *Inexpensive/Moderate*. 221 Reynolda Village (336-748-0221) and Hanes Mall Boulevard (336-760-8686). These restaurants have a relaxed atmosphere but are still upscale. The menu features sandwiches and salads in bountiful portions, as well as a few entrées. The Reynolda Village location is likely to be packed with students, since it is close to Wake Forest University. The Hanes Mall Boulevard location is larger and slightly more elegant. A full bar is offered. Lunch and dinner are served daily; brunch is served on Sunday.

West End Cafe. *Inexpensive/Moderate*. 926 West Fourth Street

(336-723-4774). You can see people from all strata of society at this cafe located in the artsy section of town. Customers in suits mingle with those with nose rings or baby strollers, and they're all here for the great food. Diners can mix and match sandwich ingredients to come up with their own creation or pick a tried-and-true favorite from the menu. If you're looking for something a little more substantial than sandwiches, entrées are offered, too, along with a limited wine and beer selection. Lunch and dinner are served Monday through Saturday.

Midtown Cafe and Dessertery. *Inexpensive/Moderate.* 151 South Stratford Road (336-724-9800). Whether you're simply looking for a late-night dessert or pancakes for breakfast (or lunch or dinner), this cafe is sure to fit the bill. Specialties include banana crunch pancakes, taco stew, and tarragon chicken salad. You absolutely can't go wrong with any of the desserts, among them chocolate hazelnut cake and five-flavor pound cake. Open daily for breakfast, lunch, and dinner.

Little Richard's Bar-B-Que. *Inexpensive.* 4885 Country Club Road (336-760-3457). For a taste of real North Carolina cuisine, try Little Richard's. Although there are three restaurants in the area that use the name "Little Richard's," this location is the original, and most authentic. The barbecue is prepared in the true Lexington tradition: pork shoulders are slow-roasted over wood coals, then chopped and served with a healthy dose of vinegar-based sauce. Don't miss the slaw or the hush puppies either. Checkered cloths adorn the tables and memorabilia decks the walls for a real down-home atmosphere.

The Horse's Mouth Coffeehouse. *Inexpensive.* 424 West Fourth Street (336-773-1311). This restaurant serves delicious sandwiches, salads, pastries, and desserts to go along with its wide variety of coffees and cappuccinos. Its downtown location makes it a favorite with business people and concert-goers at the nearby Stevens Center. Lunch is served Monday through Friday. Brunch is served on Sunday.

Greensboro ....

Greensboro's history has been an eventful one.

In 1781, some 27 years before the founding of the city, residents of the area participated in an important Revolutionary War battle just north of the present-day city limits.

During the Civil War, Greensboro served as a storehouse and railroad center for the Confederacy and was the governing seat for four days. The city was headquarters to an army of 50,000 and sheltered both civilian refugees and wounded soldiers. In April 1865, after Richmond fell into Union hands, President Jefferson Davis fled south and met General Joseph Johnston in Greensboro, where they discussed the eventual surrender to Union general William Sherman.

During World War II, Greensboro was again an important military center. Hundreds of thousands of soldiers were trained here for service overseas.

Despite the frequent presence of the military in its past, Greensboro is better known for the peaceful, accepting nature of its residents. Early settlers were Quakers, Germans, and Scots-Irish, all of whom were seeking religious and economic freedom. From the 1830s until after the Civil War, the area provided several stops on the Underground Railroad, which offered shelter and aid to escaping slaves. Shortly after the Emancipation Proclamation in 1863, a Quaker named Yardley Warner developed a new residential area in town, where he sold parcels of land to freedmen on very liberal terms.

Greensboro has long been noted for its early educational institutions for blacks and women, among them Bennett Seminary, now Bennett College; the Agricultural and Mechanical College for the Colored Race, now North Carolina A & T State University (N.C. A & T); and the Normal and Industrial School for White Girls, now the University of North Carolina at Greensboro (UNC-Greensboro).

Greensboro's tradition of tolerance undoubtedly contributed to the peaceful progress of the history-making sit-ins at the segregated lunch counter of its F. W. Woolworth store in 1960. The first sit-in included four black students from N.C. A & T, but it soon grew to include scores of protesters, among whom the young Jesse Jackson emerged as a leader.

Greensboro was founded in 1808, when county commissioners

purchased 42 acres in central Guilford County for a new county seat. The town was named Greensborough in honor of General Nathanael Greene, who led the colonial forces at the Battle of Guilford Courthouse. Greensboro grew quickly and has long since absorbed many of the small settlements that once surrounded it.

The city's economy, like its population, has been marked by diversity. Though textiles have dominated the town since Moses and Caesar Cone established their first mill in 1895, other industries have also been important. In 1912, Lunsford Richardson, a Greensboro pharmacist, developed Vick's VapoRub, a medication that became a household name during the influenza epidemic of 1918.

Greensboro's thriving business community created a large middle-class population that has historically been more transient than that of Winston-Salem. New residents, including the city's many college students and teachers, have brought with them ideas and customs that might seem alien in a less-cosmopolitan Southern city. Today, the town even has numerous bagel factories.

Greensboro has grown greatly in recent years. Several new buildings and a new streetscape have made the downtown section an enjoyable place to stroll, whether for business or pleasure. The 20-block historic section called Old Greensborough is a good place for antique shopping. New stores and restaurants seem to pop up almost every day. There's always something interesting to discover.

ACCESS:

The easternmost city of the Triad, Greensboro is located at the intersection of I-40 and I-85, which skirts the southeast section of town.

Piedmont Triad International Airport, served by eight airlines, is centrally located among Greensboro, High Point, and Winston-Salem. Many hotels offer free limousine service to and from the airport.

Amtrak makes late-night stops in Greensboro as it travels daily between New York City and New Orleans. The train station is located at 2603 Oakland Avenue; call 336-855-3382.

The Greyhound bus station is located at 501 West Lee Street; call 336-272-8950.

VISITOR INFORMATION:

Contact the Greensboro Area Convention and Visitors Bureau, 317 South Greene Street, Greensboro, N.C. 27401 (800-344-2282).

The *Greensboro News & Record*, the city's daily newspaper, publishes a comprehensive calendar in its "City Life" section every Thursday. You can also check the calendar in *Triad Style* and *ESP*, two free weekly tabloids.

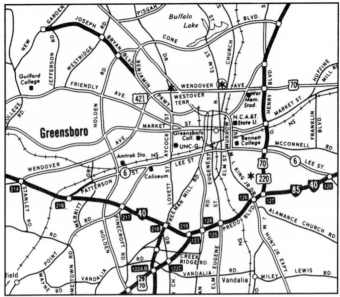

Courtesy of N.C. Department of Transportation

Attractions

Tours

The **Old Greensborough Preservation Society** offers a five-block self-guided walking tour of the historic district downtown. In addition to a close-up look at Old Greensborough's well-preserved late-19th-century architecture, the tour includes visits to some of the many antique shops in the area. Call 336-272-6617.

Historic Places

Guilford Courthouse National Military Park, six miles north of downtown off U.S. 220 on New Garden Road, was the site of an important Revolutionary War battle. On March 15, 1781, some 4,400 American troops, both veterans and raw recruits, met the 2,000 trained and well-equipped soldiers of Lord Charles Cornwallis.

Led by General Nathanael Greene, the American troops were unable to hold their ground and eventually withdrew to Virginia; even so, the Americans are generally considered to have outfought and outmaneuvered the British. A quarter of Cornwallis's forces were killed, and his losses during the encounter are said to have led to his surrender at Yorktown seven months later.

The battlefield is now a 220-acre park of rolling woods and fields, with 28 monuments and graves and a visitor center administered by the National Park Service. Dominant among the monuments is an equestrian statue of General Greene. One unusual statue honors Kerenhappuch Turner, a woman who rode on horseback from Maryland to care for her son, who had been wounded in the battle. This is thought to be one of the first monuments erected to a Revolutionary War heroine. Also on the site are the graves of William Hooper and John Penn, signers of the Declaration of Independence, and Colonel Joseph Winston, the Revolutionary War hero for whom the town of Winston (now Winston-Salem) was named.

The visitor center offers interesting displays of Revolutionary War uniforms, weapons, and other artifacts, as well as a film. It is open from 8:30 A.M. to 5 P.M. daily. Admission is free. Call 336-288-1776.

Adjacent to the Guilford Courthouse battlefield on New Garden Road is the city's **Tannenbaum Historic Park**, whose chief attraction is the restored Hoskins House (1781). This is thought to be the point from which the British started their attack; it is also said to have been a hospital for the British after the battle. The structure has remained on its original site; before restoration, it served as the den of a much larger modern house. Also on the 7½-acre grounds are a kitchen and barn. At the **Colonial Heritage Center**, visitors can learn about their cultural and ethnic heritage by seeing, touching, smelling, and even tasting the realities of 18th-century North Carolina. Through a five-by-10-foot diorama of the battle and living-history demonstrations, this heritage comes alive.

The park is open Monday through Friday from 8 A.M. to 5 P.M., Saturday from 9:30 A.M. to 5 P.M., and Sunday from 1 to 5 P.M. The Colonial Heritage Center is open Tuesday through Friday from 9 A.M. to 5 P.M., Saturday from 10 A.M. to 5 P.M., and Sunday from 1 to 5 P.M. Admission is free. Call for seasonal hours; the number is 336-545-5315.

Old Mill of Guilford, on N.C. 68 at Oak Ridge, five miles north of the airport, is a working mill that dates back to 1745. It was moved to its present location and enlarged in 1818. Cornwallis's troops took over the mill to grind meal for their use on their way to the Battle of Guilford Courthouse. Now sporting a jaunty red roof, this water-powered mill produces all manner of flour and even makes easy-to-prepare mixes. What could be better than a bag of grits to take home to a Yankee friend? The mill is open from 9 A.M. to 6 P.M. daily. Admission is free. Call 336-643-4783.

Blandwood Mansion, at 447 West Washington Street, is the former home of Governor John Motley Morehead. It is the oldest example of the Italian villa style of architecture in America. Originally a 1790s Federal-style farmhouse, the structure received an Italianate addition in 1844 by architect Alexander Jackson Davis. Many of the original furnishings are on view. In one wing is Governor Morehead's office, which features his desk and a library of old books. Behind Blandwood is a reproduction of the octagonal carriage house with the original cupola. The mansion is open Tuesday through Saturday from 11 A.M. to 2 P.M. and Sunday from 2 to 5 P.M. Admission is $5 for adults and $2 for children under 12. Call 336-272-5003.

Charlotte Hawkins Brown Memorial State Historic Site is located on U.S. 70 at Sedalia, some eight miles east of Greensboro on the campus of the former Palmer Memorial Institute, a prestigious preparatory school for African-Americans. Dr. Brown headed the school for 50 years. After it closed in 1971, its buildings fell into disrepair. The Carrie M. Stone Cottage, originally a residence for women faculty members, has been restored. It's now used as a visitor center and has exhibits and a short video on Dr. Brown's life and the history of the school. Dr. Brown's home, Canary Cottage, has also been restored and is partially furnished with her possessions. As other buildings are restored, the memorial's focus will broaden; it will become a center for the study of the educational contributions of African-Americans in North Carolina.

The site is open Monday through Saturday from 9 A.M. to 5 P.M. and Sunday from 1 to 5 P.M. in the summer; it is open Tuesday through Saturday from 10 A.M. to 4 P.M. and Sunday from 1 to 4 P.M. in the winter. Admission is free. Call 336-449-4846.

Museums/Science Centers

Greensboro Historical Museum, located at 130 Summit Avenue in a former church, has well-designed displays on the history of the city and the surrounding area. The exhibit on short-story writer O. Henry, who grew up in Greensboro as William Sydney Porter, includes photographs and letters, early editions of his books, and sketches he made when he worked in his uncle's drugstore on Elm Street; some of his relatives are buried in the graveyard just outside the museum's back door. The exhibit on First Lady Dolley Madison, also a Greensboro native, includes her snuffbox, a collection of fine china, and her French gowns. Among the other displays are room settings from historic area homes and a display of antique vehicles, including a Conestoga wagon and early automobiles. The

A reproduction of W. C. Porter's Drug Store is in the Greensboro Historical Museum
Courtesy of N.C. Travel Development

museum is open Tuesday through Saturday from 10 A.M. to 5 P.M. and Sunday from 2 to 5 P.M. Admission is free. Call 336-373-2043.

Weatherspoon Art Gallery's internationally known permanent collection comprises over 4,600 works of art, primarily by contemporary American artists. Most significant are the Cone Collection of prints by Henri Matisse, the Charles and Laura Dwan Collection of contemporary American art, and the Dillard Collection of over 400 unique works on paper acquired from the annual Art on Paper exhibition. Six galleries feature works from the collection, traveling exhibitions, and faculty and student work. Guided tours are offered monthly, and group tours are available by advance arrangement, both free of charge. Weatherspoon Art Gallery is located in the award-winning Anne and Benjamin Cone Building on the UNC-Greensboro campus at Spring Garden and Tate Streets. It is open Tuesday, Thursday, and Friday from 10 A.M. to 5 P.M., Wednesday from 10 A.M. to 8 P.M., and Saturday and Sunday from 1 to 5 P.M. Admission is free. Call 336-334-5770.

The Natural Science Center of Greensboro, located at 4301 Lawndale Drive, is a hands-on museum, zoo, and planetarium. It offers a dinosaur exhibit, a lemur gallery, an aquarium, a sea lab, a vertebrate lab, a herpetarium, and a gem and mineral gallery. The center is open Monday through Saturday from 9 A.M. to 5 P.M. and Sunday from 12:30 to 5 P.M. The zoo is open 10 A.M. to 4:30 P.M. Monday through Saturday and 12:30 to 4:30 P.M. on Sunday. There is an admission fee. Call 336-288-3769.

Mattye Reed African Heritage Center, on the campus of N.C. A & T east of downtown, features a collection of over 3,500 African art objects in the historic Dudley Building. Among the artifacts are masks, carved ivory, weapons, and handwoven kente cloths from Ghana. The collection of Nigerian bronze figures includes a four-foot leopard that was used to hold water for a hand-washing ritual. Also at the center are books on black history, paintings from African countries, and African-American artifacts. The center is open Monday through Friday from 9 A.M. to 3 P.M. and other times by appointment. Hours may vary, so it's best to call before visiting. Admission is free. Call 336-334-7874.

Cultural Offerings

The **University of North Carolina at Greensboro**, west of downtown, has strong music, art, and theater departments that offer numerous faculty and student performances throughout the year. In addition, the UNC-Greensboro Concert and Lecture Series is a great resource for touring musicians, theatrical performances, and lectures. Performances are held in the school's Aycock Auditorium on Tate Street. Call 336-334-5353.

The Greensboro Cultural Center at Festival Park, located at 200 North Davie Street, is an architectural showplace housing 25 visual- and performing-arts organizations, five art galleries, rehearsal halls, a sculpture garden, restaurants with outdoor seating, and an outdoor amphitheater. Galleries include the African-American Atelier (336-333-6885), dedicated to enhancing the exposure of African-American artists within the community; Green Hill Center for North Carolina Art (336-333-7460), which focuses on the contemporary visual arts of North Carolina; Greensboro Artists' League Gallery (336-333-7485), which promotes the visual artists of the Triad; Guilford Native American Art Gallery (336-273-6605), the first gallery in the Southeast to promote, exhibit, and sell traditional and contemporary Native American arts and crafts; and the Mattye Reed African Heritage Center Satellite Gallery (336-334-7108), which features traveling exhibits of the finest in African works. Each gallery has a shop with unique gifts in all price ranges.

The **Greensboro Symphony Orchestra** (GSO) performs a Masterworks Series of classical concerts, its Saturday concerts followed by Monday-night repeat performances. GSO performances are staged in War Memorial Auditorium, part of the Greensboro Coliseum complex. The symphony also performs a free concert each December; by accepting canned-food donations for admission, the symphony helps support families served by the Salvation Army. For ticket information, call 336-333-7490.

Greensboro Opera Company offers two major productions each fall, with guest artists singing the principal roles. Call 336-273-9472.

The Carolina Theatre, at 310 South Greene Street, is a lavishly decorated 1927 vaudeville theater that has been brought back to life. The Carolina sponsors travelogues, a popular series of classic films, and a wide variety of musical performances. In addition, the theater is frequently used for performances sponsored by other arts groups in the city. Call 336-333-2600.

The Piedmont Blues Preservation Society sponsors several concerts a year featuring blues in all its incarnations. The concerts are held in various locations. Many of the performers are North Carolinians whose music isn't well known and whose concerts are rare. The society also sponsors an all-day festival in May. Call 336-275-4944.

Recreation

Emerald Pointe Water Park, at 3910 South Holden Road, is the largest water park in the Carolinas. The Thunder Bay attraction is one of only four tsunami (giant wave) pools in the country. The park also features the new Runaway Raft Ride, where up to three people can ride a raft through thrilling water flumes. The children's area has a shipwreck replica for climbing and general swashbuckling. The over 30 aquatic attractions include water slides, waterfalls, and swimming pools. There are lockers, a picnic area, a restaurant, and a gift shop in the park. Emerald Pointe is open Monday through Thursday from 10 A.M. to 7 P.M. and Friday through Sunday from 10 A.M. to 8 P.M. on select weekends in May and September and daily from June 5 to August 24. All-day passes are $21 for adults, $15 for children under 45 inches, and $11 for seniors. Call 336-852-9721 or 800-555-5900 for additional information.

Bryan Park, six miles northeast of Greensboro off U.S. 29, is a city park on the southern shore of 1,500-acre Lake Townsend. The park includes two golf courses, four tennis courts, and facilities for picnicking, volleyball, soccer, and horseshoes. Fishing boats and small sailboats may be rented. Call 336-375-2222.

Jaycee and **Country Park** are adjacent facilities six miles north of downtown on U.S. 220. The parks offer two stocked fishing lakes, pedal and fishing boats, 10 picnic shelters with grills, three playgrounds, and fitness trails. It is also the site of the J. Spencer Love Tennis Center and the Carolina Cup Bicycle Road Race. The Natural Science Center of Greensboro is adjacent to the grounds. Call 336-373-2574 for the parks; call 336-288-3769 for the science center.

Seasonal Events

The Greater Greensboro Chrysler Classic Golf Tournament is the third-oldest tournament on the PGA tour. With a $2.2-million purse, coverage on network television, and the world's best professional golfers, it is one of the country's important tournaments. The GGCC is a fund-raiser for the Greensboro Jaycees, and its profits have been used in worthwhile projects all over the state. The tournament is held in mid-April. General admission is $18 a day; special package deals, which are much more expensive, include admission to parties, parking privileges, and other extras. Forest Oaks Country Club, the site of the tournament, is located at 4600 Forest Oaks Drive. Call 336-379-1570.

Sword of Peace, an outdoor drama by William Hardy, depicts the story of the Cane Creek Quakers during the Revolutionary War. Its climax is the Battle of Guilford Courthouse. The play runs from mid-June through mid-August at Snow Camp, about 25 miles southeast of Greensboro; call for directions. Tickets are $10 for adults, $8 for seniors, and $5 for children under 12. Group discounts are available. Call 336-376-6948.

Eastern Music Festival is a six-week series of concerts by full orchestras and chamber-music ensembles, as well as recitals by faculty and accomplished classical-music students. Concerts are held on the campus of Guilford College, located on the western edge of Greensboro, and at other locations in the area from mid-June to early August. Call 336-333-7450.

City Stage, a two-day street-fair extravaganza, is held on the first full weekend in October in downtown Greensboro. Local and nationally known musicians perform on several outdoor stages. Streets are lined with booths featuring crafts and international foods. A 10K run and a parade of bands kick off the festivities. A special area is devoted to activities for children, and there are beer gardens for adults. Call 336-333-7440.

Side Trips

See *Triad Side Trips*

Accommodations

Most of Greensboro's motels and hotels are clustered around I-85 and I-40. If you're staying awhile, you might want something closer to town.

Hilton Greensboro. *Expensive*. 304 North Greene Street (336-379-8000). On the exterior, the Hilton is a bland block of concrete. But inside, with its imposing central staircase and two-story brass columns, the hotel is among the most impressive in the Triad. This downtown facility has extensive meeting space and well-furnished rooms.

Marriott Hotel. *Expensive*. Piedmont Triad International Airport (336-852-6450). If it weren't for the low-flying aircraft, you might think you were at a country resort rather than next to an airport. The Marriott is surrounded by an abundance of space. Tennis courts, a volleyball court, and a small lake are on the grounds. The indoor-outdoor pool is quite large, and the glass-enclosed indoor section is pleasantly sunny.

Holiday Inn Four Seasons. *Expensive*. 3121 High Point Road (336-292-9161). Located next to Four Seasons Mall, this hotel offers shopping at several boutiques inside its convention center, as well in the mall. Its 1014 rooms on 27 floors make this the largest hotel in North Carolina.

Restaurants

Greensboro residents seem to have an insatiable appetite for eating out. New restaurants are constantly opening, yet there always seems to be a line on weekends. If you're on a tight schedule, it's best to eat early or find a restaurant that will take reservations.

Lo Spiedo Di Noble. *Expensive*. 1720 Battleground Avenue (336-333-9833). The third in a series of very popular restaurants by the Noble family, this establishment features a rotisserie grill and brick ovens which infuse the food with the flavors of hickory and oak. An extensive wine list complements the Tuscan and Mediterranean dishes, which have a French flair. Live jazz is offered Wednesday through Saturday. Dinner is served daily.

Paisley Pineapple. *Moderate/Expensive*. 345 South Elm Street (336-279-8488). This upscale eatery in Old Greensborough features everything from beef to game to fowl to seafood to pasta. Once dinner has settled, patrons can mosey upstairs to the sofa bar to enjoy a drink and live jazz. Dinner is served Tuesday through Saturday.

Southern Lights Bistro and Bar. *Moderate*. 105 North Smyres Place (336-379-9414). This casual cafe features chicken, pasta, and seafood dishes cooked to order. Entrées change daily, but a full sandwich and salad menu is always available. Beer and wine are offered. Lunch is served Monday through Friday and dinner nightly. Sunday brunch is also offered.

Spring Garden Brewing Company. *Moderate*. 714 Francis King Street, near Guilford College (336-299-3649). Baby back ribs, sandwiches, salads, pasta, and fish are all available here, along with a German-style lager beer brewed on the premises. Lunch and dinner are served daily. A late night menu is offered for the barroom area after the dining room closes.

Sunset Cafe. *Inexpensive/Moderate*. 4608 West Market Street (336-855-0349). The delicious entrées served here tend to have a Mediterranean touch, and the huge portions of simply prepared vegetables are better than you can imagine. The blackboard menu changes daily. Beer and wine are offered. Lunch is served Tuesday through Friday and dinner Tuesday through Sunday.

Stamey's Barbecue. *Inexpensive*. 2206 High Point Road (336-299-9888) and 2812 Battleground Avenue (336-288-9275). If you can't make it to the barbecue capital of Lexington, Stamey's is a good alternative. Both of its locations have large, busy dining rooms. The barbecue served at both restaurants is cooked in a building behind the High Point Road location, which fills the air in that part of town with a mouth-watering aroma. No alcohol is offered. Lunch and dinner are served Monday through Saturday.

High Point

There's a good chance the chair you're sitting in was made in High Point. The city has an astonishing 100 furniture-manufacturing plants, including 10 of the largest in the world and over 60 retail furniture stores. Are you wearing socks? High Point also has 14 major hosiery manufacturers that produce almost a million pairs of socks and hose a day.

A drive around downtown High Point leaves no question as to what the main business is here. The city's largest buildings house the furniture showrooms that are on display during the twice-a-year International Home Furnishings Market. In recent years, a growing number of furniture manufacturers have constructed their own buildings to house their showrooms, and others have renovated existing structures in the city. The architecture and window displays of these design-oriented facilities give High Point an unusual sophistication for a Southern factory town of 73,000 people.

The world's largest chest of drawers, at 508 North Hamilton Street, is a whimsical expression of High Point as the furniture capital of the world. Constructed in 1926 by the chamber of commerce, the 36-foot-high chest is actually the facade of the building that houses the High Point Jaycees. The neighboring town of Thomasville, also a furniture-manufacturing center, has an 18-foot cement replica of a Duncan Phyfe chair on its Main Street.

High Point was laid out in 1849, when the North Carolina & Midland Railroad was brought through the area. So determined were the surveyors to make the town exactly two miles long and two miles wide that they put the eastern boundary "through the doors of Jane Parson's house." The new city was the highest point on the railroad line and so received its name. When the Plank Road from Salem to Fayetteville was built in 1854, it also passed through High Point. That intersection of road and railroad secured the future of the town.

ACCESS:

High Point is southwest of Greensboro. It may be reached via I-85 Business or U.S. 311.

Piedmont Triad International Airport, served by eight airlines, is centrally located among High Point, Greensboro, and Winston-Salem. Some hotels offer free limousine service to and from the airport.

The Amtrak station is located at 100 West High Street; call 336-841-7245.

The Trailways bus station is located at 100 Lindsay Street; call 336-882-2000.

VISITOR INFORMATION: Contact the High Point Convention and Visitors Bureau, 300 South Main Street, P.O. Box 2273, High Point, N.C. 27261 (800-720-5255) or access its Web site at http:\\www. highpoint.org.

The city's daily newspaper, the *High Point Enterprise*, publishes an "Entertainment" section with listings of local cultural events.

Attractions

Tours

Market Square, at 305 West High Street, is a renovated chair factory that contains 100 contemporary showrooms. The 990,000-square-foot factory, built of red brick in 1901 and restored 78 years later, is listed on the National Register of Historic Places. Tours, available to groups of 15 or more, include visits to several showrooms and a look into many more. The complete tour lasts about 1½ hours but can be abbreviated on request. Reservations should be made two weeks in advance. No tours are offered during the April and October trade shows. Admission is charged. Call 336-889-4464.

Museums

At the **High Point Historical Museum**, located at 1859 East Lexington Avenue, visitors can see what it was like to live in the area in the recent past. Located on the grounds of the museum are the John Haley House (1786), a blacksmith shop, and a weaving house. The museum itself is undergoing renovations but is scheduled to reopen in the late fall of 1999. It will feature exhibits on the town's history and culture and offer traveling exhibits on loan from other institutions. Among the museum's permanent displays are military artifacts, a fascinating collection of early telephones, and a growing collection of early furniture made in High Point. The grounds of the museum will remain open during the renovation. They may be visited Tuesday through Saturday from 10 A.M. to 4 P.M. and Sunday from 1 to 4 P.M. Admission is free. Call 336-885-6859.

The Springfield Museum of Old Domestic Life, at 555 East Springfield Road, is located in the Springfield Friends Meeting House (1857), a plain brick structure with large windows and simple Greek Revival details. The building has been used as a museum since the late 1920s, when the current meeting house was built next door. The collection includes spinning wheels, farm tools, kitchen utensils, clothing, planks from the old Plank Road, and a few old tombstones from the lovely churchyard that surrounds the building. The museum is open by appointment only. Admission is free. Call 336-882-3054.

The Furniture Discovery Center, at 101 West Green Drive, is the nation's only museum devoted to the design and manufacture of home furnishings. The center offers a self-guided tour detailing the making of furniture in a simulated modern-day furniture factory. The tour guides visitors through the entire process, from the cutting of rough lumber to the production and packaging of the finished product. The case goods area tracks a Queen Anne highboy, while the upholstery area highlights the making of a love seat. Visitors are encouraged to try out an air-powered

The Furniture Discovery Center
Photograph by William Russ
Courtesy of N.C. Travel and Tourism Division

screwdriver, sprayer, or stapler. There's a talking red oak tree, a fabric-designing computer, a collection of famous Serta miniature bedrooms, and the Furniture Hall of Fame, featuring the pioneers of the furniture industry. The center is open Monday through Saturday from 10 A.M. to 5 P.M. and Sunday from 1 to 5 P.M. from April through October. It is closed Mondays from November through March. Admission is $5 for adults, $4 for seniors and students over 15, and $2 for children six to 15; children under six are free. Call 336-887-3876.

The **Angela Peterson Doll and Miniature Museum**, adjacent to The Furniture Discovery Center, is the South's largest doll museum. It contains some 2,500 pieces; its 1,700 dolls range from 15th-century pieces to modern-day collectibles. Special exhibits include a six-foot miniature mobile home, three couples of dressed "fleas" seen under a magnifying glass, over 120 Shirley Temple dolls, a dollhouse village with 15 houses, and a crèche scene with 50 dolls dating from before the 20th century. The museum is open the same hours as The Furniture Discovery Center but stops giving tours half an hour before closing time. Admission is $3.50 for adults, $3 for seniors and students over 15, $2 for children six to 15, and $1 for children three to five; children under three are free. Call 336-885-3655.

Cultural Offerings

North Carolina Shakespeare Festival (NCSF) presents three or four plays in late summer and early fall, two of them by William Shakespeare. Elaborate costumes and sets and top-notch professional actors and directors make this the most consistently satisfying theater in the Triad. In addition to the six-week season in August and September at the High Point Theatre, located at 220 East Commerce Avenue, NCSF takes a Shakespeare play on the road for a four-week tour through the Southeast each fall. Annual productions of *A Christmas Carol* are performed in High Point, Winston-Salem, and Greensboro in December. For information, call 336-841-2273; for tickets, call 336-887-3001.

The Bernice Bienenstock Furniture Library, at 1009 North Main Street, is a research library with 7,000 volumes on furniture, design, and the decorative arts. In addition, some 300 different books on furniture are offered for sale. The library is open to the public Monday through Friday from 9 A.M. to noon and from 1 to 5 P.M. Admission is free. Call 336-883-4011.

Theatre Art Galleries encompasses three exhibition areas in the High Point Theatre and Exhibition Center, at 220 East Commerce Avenue. Two galleries offer individual and group shows and competitions featuring southeastern artists; the third gallery's exhibitions are sponsored by the High Point Fine Arts Guild. Theatre Art Galleries are open Monday through Friday from noon to 5 P.M. and weekends by appointment. Admission is free. Call 336-887-3415.

Recreation

Oak Hollow Park, at 3431 North Centennial Street, has an 18-hole golf course with a practice range and a clubhouse. The park also has 10 outdoor tennis courts, four indoor tennis courts, and 90 paved campsites with full hookups. Small sailboats can be rented for use on Oak Hollow Lake, which has launching ramps for motorboats and is the site of the Oak Hollow Championship Boat Races, a two-day event held in late July. Call 336-883-3486 for general information or 336-883-3494 for the marina.

City Lake Park, on Greensboro Road, is a 969-acre site featuring a large swimming pool, a water slide, a playground, and picnic facilities. Boats can be rented for fishing in the 341-acre lake. Call 336-883-3498.

Piedmont Environmental Center, on Penny Road, maintains over 10 miles of hiking trails and offers educational programs, a nature preserve, a nature store, animal exhibits, and a bicycling trail. Kids and adults alike will be impressed by Mapscape, the 35-by-70 foot map exhibit on North Carolina and its surrounding states; the exhibit features the major rivers, mountain ranges, and even the Atlantic Ocean for visitors to touch and explore. Open daily. Admission is free. Call 336-883-8531.

Seasonal Events

Each April and October, the population of High Point nearly doubles when 2,300 furniture companies show their latest lines at the **International Home Furnishings Market**, the largest furniture exhibition in the world. For nine days, buyers wander through 7 million square feet of showrooms in 150 separate buildings. Competition is fierce, and attention-getting tactics are often spectacular. Admission is strictly limited to furniture dealers and interior decorators. In fact, if you don't have credentials to get into the market, it's a good idea to stay away from the area while it's going on. Hotels throughout the Triad are booked, and even if you can get a table at a restaurant, service from the overtaxed staff is likely to be slow.

North Carolina Furnishings Festival is held in early August in the downtown area to celebrate High Point's furnishings heritage. The festivities include appearances by noted furniture designers, auctions, a jazz brunch, and artisan demonstrations. Several stages set up around the area feature live entertainment, and kids of all ages will be amused by the attractions, which range from a children's play area to beer gardens. Call 336-956-1888.

Day in the Park is held on a Saturday in September at City Lake Park. Music, food, crafts, and children's activities are included. Call 336-889-2787.

Side Trips

See *Triad Side Trips*

Accommodations

Radisson Hotel High Point. *Expensive.* 135 South Main Street (336-889-8888). Located next to the largest of the furniture showroom buildings, the Radisson is High Point's finest and most fashionably furnished lodging. The hotel offers 252 rooms and suites, an indoor pool, an exercise room, a bar, and a restaurant. Complimentary transportation to and from the airport is available.

Howard Johnson Inn. *Moderate.* 2000 Brentwood Street at I-85 Business (336-886-4141). This HoJo offers 104 rooms and a pool, but not all those ice-cream flavors. The restaurant, unaffiliated with the chain, is called The Studio, in reference to a commercial film studio adjacent to the motel.

Super 8 Motel. *Inexpensive.* 400 South Main Street (336-882-4103). This motel can't be beat for the price and the location near furniture shopping centers. It offers 43 rooms.

Restaurants

The expense accounts of furniture buyers have done wonders for the culinary offerings of High Point. The town has more than its share of very nice places to eat.

Restaurant J. Basul Noble. *Expensive.* 114 South Main Street (336-889-3354). A converted storefront, Noble's has the relaxed atmosphere of a European bistro; its back patio is particularly appealing. The menu changes often, but you can be sure to find grilled seafood, chicken, and veal, always topped with a sauce of the chef's choosing. Pheasant, quail, and sweetbreads—uncommon offerings in this area—also turn up on the menu from time to time. A full bar is offered. Dinner is served Monday through Saturday.

Atrium Cafe. *Moderate.* 430 South Main Street (336-889-9934). Located in the Atrium Furniture Mall, which houses 36 retail and discount furniture galleries, this cafe features salads, pasta, beef, chicken, soups, special sauces, and sandwiches. Lunch and dinner are served Monday through Saturday.

Square One Restaurant at Market Square. *Moderate.* 305 West High Street (336-889-4464). This airy restaurant is located in a furniture showroom complex. The menu changes daily but always includes salads, soups, sandwiches, and hot entrées. A full bar is offered. Reservations are suggested. Lunch is served Monday through Friday.

Triad Side Trips

North Carolina Zoological Park is truly one of the state's treasures. It is located on 1,448 acres in Randolph County near Asheboro, about 25 miles south of Greensboro on U.S. 220. Animals live in environments modeled as closely as possible to their native habitats. Natural barriers or Plexiglas shields have replaced the bars and fences found at traditional zoos, and for the most part, the creatures have plenty of room to roam.

The R. J. Reynolds Aviary is a glass dome which houses 2,000 tropical plants and 150 bird specimens from Asia, Africa, South America, and the Pacific. The vegetation is so lush that seeing the birds sometimes takes effort, but that's what makes a visit exciting. The best way to proceed is to find a bench and let the birds come to you. Don't leave until you've spotted the little white-fronted bee-eater, which is red, orange, yellow, blue, green, and brown, in that order.

At the nine-story-high African Pavilion, 200 animal specimens live both indoors and out. The pavilion is divided into areas representing the major environments of the African continent; in one part, for instance, are the plants and animals of the African swamps, including the spot-necked otter, the white-faced whistling duck, and dwarf crocodiles. Other areas represent rain forests, savannas, grasslands, and semideserts. From the pavilion's overlook areas, visitors get a panoramic view of the 40 acres of plain outside, where herds of 12 species of antelope and four species of birds live together in harmony. Who needs a safari?

The best thing about the zoo is that it's only in the beginning stages. The North American section was launched in September 1993 with the opening of the Sonora Desert exhibit, and with the exception of one or two exhibits still to come, it is now completed. The North American section houses one of the most popular attractions at the zoo, the polar bear exhibit. Visitors can view the polar bears' rocky habitat from above or watch them frolicking underneath the water from a glassed viewing area. Yet to come are sections on Asia, Europe, South America, Australia, and the "World of Seas."

The zoo has plenty of amenities to assure a comfortable visit. You can take a tram instead of walking the full two miles of paths. Menu selections at the restaurants are limited, so you might want to pack a picnic. Follow the signs from U.S. 220 south of Asheboro. Admission is $8 for adults and $5 for senior citizens and children ages two to 12. The zoo is open from 9 A.M. to 5 P.M. from April to late October and closes at 4 P.M. from November through March. The zoo is open every day of the year except Christmas. Call 800-488-0444.

Within a five-mile radius of the town of **Seagrove**, located about 30 miles south of Greensboro on U.S. 220, are more than 20 potteries that carry on a 200-year tradition in the area. Some of the potteries are run by fifth-generation North Carolina craftspeople, but a growing number of area potters are newcomers, many of them trained at a local technical college. Their wares are generally quite inexpensive by current standards and range from functional pieces to elaborately decorated art pottery.

Most of the potteries are located off N.C. 705 between Seagrove and Robbins and are well marked with signs. Ask at any pottery for a map of the locale. All are closed on Sunday, and if you plan to go on Saturday, it's best to arrive in the morning, since the shelf stock is often quickly depleted at the best-known places.

Friends of North Carolina Pottery Center, located at 235 East Main Street in downtown Seagrove, features a gallery and a museum detailing the history of this local art form. Plan on making this your first stop in Seagrove, as you can learn about the different types of pottery available and also design a map of the area shops and galleries to suite your pottery tastes. Call 336-873-7887 for more information.

The **Richard Petty Museum** honors the winningest racecar driver in history. Petty, who lives near Randleman, about 15 miles south of Greensboro on U.S. 220B, retired after 200 wins in his 35-year career. Four of his racecars are on display at the museum, as are two antique cars and a show car. The museum houses numerous trophies, plaques, and awards, along with photographs of Petty shaking hands with United States presidents, winning races, and crashing. A wide-screen television shows old racing films and interviews with the racer. And of course, souvenirs are offered for sale.

The museum is on the grounds of Petty's garage complex, which is opened for public tours several times a year. Take U.S. 220 South from Greensboro and turn left at the Level Cross exit. Admission is $3 for adults and $1.50 for children ages six to 18; children under six are free. The museum is open Monday through Saturday from 9 A.M. to 5 P.M. Call 336-495-1143.

Burlington, a textile-manufacturing town 15 miles east of Greensboro on I-85/I-40, has earned a national reputation for its outlet stores. Some of the outlets are still at the factories, where you can hear the rumble of looms and be certain of getting the best deal possible. Many are in unattractive concrete-block buildings, but of course, money the outlets save on rent means money you save on shoes, luggage, housewares, sweaters, children's clothes, and other items. Most of Burlington's outlets are located within sight of I-85/I-40. Some travel agencies and bus companies offer special "outlet tours" of the area, but most visitors can manage with one of the several booklets or maps that are widely available. A number of fast-food restaurants in the area cater to people who don't want to miss a minute in the stores.

Alamance Battleground State Historic Site, six miles southwest of Burlington on N.C. 62, is the site of the battle that ended the War of the Regulation, which has been called a rehearsal for the American Revolution. On May 16, 1771, the 1,000-man army of Royal Governor William Tryon defeated 2,000 "Regulators," a group whose protest actions against corruption in the colonial government had grown more and more radical.

The battlefield includes a visitor center with exhibits and an audio-visual presentation. Also on the grounds is the John Allen House, a restored and authentically furnished log home built around 1782. The site is open Monday through Saturday from 9 A.M. to 5 P.M. and Sunday from 1 to 5 P.M. from April to October; it is open Tuesday through Saturday from 10 A.M. to 4 P.M. and Sunday from 1 to 4 P.M. from November 1 to March 31. Admission is free. Call 336-227-4785.

A few miles north of Alamance Battleground on N.C. 62 is the **Alamance County Historical Museum**, located in the birthplace of Edwin Michael Holt, one of the state's earliest and most successful textile manufacturers. The house has been restored and furnished to its appearance in the late 19th century, when Holt's son, Lynn Banks Holt, lived here. The museum is open Tuesday through Friday from 9 A.M. to 5 P.M., Saturday from 10:30 A.M. to 5 P.M., and Sunday from 1 to 5 P.M. Admission is free. Call 336-226-8254.

Hanging Rock State Park, about 30 miles north of Winston-Salem on N.C. 89, is the largest state park in the Piedmont. The

6,000-acre park is best known for its three summits with sheer rockfaces: Hanging Rock, Cooks Wall, and Moores Knob. The latter two are popular with rock climbers; climbing is not allowed on Hanging Rock. The park has campsites for tents and trailers but no hookups. The shower houses have hot water. The six cabins, which have a bath and kitchen, are especially popular; reservations are accepted in writing beginning January 1, and the cabins are usually booked for the year by the end of March. A 12-acre lake offers swimming at a beach with a lifeguard. Rowboats can be rented, and the lake is stocked for fishing. Two picnic areas with several hundred tables are offered, as are 20 miles of hiking trails. A recent addition to the park has extended it to the Dan River, where an access for canoeists is offered; the Dan is usually a pleasant, easy canoe trip. Call 336-593-8480.

Pilot Mountain, 25 miles northwest of Winston-Salem on U.S. 52, is the area's most distinctive geologic attraction. Rising dramatically out of the Piedmont landscape is a 1,500-foot mountain topped by a dome of exposed quartzite. Accessible by automobile, the mountain's summit offers a panoramic view. The mountain is part of 3,768-acre Pilot Mountain State Park, which maintains hiking trails, bridle paths, picnic areas, and campsites with hot showers but no hookups. Call 336-325-2355.

Legend has it that **Boone's Cave State Park**, on the Yadkin River 35 miles south of Winston-Salem via N.C. 150, is the site of a cabin built by Daniel Boone, who also supposedly hid from Indians in the cave on park property. Boone is known to have lived near North Wilkesboro, 50 miles northwest of the park.

The 110-acre park has a picnic area. From the parking area, a steep walk takes visitors down to the river and the cave. Open to the public, the cave is three to five feet high and extends about 80 feet into the hillside. The park is open on weekends only from 8 A.M. to 6 P.M. December through March and daily during the same hours from March through June. Call 704-982-4402.

Lexington, 20 miles south of Winston-Salem on U.S. 52, has earned a national reputation for its barbecue. That's saying something in a state where barbecue is not just a food but nearly a way of life. Lexington's renown is based partly on quantity. There are presently 14 barbecue restaurants in the town, which has a population of less than 17,000. It's often said that more barbecue is served here per square mile than any other place in the country. Quality is another factor. Lexington barbecue is made only of pork shoulder, which makes it particularly lean, and it's cooked slowly over a wood fire, usually in a small building right behind the restaurant. Generally, the sauce is a vinegar and tomato concoction, in contrast to the eastern North Carolina sauce, which usually has no tomato. Even within Lexington, the sauce varies from one restaurant to the next, and that's where personal taste comes in. Guests are served slaw moistened with barbecue sauce, rather than mayonnaise.

Here's a beginner's guide to ordering Lexington-style: if you ask for "a barbecue," you'll get it chopped with slaw on a hamburger bun. Variations include sliced and coarse-chopped meat. You can get a "tray" or a "plate" if you want more than a sandwich. Hush puppies are de rigueur, as is syrupy-sweet iced tea. Beer is the perfect beverage to have with barbecue, of course, but you'll have to get a takeout order to arrange that combination. Prices vary from one restaurant to the next, but that's because the portions do, too.

Lexington holds an annual Barbecue Festival, usually on the last Saturday in October. Some 10,000 pounds of barbecued pork shoulder are served in tents on the town square. The festival kicks off with the Parade of Pigs and ends with a concert in the civic center. In between come crafts, cheerleader competitions, and as much barbecue as you care to stand in line for.

Lazy 5 Ranch, located on NC 150 nine miles from I-77 and 14 miles from I-85, is a full day of fun for the family. The ranch features a petting zoo with animals such as llamas and camels. On a wagon ride through the countryside, the kids can feed and water buffalo and giraffes. A playground is available to those a little less daring. The ranch is open Monday through Saturday from 9 A.M. until one hour before sunset and Sunday from 1 P.M. until one hour before sunset. Admission is $7.50 for adults and $4.50 for seniors and children ages two to 11. There is an additional fee for the wagon ride. Special group rates are available. Call 704-663-5100.

Charlotte

by Edgar and Patricia Cheatham

With its massive industrial parks, bustling international airport, major-league cultural offerings, and major-league basketball and football, Charlotte has certainly come a long way from the time George Washington once called it "a trifling place." In fact, the city and the surrounding Piedmont form one of the nation's fastest-growing areas. George could never have predicted Charlotte would now be the largest metropolis in the Carolinas.

Thirty years ago, the city boasted lovely residential neighborhoods, tree-lined streets, spacious parks, and fine department stores—but only the hint of a skyline. The downtown business district—called "Uptown"—featured attractive buildings representing architectural styles dating back to the post–Civil War period. But toward the end of the 1960s, there was a palpable feeling that the city was overflowing with unleashed energy and ready for a quantum leap into the New South.

And that's exactly what has happened. Today, those old buildings are dwarfed by a futuristic skyline of soaring contemporary towers, including one of the tallest buildings in the Southeast. The skyline is a symbol of the Queen City's hope and promise.

Charlotte has a population of 471,000, with over 6 million people within a 100-mile radius. The second-largest financial center in the United States, it has attracted an impressive roster of major corporations and industries, some locating Uptown and others in planned industrial and executive centers throughout the city. Local officials are working to attract still more investment and jobs to what is considered one of the nation's up-and-coming midsize cities.

The sound of jackhammers is surely music to the ears of the city's developers, but Charlotte's cultural life is keeping pace with its physical growth. In addition to first-rate musical and theatrical productions, Charlotte hosts other cultural highlights that are well worth a detour: the historic Mint Museum of Art; Discovery Place, a terrific hands-on science and technology museum; Spirit Square, which features performances and exhibits; the North Carolina Blumenthal Performing Arts Center, with its impressive performance facilities; and the Museum of the New South, which offers history exhibits that not only inform but entertain as well.

The city's art isn't all behind closed doors. Charlotte boasts several interesting public art displays: a Martin Luther King, Jr., statue in Marshall Park; Arnaldo Pomodoro's *Il Grande Disco*, a circular metal sculpture at NationsBank Plaza; and a golden-hued, spiral-like work called *Hovering* by sculptor Charles Perry, located on the grounds of IBM in University Research Park.

One of the more interesting tickets in town is surely NBA basketball

Skyline of Charlotte
Courtesy of N.C. Travel and Tourism Division

and the Charlotte Hornets. The team first took to the court in November 1988 at the splendid, equally new, 25,000-seat, state-of-the-art Charlotte Coliseum. Teal-and-purple hornets, the team's logo, peer out of the strangest places all over town. Local stores can outfit the whole family in Hornets gear—T-shirts, sweatshirts, shorts, visors, binoculars, towels, gym bags, pennants and decals.

Charlotte's latest professional sports franchise is the Carolina Panthers of the NFL. The Panthers began play in the fall of 1995 and quickly achieved respect in the league after earning a spot in the 1996 playoffs. The Panthers play their home games in Ericsson Stadium, a state-of-the-art facility in downtown Charlotte.

George Shinn, the self-made millionaire, owns the Hornets and the city's class AAA baseball team, the Charlotte Knights. A farm team of the Florida Marlins, the team plays in a new 15,000-seat stadium known as Knights Castle.

Charlotte/Douglas International Airport has become an increasingly important terminus. USAirways has a major hub here, offering direct service to Nassau, Frankfurt, and London, in addition to a heavy domestic schedule.

As the city has flourished, many attractive residential suburbs have developed, especially in the affluent southeastern areas. The prosperity has also led to the dynamic revitalization of historic Dilworth and Uptown's Fourth Ward, a charming neighborhood that contains houses of Victorian and various 20th-century styles. Shopping centers and retail outlets have proliferated.

All of this full-speed-ahead development has brought about infuriating rush-hour traffic crunches. New thoroughfares have been constructed and existing ones widened, and others are in the planning stages.

In 1992, Charlotte's Uptown received a dramatic new symbol with the unveiling of the NationsBank Corporate Center at Trade and Tryon Streets, designed by internationally renowned architect Cesar Pelli. The complex includes the North Carolina Blumenthal Performing Arts Center and Founders Hall, a plaza offering 85,000 square feet of shops and restaurants surrounding an atrium with a glass ceiling looming 135 feet overhead. The centerpiece of the complex is a 60-story postmodern high-rise, the tallest building between Philadelphia and Miami. It is expected to dominate Charlotte's skyline through the 1990s.

The complex was an ambitious undertaking, but Charlotte has a history of bold, defiant acts. The pioneer settlers who founded Mecklenburg County in 1762 were sturdy, independent farmers, artisans, and merchants of Scots-Irish, English, German, Swiss, and French Huguenot descent. Charlotte was established three years later on a 360-acre site purchased by George A. Selwyn for the princely sum of "ninety pounds, lawful money." The town was named for Queen Charlotte, devoted wife of Britain's King George III. The county was named for her German homeland, Mecklenburg-Strelitz.

Despite its royal name, Charlotte was quick to support the colonial resistance. In fact, county leaders reportedly signed the Mecklenburg Declaration of Independence, then hastily commissioned a brave equestrian to deliver the document to the Continental Congress in Philadelphia. The declaration was apparently ignored by the Continental Congress and was later destroyed by fire in the early 1800s. Historians have been debating the validity of this proclamation of colonial independence ever since.

In an effort to extinguish the revolutionary forces in Mecklenburg County, Lord Charles Cornwallis and his redcoats occupied Charlotte for a brief period in 1780, despite rigorous resistance by local patriots. Irked by the Mecklenburgers' constant skirmishes, Cornwallis finally declared their domain "a damned hornet's nest" and retreated after less than a month. This epithet was subsequently recorded on the city seal—expletive deleted, of course. Two centuries later, it inspired the name for the city's NBA team, the Hornets.

In 1799, Charlotte again buzzed with activity when word of a farmer's discovery of gold near town triggered the nation's first gold rush. A branch of the United States Mint was subsequently opened in Charlotte. It produced gold coinage from 1837 to 1865.

In the 1850s, the coming of the railroads stimulated trade and manufacturing. During the Civil War, a large Confederate navy yard protected by troop installations enabled the city to survive the conflict unscathed.

Charlotte enjoyed a smooth economic recovery during the postwar years and began a dramatic transition from a little-known backwater town to a major urban presence. Its first suburbs, Dilworth and Myers Park, were established, and a sophisticated trolley system linked them to other parts of the city. North Carolina's earliest skyscraper, the Independence Building (c. 1905), soared a staggering 12 stories above Uptown.

In 1905, tobacco tycoon James Buchanan "Buck" Duke purchased a hydroelectric plant on the Catawba River. It became the nucleus for the vast Duke Energy system, fueling the Carolinas' burgeoning factories and textile mills. His house, called the Duke Mansion, is located in Myers Park.

The South's first fully licensed radio broadcasting station took to Charlotte's airwaves in 1922. An airline passenger terminal was built during the 1930s and served as a World War II training center.

By 1945, Charlotte's population topped 100,000. The decades that followed were exciting times, as the Queen City of the Carolinas entered the surging mainstream of New South progress.

Now, it sits comfortably in the forefront.

ACCESS:

I-77 and I-85 intersect in Charlotte, linking the city and its "Metrolina" hinterland with South Carolina, Georgia, Florida, New England, and the Great Lakes regions. The city has been relatively slow in developing links to major highways and beltline loops. The Billy Graham Parkway links I-77 and I-85 and is the major access route to Charlotte/Douglas International Airport. The Brookshire Freeway links the eastern part of the city and the central business district to the interstates.

Charlotte/Douglas International Airport offers more than 500 scheduled flights daily. Charlotte is a primary hub of USAirways. Five other major airlines and one regional carrier serve the airport.

Rail service is via the Amtrak Crescent, which runs daily north and south between New York City and New Orleans. Call 800-USA-RAIL for information and reservations. The local Amtrak station is at 1914 North Tryon Street; call 704-376-4416.

The Greyhound bus terminal is located at 601 West Trade Street; call 800-231-2222.

VISITOR INFORMATION:

Contact the Charlotte Convention and Visitors Bureau, 122 East Stonewall Street, Charlotte, N.C. 28202 (704-334-2282 or 800-231-4636).

Info Charlotte, located at 330 South Tryon Street, is a new facility with information on things to see and do in Charlotte. Call 704-331-2700 or 800-231-4636.

The *Charlotte Observer*'s "Extra" section each Friday includes extensive listings of current events and activities. So does the free tabloid newspaper *Creative Loafing*, widely distributed throughout town.

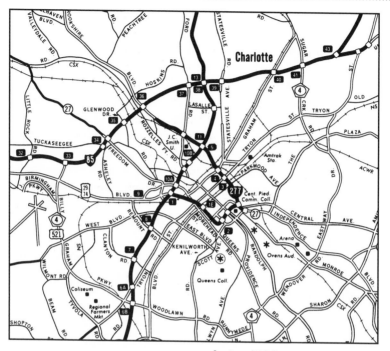

Courtesy of N.C. Department of Transportation

Attractions

Tours

A Walk Thru Historic Fourth Ward, a text-and-map folder, is a good companion for a self-guided visit to this storied Uptown neighborhood. The homes reflect various styles of architecture, from Victorian to contemporary. The complete tour includes 74 structures. An abbreviated version features those designated as Local Historic Property or listed on the National Register of Historic Places. A folder is available at Info Charlotte at 330 South Tryon Street (704-331-2700).

University of North Carolina at Charlotte covers over 200 acres about two miles from the city limits on N.C. 49 near its intersection with U.S. 29. You can pick up a free self-directed tour-guide brochure with map at the information booth just inside the entrance off N.C. 49 (University City Boulevard).

The hub of a new minicity that has sprouted northeast of town, UNC-Charlotte has an enrollment of more than 12,000 students. The campus's wooded, slightly rolling landscape is dotted with streams and ponds. Park in the visitors' lot near the entrance, the most convenient spot if you want to explore UNC-Charlotte.

UNC-Charlotte's rapid development has come in part from adjacent University Research Park, which includes such companies as IBM, the *Wall Street Journal*, AT&T, and a number of other technological research firms. Most of its architecture borders on futuristic, and visitors are welcome to drive around the grounds. Nearby, too, is the new Oasis Shrine Temple, which manages to merge fine contemporary architecture with a certain ancient Egyptian ambiance. Although it's not open to nonmembers, you're welcome to photograph the exterior.

In toto, this area makes for one of the Southeast's handsomest and fastest-growing satellite cities. It should help put to rest Charlotte's longstanding "got to keep up with Atlanta" complex.

Historic Places

Hezekiah Alexander Homesite, at 3500 Shamrock Drive, is the oldest dwelling in Mecklenburg County. The clean lines of this 2½-story stone house, completed in 1774, are reminiscent of the architecture found in Maryland and Pennsylvania, where Alexander lived before coming to the Piedmont. A blacksmith-turned-farmer, Alexander accumulated considerable wealth and influence in his new home. He was even one of the signers of the Mecklenburg Declaration of Independence on May 20, 1775. His "Rock House," listed on the National Register of Historic Places, has been faithfully restored and furnished with 18th-century antiques. Costumed staff members give tours of the house, barn, and springhouse.

The Charlotte Museum of History, located on the Hezekiah Alexander Homesite property, houses artifacts of local and regional history in permanent and changing exhibits, plus a research library and archives. The Mobcap Shoppe, named for the caps worn by 18th-century women, offers handmade crafts, books, and colonial toys for sale.

Admission to the homesite is $4 for adults, $2 for children, and $3 for senior citizens. Admission to the grounds is free. Tours of the homesite are offered at 1:15 and 3:15 during the week. The homesite is open Tuesday through Friday from 10 A.M. to 5 P.M. and Saturday and Sunday from 2 to 5 P.M. For information, call 704-568-1774.

Latta Place (5225 Sample Road, Huntersville, off I-77 North) is a distinctive two-story frame house in the Georgian-Federal transitional style. It was built as a plantation house around 1800 by James Latta, a traveling merchant whose wealth and good taste are evident in the fine carvings on the interior woodwork. After touring the main house, you can visit the slave house and the smokehouse. To make the history come alive, a kitchen garden and cotton field are planted each year and animals are kept in the barn. Admission is $4 for adults, $3 for students and seniors, and $2 for children six to 12. The site is open Tuesday through Sunday. Tours are given at 1 P.M., 2 P.M., and 3 P.M. during the week, on the hour from 11 A.M. to 4 P.M. on Saturday, and at 2 P.M., 3 P.M., and 4 P.M. on Sunday.

While you're there, plan to stay and enjoy **Latta Plantation Nature Preserve**. The 1,100-acre preserve overlooks beautiful Mountain Island Lake, formed by impounded waters of the Catawba River. The park features an equestrian center and seven miles of bridle paths, 16 miles of hiking trails, a fishing pier, and two ramps for launching canoes. The visitor center displays specimens of native wildlife and has an attractive gift shop.

The Carolina Raptor Center, Inc. located at the park, is devoted to the care of injured or orphaned birds of prey. On weekends, hawks, owls, eagles, vultures, and falcons are on display; volunteers will tell you how the birds are treated and then released to the wild.

Admission to Latta Plantation Nature Preserve is free, but admission to the Raptor Center costs $4 per adult and $2 per child over six. Latta Plantation Park is open daily from 7 A.M. to dark and closes only on Christmas. The Raptor Center is open Tuesday through Saturday from 10 A.M. to 5 P.M. and Sunday from 12 to 5 P.M. For information about Latta Plantation Nature Preserve, call 704-875-1391. For information about the Carolina Raptor Center, call 704-875-6521.

The James K. Polk Memorial, on U.S. 521 half a mile south of Pineville and about 10 miles south of Uptown Charlotte, commemorates the birthplace and boyhood home of the 11th president of the United States. The two-story log house in which Polk was born in 1795 has been re-created, as have the farm buildings. The visitor center of this State Historic Site has an orientation film and exhibits highlighting the accomplishments of Polk's administration, including tariff reduction, the Oregon Compromise, and the Mexican War, which resulted in the annexation of Texas, California, and New

Mexico. During his election campaign, Polk made the unusual promise that he'd remain in office for only one term—and he did. There are picnic tables for those who wish to have lunch on the grounds. Admission is free. The site is open Monday through Saturday from 9 A.M. to 5 P.M. and Sunday from 1 to 5 P.M. from April to October. The hours are Tuesday through Saturday from 10 A.M. to 4 P.M. and Sunday from 1 to 4 P.M. from November through March.

Museums and Galleries

The Mint Museum, at 2730 Randolph Road, is the only art museum in the country in a former branch of the United States Mint. Designed in the Federal style by the celebrated Philadelphia architect William Strickland, it was built in 1835, when the Carolina Piedmont was the primary source of gold in the United States. Its numismatic function ended in 1913, and in 1933 it was threatened with demolition. The historic building was moved from its original in-town location and carefully reconstructed in the Eastover residential neighborhood. It reopened in 1936 with great fanfare as the state's first art museum. Special wings have been added to house the Delhom Gallery of Decorative Arts, which exhibits historic ceramics, and the Dalton Gallery, which has an excellent permanent collection of American paintings (including works by Thomas Eakins and Andrew Wyeth). Permanent displays include American and European paintings, pre-Columbian and African art, and historic artifacts of the Carolinas (among them gold coins minted in Charlotte). At intervals, the museum displays special exhibitions. Admission is $6 for adults and $4 for senior citizens and students over 12; children 12 and under are free. No admission is charged on Tuesday evenings from 5 to 10 P.M. or on the second Sunday of each month. The museum is open Tuesday from 10 A.M. to 10 P.M., Wednesday through Saturday from 10 A.M. to 5 P.M., and Sunday from 12 to 5 P.M. For information, call 704-337-2000.

Discovery Place, at 301 North Tryon Street in Uptown Charlotte, is a hands-on science and technology museum popular with adults and children. In the three-story glass-and-brick building, you can find exotic birds and cascading waterfalls in a tropical rain forest, an aquarium with 21 tanks and a touch pool, a transparent mannequin showing the inner workings of the human body, and OMNIMAX

Theater, which houses the largest planetarium in the United States. Other highlights include magnetic demonstrations that will make your hair stand on end, chemical wizardry at the Piedmont Natural Gas Hearth, and an opportunity to learn about personal computers. There are four different options to choose from. Admission to one of the four options is $6.50 for ages 13 to 59, $5 for ages six to 12 and senior citizens, and $2.75 for ages three to five; each additional activity is $2. Note that OMNIMAX Theater tickets are sold separately at the museum. Discovery Place is open Monday through Saturday from 9 A.M. to 6 P.M. and Sunday from 1 to 6 P.M. from June through August. For information, call 704-372-6261 or 800-935-0553.

The Nature Museum, at 1658 Sterling Road adjacent to Freedom Park, has been specially designed for small children as a center for learning and fun. Here, little knee-grabbers can punch, poke, press, and pull various hands-on displays, observe live animals and habitat exhibits, hike nature trails, and take field trips. Admission is $2, but children under three accompanied by an adult are free. The museum is open Monday through Friday from 9 A.M. to 5 P.M., Saturday from 10 A.M. to 5 P.M., and Sunday from 1 to 5 P.M. For information, call 704-372-6261 or 800-935-0553.

The Museum of the New South, at 324 North College Street, is a hands-on interactive look at the history of North Carolina's premier city and the surrounding Piedmont area. Exhibits depict the era from 1897 to the present and reflect the humble beginnings of the area and the process through which Charlotte became one of the most influential cities in the South. The collection of oral histories is a must-hear for those wanting to get a real sense of the people and their struggles during this time. Kids will enjoy the tactile displays, such as an antique corn sheller, a tenant-farm still life, and peach and cotton seedlings that teach the story behind their growth processes. The Museum of the New South is open Tuesday through Saturday from 11 A.M. to 5 P.M. Admission is $2 for adults, $1 for students, seniors, and educators, and $5 for the entire family. Call 704-333-1887.

Gardens

The UNC-Charlotte Botanical Gardens, near the entrance off N.C. 49 (University City Boulevard), consists of three separate sections. The **Van Landingham Glen** is especially delightful in late

April and early May. That's when thousands of hybrid rhododendron plants burst into a frenzy of white, pink, red, and purple blossoms. At other times, native rhododendron, azaleas, and wildflowers are in bloom. You can stroll among hickories, oaks, poplars, and maples and even discover a rustic 120-year-old reconstructed log cabin. Adjacent is the **Susie Harwood Garden**. A year-round treat for plant lovers, it displays exotic and ornamental plants from around the world in a setting complete with gazebo, arched bridges, and a moon gate. March through May, it's vibrant with spring bulbs and early-flowering shrubs. Summer-flowering crape myrtles bloom in the moon garden, and come autumn, the hardwoods glow gold, amber, and crimson. Across the way, northeast of the campus's handsome landmark—the soaring, contemporary Belk Carillon Tower—the **McMillan Greenhouse** includes an outstanding collection of orchids and plants representing the world's diverse climates. Here, too, is the UNC-Charlotte herbarium, a national resource collection with more than 18,000 preserved specimens of native and introduced flora. The outdoor gardens are open during daylight hours seven days a week. The greenhouse is open Monday through Saturday from 10 A.M. to 3 P.M. There is no admission fee. Call 704-547-2364.

Wing Haven Gardens and Bird Sanctuary, at 248 Ridgewood Avenue, is a serene retreat in a pleasant residential neighborhood. Created by Edwin and Elizabeth Clarkson on a three-acre site at their home, it has been a labor of devotion since 1927. There are several varieties of azaleas, camellias, and rhododendron that are attractive throughout the year but especially flamboyant in spring. The retreat attracts a great number of birds; bird watchers have sighted over 130 species so far. The late Dorothy Doughty's sculpture of myrtle warblers for the Royal Worcester Doughty Bird Series of high-quality porcelain artworks was done at Wing Haven. Admission is free. The sanctuary is open Tuesday from 3 to 5 P.M., Wednesday from 10 A.M. to 12 P.M., and Sunday from 2 to 5 P.M. For information, call 704-331-0664.

Cultural Offerings

Two arts complexes in or near the central business district contribute to the city's cultural blossoming.

Spirit Square Center for the Arts, at 345 North College Street, is one of the "people places" that's breathing new life into Uptown Charlotte. It's the city's premier arts center. Located in the former

First Baptist Church, a distinctive turn-of-the-century Byzantine structure, it includes four galleries and three theaters and offers hundreds of arts workshops and classes. Admission to the galleries is free; classes and show prices vary. The center is open Tuesday through Saturday from 11 A.M. to 6 P.M.; hours are extended on the nights of shows. For information, call 704-348-5750.

The Afro-American Cultural Center, at 401 North Myers Street, is a multidisciplinary arts organization presenting art exhibits, concerts, dance and theatrical productions, and humanities and children's programs in the beautifully renovated Little Rock A.M.E. Zion Church. The center is open Tuesday through Saturday from 10 A.M. to 6 P.M. and Sunday from 1 to 5 P.M. Admission to the galleries is free, but donations are accepted. There are admission charges for the individual shows. For information, call 704-374-1565.

Charlotte Repertory Theatre, founded as Actors Contemporary Ensemble (ACE) in 1976, is a resident professional theater presenting contemporary works from drama to farce. For information, call 704-333-8587.

The Charlotte Symphony Orchestra, headquartered in the Charlotte Plaza on College Street, is a full-service, professional, regional orchestra that is over 60 members strong. It presents classical, pops, and contemporary music in at least 40 concerts throughout the year. The box office is open from 10 A.M. to 5 P.M. Monday through Friday during the winter and from 10 A.M. to 4 P.M. Monday through Thursday and from 10 A.M. to 1 P.M. Friday during the summer. For information, call 704-332-0468.

Children's Theatre of Charlotte, at 1017 East Morehead Street, offers classic and contemporary works cast with a unique combination of professional adults and young people. It also offers an education program and special mime, music, and puppetry events for children. For information, call 704-333-8983.

Opera Carolina, headquartered at 345 North College Street, Suite 409, has been in existence for over 50 years. It presents four productions each year with up-and-coming guest artists in lead roles. The company's touring program offers opera to schools and community groups. For information, call 704-332-7177.

Theatre Charlotte, at 501 Queens Road, has been Charlotte's community theater since 1927. In recent years, performances have ranged beyond standard little-theater fare to include contemporary works. For information, call 704-376-3777.

Recreation

Although commerce long ago succeeded agriculture as the Charlotte area's major economic source, the Mecklenburg County Park and Recreation Department has managed to preserve impressive rural segments in its 14,000 acres of parks and 17 recreational centers. The department administers over 100 parks, six greenways, four golf courses, four historic sites, and a model-airplane flying field.

McDowell Park and Nature Preserve, one of the county's largest parks and one of its three nature preserves, is a 1,000-acre enclave on Lake Wylie off N.C. 49 South. It offers camping, hiking, fishing, picnicking, boat ramps, guided nature hikes, and paddleboat and canoe rentals. Eight miles of trails wind through the nature preserve, and its nature center has an exhibit hall with touchable displays. You can sign up for workshops here on all types of nature topics. From I-77, take the Westinghouse Boulevard exit and turn right. At the second light, turn left onto N.C. 49. Drive five miles south to the park's entrance, on the right. The vehicle entry fee is $3 for county residents and $5 for nonresidents. For information, call 704-588-5224.

Lake Norman, a vast 32,500-acre "inland sea," was formed when Cowan's Ford Dam blocked the Catawba River in 1963 and created the largest body of fresh water in North Carolina. Shared by Mecklenburg, Catawba, Iredell, and Lincoln Counties, it's a Duke Energy lake; its waters power the generators at Cowan's Ford Dam and cool the streams that drive the turbines of Marshall Steam Station and McGuire Nuclear Station. Marinas, family campgrounds, picnic sites, and fishing areas abound at this water recreation mecca. From Charlotte, there's easy access via N.C. 16, I-77, and N.C. 73 (which skirts the southern rim of the lake and runs past Cowan's Ford Dam and McGuire Nuclear Station). You can buy supplies, groceries, and snacks and rent or store boats at sites indicated on the free Lake Norman brochure and map, available from the Corporate Communications Department, Duke Energy, P.O. Box 33189, Charlotte, N.C. 28242.

There are several public 18-hole golf courses in Charlotte and the surrounding area. For a listing, contact the Charlotte Convention and Visitors Bureau at 704-334-2282 or 800-231-4636.

Seasonal Events

Carolinas' Carrousel Parade, one of the Carolinas' largest and most lavish Christmas parades, winds through the heart of Uptown Charlotte on Thanksgiving Day. For information, call 704-372-9411.

Festival in the Park, Charlotte's oldest and largest festival, lures visitors from throughout the Southeast to Freedom Park. The festival runs from the Thursday of the third full week in September through the following Sunday. It's a merry mélange of arts, crafts, performing artists, clowns, games, food, and music. For information, call 704-338-1060.

NASCAR racing was, is, and ever shall be king in Charlotte, where hundreds of thousands of fervent fans trek to nationally renowned events at the Charlotte Motor Speedway. Top annual events include the Memorial Day weekend Coca-Cola 600, the Mello Yello 500, and All Pro Auto Parts 300. For a full schedule and ticket information, call 704-455-3200.

The Southern Christmas Show ushers in the holiday season during 11 days in mid-November at the Charlotte Merchandise Mart, at 2500 East Independence Boulevard. It includes cooking clinics, a food pavilion, decorated Christmas rooms, crafts demonstrations, gifts, dollhouses, antique toys, and, of course, jolly old St. Nick himself. For information, call 704-376-6594.

The Southern Spring Show draws thousands of visitors from throughout the nation and abroad to the Charlotte Merchandise Mart for nine days in late February and early March. The show offers a vast array of landscaped gardens, interiors decorated by professional designers, horticultural displays, crafts, and travel exhibits. For information, call 704-376-6594.

Side Trips

The **Reed Gold Mine** is the first documented gold mine in the United States. One Sunday morning in 1799, Conrad Reed, the young son of a German immigrant farmer, found a large yellow rock in Little Meadow Creek on the family property. The family thought it made a nice doorstop. Three years later, a jeweler in Fayetteville identified the 17-pound stone as a gold nugget. He bought it for the previously agreed-upon but scandalous price of $3.50—about one-thousandth of its actual value.

Farming wasn't nearly so interesting to Reed after that. He and his family began searching for gold in nearby creek beds. By 1803, Reed had formed a partnership with three local men who mined the streams. They turned up a spectacular 28-pound nugget, a find that launched the nation's first gold rush. Fortune seekers swarmed into the area, combing the streams for "color." Big investors came, too, especially after 1825, when panning in streams gave way to under-ground operations at various sites in the Piedmont. They brought with them skilled miners and technicians, many from Cornwall in England.

The value of gold recovered in North Carolina was estimated at more than $1 million dollars a year until 1848, when it was eclipsed by the mad rush to California. In 1837, the first branch of the United States Mint opened in Charlotte for coining gold in denominations of $5, $2.50, and $1. After the Civil War, mining efforts diminished. Today they have all but disappeared.

The Reed Gold Mine is a State Historic Site; its visitor center features a 20-minute orientation film and displays of mining tech-niques and machinery, historic photographs, and stunning examples of the decorative and industrial uses of our most romantic metal. You can get a look at a restored section of an underground mine shaft on the conducted tours. Outdoor exhibits include an old stamp mill and troughs where you can try your luck at gold panning during the summer. You can take a picnic lunch to eat on the grounds and walk the nature trails after your visit.

To get there, take N.C. 24/27 about 30 miles east of Charlotte. Shortly after the junction with U.S. 601, watch for the mine sign and follow the rural road to the left. Admission is free, but it costs $2 per pan to search for gold. The mine is open Monday through Saturday from 9 A.M. to 5 P.M. and Sunday from 1 to 5 P.M. from April through October; it is also open Tuesday through Saturday from 10 A.M. to 4 P.M. and Sunday from 1 to 4 P.M. from November through March. For information, call 704-786-8337.

Charlotte Motor Speedway, 16 miles northeast of Uptown on U.S. 29, hosts some of the richest and most important racing events in the National Association for Stock Car Auto Racing (NASCAR) circuit. The speedway draws as many as 160,000 fans in a day to watch their favorite drivers varoom around the course. The famous 1½-mile super speedway, home of the Coca-Cola 600, now offers tours which include a movie on the speedway's history, a ride around the track, and special exhibits. Tours leave on the hour Monday through Saturday from 9 A.M. to 4 P.M. and Sunday from 1 to 4 P.M. (No tours are offered during race weeks.) Admission is $4 per person; children under three are admitted free.

Regarded by many as America's premier NASCAR facility, Charlotte Motor Speedway is giving auto racing some prestige and social prominence without losing the loyalty of the everyday folk who have sustained the races for so many years. Condominiums built above the massive grandstand overlook the first turn on the track, offering residents and their guests comfortable havens for watching the automotive spectacles.

Even more sophisticated is the Speedway Club, an exclusive nest in an ultramodern office tower from which the views are ultragrand. The lavish interior was designed by Carleton Varney, noted for such achievements as the Greenbrier resort in West Virginia. Club membership is limited to a "select group of winners," but the club can be admired from the outside by those who lack qualifying credentials.

For information about the speedway, call 704-455-3200.

Cannon Village occupies the center of town at Kannapolis, 26 miles northeast of Charlotte via I-85. Kannapolis was established as a

Charlotte Motor Speedway
Photograph by William Russ
Courtesy of N.C. Travel and Tourism Division

Cannon Mills company town in 1887 by industrialist Charles Cannon. The community quickly became a leading textile manufacturing center, specializing in towels, blankets, and linens. When Cannon Mills was bought by the Fieldcrest Corporation, the new owner restored Cannon Village and turned it into a merchandising center.

Today the village, with its blend of colonial and early-20th-century buildings set off by brick sidewalks, mature trees, and streetlights, has become a magnet for shoppers. It offers a wide variety of merchandise in more than 40 boutiques, specialty stores, and factory outlets of leading manufacturers—most prominently the Cannon Bed and Bath Outlet, where you can still buy towels by the pound. There are also restaurants where you can regroup and recharge before returning to serious shopping. Admission to the village is free, but bring money.

In the Cannon Visitor Center, you can see the history of Cannon Mills' production and merchandising, plus displays of textile manufacturing. The visitor center is open Monday through Saturday from 9 A.M. to 5 P.M. and Sunday from 1 to 6 P.M. For information, call 704-938-3200.

Paramount's Carowinds, 10 miles south of Charlotte via I-77, lies astride the border of the Carolinas. The 100-plus-acre theme park appeals mightily to children who know they're children, adults who think they're children, and anyone in between who has yet to make up their mind. Areas are organized around aspects of life and culture in the Carolinas—all feature food, amusements, and entertainment. Among the rides are sternwheeler cruises, flume and mine-train ventures, the Rip Tide Reef water section, and Vortex—a roller coaster you ride standing up. You can take younger or tamer friends to meet Yogi Bear and Fred Flintstone in Animation Station. Smurf Island has a playground, a fantasy village, and other delights for the tiniest tots. Among the other options are Blue Ridge Junction, which celebrates the traditions of the southern Appalachians; County Fair, which showcases a 1923-vintage carousel with hand-carved wooden horses; and Old World Market Place, where you can enjoy foods from places abroad.

After Paramount purchased the park, it added two innovative racing-simulator theaters based on the film, *Days of Thunder*. It also introduced Paramount on Ice, an ice-skating extravaganza saluting the company's movie and TV productions. The most recent addition is Wayne's World, an entire section of the park dedicated to the popular movie.

Characters from *Star Trek* also join the Smurfs and Hanna-Barbera favorites in the park. On weekends and holidays during the summer months, headline rock and country entertainers perform at the Paladium amphitheater.

To make visits easier for families, there are first-aid and infant-care stations, a free pet kennel, fast-food services, and a campground. Wheelchairs are available free at the guest-relations office near the entrance.

The park is open daily from 10 A.M. to 8 P.M. It remains open until 9 P.M. on Sundays and 10 P.M. on Saturdays in the summer. Admission changes annually. For information, call 704-588-2606 or 800-888-4FUN.

Waxhaw, a small, quaint town about 13 miles south of Charlotte on N.C. 16, may have the largest number of antique shops per capita in the nation. With its carefully preserved turn-of-the-century architecture, Waxhaw is a delightful spot for ambling and browsing for that special bargain in the various shops scattered about town. Shop owners set their own pace and don't always adhere to strict opening and closing times. And no matter the weather the last weekend of February, big crowds attend the Waxhaw Woman's Club's antiques show in the American Legion Hut.

The **Schiele Museum of Natural History** is located at 1500 East Garrison Boulevard in Gastonia, approximately 20 miles west of Charlotte at the New Hope exit off I-85. Opened in 1961, the Schiele is devoted to interpreting the wonders of the natural world. It has well-designed displays and more than 10,000 items in its collection, and ranks as the most frequently visited museum in North Carolina. You'll see lifelike dioramas depicting animal habitats and vivid exhibits on forestry, geology, archaeology, and astronomy. Some of the best interpretive educational programs in the South are presented here for all grade levels, with concentration on earth and space sciences. A nature trail leads along the shore of Slick Rock Branch through a wilderness of Piedmont flora and fauna. Workshops, field trips, special events, research facilities, and planetarium shows round out the museum's multifaceted offerings. Admission to the museum is free, but the planetarium shows cost $2.50 per adult and $1 for senior citizens. The museum is open Monday through Saturday from 9 A.M. to 5 P.M. and Sunday from 1 to 5 P.M. Planetarium shows run on Saturday at 1 P.M., 2 P.M., and 3 P.M. and Sunday at 2 P.M. and 3 P.M. For information, call 704-866-6900.

After a visit to the museum, you might consider a picnic lunch at **Crowders Mountain State Park**. Six miles west of Gastonia on U.S. 321, it's a 3,122-acre wooded tract in the Kings Mountain area, the site of a major Revolutionary War battle. (The actual battlefield is preserved at Kings Mountain National Military Park, just over the line in South Carolina.) Notable for its abundant bird life—more than 90 species have been spotted here—the park offers wilderness camping, pond fishing, hiking, rock climbing, and picnicking. For information, call 704-853-5375.

Morrow Mountain State Park, located seven miles east of Albemarle and 42 miles east of Charlotte off N. C. 740, preserves a scenic 4,693-acre segment of the ancient Uwharrie Mountains, which are older than the Appalachians. There's good fishing for catfish and white bass in the Pee Dee River, along with boating and boat rentals on Lake Tillery. The park has a modern swimming pool, a bathhouse, and hiking and horseback-riding trails. Park rangers conduct year-round nature programs. You can also visit Kron House, a reconstructed residence of an early area physician. Tent and trailer campsites and several family vacation cabins are available by reservation only. For information, contact the Superintendent, Morrow Mountain State Park, 49104 Morrow Mountain Road, Albemarle, N.C. 28001 (704-982-4402).

Uwharrie National Forest, seven miles east of Albemarle on N.C. 24/27, is a 50,000-acre forest which ranges through parts of three counties. Appealingly rustic and scenic, it offers campgrounds, boat ramps, and fitness and nature trails. Most are located near and around 8,000-acre Badin Lake in Troy. For serious hikers, there's the 20-mile Uwharrie Trail. For information, drop by the ranger station two miles east of Troy on N.C. 27 or call 910-576-6391.

Town Creek Indian Mound State Historic Site, five miles southeast of Mount Gilead on an unmarked road between N.C. 731 and N.C. 73, is the restored and reconstructed cultural and religious center of a 16th-century group related to the Creek Indians. They farmed bottomlands of the Little River and selected this nearby site as their ceremonial center. A palisade surrounds the grounds, and there's a restored temple atop a man-made earthen mound. The visitor center features interpretive exhibits and a film and slide show of the reconstructed ceremonial center. Picnic facilities are on the grounds. The site is open Monday through Saturday from 9 A.M. to 5 P.M. and Sunday from 1 to 5 P.M. from April through October. It is open Tuesday through Saturday from 10 A.M. to 4 P.M. and Sunday from 1 to 4 P.M. from November through March. Admission is free. For information, call 910-439-6802.

The lovely historic city of **Salisbury**, 42 miles northeast of Charlotte via I-85, was an important frontier town founded in 1753. Pioneers including Daniel Boone outfitted themselves here before pushing westward. This is also where Andrew Jackson came to study law. During the Revolutionary War, Salisbury was headquarters in turn for British general Cornwallis and American general Nathanael Greene, hero of the Battle of Guilford Courthouse (see *Greensboro: Historic Places*). The city had one of the Confederacy's largest prison camps during the Civil War. About 5,000 Union soldiers are buried in a national cemetery on its site.

Salisbury is also the home of Cheerwine, a soft drink with a taste somewhere between Dr. Pepper and Cherry Coke. Cheerwine has acquired a marginal cult following in Piedmont North Carolina. Since it's not widely distributed elsewhere, devotees have been known to carry cases of it with them if they move outside the area.

A 23-block section in the town of 23,000 is a National Historic District, preserving homes, offices, and much of the downtown area. You can pick up a self-guided tour map in room 206 of the Historic Salisbury Foundation Headquarters, on the corner of Innes and Main Streets. The headquarters is open from Monday through Friday from 9 A.M. to 5 P.M. Many historic buildings are private residences or offices; one that is open to visitors is the **Rowan Museum**, located at 202 North Main Street in the 1819 Judge James Martin House. It has Federal-era furnishings, Civil War artifacts, and local-history displays. The grounds include a 19th-century garden. There is an admission fee. The museum is open Thursday through Sunday from 2 to 5 P.M. Call 704-633-5946.

If you are looking for accommodations in Salisbury, try the **Rowan Oak House**. Located in the historic district at 208 South Fulton Street, this is a small bed-and-breakfast inn with four individually decorated rooms that include such niceties as a double Jacuzzi in one room and a green marble bath for two in another. The 1902 Queen Anne mansion has intricately carved woodwork, stained and leaded glass, and seven mantels. You can enjoy complimentary beverages on the porch, in the garden, or in the sunroom and have a gourmet breakfast in your room or the dining room. For information, call 704-633-2086 or 800-786-0437.

The **North Carolina Transportation Museum/Historic Spencer Shops**, are located in the small community of Spencer, about two miles north of Salisbury via I-85. The Southern Railway established a primary staging area and repair facility here. Although the shops have long since closed, their significance is being preserved through restoration. The massive buildings are used for displays of transportation artifacts ranging from a prehistoric Indian canoe to a vast variety of railroad rolling stock. Development of this State Historic Site is ongoing as the collection grows. A 45-minute train tour operates seasonally. Admission to the museum is free; the train ride costs $5 for adults and $4 for children and senior citizens. The shops are open Monday through Saturday from 9 A.M. to 5 P.M. and Sunday from 1 to 5 P.M. from April through October; they are open Tuesday through Saturday from 10 A.M. to 4 P.M. and Sunday from 1 to 4 P.M. from November to March. For information, call 704-636-2889.

Accommodations

There seems to be no end in sight to Charlotte's hotel boom of recent years. The pricier Uptown, South Park Mall, and University Place hostelries are popular with meeting and convention groups. On weekends, many of these offer very attractive bargains. The economy chains are well represented, especially in the airport area and along the I-77 and I-85 corridors.

Park Hotel. *Expensive/Deluxe*. 2200 Rexford Road (704-364-8220). In tone and ambiance, this elegant 193-room hotel opposite upscale South Park Mall is reminiscent of the grandeur of a European hotel. Oriental ceramics, porcelains, and artwork adorn the lobby area. The rooms are tastefully furnished in 18th-century style. The amenities include a concierge, an outdoor pool, and a health club with a Jacuzzi and a steam room.

Adam's Mark Hotel. *Expensive/Deluxe*. 555 South McDowell Street (704-372-4100). This 613-unit hotel overlooking Marshall Park has established a reputation for the quality of its services and amenities. The city's largest lodging, the hotel has oversized, stylishly decorated guest rooms with striking city views. It also offers extensive meeting space, two heated pools, an exercise room, and a jogging track.

The Dunhill Hotel. *Expensive/Deluxe*. 237 North Tryon Street

(704-332-4141). Uptown's movers and shakers have displayed a feverish glee in imploding vintage structures to make way for yet another glass or bronze tower. A notable exception is the Dunhill, a 1929 hostelry that has been transformed into an elegant European-style hotel. Its deluxe rooms, replete with well-stocked refrigerators, are handsomely decorated with traditional furniture and hand-sewn draperies. A staff chauffeur will whisk guests to appointments in the hotel's Rolls Royce.

Hilton at University Place. *Expensive/Deluxe*. 8629 J. M. Keynes Drive (704-547-7444). One of the city's newest luxury hotels, this 12-story, 243-unit lakeside postmodern structure near I-85 and Harris Boulevard is the showpiece of handsome University Place. Within half an hour of a wake-up call, each guest receives complimentary coffee, juice, and daily newspaper.

The Hilton Charlotte and Towers. *Expensive/Deluxe*. 222 East Third Street (704-377-6664). This 407-room hotel also houses the Uptown YMCA, which guests may use. The rooms have refreshment centers and two telephones. Valet parking and an airport shuttle are available.

Radisson Plaza Hotel. *Expensive/Deluxe*. NationsBank Plaza, Trade and Tryon Streets (704-377-0400). This sleek, 15-story tower was a bit startling when it made its debut as Charlotte's first Uptown luxury hotel. The rooms have contemporary decor, and concierge service is offered on the Plaza Club floor. Other amenities include a sauna and steam and exercise rooms. Complimentary parking and airport transportation are also available.

Charlotte Marriott City Center. *Expensive*. 100 West Trade Street (704-333-9000). The Marriott Corporation has emerged as a major presence in the Charlotte area, and this tower in the heart of Uptown was its initial entry. The front-desk staff is especially friendly and efficient—a trademark of this first-rate system. The attractive rooms are furnished with 18th-century reproductions, and an executive floor offers concierge services and other perks. The hotel also offers one of the city's largest ballrooms, a heated indoor pool, an exercise room, valet parking, and airport transportation.

Residence Inn by Marriott Charlotte-North. *Expensive*. 8503 U.S. 29 (704-547-1122). Marriott acquired the all-suite Residence Inn chain in 1987, and this Charlotte property was the first in the nation to hoist the "Residence Inn by Marriott" sign. Near UNC-Charlotte and University Research Park, it offers two-bedroom suites and one-bedroom studios with a separate living-room area. All have contemporary furnishings. Amenities include a free daily newspaper, continental breakfast, a hospitality hour in the spacious lobby, a swimming pool, and a whirlpool. You can rent a VCR (there's a Blockbuster Video conveniently located around the corner) and even purchase frozen foods for microwaving in your unit.

Holiday Inn Woodlawn. *Moderate.* 212 Woodlawn Road (704-525-8350). Before major hotel chains discovered Charlotte, this lodging with its huge satellite dish was the primary destination for groups and business travelers who wanted a location near the airport. Today it's just as popular with family vacationers beating a retreat from the interstates. Amenities include a pool and complimentary airport transportation.

Hampton Inn Executive Park. *Inexpensive/Moderate.* 440 Griffith Road (704-525-0747). Affiliated with the economy arm of Holiday Inn's parent company, this contemporary inn has cheerful, spacious rooms and is an excellent buy for business travelers and family vacationers. It has a pool, an exercise room, nonsmoking rooms, free continental breakfast, and a hospitality suite for small meetings.

La Quinta Inn. *Inexpensive/Moderate.* 7900 Nations Ford Road (704-522-7110). With its Spanish-style ambiance and squeaky-clean accommodations, this San Antonio–based chain has spread its reputation eastward. Its rooms are attractively furnished in a contemporary decor and have work areas and oversized beds. Amenities include a pool, nonsmoking rooms, free copies of *Newsweek*, and morning coffee.

Econo Lodge. *Inexpensive.* 1415 Tom Hunter Road (704-597-0470). This fast-growing budget chain, based in Charlotte, plans major expansion in North Carolina. It offers predictably clean, comfortable, no-frills accommodations.

Inns and Bed-and-Breakfast Guest Houses

The Morehead. *Expensive/Deluxe.* 1122 East Morehead Street (704-376-3357). This 1917 residence near the central business district, patterned after an 18th-century Pennsylvania farmhouse, was transformed into a "country inn" in 1984. The rooms have phones and TVs, and one offers a refrigerator and a coffee maker. The Morehead also offers meeting areas and swimming and exercise privileges at the nearby YMCA, as well as an extended continental breakfast.

The Homeplace Bed-and-Breakfast. *Expensive.* 5901 Sardis Road (704-365-1936). Set on a large, tree-shaded lot in an attractive residential district, this cream-colored 1902 Victorian home makes you want to move right in. When you walk onto its wraparound porch and step into its foyer with a 10-foot beaded ceiling and a handcrafted staircase, you'll become even more captivated. The two guest rooms are decorated with quilts and family antiques, and the two-room suite features a sitting room with a television. A full breakfast is served in the dining room, and complimentary beverages are offered in the evenings. No small children are accepted.

Restaurants

Some of Charlotte's best dining rooms are admittedly still found in hotels, but in recent years the city has witnessed an influx of top-quality restaurants. Many cater to sophisticated tastes—indeed, it's easier to find baked Brie and sushi than boiled collard greens and cornbread.

McNinch House Restaurant. *Expensive.* 511 North Church Street (704-332-6159). This establishment is unique in that you can't just walk in off the street to dine. It is open only for those who make advance reservations, but Charlotteans think it's worth the extra effort. McNinch House is a historic Victorian manor, and the reservations-only requirement makes you feel like a guest invited for dinner. There is a set menu of six courses, but the staff will try to accommodate personal tastes.

La Bibliothèque. *Expensive.* 1901 Roxborough Road (704-365-5000). French and American cuisine are the specialties of this restaurant honored three years in a row with a Four Diamond rating from AAA. You can expect to see international delicacies such as escargot and chateaubriand on the menu alongside such American classics as a tuna salad sandwich (served, of course, with more flair than what your mom packed you for lunch every day). During the summer months, the restaurant expands onto a deck and takes on the atmosphere of a European cafe. An extensive wine list is available.

Reservations are suggested. Lunch is served Monday through Friday; dinner is available Monday through Saturday.

The LampLighter Restaurant. *Moderate/Expensive.* 1065 East Morehead Street (704-372-5343). Housed in a Mediterranean-style house built in 1925, this restaurant has earned several awards, including the Distinguished Restaurants of North America Award. The interior sports high-quality birch paneling and Doric columns. The award-winning cuisine includes veal, beef, duck, chicken, and seafood. Dinner is served nightly.

Cino Grille. *Moderate/Expensive.* 6401 Morrison Boulevard (704-365-8226). This upscale eatery features a menu that's long on authenticity and short on the watered–down American version we typically think of as southwestern food. The desserts are amazing—the pumpkin crème brûlée with ginger whipped cream is sure to please even the biggest sweet tooth. Live jazz is featured on Friday and Saturday nights and during brunch. No checks are accepted. Brunch, lunch, and dinner are served daily.

Bistro 100. *Moderate/Expensive.* 100 North Tryon Street (704-344-0515). This upscale bistro is located in Founders Hall of the NationsBank Corporate Center. Owned by the same company that owns the Bistro 100 in Chicago, it features French, Italian, and American cuisine with an emphasis on wood-oven specialties. The restaurant is open for lunch and dinner Monday through Saturday and for brunch and dinner on Sunday.

Olé Olé. *Moderate/Expensive.* 709 South Kings Drive (704-358-1102). This restaurant features Spanish and Mexican food that is presented authentically, not watered down by American influence. The atmosphere is a nice contrast to the fiesta mood of many such places. Lunch is served Monday through Friday and dinner seven days a week.

The Cajun Queen. *Moderate.* 1800 East Seventh Street (704-377-9017). New Orleans cookery is alive and well in this turn-of-the-century house. Crawfish or shrimp étouffée and blackened seafood are among the luscious specialties. Side dishes include red beans and rice, gumbo, and shrimp rémoulade. There are even New Orleans–style drinks and live jazz at night. Dinner is served daily. No reservations are accepted on the weekends.

The Pewter Rose Bistro. *Moderate.* 1820 South Boulevard (704-332-8149). Aged-brick ceiling beams, lace curtains, and pink accents highlight this airy, open restaurant on the second floor of a renovated textile mill. But it's the imaginative menu that's made the Pewter Rose so popular. There are hearty sandwiches for lunch, such as the "Quatre Fromages"—with provolone, mozzarella, fontina, and Gorgonzola cheeses. Dinner standouts include grilled grouper and fettucine *á la Rose*—with smoked salmon and red and black caviar topped with fresh Parmesan. The salads are lavish, the desserts decadent. The restaurant is open daily for lunch and dinner and now has a cigar bar.

Frank Manzetti's Bar and Grill. *Moderate.* 6401 Morrison Boulevard, Specialty Shops on the Park (704-364-9334). From the day it opened, this cousin of South Carolina's popular California Dreaming restaurants has had lines stretching beyond the door on weekend nights. High ceilings, a mirrored wall, and a dramatic floor-to-ceiling lighted bar display make it appear larger than it is. The shrimp Manzetti, sautéed with mushrooms and garlic and served over fettucine, is exceptional; the 10-ounce center-cut fillet of beef practically melts in the mouth. The burgers and sandwiches show the same attention to quality. Dinner and lunch are served daily.

Southend Brewery and Smokehouse. *Moderate.* 2100 South Boulevard (704-358-4677). Warm wooden tables and partitions make the huge space in this brewpub feel intimate. There's also a patio for enjoying a microbrewed beer on a warm summer evening. Lunch and dinner are served daily.

Alexander Michael's. *Inexpensive/Moderate.* 401 West Ninth Street (704-332-6789). This restaurant and neighborhood tavern is located in Uptown's historic Fourth Ward in an old store that served as the center for the ward in earlier days. The lunch menu focuses on sandwiches, salads, and homemade soups. Dinner features pasta with a variety of sauces and fresh seafood. Lunch and dinner are served daily.

The Fish Farm. *Inexpensive.* 1200 Sam Newell Road, Matthews (704-847-8578). Drive east on Independence Boulevard, turn right at the large Fish Farm sign, and go a short distance through surprisingly bucolic countryside to this red-and-white barnlike building that once was a dinner theater. With knotty-pine booths, ladder-back chairs, and tables topped with blue-and-white-checked cloths, it's a bit fancier than a real fish camp, but it serves the same no-nonsense fare. All-you-can-eat flounder, bass, shrimp, perch, and trout are offered. One departure—blackened catfish fillets New Orleans–style served on Cajun rice—is delicious. Children under five eat free if they settle for chicken or perch. Dinner is served Tuesday through Sunday.

*The Mile-High Swinging Bridge
on Grandfather Mountain*
Photograph by William Russ
Courtesy of N.C. Travel and Tourism Division

The Mountains

The mountain region is the smallest of North Carolina's three major sections, extending over only 17 of the 100 counties. But it is by far the most picturesque, both in scenic beauty and quaintness of custom.

The rugged Appalachian Mountains stretch from Quebec to Alabama, and as they reach North Carolina, they split into two major formations. The eastern arm is the soft-silhouetted Blue Ridge Mountains; the western arm is the hazy Great Smoky Mountain range.

Courtesy of N.C. Department of Transportation

Between the two is a high plateau slashed by smaller east-west cross-ranges. The greatest mass of mountains in the eastern United States, the North Carolina ranges cover 11,000 square miles, with more than 40 peaks over 6,000 feet high. Mount Mitchell, at 6,684 feet, is the highest peak in the eastern United States.

The people who settled these mountains had to be rugged. Many were hardy Scots who had been brutally evicted from the Scottish Highlands. The mountains did not afford an easy living, and settlers became hunters, woodsmen, and small-scale farmers. A few were so isolated that some of their descendants still exhibit quirks of speech and pronunciation that hark back to 18th-century English or Scottish dialects. Many North Carolina mountain people had such a different economy and way of life that they opposed the state's secession during the Civil War.

Also living in the Smoky Mountains were the Cherokees—one of the five civilized tribes of Native Americans and the first to have a written language. Westward expansion by white settlers led to a devastating treaty that removed thousands of Cherokees to inferior land in Oklahoma. The migration was dubbed the "Trail of Tears"; an outdoor drama in the town of Cherokee depicting the event is one of the most popular attractions in the state.

Two of the most beneficial events for the mountain area's economy were the construction of the Blue Ridge Parkway in 1935 and the opening of Great Smoky Mountains National Park in 1934. These attractions have enabled millions of visitors to discover the breathtaking beauty of the mountains—especially in the colorful spring and fall seasons. As a result, many people of the mountains have turned to tourism for their living, but in a different way from their counterparts along the seacoast. They sell products now associated with the Appalachian culture—patchwork quilts, hammered dulcimers, handmade toys, pottery, and handwoven goods. Once here, visitors discover that North Carolina's mountains offer a wealth of recreational opportunities, from skiing to trout fishing to whitewater rafting.

In the years before air conditioning, affluent Southerners came to the mountains for the summer, enjoying temperatures 10 to 15 degrees cooler than the flatlands. Some of their large homes have been turned into striking bed-and-breakfast inns, and a number of new resorts have been built, so you no longer have to be rich to enjoy tennis and golf in the clear mountain air.

In the heart of the mountains is the city of Asheville, situated in a natural bowl rimmed by mountain peaks. Most visitors start their exploration here with a visit to Biltmore Estate, completed in 1895 by George W. Vanderbilt in the manner of a French chateau. From Asheville, driving through the mountains is a joy. On the Blue Ridge Parkway, you'll follow the crest of the mountain range and frequently see vistas that will make you reach for your camera—often, you'll see a succession of gentle mountain peaks that fade to lighter blue in the distance, looking almost like ocean waves.

And there's more driving pleasure in store. The two-lane roads linking small mountain towns throughout the area will present you with lovely surprises—tumbling waterfalls, winding routes that rise and fall dramatically, and roadside entrepreneurs with animal carvings or sourwood honey for sale.

There may be mountain areas in the United States that are taller, steeper, and snowier, but you won't find any more delightful to visit than that in North Carolina.

The Mountains

The Blue Ridge Parkway
The High Country
Asheville
The Southern Mountains
The Great Smoky Mountains

by Ginny Turner

The Blue Ridge Parkway

The Blue Ridge Parkway is unique in the national park system in that it was designed not as a *destination* but as a *journey*. Weaving around mountain slopes and skirting their towering peaks, the parkway covers 469 miles, from Shenandoah National Park in Virginia to Great Smoky Mountains National Park on the North Carolina–Tennessee border.

As you drive the parkway, you feel like a soaring bird. You swoop down gradually into valleys of wilderness timber, then up again over the mountain crests to view on the other side long ravines of forested mountain slopes bright with spring blooms, the lush green of summer, or the striking autumn finery. In the distance, the mountains are soft blue, the peaks becoming lighter in color as they progress to the horizon—the image most often associated with the Blue Ridge Mountains.

Other parts of the parkway are less spectacular but no less pleasing. Weathered split-rail fences line some stretches of the road, separating the trimmed grassy areas next to the asphalt from meadows of wildflowers. Occasionally, you'll see an old farm building, but you won't see many signs of commercial development. At regular intervals, there are places to stop and rest, take pictures, or walk on a nature trail.

An important thing to know about the parkway is that the speed limit is only 45 miles per hour, and sometimes it's even slower if it's crowded or you get stuck behind a dawdling driver of a lumbering RV. If you chafe under that restriction, you should travel other routes (though on the two-lane state roads you won't really average much more than that).

Keep in mind, too, that mountain weather is different from that down below. It's always cooler and considerably more changeable. You may drive up on a mild spring day, only to discover that a parkway section is closed due to snow or ice. The flip side is that you can enjoy a second spring up in the mountains about a month later. It's always a good idea to have a jacket or sweater with you, even in summer.

You may want to take the parkway in small bites, interspersing it with excursions to other areas of the mountains. Despite its great natural beauty, if you stay on the parkway for its 253 miles in North Carolina, you'll miss a lot of what this part of the state has to offer. Don't hesitate to detour into nearby towns—it's easy to get back on the parkway a little farther down the road.

Below is a list of attractions, facilities, and recreational options along the parkway. They're identified by milepost markers, which start at 0 at Shenandoah National Park and increase as you go south, ending with 469 at Great Smoky Mountains National Park. Occasionally, you'll see a sign with a squirrel gun and powder horn noting a spot where an interpretive marker explains a legend, historic building, or place of scientific interest.

VISITOR INFORMATION:

Stop at any of the visitor centers to pick up parkway information or to learn about interpretive exhibits and guided nature walks. The centers are open from 9 A.M. to 5 P.M. from June through October. Or you can request a map and brochure from the Office of the Superintendent, Blue Ridge Parkway, 400 BB&T Building, Asheville, N.C. 28801 (828-271-4779).

At nearby restaurants and attractions, you'll find a couple of free publications that cover the parkway. *Blue Ridge Parkway Directory* is a thin magazine that lists lodgings and attractions near each exit. *Blue Ridge Parkway Milepost* is a tabloid that has news stories as well as general parkway information.

The emergency number for aid on the parkway is 800-727-5928. Be sure you know your location by milepost marker when you call.

The Parkway

Milepost

217.5   Cumberland Knob Visitor Center, the northernmost visitor center in North Carolina, has a 1,000-acre picnic area and two trails—a 15-minute walk to Cumberland Knob and a two-hour hike into Gully Creek Gorge. The altitude here is 2,740 feet.

218.6   Fox Hunter's Paradise is an overlook, parking area, and trailhead for a 10-minute trail to Paradise Valley. The altitude is 2,805 feet.

229   U.S. 21 crossover is seven miles east of Sparta and four miles west of Roaring Gap.

238.5-244.7   Doughton Park has picnic areas and campsites and 20 miles of hiking trails. In the restored Brinegar Cabin, you can see weaving demonstrations in the summer. The altitude is 3,710 feet.

248.1   N.C. 18 crossover is two miles east of Laurel Springs and 24 miles west of North Wilkesboro.

259   The Northwest Trading Post operates a major crafts center here. The side road beside the center leads to Glendale Springs, the site of the famous frescoes at Holy Trinity Episcopal Church (see *Boone: Side Trips*).

261   N.C. 16 crossover is five miles east of Glendale Springs and 20 miles west of North Wilkesboro.

272   E. B. Jeffress Park has an overlook, a picnic area, and a short trail to nearby cascades.

276.4   U.S. 421 crossover is 11 miles east of Boone.

291.9   U.S. 221 crossover is seven miles south of Boone and two miles north of Blowing Rock.

292.7-295   Moses H. Cone Memorial Park and Visitor Center, the former estate of the Greensboro textile magnate, encompasses 3,600 acres and miles of trails. The beautiful white manor house overlooks a sparkling lake. Inside is a craft shop exhibiting the wares of the Southern Highland Craft Guild (see *Blowing Rock: Special Shopping*). You can also hike around the two nearby trout ponds or take a short hike to the Cone grave site. The altitude is 4,000 feet.

295-299   Julian Price Memorial Park encompasses 4,344 acres and has a campground and a picnic area. There is a popular 2.5-mile loop trail around the lake. The park is also one of the trailheads for the popular 13-mile Tanawha Trail. Because hiking the entire trail is a strenuous task, many people park one car here and hike down from the other end near the Linn Cove Viaduct.

302   Rough Ridge Parking Area offers one of the best places to photograph the famous Linn Cove Viaduct. You can take your photo from the wooden platforms above the parking area.

304   The Linn Cove Viaduct winds 1,243 feet around the side of rugged Grandfather Mountain. The last link in the 469-mile parkway to be completed, this engineering feat offers spectacular views of the valleys

The Linn Cove Viaduct
Photograph by William Russ
Courtesy of N.C. Travel and Tourism Division

below and Grandfather Mountain above. This is also a good place to pick up the Tanawha Trail. You can find more information about the trail at the visitor center located here.

305.9   U.S. 221 crossover is three miles east of Linville and one mile east of the entrance to Grandfather Mountain. (See *Banner Elk/Beech Mountain/Linville: Attractions.*)

308.2   Flat Rock Overlook has a nature trail that leads to a panoramic view of Linville Valley and Grandfather Mountain. The altitude is 3,995 feet.

312   N.C. 181 crossover is two miles south of Pineola and 32 miles northwest of Morganton.

316.3   Linville Falls has a campground, a picnic area, and trails leading to overlooks of the falls and Linville Gorge. (See *Banner Elk/Beech Mountain/Linville: Attractions.*)

317.4   Linville Falls Visitor Center has a picnic area and a bridge over the Linville River, where you can fish. The altitude is 3,250 feet.

320.7	Chestoa View offers a beautiful vista from atop a cliff on Humpback Mountain. The altitude is 4,090 feet.
331	N.C. 226 crossover is six miles south of Spruce Pine and 14 miles northwest of Marion.
331	The Museum of North Carolina Minerals displays specimens of gems and minerals found in the state. A gift shop sells books on gems, mining, and parkway natural history. (See *Spruce Pine/Burnsville: Attractions.*)
339.5-340.3	Crabtree Meadows Visitor Center encompasses 250 acres, a picnic area, and hiking trails, including a 40-minute walk to Crabtree Falls. The altitude is 3,735 feet.
355.4	N.C. 128 leads to Mount Mitchell State Park, which boasts the highest peak in the eastern United States. It has picnic tables, campsites, hiking trails, and a natural-history museum. (See *Spruce Pine/Burnsville: Attractions.*)
364.4	Craggy Gardens Visitor Center has a picnic area, an interpretive center, and several trails that offer close-up views of the sensational purple rhododendron that blankets the mountains in mid-June. (See *Asheville: Side Trips.*)
382	Folk Art Center, headquarters of the Southern Highlands Craft Guild, has craft demonstrations and exhibits, plus the Allanstand Craft Shop. (See *Asheville: Special Shopping.*)
382.6	U.S. 70 crossover is five miles east of Asheville and 10 miles west of Black Mountain.
384.7	U.S. 74 crossover is three miles east of Asheville and 17 miles west of Chimney Rock.

388.8   U.S. 25 crossover is five miles south of Asheville and 17 miles north of Hendersonville.

393.6   N.C. 191 crossover is six miles south of Asheville and 20 miles north of Hendersonville.

408.6   Mount Pisgah Visitor Center, located at 5,749 feet, is the highlight of Pisgah National Forest. The center has picnic tables, campsites, several hiking trails, and an inn. (See *Brevard: Recreation.*)

412   U.S. 276 crossover is eight miles south of Cruso and 18 miles north of Brevard. The Cradle of Forestry is located on the way to Brevard. (See *Brevard: Historic Places.*)

418.8   Graveyard Fields Overlook has a loop trail to Yellowstone Falls.

422.4   Devil's Courthouse features a 40-minute walk to the rock formation and a 360-degree view of the mountains. The altitude is 5,462 feet.

431.4   Richland Balsam Overlook is the highest point on the parkway, at 6,047 feet.

443.1   U.S. 19A/23 crossover is seven miles south of Waynesville and 12 miles north of Sylva.

451.2   Waterrock Knob Visitor Center boasts a four-state view. It also has an interpretive center and a loop trail to the knob. The altitude is 5,718 feet.

458.2   Heintooga Ridge Road is a parkway spur that leads to Mile High Overlook and Great Smoky Mountains National Park. The altitude is 5,325 feet.

469.1   The parkway ends at Great Smoky Mountains National Park and the intersection with U.S. 441.

Attractions

The parkway draws thousands of visitors each year in the spring and fall, when nature provides an array of color. In the spring, the color is provided by wildflowers and native shrubs like rhododendron, mountain laurel, and azalea. The spring wildflowers do not start to appear until late April. The blooming period changes with altitude, but mid-May to late June usually provide ample color. The peak of the fall color varies according to weather and altitude but usually is at its height in mid-October. Be forewarned that the parkway is crowded during this time, and accommodations need to be reserved well in advance. For information and updates on the fall foliage, call 828-298-0398.

Recreation

Camping is available at Doughton Park, Julian Price Memorial Park, Linville Falls, Crabtree Meadows, and Mount Pisgah. Sites are allotted on a first-come, first-served basis, with stays limited to 14 days. There are few RV sites, and they fill up fast. Campgrounds are open from May through October.

Many areas along the parkway are designated for **picnicking**, and offer tables, grills, and restrooms. However, you will notice that most people simply pull over and spread their blankets on the well-maintained grassy shoulders. This is legal as long as the vehicles are five to 10 feet off the parkway. Parking is not allowed within 200 feet of an intersection.

Hiking trails of varying degrees of difficulty are to be found throughout the parkway area. Inquire at any visitor center for suggestions to meet your interest and skill level.

Trout fishing is available at Doughton Park, Moses Cone Memorial Park, Julian Price Memorial Park, and Linville Falls. You must have a state fishing license, obtainable at hardware and sporting-goods stores. Swimming, littering, and letting pets run loose are prohibited.

Accommodations

In mountain towns just off the parkway, there are plenty of lodgings to choose from, as you'll notice in our listings. But if you want to stay on parkway property, only two options are available. These are National Park Service concessions let to private owners.

Pisgah Inn. *Moderate*. Milepost 408.6 (828-235-8228). At an altitude of 5,000 feet, Pisgah Inn has a mountain view from each room so striking you may not want to leave. It's a modern facility but has a rustic atmosphere. A gift shop, a service station, a restaurant, and a campground are offered. The inn is open from April through October.

Bluffs Lodge. *Moderate*. Milepost 241 (336-372-4499). This rustic lodge in Doughton Park, built in 1949, has spectacular views of the surrounding Blue Ridge Mountains. At 3,750 feet in elevation, the area can be cool for morning walks in the meadow. The lodge's rooms are not fancy and do not have TV or telephones. A gift shop, a service station, and a full-service restaurant are offered. The lodge is open from May until November.

The High Country ....

North Carolina's northern mountain region around Boone, Blowing Rock, Banner Elk, Spruce Pine, and Burnsville is known as the High Country. In addition to spectacular scenery, it offers a year-round variety of recreational options, children's attractions, an annual Scottish festival, and the best ski resorts in the Southeast. And because the towns are relatively close together, you can easily visit any of the attractions listed in this section no matter where you stay.

Tourism is a booming industry in the High Country—you'll see lots of condominiums, vacation houses, and other developments under construction. Prices in antique shops are on the high side here; on the other hand, you'll find local people selling jam, cider, and sourwood honey at roadside stands.

Boone

Named for Daniel Boone, who supposedly camped here while exploring the area, Boone is the largest town in the region. Situated on a plateau surrounded by high peaks, it's regarded as the heart of the High Country.

Boone is a sprawling, bustling town that serves as the seat of Watauga County. It's also home to Appalachian State University, one of the 16 state-supported four-year institutions in the University of North Carolina system. Its students keep things lively and ensure that eclectic stores, restaurants, and bars have more than tourism to keep them solvent. The downtown area offers an alternative to the sprawl found on the city's outskirts.

To honor frontiersman Boone, there are namesake gardens and an outdoor drama—one of the biggest summer attractions in the northern mountains.

You'll find more restaurants and accommodations in Boone than in the smaller surrounding towns, so it may be a good choice for your base camp. However, you may find a wider range of accommodations in nearby Blowing Rock.

ACCESS:
U.S. 321 and U.S. 421 both travel through Boone, while N.C. 105 and N.C. 194 terminate here.

VISITOR INFORMATION:
Contact the Boone Chamber of Commerce, 208 West Howard Street, Boone, N.C. 28607 (828-264-2225) or North Carolina High Country Host, 1700 Blowing Rock Road, Boone, N.C. 28607 (828-264-1299 or 800-438-7500); the latter agency promotes the entire region.

The *Watauga Democrat* is published three times a week. The *Mountain Times*, a free weekly, offers news and events listings.

Attractions

Daniel Boone Native Gardens are adjacent to the outdoor theater where *Horn in the West* is performed; signs for the outdoor drama are prominent. The gardens feature a collection of plants native to North Carolina. Sponsored by the Garden Club of North Carolina, the gardens opened in 1966 to preserve the plants in a pleasing setting and educate visitors about them. A sunken garden, a wishing well, a rustic bridge leading to a fern garden, a reflection pool, and a historic cabin are offered. The wrought-iron entrance gates were made by Daniel Boone VI, a direct descendant of the pioneer. The gardens are open daily from 9 A.M. to 6 P.M. from May through October. They are open until 8 P.M. when *Horn in the West* is being performed. Admission is $2. For information, call 828-264-6390.

The Mast General Store at Valle Crucis
Photograph by Clay Nolen
Courtesy of N.C. Travel and Tourism Division

Special Shopping

Mast General Store, on N.C. 194 in Valle Crucis, opened for business in 1883, eight years before Mr. Sears and Mr. Roebuck got together. The store offers a trip back in time to the days when one enterprise sold everything for the home and farm. Here, you can still buy thread or work boots, harmonicas or kerosene lanterns. The store sells nostalgia, too, such as modern replicas of shaving mugs and enamel advertising signs. It's fun to take the kids, but they probably won't believe this is what shopping used to be like.

Shortly before reaching the original store, you'll see the Mast Annex, a part of the Mast Store complex which specializes in clothing and candy. You'll see varieties of candy from your childhood that you assumed weren't even manufactured anymore.

The store has proved so popular that other Mast Stores have opened in Waynesville and Hendersonville. There is also a Mast Store in the downtown section of Boone. It carries similar merchandise to the original store, though it lacks the atmosphere of the Valle Crucis original, with its working post office, potbelly stove, and creaky wooden floors. For store hours, call 828-963-6511.

Wilcox Emporium Warehouse, 161 Howard Street in downtown Boone, houses over 180 vendors of antiques, art, collectibles, and food. Included among these establishments is **Blue Ridge Hearthside Crafts**, a sales outlet for a craft cooperative that was formed in 1968 to represent over 200 artisans. This store offers handmade items like those shipped to retail stores all over the country, but at lower prices. For information about Blue Ridge Hearthside Crafts, call 828-265-4004. For information about Wilcox Emporium Warehouse, call 828-262-1221.

Recreation

The North Carolina High Country Host, at 1700 Blowing Rock Road, provides a complete list of outfitters for the whitewater-rafting and canoeing trips available at several locations throughout the High Country, as well as information about public golf courses. The High Country offers some of the best golf courses in the country—although the better ones are private. For information, call 828-264-1299 or 800-438-7500.

Skiing is available close to Boone at **Appalachian Ski Mountain**, which has eight slopes, vertical drops of 365 feet, and rental equipment. The lodge offers accommodations and dining. For information, contact Appalachian Ski Mountain, P.O. Box 106, Blowing Rock, N.C. 28605 (828-295-7828). For other ski resorts in the area, see the *Banner Elk/Beech Mountain/Linville* section.

Seasonal Events

Horn in the West, an outdoor drama by Kermit Hunter, depicts the activities of Daniel Boone and other mountain men during the Revolutionary War. Produced at the Daniel Boone Amphitheater, just east of U.S. 421 in Boone, this has been a durable attraction since it was first performed in 1937. Remember that even in the summer, Boone can get quite cool in the evenings. The drama runs nightly except Monday from mid-June through mid-August. For ticket prices and reservations, call 828-264-2120.

An Appalachian Summer is a diverse arts festival at Appalachian State University. It features seminars, lectures, and performances of dance and music by guest artists and orchestras. The season traditionally ends with an outdoor fireworks concert in Kidd Brewer Stadium. Tickets to events are available singly or in season packages; some presentations are free. For information, call 828-262-4046 or 800-841-ARTS.

Side Trips

If you head north into Ashe County, you will find two attractions different from anything else in the area.

You can see cheese being made at the **Ashe County Cheese Company,** at Main and Fourth Streets in West Jefferson, about 45 minutes from downtown Boone or Blowing Rock. A viewing window allows you to watch several of the processes, and you can sample and buy the product in the store. Tours of the plant are given Monday through Saturday from 8:30 A.M. to 5 P.M. However, if you want to see cheese being made, you will need to arrive in the early morning. For information, call 336-246-2501. There is also a sales outlet for the cheese company in Blowing Rock; call 828-295-0768.

At St. Mary's Episcopal Church in Beaver Creek, just outside West Jefferson, you can see some of the **frescoes** created by North Carolina native Ben Long. There are prominent signs directing you to the frescoes. Long, who studied fresco painting with a Florentine master, is one of the few American artists still working in this ancient tradition. Admission to the frescoes is free. The church is open daily.

Less than 10 miles to the east on N.C. 16 in Glendale Springs, Holy Trinity Episcopal Church features a larger fresco, Long's interpretation of the Last Supper. It may also be viewed daily for free.

If you work up a hunger while in the area, two local dining establishments draw crowds from miles around for bountiful country cooking served family-style. **Greenfield Restaurant** is located just off U.S. 221 between Jefferson and West Jefferson. It serves breakfast, lunch, and dinner daily. Off-season hours vary. For reservations and hours, call 336-246-9671. **Shatley Springs Inn**, located five miles north of Jefferson on N.C. 16, serves breakfast, lunch, and dinner from May through October. You can also take a sip of the mineral water that once made this inn a famous resort. For information, call 336-982-2236.

Glendale Springs Inn and Restaurant is located on N.C. 16 in Glendale Springs, near Milepost 259 on the Blue Ridge Parkway. The inn and restaurant are housed in a restored home which was built in 1892. There are nine guest rooms, some with fireplaces and Jacuzzis. The restaurant serves lunch, dinner, and Sunday brunch. During the off-season, meals are served only on the weekends. For information or reservations, call 336-982-2103 or 800-287-1206.

Accommodations

Keep in mind that the "season" for Boone is all summer, the month of October, and the winter months, when the skiers arrive in droves. However, many lodgings do offer lower rates off-season.

Quality Inn–Appalachian Conference Center. *Moderate.* 344 Blowing Rock Road, at the intersection of U.S. 321 and N.C. 105 (828-262-0020). This six-story hotel is one of Boone's top-of-the-line accommodations. It offers a spacious lobby with wing chairs and antique reproductions, along with attractively decorated rooms. A restaurant and a lounge are on the premises, as well as meeting rooms and an indoor pool.

High Country Inn. *Moderate.* N.C. 105 South (828-264-1000 or 800-334-5605). The huge waterwheel out front makes this inn easy to spot. The attractive stone-and-wood building gives the impression of rusticity, but you won't feel it inside. The inn has a sauna, a hot tub, a weight room, indoor and outdoor pools, and comfortable rooms. Some suites have brick fireplaces. A restaurant and a lounge are on the premises.

Broyhill Inn and Conference Center. *Moderate.* 775 Bodenheimer Drive (800-951-6048). This facility, which is run by Appalachian

State University, is located on a hill overlooking the campus. It's probably best known as a place to hold meetings, but the 83 rooms are comfortable and the rates are reasonable. The views of the mountains are outstanding, and it's conveniently located close to downtown Boone. On the premises is "The Commons," a full-service restaurant offering breakfast, lunch, and dinner daily. For reservations, call 828-262-2204.

And of course, you can always find reliable lodging at one of these chains:
Comfort Suites. *Moderate.* 1184 N.C. 105 (828-268-0099).
Hampton Inn. *Moderate.* 1075 N.C. 105 (828-264-0077).
Holiday Inn Express. *Moderate.* U.S. 321 (828-264-2451).

Inns and Bed-and-Breakfast Guest Houses

Mast Farm Inn. *Expensive/Deluxe.* S.R. 1112 in Valle Crucis, three miles from N.C. 105 (828-963-5857). Mast Farm Inn occupies a huge, rambling three-story farmhouse with a wraparound porch. Built in 1885, it was first operated as an inn in the early 1900s. In 1972, the farm was placed on the National Register of Historic Places as a fine example of a self-contained mountain homestead. The guest rooms, most with private baths, are furnished with country antiques and old quilts; other quilts hang over banister railings. There's also a two-room cabin that used to be a loom house. The inn serves a hearty breakfast and generous family-style meals in two dining rooms.

Lovill House Inn. *Expensive/Deluxe.* 404 Old Bristol Road (828-264-4204 or 800-849-9466). Housed in an 1875 farmhouse with a wraparound porch, this inn offers private baths, cable TV, and telephones in each room. A home-cooked country breakfast is served in the mornings.

Bluestone Lodge. *Expensive/Deluxe.* Off N.C. 105 on the way to the Mast General Store (828-963-5177). Although breakfast is served with your lodging here, this establishment is more of an inn than a restored home. The amenities include an outdoor pool, whirlpool tubs, fireplaces, twig beds, and six-foot skylights. Cottages are also available. All of this is located on seven secluded acres with spectacular mountain views.

The Inn at the Taylor House. *Expensive.* 0.8 mile from the Mast General Store on N.C. 194 in Valle Crucis (828-963-5581). The Taylor House, built in 1910, has been described as "country elegant." The bedrooms have private baths, and there are four cabins which range in size from one to three bedrooms.

Restaurants

Boone offers abundant fast-food restaurants full of people in a hurry to get to the hiking trails and ski slopes. Here are some alternatives.

Mast Farm Inn. *Moderate*. S.R. 1112 in Valle Crucis (828-963-5857). Mast Farm Inn serves family-style gourmet country meals with so many serving dishes the tables almost sag. The menu changes daily and offers everything from chicken and dumplings to moussaka. Any restaurant that has its own best-selling cookbook must be good. Dinner is served Tuesday through Saturday. Lunch is served on Sunday. Reservations are requested.

Dan'l Boone Inn. *Inexpensive/Moderate*. 105 Hardin Street, at the junction of U.S. 321 and U.S. 421 (828-264-8657). This casual family restaurant features country fare such as fried chicken, country ham, hot biscuits, and a large assortment of fresh vegetables, all served family-style. From Memorial Day through October, breakfast is served on Saturday and Sunday and dinner is served from 11 A.M. to 9 P.M. daily. During the winter, breakfast is served on Saturday and Sunday and dinner is served Monday through Friday from 5 to 9 P.M. and Saturday and Sunday from 11 A.M. to 9 P.M.

Red Onion Cafe. *Inexpensive*. 214 Hardin Street (828-264-5470). This is a good place for a quick lunch—sandwiches, salads, or pizza. The cafe is open for lunch and dinner daily.

The Cottonwood Brewery at Howard Street Grill. *Inexpensive*. At the Wilcox Emporium Warehouse on Howard Street in downtown Boone (828-264-7111). This is currently Boone's only brewpub, so it attracts a lively crowd. The food is not exceptional but is fine for bar food. Lunch and dinner are served daily.

Pepper's. *Inexpensive*. 240 Shadowline Road, just off Blowing Rock Road (828-262-1250). Pepper's opened in 1975 and has been a Boone favorite ever since. The menu includes sandwiches, seafood, pasta, and homemade desserts. Lunch and dinner are served daily.

The Caribbean Cafe. *Inexpensive*. 489B East King Street (828-265-2233). Jerk chicken platters, conch fritters, fried plantains—all indicate that this is the real stuff. The owner has extensive experience as a chef in south Florida. The cafe also boasts that it has the best imported-beer list in the area. Lunch and dinner are served daily.

Blowing Rock

This attractive little town was named for a natural phenomenon on a rocky outcrop of the cliff overlooking the Johns River Gorge. Lightweight objects tossed over the edge of the rock occasionally come flying back, lifted by the air currents below. In winter, the snow seems to be falling upside down.

The village of Blowing Rock is only eight miles from Boone, but the feeling here is completely different. It's been a resort area for a century, and miraculously, it seems to have been spared commercial exploitation—the commercial strip has been zoned to the outskirts of the community. Blowing Rock has a pretty town park with summer art shows, antique and gift shops, and benches on Main Street where you can sit and enjoy an ice-cream cone and watch the people passing by. If you're looking for charm, it's in Blowing Rock.

ACCESS:
Blowing Rock is located eight miles south of Boone where U.S. 321 and U.S. 221 join and become Blowing Rock Road.

VISITOR INFORMATION:
Contact the Blowing Rock Chamber of Commerce, P.O. Box 406, Blowing Rock, N.C. 28605 (828-295-7851 or 800-295-7851). The town also falls under the purview of the North Carolina High Country Host, 1700 Blowing Rock Road, Boone, N.C. 28607 (828-264-1299 or 800-438-7500).

Attractions

The Blowing Rock is south of town, just off U.S. 321. When you drive up to the site, you'll see only a flower-bedecked fieldstone gift shop. Once you go through the shop, you'll walk a short gravel trail, then go up a few steps to a lookout platform just below the overhanging rock. You can feel strong breezes there all the time and surprising gusts on windy days.

There's a splendid panoramic view. From the 4,090-foot height, you can see Table Rock, Grandfather, Grandmother, and Hawksbill Mountains.

The attraction is open from 8 A.M. to 8 P.M. from June through October. It is also open during the winter, weather permitting. Admission is $4 for adults, $3 for senior citizens, and $1 for children ages six to 11; there is no charge for children under six. For information, call 828-295-7111.

Tweetsie Railroad, a combination amusement park and frontier village on U.S. 221/321 between Boone and Blowing Rock, re-creates a bit of the Old West. A narrow-gauge locomotive pulls a sightseeing train for three miles through the park. In open-air coaches, passengers witness a train holdup, an Indian raid, and a Western shootout. The train stops at Tweetsie Junction—a replica of a turn-of-the-century town with a general store and ice-cream parlor—and at the country-fair area, which offers rides, shooting galleries, food, and family entertainment.

In operation since 1957, Tweetsie Railroad is open daily from 9 A.M. to 6 P.M. from the mid-May through Labor Day. From Labor Day until the end of October, the hours are 9 A.M. to 6 P.M. on Friday, Saturday, and Sunday. Admission is $16 for adults and $13 for senior citizens and children ages three to 12; children under three are free. For information, call 828-264-9061 or 800-526-5740.

Mystery Hill, on U.S. 221/321 between Boone and Blowing Rock, is a house where you can see puzzling phenomena of gravity and perspective, along with a dancing hologram. The complex also includes the **Appalachian Heritage Museum**. It is open from 8 A.M. to 8 P.M. from June to August and from 9 A.M. to 5 P.M. from September to May; the complex does not open until 1 P.M. on Sunday. Admission is $5 for adults, $4.50 for senior citizens, and $3.50 for children ages five to 12; children under five are admitted free. For information, call 828-264-2792.

Special Shopping

Goodwin Guild Weavers, on U.S. 321 Bypass, sells beautiful all-cotton pillows, place mats, tablecloths, and lap blankets made with Jacquard looms, which produce pictorial designs. This family business was started in 1812 in England; a fourth-generation Goodwin set up shop in Blowing Rock in 1950, and three more generations of Goodwins are continuing the work. You'll be intrigued by the colors and old designs they produce. The showroom is open Monday through Saturday from 9 A.M. to 5:30 P.M. and Sunday from 10 A.M. to 5 P.M. For information, call 828-295-3394.

Parkway Craft Center, in the manor house at Moses H. Cone Memorial Park, located at Milepost 294 on the Blue Ridge Parkway, is a sales outlet for the many professional craftspeople of the Southern Highland Craft Guild. You'll find traditional and contemporary crafts—pottery, weavings, dulcimers, woodcarvings. The center is open from 9 A.M. to 6 P.M. daily from May to October and from 9 A.M. to 4 P.M. the rest of the year. For information, call 828-295-7938.

Recreation

Appalachian Ski Mountain, off U.S. 321 between Blowing Rock and Boone, has eight slopes and a vertical drop of 365 feet and is also home to the South's largest ski school. It also has a large restaurant, a ski shop, and rental equipment. For information, contact Appalachian Ski Mountain, P.O. Box 106, Blowing Rock, N.C. 28605 (828-295-7828 or 800-322-2373).

Glen Burney Trail is a historic trail constructed in the late 1800s, when tourists began to flock to Blowing Rock. It is a 1.5-mile mountain trail that can be used only by hikers. The elevation drop makes it a moderately strenuous hike, but the waterfalls along the way are worth the effort. To find the trail, turn off Main Street onto Laurel Lane, continue straight at the first stop sign, and make the next left into the parking area across from the lake in Anne Cannon Park. To receive a free trail map, call the Blowing Rock Chamber of Commerce.

Seasonal Events

Art in the Park is a series of juried arts-and-crafts shows in downtown Blowing Rock, featuring up to 120 selected exhibitors. The event is held one Saturday a month from May through October. For information, call 828-295-7851.

Accommodations

Because Blowing Rock has a long history as a resort community, it comes naturally to proprietors here to make their lodgings appealing. Rates may vary according to the season.

The Chetola Resort. *Expensive/Deluxe.* North Main Street (800-

243-8652). The resort offers accommodations in the hotel, which is housed in a beautiful stone mansion overlooking the seven-acre Lake Chetola, and in one-, two-, and three-bedroom condominiums. Some of the hotel's rooms offer balconies and whirlpool baths. Guests can rent VCRs and movies, hike the resort's trails, boat and fish on the lake, play tennis and racquetball, and swim in the indoor pool.

Westglow Spa. *Expensive/Deluxe*. On N.C. 221 outside Blowing Rock, heading toward Linville (800-562-0807). Westglow is a European-style spa located in the former home of artist Elliott Daingerfield. The resort offers overnight and day packages.

Meadowbrook Inn. *Moderate/Expensive*. 294 North Main Street (828-295-4300 or 800-456-5456). This hotel is within easy walking distance of downtown Blowing Rock. The amenities include a restaurant, a lounge, golf privileges, a fitness center, an indoor pool, and a laundry.

Azalea Garden Inn. *Moderate/Expensive*. U.S. 321 (828-295-3272). This inn is actually a motel, but it's one of the nicest you'll ever see. Flowers cascade from window boxes in front of each room. From the sitting area on the brick walkway, you can view the three-acre garden with a log cabin in the center. The rooms are blindingly clean and neat.

Cliff Dwellers Inn. *Moderate*. U.S. 321 Bypass (828-295-3121 or 800-322-7380). This inn is literally perched on the side of a cliff overlooking Lake Chetola and its scenic rock dam. All rooms in this Swiss Alpine–style inn have balconies that overlook the lake. The one- and two-bedroom suites offer kitchenettes and fireplaces. A whirlpool and a pool are also offered.

Hillwinds Inn. *Inexpensive/Moderate*. Sunset Drive and Ransom Street (828-295-7660). Hillwinds' style and decor, reminiscent of Colonial Williamsburg, with brick exterior and Colonial furniture, is very pleasing. Its units have cable TV and refrigerators. A few efficiencies with full kitchens are available by the week.

Inns and Bed-and-Breakfast Guest Houses

Gideon Ridge Inn. *Expensive*. P.O. Box 1929, 6148 Gideon Ridge Road (828-295-3644). Perched on a ridge overlooking the Johns River Gorge, this beautiful resort home was built in the 1930s by a nephew of Mrs. Moses Cone. The guest rooms all have private baths, and some have private entrances that lead to the stone terrace that wraps around the entire house. From the terrace you can enjoy one of the most magnificent views in Blowing Rock. On a clear day, you can see not only Table Rock and Hawksbill, but all the way to Pilot Mountain in the Piedmont.

The Inn at Ragged Garden. *Moderate/Expensive*. 203 Sunset Drive (828-295-9703). This charming old stone house is set on an acre of land with roses, rhododendron, and enormous shade trees. Each of the 12 guest rooms has a gas-burning fireplace and a private bath (some with a Jacuzzi).

Restaurants

Although Blowing Rock is a very small town, there are several nice places to eat. Some are closed during the winter months.

The Gamekeeper Restaurant. *Expensive*. On Shulls Mill Road at Yonahlossee Resort (828-963-7400). This restaurant offers steak, chops, wild game, and seafood in an interesting stone home with a great view. If you wish alcoholic beverages, you'll have to brown-bag here. Dinner is served Tuesday through Saturday at 6 P.M.

The Best Cellar Restaurant. *Moderate/Expensive*. Off U.S. 321 Bypass in Blowing Rock; call for directions (828-295-3466). This restaurant is located in a 1938 log cabin. The winding road that begins at the side of the Food Lion parking lot may be difficult to find, but the imaginative entrées and scrumptious desserts are truly worth the effort. The old-fashioned decor includes decorative quilts, beam ceilings, and wood-burning fireplaces. Be sure to call for a reservation, because this is one of Blowing Rock's most popular restaurants, and it's often booked. Dinner is served Monday through Saturday year-round.

Village Cafe. *Moderate/Expensive*. Next to Kilwin's on Main Street (828-295-3769). This restaurant is a bit hard to locate—follow the stone path behind the ice-cream stand on Main Street. Housed in an old home, the Village Cafe serves gourmet breakfasts and lunches. Guests can dine inside the house or on the patio. The cafe is open daily except Wednesday and is closed during the off-season. Reservations are recommended.

Knight's on Main. *Moderate*. North Main Street (828-295-3869). Knight's serves good food all day in a casual, country atmosphere. There's a good selection of burgers and sandwiches for lunch and fried chicken, flounder, mountain trout, and steaks for dinner. Beer and wine are available. The restaurant serves breakfast, lunch, and dinner daily.

Woodlands. *Inexpensive.* U.S. 321 Bypass (828-295-3651). This is where the locals go for their barbecue, whether it's chopped or sliced, ribs or chicken, beef or pork. The restaurant also serves Mexican food and offers live entertainment which leans toward folk and bluegrass.

Banner Elk / Beech Mountain / Linville

Banner Elk, Beech Mountain, and Linville are at the center of some of the best outdoor recreation in this region. Looming above the village of Banner Elk are mountain peaks of 5,000 to 6,000 feet, and several ski resorts are located only a few miles from its one stoplight.

The township of Beech Mountain, which prides itself on being the highest incorporated town east of the Mississippi, is located three-fourths of the way up the mountain near the base of the ski slopes.

Immediately south of Banner Elk, with an entrance near Linville, is Grandfather Mountain, a wilderness area that has been thoughtfully developed into a private park. With hiking trails, picnic tables, and well-chosen overlooks, it's an enormously popular family attraction through most of the year. On summer weekends, you may have to wait in line at the entrance.

ACCESS:

Banner Elk is less than 20 miles southwest of Boone, at the intersection of N.C. 194 and N.C. 184.

To reach Beech Mountain, go to Banner Elk and follow the signs to the ski resort.

Linville is at the intersection of U.S. 221, N.C. 105, and N.C. 181 three miles west of Milepost 305.9 on the Blue Ridge Parkway.

VISITOR INFORMATION:

Contact the Avery/Banner Elk Chamber of Commerce, High Country Square, Banner Elk, N.C. 28604 (828-898-5605 or 800-972-2183) or on the Web at www.averycounty.com or www.banner-elk.com. Or contact the Beech Mountain Chamber of Commerce, 403-A Beech Mountain Parkway, Beech Mountain, N.C. 28604 (828-387-9283 or 800-468-5506). This area is also covered by the North Carolina High Country Host, 1700 Blowing Rock Road, Boone, N.C. 28607 (828-264-1299 or 800-438-7500).

The *Mountain Times*, a free weekly, includes information about the area.

Attractions

Grandfather Mountain is located two miles northwest of Linville on U.S. 221; the closest exit off the Blue Ridge Parkway is at Milepost 305.9. It is a private park that encompasses the 5,964-foot

Grandfather Mountain, so named because its profile suggests an old man sleeping. Once through the gates, guests drive up a winding road toward the summit. The visitor center—a stone building perched on top of the mountain—sells snacks, film, and souvenirs. If you're game, you can walk across the Mile-High Swinging Bridge, a suspension span that sways with the gusting winds that whip the mountain.

On the drive up or down, you can stop at several overlooks (all of which have picnic tables) to see expansive views of other Blue Ridge peaks. You can also stop at the nature museum and the animal habitat. The nature museum has exhibits about the area's flora, minerals, wildlife, birds, and history; it also offers a nature film, a souvenir shop, and a snack bar. At the animal habitat, you can glimpse the mountain's famous black bears, otters, cougars, bald and golden eagles, and deer. The best time to see the animals is shortly after the park opens, when they have just been fed and the crowds are sparse.

The park also maintains over 30 miles of hiking trails, but to use them, you must purchase a daily permit, which will also get you a trail map. Passes can be purchased at the entrance gate.

The mountain is open during the summer from 8 A.M. to 7:30 P.M. During the spring, the park closes at 6 P.M., and during the winter, if weather permits the park to open at all, it closes at 5 P.M. Admission is $10 for adults and $5 for children ages four to 12; children under four are admitted free. For information, call 828-733-4337 or 800-468-7325.

Linville Falls cascades 90 feet into Linville Gorge, a national wilderness preserve second only to the Grand Canyon in length and depth. You can view the falls by taking Linville Falls Trail from the Linville Falls Visitor Center, located at Milepost 317.4 on the Blue Ridge Parkway. The trail is a 2.1-mile round-trip hike which offers

The Mile-High Swinging Bridge on Grandfather Mountain
Photograph by William Russ
Courtesy of
N.C. Travel and Tourism Division

views of the upper and lower falls. The hike to view the upper falls is easy. Viewing the lower falls is more strenuous—but the lower waterfall is the one you usually see on postcards.

Linville Gorge is part of the Grandfather Ranger District of Pisgah National Forest. It has been declared a wilderness area, so its wild beauty will be preserved. The gorge is a favorite hiking spot for locals, but its designation as a wilderness area means that paths are not always obviously marked. A topographical map and a compass are necessities. For more information about the hiking trails in the gorge, contact the Pisgah National Forest office at 828-652-2144.

Two of the main features of the gorge area are Table Rock and Hawksbill Mountains. For a good view of these promontories without taking a hike in the wilderness, drive to the overlook at Wiseman's View. To reach it, take N.C. 183 North from Milepost 316.3 on the Blue Ridge Parkway. It is 0.7 mile from the town of Linville Falls to a gravel road which runs four miles to the parking area. This route may be too rough for an RV.

Linville Caverns, on U.S. 221 between Linville and Marion four miles south of the Blue Ridge Parkway at Milepost 317.4, is a series of massive limestone caves under Humpback Mountain. During the Civil War, the caverns sheltered deserters, but now they amuse and amaze visitors who come to see the centuries-old stalactites and stalagmites, whose peculiar shapes and varying colors make them resemble fantastic animals. The pathway leads along an underground stream and into several lighted chambers. The caverns are open from 9 A.M. to 6 P.M. from June through Labor Day. They close at 5 P.M. in the spring and fall and at 4:30 P.M. November through March. They are open on weekends only during December, January, and February. Admission is $5 for adults and $3 for children ages five through 12; children under five are admitted free. For information, call 828-756-4171.

Recreation

For even more hiking possibilities, try the Lost Cove, Wilson Creek, and Harper Creek areas of Pisgah National Forest. There are several hiking trails that lead to scenic views and beautiful waterfalls such as South Harper Creek Falls and Hunt Fish Falls. For appropriate topographical maps and information, call 828-652-2144.

Skiing and more skiing. The highest, steepest slopes in the state are here, and this is where you'll find the serious skiers. The first two listings are the giants of the North Carolina ski industry.

Ski Beech has a Banner Elk post office address but is actually in the town of Beech Mountain, four miles north. It's the largest ski resort in North Carolina, and at an elevation of 5,505 feet, the highest in the eastern United States. It has 14 slopes and 830 feet of vertical drop and offers four restaurants, a pub, a ski school, and an outdoor ice rink for visitors who don't ski. It also has a children's program and a nursery. For information, contact Ski Beech, P.O. Box 1118, Banner Elk, N.C. 28604 (828-387-2011 or 800-438-2093).

Sugar Mountain Resort, immediately north of Banner Elk, boasts 18 slopes with 1,200 feet of vertical drop, the steepest in the state. Ski lessons and equipment rental are available, as are two cafeterias, a restaurant, and a lounge with live entertainment. For information, contact Sugar Mountain Resort, P.O. Box 369, Banner Elk, N.C. 28604 (828-898-4521).

Ski Hawksnest is off N.C. 105 in the town of Seven Devils. It offers 14 slopes with 669 feet of vertical drop, plus ski instruction and full-scale facilities at the lodge. For information, contact Ski Hawksnest, 2058 Skyland Drive, Banner Elk, N.C. 28604 (828-963-6561).

For whitewater canoeing and guided hiking and backpacking trips, call North Carolina High Country Host.

Seasonal Events

Highland Games and Gathering of the Clans is held at Grandfather Mountain in Linville the second full weekend in July. This is the largest Scottish-clan gathering in the eastern United States. The extravaganza includes Highland dancing, sheep-dog demonstrations, parading pipers, world-class athletes running in track-and-field events, and traditional Scottish events like tossing sheep sheaves and cabers. The circular track at MacRae Meadow is surrounded by decorative tents manned by members of the various clans. Scottish and American food is for sale, along with tartans, Celtic tapes, and other Scottish souvenirs.

The festivities begin on Thursday night with the dramatic Torch-light Opening Ceremony. The parade of torchbearers in traditional Scottish dress accompanied by drums and bagpipes is a stirring climax to an evening of Scottish entertainment. Friday's activities focus on contests for bagpipers and traditional Scottish dancers and the Celidh, a concert of Scottish folk music, song, and dance. Saturday includes more contests for dancers, bagpipers, Scottish fiddlers, harp players, and drummers. Sunday, there is more competition, plus the Clan Tug of Wars and the closing Parade of Tartans.

Parking near the meadow is restricted unless you arrive early in the week and camp nearby. Everyone else must take the shuttle buses that run from Linville, but fortunately, they tend to be amazingly efficient. An admission fee is charged. For information, call 828-733-1333.

Singing on the Mountain, held the fourth Sunday in June at Grandfather Mountain, is an outdoor gospel concert that originated in 1930. Gospel choirs and singers perform in MacRae Meadow. At times, the audience sings along. For information, call 828-733-4337.

Woolly Worm Festival, which is usually scheduled for a weekend in mid-October, is a great event for children. The festival includes food vendors, craft exhibits, and musical entertainment, but the main attraction is the woolly worm races. Fluffy caterpillars with orange and black stripes crawl up three-foot-long lanes. By "reading" the stripes on the overall winner, officials forecast the severity of the approaching winter. If you don't have your own worm, plenty are available for purchase. There is a small admission fee. Call 800-972-2183 for information.

Accommodations

There are numerous private home and condominium rentals in this area. For information, call the Avery/Banner Elk Chamber of Commerce at 800-972-2183.

Holiday Inn Banner Elk. *Moderate/Expensive*. N.C. 184 (828-898-4571 or 800-HOLIDAY). This is a predictable but comfortable hostelry. It offers pleasantly decorated rooms, plus an outdoor pool and a restaurant open for all meals.

The Beech Alpen Inn. *Moderate*. 700 Beech Mountain Parkway, Beech Mountain (828-387-2252). This charming country inn offers beautiful views of the Blue Ridge and easy access to the Beech Mountain ski slopes. Many of the rooms have fireplaces. There is also a huge fireplace in the lodge-style dining room.

Inns and Bed-and-Breakfast Guest Houses

Eseeola Lodge. *Deluxe*. Near the intersection of U.S. 221, N.C. 105, and N.C. 181 in Linville (828-733-4311). This beautiful two-story inn has a rustic look from the outside, with its chestnut-shingle siding and riot of colorful flowers in carefully tended beds, but it's graced with a country elegance inside. One of the first things you will see is the massive fieldstone fireplace. Each of the rooms is comfortably furnished and has a private porch, window boxes, and a lovely mountain view. If you want to do more than just rest, you can golf at some of the best courses in the country, play tennis, or ride horses. The rates include two meals.

Archers Mountain Inn. *Moderate/Expensive.* Beech Mountain Parkway, Beech Mountain (828-898-9004). Perched on the side of Beech Mountain, this country inn offers a spectacular view of the Elk River Valley and the surrounding mountains. Each of the 14 rooms has a private bath and a fireplace. Rocking chairs on the porches allow you to take advantage of the view.

Azalea Inn Bed and Breakfast. *Moderate/Expensive.* Azalea Circle in Banner Elk, behind the Village Shops (828-898-8195). This is a comfortable bed-and-breakfast complete with an acre of flower gardens, a living room with wormy chestnut paneling, two sun porches, and a white picket fence. Each of the five guest rooms has a private bath (some with a claw-foot tub), and remote-control TV.

The Inn at Elk River. *Moderate.* On N.C. 194 between the entrance to Elk River Club and N.C. 184, Banner Elk (828-898-9669). This Williamsburg-style inn has eight guest rooms, each with a private bath. The rooms have fireplaces and balconies that offer mountain vistas. There is a full-service restaurant on the premises.

Restaurants

Eseeola Lodge. *Expensive.* Near the intersection of U.S. 221, N.C. 105, and N.C. 181 in Linville (828-733-4311). The surroundings here are elegant—for dinner, a coat and tie for men and appropriate dress for women are required. The restaurant has won the prestigious Mobil Four-Star Award, so you know it's special. It features French and New American cuisine. A special seafood buffet is served on Thursday evenings. Breakfast and dinner are served daily. Reservations are required.

Morels Restaurant. *Expensive.* 1 Banner Street, Banner Elk (828-898-6866). This restaurant is small, but its bistro style has a chic ambiance. That may be due to the chef, who established a fine reputation at several well-known Florida restaurants before coming to Linville Ridge as that club's executive chef. Later, he opened Morels. The cuisine is continental, featuring dishes such as fresh salmon seared in honey. Dinner is served nightly.

Louisiana Purchase Food and Spirits. *Moderate/Expensive*. N.C. 184, Banner Elk (828-898-5656). This establishment specializes in Cajun, Creole, and French cuisine and boasts the largest wine list in the area. Open daily for dinner only. Reservations are suggested.

Stonewalls. *Moderate*. N.C. 184, Banner Elk (828-898-5550). Located in a rambling fieldstone house with crosshatched windows, this restaurant has a relaxed country atmosphere. Teriyaki chicken, top sirloin, and broiled fish are the main entrées. Dinner is served daily.

Fred's Deli. *Inexpensive*. In Fred's General Mercantile Company on Beech Mountain Parkway, Beech Mountain (828-387-4838). Fred's General Mercantile resembles an old-fashioned general store in more ways than its name. It's here that the locals gather. Although they may be more affluent than the typical patrons of the old general store, the customers here still buy a sandwich, a salad, or a cup of coffee to enjoy inside or on the deck while they read the newspaper or chat with their neighbors. The restaurant offers a wide selection of deli meats and cheeses and encourages you to build your own sandwich. Every Saturday, it offers a "Great American Backyard Cookout." The owners also sponsor several concerts and community events in front of their store during the summer and fall.

Nick's. *Inexpensive*. In the Shoppes at Tynecastle, at the junction of U.S. 105 and N.C. 184 (828-898-9613). Located in an upscale shopping center, this restaurant offers sandwiches and salads, along with a good selection of wines and imported beers.

Spruce Pine / Burnsville

Spruce Pine, although a small town by most standards, is still the largest in Mitchell County, an area known for its rugged landscape and gem mining. In Mitchell County, the North Toe River has carved out a valley among the highest mountain ranges in the eastern United States. Immediately southwest are the Black Mountains, where Mount Mitchell presides over a dozen peaks more than 6,000 feet high.

Burnsville is the seat of Yancey County, which includes the Black Mountains. It is a pretty little town with a statue in the town square of Captain Otway Burns, the Revolutionary War privateer for whom the town was named. Reportedly, he so harassed the British fleet in his ship, *Snap Dragon*, that King George put a price on his head.

Both counties were settled by tough mountaineers, and the community names reflect the environment they found—Hoot Owl, Bear Creek, Possum Trot, Pigeon Roost.

Some evidence indicates that the first miners in the area may have been Spaniards looking for gold in 1665. Gemstones—emeralds and aquamarines in particular—were discovered about 100 years ago and were mined commercially. But for the past 75 years or so, the mines have attracted only rock hounds and tourists who like the idea of searching for their own gems. Spruce Pine is the site of the annual North Carolina Mineral and Gem Festival.

Visitors who aren't interested in minerals will find some beautiful high-mountain scenery in this area, without the garish development that usually follows an increase in tourism. In fact, compared to other mountain areas, Spruce Pine and Burnsville are underdeveloped, although this is quickly changing.

ACCESS:
Spruce Pine is at the intersection of
U.S. 19E and N.C. 226 only six miles
off the Blue Ridge Parkway at Milepost
331.

Burnsville is located at the intersection of U.S. 19 and N.C. 197. From
Milepost 344 on the Blue Ridge Parkway, follow N.C. 80 to U.S. 19.

VISITOR INFORMATION:
For information about the Spruce Pine
area, contact the Mitchell County Chamber of Commerce, Route 1, Box 796,
Spruce Pine, N.C. 28777 (828-765-
9483 or 800-227-3912). The offices
are located at the Museum of North
Carolina Minerals, where the Blue Ridge
Parkway intersects N.C. 226.

For information about the Burnsville
area, contact the Yancey County Chamber of Commerce, 106 West Main
Street, Burnsville, N.C. 28714 (828-
682-7413).

Attractions

The **Museum of North Carolina Minerals** is part of the Blue Ridge Parkway Visitor Center, located at Milepost 331. Exhibits display the wide range of minerals found in North Carolina, and the gift shop carries books on gems and mining. The museum is open from 9 A.M. to 5 P.M. daily. Admission is free. Call 828-765-2761.

If you want to go mining for your own gems, there are several mines open to the public. They generally operate the same way. You pay about $5 for admission to the mine area, then a small fee for three or four buckets of gravel excavated from the mine shaft, which you rinse in a flume a little at a time, looking for raw gemstones. Although it's unlikely you'll find high-quality gems, you can take home garnets and pretend they're rubies.

Emerald Village, on McKinney Mine Road in Little Switzerland, offers an underground museum in an old mine. You can see equipment and methods used for mining gems a century ago. A gem and mineral gift shop is also on the premises, and snacks and hot foods are available. The mine offers enriched gravel, which increases your chances of finding gems—a good idea if you're taking children. The village is open daily from 9 A.M. to 6 P.M. from Memorial Day to Labor Day and from 9 A.M. to 5 P.M. during May, September, and October. Fees are charged only for the mine tour and mining buckets. For information, call 828-765-MINE.

For mines that are open for tourists, call the Mitchell County Chamber of Commerce at 828-765-9483.

Orchard at Altapass offers a view into the history and lore of the mountains and the growing of some of the best apples in the country. Located in Little Switzerland, this is the only private business with direct access to the Blue Ridge Parkway (the parkway actually bisects the orchard). Hayrides, mountain music, and storytelling are only a few of the entertainments to be found here. The gift shop, located in the packing house, sells homemade crafts, sweets, and, yes, apples. Groups are offered special rates, and lunches are available. Call 888-765-9531 or visit their Web site at http://blowingrock.com/northcarolina/altapass-orchard.

Mount Mitchell State Park, located in Yancey County, boasts the highest peak east of the Mississippi River. Accessible at Milepost 355 of the Blue Ridge Parkway, the park has picnic areas, nature trails, a lookout tower offering a spectacular mountain view, camping areas, a concession stand, and a ranger station, where you can get maps of hiking trails and further information. The park and ranger stations are open year-round except Christmas Day; the concession stand is only open May through October. For information, call 828-675-4611.

Special Shopping

Pine Crossing, on N.C. 226 just north of the parkway in Spruce Pine, is a charming 1920s country store with a traditional crafts gallery specializing in country primitives. As you browse through the store, you'll find regional antiques, tools, country-store items, prints, and collectibles. The store is open Tuesday through Saturday from 10 A.M. to 5 P.M. from May through late October. Call 828-765-8400.

Recreation

You'll find 18 miles of hiking trails at Mount Mitchell State Park. To receive a trail map, you can visit the ranger station at the park or call 828-675-4611.

A popular summer activity is **tubing** on the South Toe River. At Carolina Hemlocks Recreation Area on N.C. 80, you will notice crowds of people bobbing along the river in rubber inner tubes. The gentle cascades and slow-moving current lend just enough excitement to make the activity exhilarating but not too dangerous. Remember, these mountain streams are cold, so you may want to wait for a hot summer day. You will see signs for tube rentals at the small convenience marts near the recreation area.

Seasonal Events

North Carolina Mineral and Gem Festival, held the first week of August in Spruce Pine, presents exhibits and demonstrations. For information, call 828-765-9483.

Mount Mitchell Crafts Fair is held on Burnsville's town square the first weekend in August. For information, call 828-682-7413.

Side Trips

Take N.C. 226 south from Spruce Pine for 10 miles to **Little Switzerland**. If you can, stop for lunch at The Chalet Restaurant, which features Swiss architecture and an awe-inspiring view of a beautiful mountain valley.

Penland School, founded in 1929, has earned an international reputation for nurturing craftspeople to attain the highest artistic levels. In a remote mountain setting, courses are offered in traditional media: clay, fibers, paper, wood, glass, iron, and jewelry. The school's craft shop sells some of this work. It is open from April through November. The hours are 10 A.M. to noon and 1 to 4:30 P.M. from Tuesday through Saturday and noon to 4:30 P.M. on Sunday. To get there, take S.R. 1162 (Penland Road) off U.S. 19E between Spruce Pine and Burnsville. It is 2.9 miles to a left turn onto S.R. 1164. It is then 1.8 miles on this winding road to the school. For information, call 828-765-2359.

Accommodations

Switzerland Inn. *Moderate.* N.C. 226A at the Blue Ridge Parkway exit at Milepost 334, Little Switzerland (828-765-2153). This inn is wonderfully evocative of Switzerland, with chalet-style architecture, paintings of storks on the chimney, and a magnificent panoramic view. An entire wall of the fieldstone-floored lobby is a window framing a sweeping view of well-groomed lawns and the Black Mountain Valley beyond. The rooms are decorated with hand-painted Alpine murals. For more privacy, small cottages and cottage suites are available. Outside the lodge is a small cluster of similarly styled shops. The high-ceilinged restaurant is open for all meals. Reservations are usually necessary well in advance.

Pinebridge Inn. *Inexpensive/Moderate*. 101 Pinebridge Avenue, Spruce Pine (828-765-5543 or 800-356-5059). This hotel and executive center is a renovated elementary school. The exterior is brick surrounded by a lot of asphalt, but the interior has been attractively redone. The rooms—former classrooms—are so large that the furniture is out of proportion, but all the same, they're comfortably furnished. The former auditorium has been transformed into a presentation hall, and the complex has access to the neighboring physical-fitness facility, which has an indoor pool and an ice-skating rink.

Inns and Bed-and-Breakfast Guest Houses

The Castle Inn on English Knob. *Deluxe*. Castle Way, Spruce Pine (828-765-0000 or 800-925-2645). This royally appointed inn features five private suites, each with its own individual climate controls, TV, VCR, stained glass windows, and French-style leaded doors that lead to balcony areas. One of the area's best restaurants is located in the inn, too.

Nu-Wray Inn. *Moderate*. On the town square in Burnsville (828-682-2329). Nu-Wray Inn has been operating since 1833, though it has been expanded from a log cabin into a handsome three-story clapboard structure with rocking chairs on the porch. Inside, the lobby has a cluttered but friendly feeling, with its cuckoo clocks and collection of old musical instruments. The parlor is furnished with Victorian pieces and a player piano. The rooms are a bit on the small side, with floral-print wallpaper and white chenille bedspreads. For more privacy, ask for a room away from the square, to avoid the handful of young townspeople who like to cruise at night around the square in front of the inn. The atmosphere here is casual and friendly; you're likely to strike up a new friendship, especially around the large dinner tables in the dining room. Breakfast is included.

Restaurants

Although a few fast-food outlets have opened near Spruce Pine and Burnsville, there is a scarcity of restaurants in this area.

The Castle Inn on English Knob. *Expensive*. At the Castle Inn in Spruce Pine (828-765-000 or 800-925-2645). This restaurant is definitely one of the most exclusive in the area. Adults only are permitted, and then only in appropriate attire. Once you've gained admittance, though, the food will more than make up for having to dress formally. Seven-course gourmet dining is offered seven nights a week year-round. The four-course Sunday meal from noon to 5 P.M. features such fare as fresh salmon fillets stuffed with backfin crab. Afternoon tea is available Tuesday, Thursday, and Saturday.

The Chalet Restaurant. *Moderate.* At the Switzerland Inn in Little Switzerland (828-765-2153). The Chalet offers continental fare in a large, open room with a view of the mountain valley. Entrées include pasta, pork loin, chicken with avocado, and roast beef. Open daily for breakfast, lunch, and dinner.

Nu-Wray Inn. *Inexpensive.* On the town square in Burnsville (828-682-2329). Nu-Wray serves up a whopping dinner of country food. For example, your meal might include roast beef and potatoes, corn soufflé, lima beans, carrots, slaw, and biscuits—plus dessert. All guests enter and are seated at the same time, family-style, at large tables. You're instructed as to which way the dishes should be passed, and then you're on your own. Unless you're a total recluse, you'll have fun. Breakfast offerings are equally generous. Nu-Wray is open nightly for dinner at 6 P.M. from May through late October, and reservations are necessary. Dinner is served Friday and Saturday nights only and lunch Sunday only during the off-season.

Asheville

If you approach Asheville from the east on I-40, the Blue Ridge Mountains appear low in the distance, pale as a mirage. As you come closer, they seem to grow taller and bluer, and the road begins an incline. Soon, mountains fill the horizon. The air gets cooler, and the road rises and falls as if the mountains were softly breathing.

As the road cuts through Pisgah National Forest, the signs of civilization are left behind for a while. There's only the forest and the ascending ribbon of asphalt. Suddenly, the road curves strongly to the left, presenting a fabulous view of the forested slopes you've just climbed. At last, you're really in the mountains. It's still a half-hour to Asheville, but once you round that curve, you feel you're already there.

A favorite view of Asheville for many people is from the Sunset Terrace of the Grove Park Inn late in the day. High on a hill north of the city, you can look down across the golf course and the surrounding trees to the city beyond. Asheville is situated on a plateau, and its skyline is set against a backdrop of softly rounded mountains. When the sun goes down, the sky turns bright salmon, the mountains deepen to violet, and the city lights come on.

Asheville is a dream destination for a publicity team. The city has regional culture, a strong craft tradition, a stunning French Renaissance chateau, historic buildings, a good selection of restaurants and accommodations, and superior recreational options. No wonder visitors choose it as their base from which to explore the Blue Ridge and Great Smoky Mountains.

Asheville, incorporated in 1797, was named for Governor Samuel Ashe. The area was settled by Scots-Irish immigrants from Northern Ireland, who set up homesteads in the mountains. These early settlers were so isolated from other parts of the state that they developed a unique Appalachian culture that is still visible today in their music and crafts.

In the 1880s, the railroad came to Asheville, and the town of 2,600 became the focus of a development boom. Rich people from the flatlands, discovering how cool and restorative mountain summers could be, built large homes—the grandest of which was George W. Vanderbilt's 250-room Biltmore Estate—and made lengthy visits to elaborate resort hotels such as the Grove Park Inn. Asheville's population quickly grew to 10,000.

Asheville had another boom period during the 1920s. Art Deco was a favored style of that era, and you'll see many buildings with "shoulders" in their silhouettes, embellished with colorful bas-relief carvings. City hall has an octagonal domed roof covered with pink and green tiles. When it was built, officials decided it was too opulent looking and canceled the architect's contract for the county courthouse next door. The result was a structure so severe that it looks like Clark Kent's *Daily Planet* building. The most strikingly beautiful building in Asheville may be the Spanish Baroque–style St. Lawrence Church on Haywood Street, the first Catholic church in North Carolina. It has a copper-covered dome, two domed towers, and a polychrome terra-cotta bas-relief over the entrance. Though the building looks as if it belongs in Seville, the bricks were made in the South.

There's a lot of historic restoration going on, both to save the buildings and to inject more life into the downtown area, which declined—as in so many American cities—as shoppers were drawn to neighborhood malls. In recent years, downtown has gained a reputation as a lively spot, thanks to its eclectic boutiques, shops,

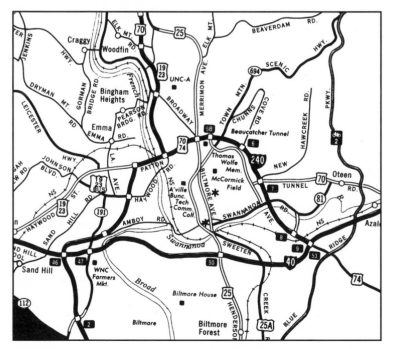

Courtesy of N.C. Department of Transportation

restaurants, bars, and Pack Place. Historic Montford, a residential area just north of downtown, is also seeing its turn-of-the-century houses restored.

When you come to Asheville, plan to visit the downtown area. Guided walking tours are available; for information, call 828-254-2343. Or you can visit the Thomas Wolfe Memorial or shop at over 100 retail shops, many of which sell antiques and crafts.

You'll probably discover you want to extend your stay in Asheville, because you'll keep finding things to do. And once you see those gorgeous sunsets, you won't want to leave them behind.

ACCESS:

Asheville is at the intersection of I-40 and I-26.

Asheville Regional Airport is served by three major carriers.

The Greyhound bus station is at 2 Tunnel Road (828-253-5353).

VISITOR INFORMATION:

Stop by the Asheville Visitor Center at 151 Haywood Street, just off I-240 at Exit 4C. The center is open daily. If you're planning a visit, contact the Asheville Convention and Visitors Bureau, P.O. Box 1010, Asheville, N.C. 28802 (828-258-6109 or 800-257-1300).

The daily newspaper is the *Asheville Citizen-Times*, which has a special "Take Five" entertainment section on Thursdays. You can also find event and restaurant listings in the free weekly tabloid *Mountain X-Press*.

Attractions

Historic Places

Biltmore Estate, located on U.S. 25 three blocks north of Exit 50 on I-40, is, quite simply, spectacular. Built for George W. Vanderbilt, Biltmore was modeled after the elaborate 16th-century chateaus of France's Loire Valley. Surrounded by rolling forestland and enhanced by a lagoon, an arboretum, and azalea, rose, and formal walled gardens, Biltmore is one of North Carolina's most frequently visited tourist attractions.

Ever since it opened as a private home in 1895, Biltmore has excited interest for the balance and beauty of its design and the luxury of its amenities. Not only did it have the unheard-of luxuries of central

Biltmore House and Gardens
Photograph by William Russ
Courtesy of N.C. Travel and Tourism Division

heating, indoor plumbing, electric lights, and mechanical refrigeration, but guests could also enjoy a bowling alley, a gymnasium, and an indoor pool—astonishing features at the time.

The grandson of industrialist Cornelius Vanderbilt, George Vanderbilt decided to build his home in Asheville because the mountain views and climate pleased him. He purchased 125,000 acres of forestland and hired two of America's foremost designers to plan the estate.

Architect Richard Morris Hunt oversaw construction of the 250-room mansion, which took 1,000 men five years to complete. Brick kilns and woodworking shops were set up. Indiana limestone was transported on a private railroad spur and dressed on the property. Artisans were brought from Europe—master carvers, plasterers, and metalworkers.

Landscape architect Frederick Law Olmsted, who designed New York's Central Park, laid out the gardens and the park area surrounding the house, including the curving three-mile approach road from the main gate. The 250 acres of gently undulating land surrounding the house are studded with mature oak and elm in the natural style Olmsted made famous. The formal flower gardens adjacent to the house were based on those at the Vaux le Vicomte chateau near Paris.

Unlike some of his relatives, who had their mansions and summer social scene in Newport, Rhode Island, Vanderbilt was concerned about land management, and he developed his estate into a productive farming and forestry enterprise. Although Biltmore Estate is still owned by Vanderbilt's descendants, today only 8,000 acres of the original property remain; the rest was sold to the federal government and became part of the Blue Ridge Parkway or Pisgah National Forest.

You must pay admission at the Lodge Gate, then drive the three miles to the parking area. You first see the French Renaissance house across a long lawn with a reflecting pool in the center. It's enormous, and the complexity of the design—such as the carved archways, columns, gargoyles, and window frames—is stunning. But that only begins to prepare you for the visual feast inside.

Each room has a distinctive tone. The medieval-style banquet room has a 70-foot ceiling arching over a table that seats 64. Flemish tapestries and a dozen elk and moose heads hang on the walls, and a carved mantel spans three fireplaces. The two-story Baroque-style library has elaborately carved walnut paneling, a marble mantel, and an 18th-century ceiling painting imported from a Venetian palace.

You should set aside at least half a day for your visit to the estate. The tour lasts about two hours, taking you through nine major rooms on the main floor, the small trophy and smoking rooms, and other rooms upstairs. The tour then leads downstairs to the service area—the laundry, kitchens, pantries, and servants' rooms, as well as the gymnasium, bowling alley, and pool. You may also roam the gardens and visit the Biltmore Estate Winery.

Anytime you visit Biltmore, it will be crowded, but it's well worth seeing even if you have to share the experience with scores of others. You'll enjoy it more if you get there early in the day and if you avoid school holidays. Two times of year draw especially large crowds—the holiday season, when the entire house is lavishly adorned in Victorian Christmas finery, and April and May, when spring blossoms are at their peak and each room has a different floral display.

If you get hungry, there are a few dining options. The Stable Cafe, inside the stable next to the main house, offers entrées, sandwiches, drinks, and ice cream. The Deer Park Restaurant and the Winery Bistro offer a more upscale menu selection.

The ticket office is open from 8:30 A.M to 5 P.M. Monday through Friday and from 8:30 A.M. to 4 P.M. on the weekends. The house is open from 9 A.M. to 5 P.M. daily, and the winery is open Monday through Saturday from 11 A.M. to 7 P.M. and Sunday from noon to 7 P.M.; both are closed on Thanksgiving Day and Christmas. Admission is charged, and it is not inexpensive. However, when you consider that it includes at least half a day's entertainment, it doesn't seem quite as steep. For information, call 828-255-1700 or 800-543-2961.

Visitors to the **Thomas Wolfe Memorial**, located at 52 North Market Street downtown, will be in for a shock when they learn that the house is closed for repairs due to an arsonist's fire. Luckily, over 85 percent of the artifacts and personal belongings of the Wolfe family were recovered from the July 24, 1998, fire, and are now in storage or on display at the adjoining visitor center. They will remain there until the house reopens sometime in 2001 or 2002. The visitor center will remain open throughout the repairs to educate and inform visitors about the formative years of one of America's premier writers. For example, you'll learn that young Thomas didn't have a room of his own in the 28-room house because his mother used all the available bedroom space for lodgers in her boardinghouse.

When Wolfe published his 1929 novel, *Look Homeward, Angel*, about the "Dixieland" boardinghouse in "Altamont," people and incidents in Asheville were only thinly disguised. Wolfe and his work were not appreciated by his hometown residents, and the book was even banned from the Asheville Public Library for more than seven years. But in 1948, only 10 years after Wolfe's early death, the Asheville Chamber of Commerce helped to purchase the house as a memorial to the Asheville native who had become recognized as one of this century's great novelists. In 1976, the city turned it over to the state, and it was designated a State Historic Site.

The visitor center is open Monday through Saturday from 9 A.M. to 5 P.M. and Sunday from 1 to 5 P.M. Hours are shortened in the winter. For information, call 828-253-8304.

Museums

Pack Place, located at 2 South Pack Square in downtown Asheville, opened in 1992. The $14-million complex is western North Carolina's arts-and-science center. It houses several local organizations associated with the arts, as well as galleries and studios for artists. The **Asheville Art Museum** has a modest collection of contemporary and traditional paintings and some sculpture by Southern artists, particularly southern Appalachian artists. The **Colburn Gem and Mineral Museum** has over 1,500 gems, semiprecious stones, mineral specimens, and fossils on display. The complex also includes **Health Adventure, YMI Cultural Museum** (Asheville's African-American cultural center), and a 514-seat performing-arts theater. It is open Tuesday through Saturday from 10 A.M. to 6 P.M. and Sunday from 1 to 5 P.M. from June through October; it is closed Sundays during the winter season. For information, call 828-257-4500.

Smith-McDowell Museum of Western North Carolina History, at 283 Victoria Road, is a museum in Asheville's oldest existing house. The three-story brick house with double-tiered full-length porches was built around 1840 on a land grant that opened the area to permanent settlement. In 1974, the Western North Carolina Historical Association leased the house and raised funds to restore it. Furnished with period furniture, it features temporary exhibits such as Victorian wedding gowns and antique watches. The museum is open Tuesday through Saturday from 10 A.M. to 4 P.M. and Sunday from 1 to 4 P.M. from May through December. It is open Tuesday through Friday from 10 A.M. to 4 P.M. from January through April. A small admission fee is charged. Group tours are available by arrangement. For information, call 828-253-9231.

Western North Carolina Nature Center, located at 75 Gashes Creek Road on the grounds of the former Asheville Zoo, was designed to show the interaction between plants and animals in the southern Appalachian environment. The nature center presents animals in natural-habitat exhibits. For example, you can see the underground den of a live chipmunk beneath a tree's roots. Aimed at family audiences, exhibits are aimed at several levels to interest both children and adults and invite repeat visits. The center's Educational Farm allows close inspection of a number of domestic animals—children can see a cow being milked, for example. A small gift shop offers nature-related books and souvenirs. The center is open daily from 10 A.M. to 5 P.M. A small admission fee is charged. For information, call 828-298-5600.

Gardens

Botanical Gardens at Asheville, at 151 W. T. Weaver Street, were designed to preserve and display trees, plants, and flowers native to the southern Appalachians. In 1960, several garden clubs participated in planting the grounds, which extend over 10 acres of the University of North Carolina at Asheville. Now operating as a nonprofit organization, the gardens provide a study area and information center for those interested in horticulture and a place of quiet beauty for everyone. Unpaved trails wind through various areas, including the azalea garden and the garden for the blind. A wheelchair accessible ramp is available. The gardens are open daily during daylight hours. Admission is free. For information, call 828-252-5190.

Special Shopping

Folk Art Center, located just east of Asheville at Milepost 382 on the Blue Ridge Parkway, displays the work of the Southern Highland Craft Guild craftspeople, who make—among other things—pottery, baskets, quilts, candles, brooms, weavings, furniture, jewelry, dolls, musical instruments, and woodcarvings. Surrounded by trees and azaleas, the stone building with a low-slung roof opened in 1980 to serve as an educational center, exhibition space, research library, and craft shop. At various times, you can see folk dancing, a lecture series, demonstrations of traditional handicrafts, and exhibits of work by individuals. The Allanstand Craft Shop, part of the center, offers the largest and most diverse collection of high-quality handmade crafts anywhere in the North Carolina mountains. Bring money—you can take care of your Christmas list here. The center is open from 9 A.M. to 6 P.M. daily; it closes an hour earlier during January, February, and March. Admission is free. For information, call 828-298-7928.

Biltmore Village, across from Biltmore Estate, is a small neighborhood of houses built for the artisans and craftsmen who helped construct the estate house. In recent years, the two-story stucco houses have been turned into restaurants and shops selling gifts, stationery, jewelry, clothing, knitting supplies, and household accessories. Some of the houses are brightly painted—pink or turquoise, for example—and appealing displays in their front windows beckon passersby to stop.

Western North Carolina Farmers Market, on Brevard Road off N.C. 191 and I-40, is the place to go for fresh local fruit and vegetables, dried flowers, jams and jellies, and homemade craft items. This modern facility, operated by the North Carolina Department of Agriculture, is open year-round. The market is open Monday through Friday from 8 A.M. to 6 P.M. Admission is free. Call 828-253-1691 for information.

Grovewood Gallery, on Grovewood Road adjoining the Grove Park Inn, used to be known as the Biltmore Homespun Shops. The shops were established in 1901 by Mrs. George Vanderbilt as a school to preserve the dyeing, spinning, and weaving skills mountain residents learned from their English and Scottish immigrant ancestors. In addition to the gallery and shops, there's a museum where you can see a brief film about the history of the Biltmore weaving industry. In the shops, you can buy lengths of handwoven wool, along with many kinds of handmade crafts and gifts. The gallery and shops are open Monday through Saturday from 10 A.M. to 6 P.M. and Sunday from 1 to 5 P.M. from April through December; they are open Monday through Saturday from 10 A.M. to 5 P.M. from January through March. The museum is open Monday through Saturday from 10 A.M. to 5 P.M. and Sunday from 1 to 5 P.M. during the spring, summer, and fall, but is open only on Friday and Saturday from 10 A.M. to 5 P.M. during the winter. Admission to the museum is free. Call 828-253-7651 for information.

Over the past several years, downtown Asheville has experienced a revitalization. The hilly streets are now dotted with coffee houses, antique shops, boutiques, and restaurants. **Wall Street** is a concentration of these interesting shops and restaurants. Part of the street has been blocked off to create a pedestrian mall. Just around the corner at 55 Haywood Street is **Malaprop's**, one of the finest bookstores in western North Carolina. Be sure to check out the fine selection of regional books before heading for a cappuccino in the eclectic coffee house.

Cultural Offerings

The Asheville Symphony is a fine regional orchestra. Founded in 1960, the symphony offers a series of classical concerts usually featuring an internationally known guest artist. For information, call 828-254-7046.

Asheville Community Theatre, at 35 East Walnut Street, presents six productions—including comedies, dramas, and a musical—in its own theater annually. A reader's theater, a children's theater, and classes are also offered. For information, call 828-254-1320.

Recreation

You'll find no shortage of outdoor activities around Asheville— you're surrounded by three park areas comprising more than a million acres of national forest, with ample opportunities for camping, hiking, fishing, and river rafting.

If you're interested in visiting **Great Smoky Mountains National Park**, call 423-436-1200 for information. For camping in the six campgrounds of the **Blue Ridge Parkway**, call 828-298-0398. For camping in **Pisgah National Forest**, call 828-257-4200.

Hiking opportunities include the legendary **Appalachian Trail**, which cuts through Pisgah National Forest and Great Smoky Mountains National Park. Check with the park offices listed above.

For **fishing**, consider Lake Julian, south of Asheville on N.C. 280, off U.S. 25; Lake Powhatan, on N.C. 191 just off the Blue Ridge Parkway south of Asheville; or Lake Lure, on U.S. 74 southeast of Asheville. You'll need a state fishing license, available from any license agent (K-marts and many hardware and sporting-goods stores, for example). For information about hunting and fishing regulations, call the chamber of commerce at 828-258-6101.

Whitewater rafting is available June through August on the French Broad River, about 30 minutes north of Asheville. If you're serious about rafting and want to try other rivers, see *Franklin: Recreation* for companies that raft the Nantahala Gorge.

Although enjoying the outdoors in North Carolina doesn't immediately suggest **skiing**, the highest mountains in the eastern United States are in this state. Man-made snow enhances the base of natural snow. Closest to Asheville are Wolf Laurel Ski Resort (828-689-4111), near Mars Hill, and Cataloochee Ski Resort (828-926-0285 or 800-768-0285), in Maggie Valley. Check the recreation listings under *Boone* and *Banner Elk/Beech Mountain/Linville* for other ski resorts.

Golf is a special pleasure in the mountains, thanks to the sparkling clear air and striking views. In the city, consider the Buncombe County Golf Club (828-298-1867), Black Mountain Golf Course (828-669-2710), Reems Creek Golf Club (828-645-4393), and

Grove Park Inn and Country Club (828-252-2711).

There's **baseball** here, too. The Asheville Tourists, a class A farm team for the Colorado Rockies, play from April through August at McCormick Field, off U.S. 25. For information, call 828-258-0428.

Seasonal Events

The **Mountain Dance and Folk Festival** is held on the first weekend in July to showcase the best mountain crafts, musicians, and dancers—cloggers and folk dancers—in the region. This is considered the "Granddaddy of Mountain Festivals" and has been going since 1927, when Bascom Lamar Lunsford started it. For information, call 828-258-6107 or 800-257-1300.

Southern Highlands Handicraft Guild Fair is held the third weekend in July and the third weekend in October. More than 100 craftspeople from the South demonstrate their skills and exhibit and sell their works. There's also mountain music and dancing. For information, call 828-298-7928.

Bele Chere Downtown Community Celebration, held the last weekend in July, features bands (many of them nationally known), international food vendors, races, and contests in the downtown area, which is closed to vehicles. For information, call 828-259-5800.

Shindig on the Green is a series of bluegrass music concerts held on Saturday nights throughout the summer. The concerts take place on City-County Plaza and are free to the public. For more information, contact the Asheville Convention and Visitors Bureau at 828-258-6109 or 800-257-1300.

Side Trips

Black Mountain, a small community in the Swannanoa Valley about 10 miles east of Asheville, has a history of attracting nonconformist freethinkers. Once a spiritual center for the Cherokee Indians, and home of the experimental Black Mountain College from 1933 to 1956, it's now the center of the largest concentration of religious retreats in the United States. There are 20 in a 35-mile radius.

Surrounded by mountain scenery that changes moods with the changing light, Black Mountain draws visitors to see the beautiful Montreat Conference Center and to enjoy shopping for antiques and crafts. On one long block of Cherry Street, you'll find Seven

Sisters Gallery and Shop, the Old Depot Association Arts and Crafts Center, and half a dozen other shops selling antiques and those ubiquitous collectibles.

An amusing place for lunch is **Pepper's** sandwich shop, at 122 Cherry Street, so named for its remarkable display of Dr. Pepper memorabilia. It is open for lunch Monday through Saturday. For information, call 828-669-1885.

For an overnight stay, consider the **Red Rocker Inn**, at 136 North Dougherty Street. This is an old-fashioned inn with a wide porch that looks out onto a tree-shaded yard. Each of its rooms is different; most have private baths, and all feature homey decor with country antiques. Country breakfasts, à la carte lunches, and family-style dinners are served in the dining room. The inn is open from mid-February through December. No credit cards are accepted. For information, call 828-669-5991.

Craggy Gardens, located between Milepost 363 and Milepost 369 on the Blue Ridge Parkway, weren't laid out as formal gardens, but they are an ideal place for viewing slopes aglow with blooming mountain laurel and rhododendron in June and the flaming colors of autumn leaves in October. Trails wind through high-mountain trees, shrubs, and flowers, and a picnic area commands a striking view of Blue Ridge peaks. The visitor center has displays of the area's geology; occasionally, the rangers present interpretive programs. For information, call 828-298-0398.

Zebulon B. Vance Homestead, about 12 miles north of Asheville near Weaverville, is a State Historic Site that features a reconstruction of the mountain home of one of North Carolina's great statesmen, best known as its Civil War governor. The two-story structure of hewn pine logs is furnished with period pieces, a few of them from the original house, built in 1790. The log outbuildings served as a corncrib, a springhouse, a smokehouse, a loom house, a slave house, and a tool house. The visitor-center displays illustrate the life of that time, and a guide explains how the Vances and other homesteaders in the mountains lived. You might want to take a picnic lunch to enjoy on the grounds. The homestead is open Tuesday through Saturday from 10 A.M. to 4 P.M. and Sunday from 1 to 4 P.M. from November to March. It is open Monday through Saturday from 9 A.M. to 5 P.M. and Sunday from 1 to 5 P.M. from April to October. There is no admission charge. For information, call 828-645-6706.

Carl Sandburg National Historic Site—See *Hendersonville: Historic Places.*

Cherokee Indian Reservation—See *Cherokee.*

Chimney Rock Park—See *Hendersonville: Side Trips.*

Accommodations

Asheville is well supplied with accommodations, with over 5,000 rooms ranging from economy motels to sophisticated urban hotels, from country inns to glorious, historic mountain resorts. Because many visitors use the city as the center for their mountain explorations, it's a good idea to have reservations before you arrive. This is an absolute must during the fall foliage season. For an October visit, you need reservations months in advance. Rates vary significantly between summer and winter.

The Grove Park Inn and Country Club. *Deluxe.* 290 Macon Avenue (828-252-2711 or 800-438-5800). The Grove Park Inn is one of those grand hotels where a stay is a romantic experience. In 1913, the staff polished all the coins every day so no guest would receive a tarnished silver dollar. Although they don't do that today, you'll find a similar attention to detail during your visit.

The Grove Park Inn was the dream of Wiley Grove, the owner of a pharmaceutical firm famous for Grove's Tasteless Chill Tonic. Grove found the climate of Asheville beneficial to his health and conceived of building the finest resort hotel in the world. He wanted it to look like a rustic inn. After it opened in 1913, it became a favorite of the rich and famous. Thomas Edison, Henry Ford, and Harvey Firestone vacationed here together. Now, a long hallway forms a photo gallery of other illustrious guests: Presidents Wilson, Taft, Coolidge, Hoover, and Eisenhower, along with Enrico Caruso, Bela Bartok, and Mikhail Baryshnikov, among others. Many of the rooms have brass plaques on the door that tell the date some famous person stayed in that room. For example, you may stay in the room where F. Scott Fitzgerald lived and wrote for several months. In 1973, the inn was listed on the National Register of Historic Places.

In the 1970s, the inn added a championship golf course, an indoor pool, a sports center, Nautilus equipment, and a clubhouse. And in the 1980s, wings were added to provide 510 deluxe rooms, two ballrooms, and a conference center. The new structures harmonize with the inn's original design.

As you approach the inn along a wooded drive, you'll see a massive stone structure softened by the use of rounded boulders and rounded edges on the rust-colored roofing tiles. Guests sit on the porch in rocking chairs, and a horse and open carriage await the next visitor for a drive around the property.

In the Grand Hall—an enormous room with a high ceiling— Mission furniture is clustered in groups before two massive fireplaces that can hold 10-foot logs. There is even an elevator built into the stonework behind one of the fireplaces. Guests can walk through the hall and out onto the Sunset Terrace, where the view includes the two tennis courts, part of the golf course, and the city of Asheville in the distance. If you arrive at the right time, you can watch the sun go down behind the Great Smoky Mountains.

All the guest rooms are luxurious. Accommodations in the original part of the inn have some antiques and an old-fashioned elegance. There are oversized rooms on the club floor, where guests receive complimentary breakfast, cocktails, and extra services.

Haywood Park Hotel and Promenade. *Expensive/Deluxe*. 1 Battery Park Avenue (828-252-2522 or 800-845-7638). Haywood Park is an ultrasophisticated suite hotel in the heart of downtown. The lobby is of very modern design, with open space and little clutter, highlighted with polished brass railings. The color scheme of mauve and gray continues through the luxurious suites, where you'll find marble and ceramic bathtubs. The hotel has computer hookups and a fitness center, 24-hour room service, an elegant restaurant, and an arcade of shops.

Radisson Hotel Asheville. *Expensive*. 1 Thomas Wolfe Plaza (828-252-8211 or 800-222-0859 in N.C., 800-438-3960 outside N.C.). Across the street from the Thomas Wolfe Memorial, the Radisson offers 281 attractively furnished rooms with contemporary decor—many with an enviable view of the mountains to the north.

Holiday Inn SunSpree Resort. *Moderate/Expensive*. 1 Holiday Inn Drive (828-254-3211). This resort and conference center is set on 120 parklike acres just a stone's throw from downtown Asheville. Its low-rise profile fits smoothly into the woods around it, and the dark green and brown decor reflects its sylvan setting. Some of the comfortable rooms have views of the city, which is very pretty at night; others look out onto the mountains. For work, there are extensive meeting and banquet facilities; for play, there's an 18-hole championship golf course, an indoor soccer center, and outdoor tennis courts.

Ramada Limited. *Moderate*. 180 Tunnel Road (828-254-7451 or 800-RAMADA). The Ramada has 114 pleasant rooms supplied with all the necessities but not loaded with extras. The amenities include HBO, in-room coffee, and a heated pool. The rates do go up for the fall season.

Comfort Inn. *Moderate*. 800 Fairview Road (828-298-9141). Calling itself a "luxury budget hotel," Comfort Inn offers 178 comfortable, spacious rooms and 24 suites with kitchenettes, Jacuzzis, and a queen-size sleeper-sofa in the living room area. A complimentary continental breakfast is offered in the lobby.

Inns and Bed-and-Breakfast Guest Houses

Richmond Hill Inn. *Deluxe*. 87 Richmond Hill Drive (828-252-7313 or 800-545-9238). This mansion, built in 1895, is considered Asheville's premier example of Queen Anne–style architecture. Designed as a private residence for Richmond Pearson, a former congressman and ambassador, the inn overlooks the French Broad River, the Asheville skyline, and the mountain peaks. There are 12 guest rooms inside the mansion and a row of charming cottages nearby. The inn added a new building of guest rooms called the Garden Pavillion a few years ago, increasing the number of options for its guests and bringing the number of rooms to a total of 36. The rooms are individually decorated and include a private bath, a television, and a telephone. The cottages all have fireplaces, porches, televisions, telephones, and refrigerators. A full-course gourmet breakfast is provided, as is afternoon tea.

Abbington Green Bed-and-Breakfast Inn. *Expensive/Deluxe*. 46 Cumberland Circle (800-251-2454 or www.abbingtongreen.com). Perched on a hill in a residential section of Asheville, this stately, award-winning bed-and-breakfast has a definite English flavor. The five guest rooms and the two-bedroom carriage-house suite are even named after parks and gardens in London. Each room has a private bath, and three of them have working fireplaces. A full breakfast is offered. Be sure to enjoy a stroll around the prize-winning gardens.

Cedar Crest Victorian Inn. *Expensive/Deluxe*. 674 Biltmore Avenue (828-252-1389). Cedar Crest is many people's idea of the perfect inn—strikingly attractive, with gracious service. Almost across the street from Biltmore Estate, this 1891 Victorian house has undergone extensive restoration, and the period decor is so consistent throughout that you'll feel you've stepped back in time. The entry hall and stairwell have floor-to-ceiling carved-oak paneling polished to a gleam. In front of the hall fireplace are plush rockers with antimacassars and shawls draped over the arms. The sitting room has lamps with fringed shades and ferns in the corners. Each of the guest rooms is different, but all have antique furnishings and turn-down service. A delicious full breakfast is served in the dining room.

The Lion and The Rose. *Moderate/Expensive*. 276 Montford Avenue (828-255-ROSE). Even this inn's name reflects its English manners and style. Located on a large, sloping lot in the historic Montford area, this 1895 house is a stately combination of the Queen Anne and Georgian styles. The four spacious rooms and the suite have private baths and are lavishly decorated with fresh flowers, fluffy comforters, and Victoriana. English tea is served with porcelain and silver in the afternoon. A gourmet breakfast is offered in the dining room each morning.

Flint Street Inn. *Moderate*. 116 Flint Street (828-253-6723). Flint Street Inn is located in two turn-of-the-century houses that sit side by side on a shady street in Asheville's oldest neighborhood. The atmosphere is relaxed, with lemonade or iced tea offered on hot days. The rooms, each with a private bath, are carefully furnished with country and Victorian antiques. A complete Southern-style breakfast is served in the dining room.

Pisgah View Ranch. *Inexpensive/Moderate*. Fifteen miles south of Asheville in Candler (828-667-9100). Pisgah View Ranch offers a delightful change of pace, especially if you have children who're tired of traveling; the ranch is geared for families. There's a minimum stay of two nights. Guests stay in small cottages on the sloping property, which has a view of Mount Pisgah. There's a tennis court, a heated swimming pool, lawn games, and a recreation room where you can join in mountain singing and dancing in the evenings. And you can hike or ride horseback on trails through the ranch's 2,000 acres. But what you're likely to remember most is the eating—family-style meals featuring fried chicken, ham, and homemade breads and desserts. You'll need reservations here—the ranch has a loyal clientele who make reservations for the following year as they check out. It is open from May through November. No credit cards are accepted. Rates include three meals and all recreation except horseback riding.

Restaurants

Although Asheville doesn't offer the range of restaurants you'd find in bigger cities, you won't have trouble finding a good meal.

Gabrielle's at Richmond Hill. *Expensive*. 87 Richmond Hill Drive (828-252-7313 or 800-545-9238). Guests can enjoy the fine cuisine in Richmond Hill's formal dining room or in the less formal glass-enclosed sun porch. The dining room offers Victorian ambiance, rich cherry paneling, and a three-tiered brass chandelier. The sun porch features wicker furniture, ceiling fans, and a spectacular view of the mountains. For a set price, you can order a five-course meal with a few choices for each course, or you can order from the menu. The restaurant is open for dinner every evening.

The Market Place. *Moderate/Expensive*. 20 Wall Street (828-252-4162). The owner-chef has lavished a great deal of attention on this small, intimate downtown restaurant. The continental menu changes daily. It might include an appetizer such as seafood strudel with basil cream sauce and entrées of roasted rack of lamb and mushroom flan or roasted duckling in tart cider. Dinner is served Monday through Saturday.

23 Page Restaurant/New French Bar. *Moderate/Expensive*. 1 Battery Park (828-252-3685). Located downtown, these "two restaurants in one" draw a large local and out-of-town following. Those looking for a casual cafe experience may dine at New French Bar, while those wanting fine dining might try 23 Page. Dinner is served daily at both establishments, and lunch is also offered at New French Bar.

Windmill European Grill. *Moderate*. Innsbruck Mall, Tunnel Road (828-253-5285). Windmill European Grill has a casual atmosphere—glass-topped tables and ceiling fans—and a menu that specializes in East Indian and various European cuisines. You'll find cold cherry soup and escargot Bourguignon as appetizers; entrées include Polish kielbasa, veal scaloppine, and Indian chicken tikka. Dinner is served Tuesday through Saturday.

The Laughing Seed. *Inexpensive/Moderate*. 40 Wall Street (828-252-3445). This popular downtown restaurant features a vegetarian menu with some truly innovative and delicious creations. Even non-vegetarians will go home satisfied. The atmosphere is open and casual, but expect a wait, especially on the weekends. Lunch and dinner are served daily.

Mountain Smoke House. *Inexpensive/Moderate*. 20 South Spruce

Street (828-253-4871). Though it's tucked away in the back of a building in downtown Asheville, Mountain Smoke House is worth finding. The restaurant offers a variety of beef, chicken, and pork barbecue dishes. The real specialty, however, is the entertainment—foot-stompin' mountain and bluegrass music, along with clogging and square dancing. Be sure to call ahead, as entertainment is not offered every night. Open Tuesday through Saturday for dinner, with extended hours for lunch during the leaf season. Call ahead during the off-season, as many private parties are booked during this time.

Barley's Tap Room. *Inexpensive/Moderate.* 42 Biltmore Avenue (828-255-0504). If you are a beer connoisseur, try this Asheville favorite. There's an amazing assortment of American and imported beers on tap, and even more in bottles. The menu offers a wide assortment of food, but pizza is the specialty (the stromboli's pretty darn good, too). Be sure to check out the live jazz or bluegrass featured weekly. Open daily for lunch and dinner.

The Southern Mountains ....

Most people love the southern mountains. The air is fresh, the people friendly, and the mountains gently rolling. The region encompasses roughly the four-county area south of Asheville, extending from Chimney Rock and Lake Lure in the east to Franklin in the west. You'll find natural beauty in Pisgah National Forest, including waterfalls to slide down, walk behind, and drive under; the historic home in Flat Rock of one of our greatest poets; a world-class music festival in Brevard; posh shops in Highlands; and ruby mines in Franklin. Even if each member of your family has a different interest, you'll all find something to like in this richly endowed area.

The towns are listed in the order in which you'd come to them on a clockwise trip through the region.

Hendersonville

Established around 1840 on a gently rolling plateau between the Blue Ridge and Great Smoky ranges, the town of Hendersonville attracts people who appreciate its mild climate, 2,200-foot altitude, and proximity to the surrounding mountains.

As one local resident described it, "There are more retired millionaires here than anyplace else in the country. You can walk on the street here 12 months a year and golf 11 months a year. There is no crime, no pollution. And it's full of friendly folks. They say you can live 10 years longer if you come here to live."

There are a lot of retired people in Henderson County. The tax base is supported by a handful of manufacturing facilities and increasingly by tourism. Many people visit the area to enjoy the mild temperatures and to experience the Apple Festival in the late summer.

The North Carolina Apple Festival takes place in Hendersonville on Labor Day weekend. Henderson County raises 70 percent of the state's leading fruit crop; regional farmers produce about 8 million bushels of Red and Golden Delicious, Rome Beauty, and Stayman apples each year.

Hendersonville also has an unusual landmark that many people stop to see on their way out of town. In Oakdale Cemetery, west of town on U.S. 64, is the carved angel that Thomas Wolfe wrote about in *Look Homeward, Angel*. Surrounded by a fence, it marks the grave of a minister's wife. It was this statue that Wolfe's father loved so dearly and kept on display in his gravestone-carving shop in Asheville.

ACCESS:

Hendersonville is 22 miles south of Asheville on U.S. 25, also called the Hendersonville/Asheville Highway. It is also just off I-26 heading south from Asheville. Both highways intersect with U.S. 64 in Hendersonville.

Asheville Regional Airport lies midway between Asheville and Hendersonville.

The Greyhound-Trailways bus terminal is at 337 East Seventh Avenue (828-693-1201).

VISITOR INFORMATION:

Contact Henderson County Travel and Tourism, P.O. Box 721, Hendersonville, N.C. 28793 (800-828-4244).

The daily newspaper is the *Times-News*. *This Week in WNC* is a free publication that carries event listings and lots of ads that are useful if you're shopping or looking for a place to eat.

Attractions

Historic Places

Carl Sandburg Home National Historic Site, just south of Hendersonville in Flat Rock, is the 240-acre farm where the Pulitzer Prize–winning poet and biographer spent the last 22 years of his life. In 1945, Sandburg bought the farm, called Connemara, and moved here with his wife, Paula, who was herself renowned for raising champion goats. He was so well known in the area that mail was addressed to him simply, "Carl Sandburg, Flat Rock, N.C." In 1967, shortly after his death at the age of 89, Connemara became a National Historic Site.

When you visit Connemara, you immediately get a sense of its peacefulness as you walk up the trail from the information center to the white three-story house. Built around 1838, it's surrounded by trees and situated with a view over rolling countryside, where you hear nothing but birds. Nearby are several outbuildings, and about a

Connemara,
home of Carl Sandburg
Photograph by William Russ
Courtesy of
N.C. Travel and Tourism Division

quarter-mile away is the barn where the goats were housed and tended. A few goats are still kept here.

In the reception area of the house, you can see a filmed interview of Sandburg by Edward R. Murrow. In the living room and especially in Sandburg's study, the furnishings, family pictures, shelves of books, and huge stacks of papers and magazines have been left just as they were when he was in residence. On the dining room table are his thermos of coffee, goat's milk, and a handful of letters to be opened. You feel as if at any minute he might walk in behind you. After your 30-minute tour of the house, you may enjoy walking two trails on the wooded property.

In the summer, actors and actresses from the nearby Flat Rock Playhouse dramatize stories from Sandburg's *Rootabaga Stories*, a book of children's folk tales, in a small outdoor amphitheater located on the grounds. Other performances are *World of Carl Sandburg* and *Sandburg's Lincoln.* Performances are held Tuesday through Saturday. Admission is free.

The Carl Sandburg Home is open daily except Christmas from 9 A.M. to 5 P.M. Admission to the grounds is free. The house tour costs $3 for adults; children under 17 are admitted free. For information, call 828-693-4178.

Special Shopping

Henderson County Farmers Mutual Curb Market, at 221 North Church Street in Hendersonville, offers home-grown flowers, fresh fruits and vegetables, baked goods, handmade crafts, and an impressive array of pickles, relishes, jellies, and jams. The Curb Market, as it's known, is a nice place to chat with locals, too. The market is open Tuesday, Thursday, and Saturday from 8 A.M. to 2 P.M. For information, call 828-692-8012.

Bonesteel's Hardware and Quilt Corner, at 150 White Street in Hendersonville, attracts a lot of visitors. Georgia Bonesteel is a well-known expert on quilting, largely because of her program on public television, called *Lap Quilting*. She has opened a shop offering quilting fabrics and supplies in a section of her husband's hardware store. So if you stop in to shop for patterns or fabric swatches or to look at the quilts on display, you'll be among people buying plywood and plumbing supplies. Call 828-692-0293.

Downtown Hendersonville has been revitalized over the last few years with an infusion of antique shops, art galleries, and specialty stores. **Honeysuckle Hollow**, located at 512 North Main Street, is a unique gift store that has a wide variety of merchandise such as potpourri, cards, and jewelry. **Touchstone Gallery**, at 318 North Main Street, features modern art exhibits, as well as affordable and creative gifts and crafts. **Days Gone By**, at 303 North Main Street, is an old-fashioned soda fountain. Visitors can go back in time with shakes, malts, and ice-cream sodas. Located in an old pharmacy that has occupied the same spot on Main Street since the turn of the century, this is the real deal, not a historic recreation. The **Mast General Store** is also an attraction you may want to explore. For information on the store, see the listing in the Boone section or call 828-696-1883.

Cultural Offerings

Flat Rock Playhouse Theatre, just south of Hendersonville in Flat Rock, is the state theater of North Carolina. It's a professional summer theater that presents eight or nine comedies, mysteries, and musicals from late May to mid-October. Periodically, Thomas Wolfe's *Look Homeward, Angel* is presented in honor of the local boy. This is not outdoor drama; it's in an air-conditioned building. For information, call 828-693-0731.

Recreation .....

Holmes State Forest, about eight miles southwest of Hendersonville on Crab Creek Road, is a managed forest with picnic areas, hiking trails, and sites for tent camping. Some of the trees have button-activated recordings about aspects of the forest. The forest is open for visitors Tuesday through Sunday from mid-March to the Friday before Thanksgiving. For information, call 828-692-0100.

For information about golf and tennis facilities, call Henderson County Travel and Tourism at 800-828-4244.

Seasonal Events

North Carolina Apple Festival, held during Labor Day weekend, celebrates the apple harvest with street dancing and crafts for sale. The King Apple Parade takes place downtown on Labor Day. For information, call 828-697-4557.

Jubilee, held in May, presents a number of musical and dance performances and arts-and-crafts displays. For information, call 828-693-8504.

Sidewalk Art Show, held the first full weekend in August, features regional artists displaying and selling their framable artwork. For information, call 828-696-7926.

Annual Quilt Fest, held in October, is a display and sale of new and old quilts sponsored by the Tar Heel Piecemakers and the Western North Carolina Quilters Guild. Boutiques sell associated merchandise. For information, call 800-828-4244.

Side Trips

Chimney Rock Park, about 15 miles east of Hendersonville at Chimney Rock, is a private park that includes the massive rock formation known for its tall, narrow shape. Chimney Rock rises 225 feet above the entrance to Hickory Nut Gorge and provides an unparalleled view of Lake Lure below and the misty Blue Ridge Mountains rising to the west. The 75-mile panorama encompasses thickly forested slopes, with dark green changing to blue on the horizon. In spring, blooming native dog-

Chimney Rock
Photograph by William Russ
Courtesy of N.C. Travel
and Tourism Division

woods and azaleas brighten the hillsides; in fall, the slopes glow with red and yellow leaves.

Visitors cross the Rocky Broad River just past the entrance to Chimney Rock Park. From there, the three-mile drive to the base of the rock formation leads through pretty woodland. To get to the top of the rock formation, you take an elevator up through a 26-story shaft hewn in the granite. Or if you wish to walk, you can follow the plank steps between rocky outcrops and at one point take a trail inside the rock. Once on top, you can enjoy the view from the fenced-in overlook or from inside the Sky Lounge, which has a gift shop and a snack bar.

Though the overlook is the major attraction here, there's good reason to stay awhile in the park. You'll find picnic areas with grills, a playground for children, and hiking trails with beautiful views. One trail is a two-hour round trip to the top of Hickory Nut Falls; this hike is not suitable for young children. The other trail offers an easy 40-minute round trip to the bottom of the falls.

To reach Chimney Rock from Hendersonville, take U.S. 64 east to Bat Cave and turn right on U.S. 74. Chimney Rock Park is open daily except Thanksgiving, Christmas, and New Year's. The ticket office is open from 8:30 A.M. to 4:30 P.M. during daylight saving time; otherwise, it's open until 5:30 P.M. The park closes 90 minutes after the ticket office. Admission is $9.95 for adults and $5 for children ages six to 15; children under six are admitted free. For information, call 828-625-9611 or 800-277-9611.

If you want to stay overnight, consider the **Lake Lure Inn**. *Moderate/Expensive.* U.S. 64 in Lake Lure (828-625-2525). This is definitely a one-of-a-kind inn in the mountains. It's a three-story, old-style hotel with Victorian furniture and chandeliers in the lobby and antique furnishings in the guest rooms.

You might also consider **The Esmeralda Inn**. *Moderate.* U.S. 74 between Bat Cave and Lake Lure (828-625-9105). There has been an inn at this location since 1892. Some of its famous visitors have included Mary Pickford, Gloria Swanson, Douglas Fairbanks, and Clark Gable. A fire damaged the inn in 1997, but it's scheduled to reopen its doors in 1999.

Saluda, located about 12 miles southeast of Hendersonville on U.S. 176, is a small community where a number of craftspeople live and work. You can see some of their work and an array of regional country antiques in Saluda's old train depot, which has been converted to shops. Flower baskets hang from the eaves, and old quilts are draped over the railings. Saluda is home to the famous Saluda Grade, the steepest main-line railroad grade in America.

If you want to spend the night in the area, try **The Orchard Inn**. *Moderate/Expensive*. U.S. 176 a half-mile southeast of Saluda (828-749-5471). This inn is housed in an old vacation retreat built for the Brotherhood of Railway Clerks. It offers a complimentary breakfast.

Eight miles farther east on U.S. 176 (and 1,000 feet lower) is the town of **Tryon**, named for the British governor of the original North Carolina colony. It's larger than Saluda and has a pretty main street with a steep slope to it. There are gift and craft shops; you can also see works by local artists and craftspeople at the Tryon Fine Arts Center. The area is well known for its famous steeplechase races, held in April and October.

If you're looking for a place to stay, try **The Pine Crest Inn**. *Deluxe*. 200 Pine Crest Lane (828-859-9135). A tuberculosis sanatorium was transformed into this rustic inn in 1918 and has been charming its patrons ever since.

If you're in the area, don't miss **Pearson's Falls**. You will see a sign to turn off U.S. 176 approximately three miles from Saluda. It is then one mile on S.R. 1102 and an easy quarter-mile trail to the 90-foot falls. The area is maintained by the Tryon Garden Club. A small admission fee is charged, but it is worth the price.

Accommodations

Hampton Inn. *Moderate*. 155 Sugarloaf Road, Exit 18 off I-26, Hendersonville (828-697-2333 or 800-HAMPTON). The Hampton Inn is a chain hotel, but you can expect a spanking-clean room for a reasonable price, a free continental breakfast, and access to the outdoor pool.

Comfort Inn. *Moderate*. 206 Mitchell Drive (828-693-8800 or 800-882-3843). This is one of Hendersonville's newest chain motels. It is conveniently located off I-26 and close to several restaurants. The rooms are pleasant, and there's an outdoor pool and a Jacuzzi.

Quality Inn and Suites. *Inexpensive/Moderate*. 201 Sugarloaf Road, Exit 18 off I-26, Hendersonville (828-692-7231). Virtually the same as others in the chain, this Quality Inn offers comfortable rooms and good service. An indoor pool, a sauna, and a hot tub are also available. The restaurant is open for all meals.

Inns and Bed-and-Breakfast Guest Houses

Woodfield Inn. *Moderate/Expensive*. U.S. 255, Flat Rock (828-693-6016 or 800-533-6016). Woodfield Inn has been receiving guests since 1852. It is a landmark establishment with a long tradition of Southern hospitality. A three-story frame hotel with a huge front lawn, the Woodfield has an enormous entry hall, a large sitting room, and three dining rooms downstairs. On the upper floors, where the floors slant slightly, are Victorian bedrooms with high ceilings and French doors opening onto a veranda. Only three of the guest rooms have private baths. Throughout the inn are antique furnishings, some of which have been in the inn since the Civil War. A continental breakfast is included.

Echo Mountain Inn. *Moderate/Expensive*. 2849 Laurel Park Highway, Laurel Park (828-693-9626). To reach this inn, guests wind their way up a mountain through a residential area called Laurel Park. This flagstone house was built in 1896. Several of the country-style bedrooms overlook the mountains and the valley below. An outdoor pool and an excellent restaurant are on the premises.

Claddagh Inn. *Inexpensive/Moderate*. 755 North Main Street, Hendersonville (828-697-7778 or 800-225-4700). This three-story frame house with a wraparound porch has been an inn for 90 years. The homey decor lends the same feeling you might get if you were visiting your grandmother. Each of the guest rooms has a private bath. A full country breakfast is served in the dining room.

The Waverly. *Inexpensive/Moderate*. 783 North Main Street, Hendersonville (828-693-9193 or 800-537-8195). Located next door to Claddagh Inn, this inn isn't quite as homey as its neighbor, but the helpful service and casual mood create a pleasant ambiance. Also a three-story frame house, The Waverly has a porch extending across the front. All of the guest rooms have private baths. Rates include a very good home-cooked breakfast.

Restaurants

The many franchise restaurants around Hendersonville and a good number of mom-and-pop eateries offer plenty of dining choices.

Highland Lake Inn. *Expensive*. Highland Lake Road, Flat Rock (828-696-9094). This restaurant is part of a conference center at Highland Lake that was a Catholic camp in an earlier incarnation. The French chef is a true gourmet, and the restaurant prides itself on fresh ingredients, including vegetables from its own garden. Dinner is served Tuesday through Saturday, and brunch is offered on Sunday. Reservations are requested.

Expressions. *Moderate/Expensive*. 114 North Main Street, Hendersonville (828-693-8516). Expressions offers continental dining in a renovated storefront. Plum wallpaper, dark green carpeting, and brass lamps on the tables set the mood for the sophisticated menu and its seasonal specialties. This chef-owned restaurant is a Mobile Three-Star establishment and has been listed as an award winner in *Wine Spectator* magazine. Dinner is served Monday through Saturday.

Woodfield Inn. *Moderate/Expensive*. U.S. 25 South, Flat Rock (828-693-6016). This inn has been a dining tradition since 1852, when it was a stop on the stagecoach line. It's a favorite for special-event meals. The menu includes fried chicken, baked ham, prime rib, and trout amandine, plus warm muffins. After a delicious homemade dessert, you'll want to linger on the veranda. The restaurant is open for dinner Wednesday through Sunday and for brunch on Sunday.

McGuffey's. *Moderate*. Blue Ridge Mall, Hendersonville (828-697-0556). This is an amusing restaurant with a schoolhouse theme based on the old McGuffey readers. Its tasty offerings will appeal to everyone in the family; several varieties of hamburgers and chicken sandwiches, pasta, vegetable stir-fry, and a few steaks are offered. Lunch and dinner are served daily.

Jimmy's Italian Villa. *Inexpensive/Moderate*. 1903 Asheville Highway (828-693-0980). This has been Hendersonville's most popular Italian restaurant for over 21 years. The interior has a pleasant Mediterranean decor. The pizza and the Italian dishes are excellent, and be sure to try Jimmy's famous garlic rolls. Open for dinner Tuesday through Saturday.

Alykat. *Inexpensive*. Four Seasons Boulevard, Hendersonville (828-697-0311). This sandwich shop is a favorite among locals. There's nothing fancy on the menu, just good sandwiches and subs served by a friendly wait staff. Open for lunch Monday through Saturday.

Hannah Flanagan's Pub. *Inexpensive*. 300 North Main Street, Hendersonville (828-696-1665). As in any good pub, the bar is the focus in this local hangout, though there are several tables up front. During the day, patrons enjoy the hearty soups and sandwiches; during the night, the fine selection of imported beers tends to get more attention. Either way, you'll enjoy yourself in this casual watering hole.

Brevard

Brevard is a pretty little town with a population of 6,000 that swells to many times that number during the annual Summer Festival of Music, a major arts event in the Southeast which began in 1936. On the edge of Pisgah National Forest, Brevard is in the heart of what is called "the land of waterfalls," which makes for beautiful driving. It's the county seat of Transylvania County, which means "across the woods."

To reach Brevard, take N.C. 280 from Asheville or U.S. 64 from Hendersonville. When you reach the intersection of N.C. 280 and U.S. 64 with U.S. 276, follow U.S. 64/276 south about three miles into Brevard. Downtown, about four blocks long, features shops, restaurants, a movie theater, antique malls, and the picturesque brick courthouse. Beyond downtown, you'll see attractive turn-of-the-century homes with big porches on shaded residential streets.

The friendly people, mild climate, and attractive setting draw a lot of retirees to the Brevard area. But it also attracts large numbers of summer residents and tourists. It's an ideal place to stay if you enjoy driving through the mountains and stopping at waterfalls.

ACCESS:
Brevard is located three miles south of the intersection of U.S. 276 and N.C. 280, about 30 miles south of Asheville.

VISITOR INFORMATION:
Contact the Brevard Chamber of Commerce, 35 West Main Street, Brevard, N.C. 28712 (828-883-3700 or 800-648-4523).

The *Transylvania Times* is a semi-weekly local newspaper.

Attractions

Historic Places

Cradle of Forestry in America, on U.S. 276 in Pisgah National Forest, is another legacy of George W. Vanderbilt (see *Asheville: Historic Places*). When he bought the property in 1889 to create Biltmore Estate, Vanderbilt hired Gifford Pinchot to manage the forestland. It was the first time in America that anyone had set up a system that allowed for selective timber cutting and processing without wholesale damage to the forest. Pinchot's successor, Dr. Carl Schenck, initiated the first school of forestry in America, the Biltmore

Forest School, which lasted from 1898 to 1913 and established modern forestry-management techniques. In 1968, Congress established the 6,400-acre Pisgah National Forest to preserve the birthplace of forestry education.

The visitor center at the facility has an 18-minute film that outlines the history of the forestry school. You can see a ranger's dwelling and the wood-shingled school building. Along two paved interpretive trails are exhibits—such as a portable sawmill and a log loader from the early 1900s—that illustrate early timber-cutting techniques.

The Cradle of Forestry is open daily from 9 A.M. to 5 P.M. from May through October. Admission is $4 for adults and $2 for senior citizens and children ages six to 17; children under six are admitted free. For information, call 828-877-3130.

Special Shopping

Brevard's downtown has recently blossomed with new shops, restaurants, antique malls, galleries, and coffee shops. In addition to the immediate downtown shopping area, there are outfitters' shops at the entrance to Pisgah National Forest, as well as guide services for mountain climbing, canoeing, and other outdoor activities.

Southern Expressions Gallery & Studios, five miles east of Brevard on U.S. 64, is one of the best places in the mountains for contemporary crafts. Carrying the work of only the finest craftspeople, this shop sells a variety of ceramics, pottery, beautifully polished wooden boxes, baskets, brooms, weavings, quilts, toys, and musical instruments. For information, call 828-884-6242.

Cultural Offerings

The Summer Festival of Music, held at the Brevard Music Center, runs from the end of June through the second week in August. It is a cultural highlight of the entire mountain region.

The Brevard Music Center began in 1936 as a summer music camp at Davidson College in Davidson, North Carolina, and moved to an abandoned summer camp in Brevard in 1943. Three years later, the director and a few Brevard residents started the Brevard Music Festival, a one-week series of performances by those attending the music camp. It was very well received. With increasing visibility and reputation over the years, Brevard Music Camp improved its performance facility with an 1,800-seat auditorium and expanded its educational offerings; now, students can earn college credits.

Brevard Music Camp offers private lessons, a concerto competition, an opera workshop, and performance experience with the Transylvania Symphony, the Brevard Music Center Orchestra, brass, wind, and woodwind ensembles, and a chamber choir. The Summer Festival of Music, which lasts for approximately six weeks, presents polished student musicians and singers and appearances by guest artists. The schedule includes a rich mixture of concerts, recitals, and six fully staged operas and musicals.

The festival has many devoted followers who buy season tickets and attend every performance, so be sure to make room reservations long in advance, or you'll have to drive miles from your lodging to the concerts. It's a good idea to buy tickets in advance, because they're not often available at the door. Ticket prices range from $7 to $25 for adults and from $7 to $12 for children, depending on the performance, seat location, and day of the week. Tickets are sold by mail or credit-card phone order. For information, contact the Brevard Music Center, P.O. Box 312, Brevard, N.C. 28712-0592 (828-884-2011).

Recreation

Pisgah National Forest offers picnic sites, campgrounds, areas for canoeing and swimming, hiking trails, and streams loaded with trout. If you plan to fish, you'll need a fishing license, which you can get at Shook's Field and Stream, a sporting-goods store a mile west of Brevard on U.S. 64; call 828-877-4574.

For more information on facilities, hiking, and biking, stop at the information center, located in the ranger station about a mile into the forest on U.S. 276 from U.S. 64. Or contact the Pisgah National Forest Supervisor, P.O. Box 2750, Asheville, N.C. 28802 (828-257-4200) or the district ranger at 828-877-3265.

Seasonal Events

Festival of the Arts, held in early July, is a week-long celebration of performing and fine arts. Indoor and outdoor displays and performances are held. For information, call 828-884-2787.

Side Trips

One of the favorite pastimes in this area is taking a scenic drive—and there are a lot of possibilities here.

The most popular drive goes north from Brevard on U.S. 276 and along the winding road through Pisgah National Forest, with stops at the Cradle of Forestry and Looking Glass Falls. If you're limber, try skimming down Sliding Rock in your bathing suit. Even if you don't want to take the plunge down the 60-foot natural water slide, it's fun to watch the people who do. There's a lifeguard on duty in the summer and a bathhouse for changing out of those cold, wet clothes. The parking lot is usually crammed to capacity on hot summer days.

You can continue past Sliding Rock to the Blue Ridge Parkway. A right turn will take you to Mount Pisgah, and a left will lead you past Devil's Courthouse. The parkway, which curves around the crest of the Blue Ridge range, is an endless delight of mountain vistas unmarred by development. You can drive to within one mile of the summit of Mount Pisgah and take a trail to its 5,749-foot peak.

Continuing straight onto U.S. 276 will take you to Waynesville. From Waynesville, take U.S. 74 back to the parkway. Or you can go even farther west on U.S. 23/19A to visit craft shops in Dillsboro before returning south on N.C. 107 and east on U.S. 64 to Brevard. Mount Pisgah, Waynesville, and Dillsboro are all covered in other sections of this book.

For another drive, take U.S. 64 west to Highlands to visit its antique shops. You will enjoy a very winding road that goes higher into the mountains, where you'll see golf resorts and expensive summer homes. Between Cashiers and Highlands, the road twists and turns so much that the driver will not be able to enjoy the views of the steep slopes with wildflowers and dense foliage. Along the way, you can stop to see Bridal Veil, Rainbow, Cullasaja, Toxaway, and Whitewater Falls (see *Highlands: Attractions*).

Accommodations

Lodging in Brevard is limited. You should have reservations if you visit at any time during the summer, but they're essential between late June and early August, during the Summer Festival of Music. Rates may be lower in winter.

Hampton Inn. *Moderate*. At the junction of N.C. 280 and U.S. 64 (828-883-4800). Perhaps the most noteworthy thing about this chain motel is its location—right at the entrance to Pisgah National Forest. The swimming pool offers a cool respite after a day of hiking or mountain biking. Continental breakfast is provided.

Brevard Motor Lodge. *Inexpensive/Moderate*. 750 North Caldwell Street (828-884-3456). Close to the Brevard Music Center, the Brevard Motor Lodge has 34 rooms with small refrigerators and three apartments and mobile homes featuring kitchens, making it an option for a long stay during the music festival. There is also an outdoor pool.

Imperial Motor Lodge. *Inexpensive/Moderate*. Half a mile north of Brevard on U.S. 64 (828-884-2887). Close to the Brevard Music Center, this motel offers 95 comfortable rooms, all featuring refrigerators. There is an outdoor pool.

Inns and Bed-and-Breakfast Guest Houses

Greystone Inn. *Expensive/Deluxe*. Greystone Lane in Lake Toxaway, 17 miles west of Brevard (828-966-4700 or 800-824-5766). Built in the early 1900s as a family retreat on the shore of Lake Toxaway, this mansion was converted to a luxury resort in 1984. Greystone now offers 33 guest rooms decorated with antiques and reproductions. Each has a view of the lake and the surrounding forest. Facilities include a golf course, outdoor tennis courts, a heated pool, two docks, and boats and gear for fishing and water-skiing. Rates include breakfast, afternoon tea, and an elegant dinner.

Earthshine. *Moderate/Expensive*. Golden Road in Lake Toxaway (828-862-4207). This large lodge is built entirely of logs on a 70-acre farm. The eight rooms all have modern baths and sleeping lofts. The lodge is decorated with log furnishings throughout. The real attraction, however, is the activities available for guests. There is a rope-climbing area which resembles those at Outward Bound, as well as opportunities for horseback riding, hiking, and rock climbing. A barnyard on the premises is filled with animals for the children. And there's always entertainment for the guests after dinner. All three meals are included.

The Pines Country Inn. *Moderate*. 719 Hart Road in the town of Pisgah Forest (828-877-3131). This inn, located a short distance from Brevard, is in a peaceful farming area overlooking the Little River Valley. You can see horses grazing and wake to the songs of the birds. The house, built in 1883, has been an inn since 1905. The atmosphere is homey. The furniture isn't fancy, but comfortable. There are 26 guest rooms, including some separate cottages. Breakfast is included in the room rate. No credit cards are accepted.

The Womble Inn. *Moderate*. 301 West Main Street (828-884-4770). This New Orleans–style house three blocks from the middle of town is the place where guest artists at the music festival often stay. Each of the rooms has a private bath. Continental breakfast is served, but a full breakfast is also available for an additional fee. The inn serves lunch Monday through Friday and will pack a picnic basket for a takeout lunch.

The Red House Inn. *Inexpensive*. 412 West Probart Street (828-884-9349). The Red House Inn sits on a corner shielded from traffic by high hedges. Porches extend across the front of the two-story house, built in 1851 as a trading post. The oak woodwork is polished to a high gloss, and the comforters are fluffed on the antique beds. A full breakfast is served in the dining room.

Restaurants

The Falls Landing. *Moderate*. East Main Street (828-884-2835). This restaurant specializes in steaks and seafood and has full ABC permits. It is open for lunch Monday through Saturday and dinner Tuesday through Sunday.

Chianti's. *Moderate*. At the junction of N.C. 280 and U.S. 64 (828-862-5683). This establishment features authentic Italian cuisine, from spaghetti and meatballs to New York–style fresh tossed pizzas. Dinner is served daily.

The Corner Bistro. *Inexpensive/Moderate*. Corner of Main and Broad Streets (828-862-4746). A casual atmosphere and unique cuisine are the highlights of this restaurant. Patrons can sample such fare as veggie burgers, turkey chili, tortilla wraps, and gourmet sandwiches. Entertainment is offered on Wednesday evenings seasonally. Lunch is served Monday through Saturday; dinner is served Tuesday through Saturday.

Essence of Thyme. *Inexpensive*. East Main Street (828-884-7171). This friendly little shop features fresh fruit smoothies, espresso and coffee, deli-style sandwiches, and pastries and pies. Lunch and dinner are served daily.

Highlands

Highlands is an anomaly in the Southern mountains—you'll see a different kind of tourist here. Affluent visitors from all over the South—and beyond—patronize the local resorts and make their summer homes in this rarefied retreat. It's the only town in the area where you'll find shops selling $400 sweaters.

Highlands was founded as a health resort, and over the years, as its pleasant summer climate and exceptional natural beauty were discovered, it eventually became a resort community. At an altitude of 4,115 feet, it's always cool, even when the flatlands are baking. The two-lane roads curve in and out through the thick woods of Nantahala National Forest, and wildflowers bloom by the roadside. The 10 miles between Cashiers and Highlands are so winding that only passengers can enjoy the scenery.

The permanent population is less than 1,000, but the downtown area—only two blocks long—bustles with activity in summer, when the population swells to 20,000. In early morning, a few elderly local residents gather on benches in the tiny park, chatting as they watch the storekeepers open their shops to sell antiques, clothing, gifts, and artworks. If you ask, they'll tell you they preferred Highlands the way it was before the boom of the past 10 years. Because the town is almost entirely surrounded by the national forest, property is at a premium; an acre along Main Street that might have sold a few years ago for $60,000 now commands $350,000.

As you drive west from Brevard or south from Franklin to Highlands, you'll see numerous realty signs offering raw property or lots in exclusive mountain developments. And who knows? Once you visit Highlands—to enjoy one of its inns, window-shop for antiques, and cruise through the lush woodlands—you may want to talk to a realtor about a longer stay.

ACCESS:
Highlands is located at the intersection of N.C. 106/28 and U.S. 64, which makes a 90-degree turn at the main intersection.

VISITOR INFORMATION:
Contact the Highlands Chamber of Commerce, Town Hall, P.O. Box 404, Highlands, N.C. 28741 (828-526-2112).

The semiweekly newspaper is The *Highlander*.

Attractions

One of the main attractions in this area is the scenery. There are two routes that are particularly scenic.

From Highlands to Franklin, U.S. 64 follows the Cullasaja River Gorge. The river cascades over falls, ripples over rapids, and drifts in deeper areas—all within sight of the road. This drive is downhill, and the road winds at first, then widens and curves more gently. Then, as the topography opens up into flatter farmland, it straightens into a four-lane highway close to Franklin. Along the route, you may want to stop to take a photograph of Bridal Veil Falls. You can see where the highway went underneath the falls at one time. The next stop is the parking area for Dry Falls. You can actually walk behind this 75-foot waterfall. The most spectacular waterfall on this route is Lower Cullasaja Falls, a dramatic series of cascades dropping more than 250 feet in a quarter-mile. It is difficult to find a parking space here because the narrow road literally hangs on a cliff. You may have to drive past the falls and hike back to see them, but it's worth the effort.

From Highlands to Cashiers, U.S. 64 is sharply curved but well paved and marked. The trees and tall rhododendron are thick and close to the road except where a great valley vista opens to the south, revealing a bird's-eye view of nearby Whiteside Mountain, which rises 2,100 feet from the valley floor. Its summit has an elevation of 4,930 feet. Both the north and south faces feature stunning, sheer cliffs ranging from 400 to 750 feet in height. The route travels on to Cashiers, a town at the crossroads of U.S. 67 and N.C. 107. There, you will find several pottery shops, gift shops, and resorts.

Museums/Science Centers

Highlands Nature Center, on East Main Street half a mile east of the U.S. 64/N.C. 28 intersection, interprets the flora and fauna of the Nantahala Forest region. It offers a small botanical garden with trails and a nature center displaying mineral samples and a few Cherokee artifacts. The center is open Monday through Saturday from 10 A.M. to 5 P.M. from May 15 to Labor Day; variable hours continue through October. Admission is free. For information, call 828-526-2623.

Special Shopping

When you're not hiking or driving, you can go shopping. It's fun even if you're not buying. You can see most of the shopping area from the main intersection, so park and stroll around. The area is so compact that shops don't even list their street numbers—"Main Street" is adequate. The shops feature upscale clothing and accessories, Christmas decorations, jewelry, antiques, and folk and Asian artworks, but you can also find a good ice-cream cone.

Cultural Offerings

Highlands Playhouse, on Oak Street, presents a summer season of professional theater featuring contemporary dramas and comedies. For schedule and ticket information, contact the box office at 828-526-2695.

Highlands Chamber Music Festival features several concerts by renowned artists held in several different venues, often local churches. The concerts take place from mid-July to the first weekend of August. For information, call 828-526-9060.

Recreation

Nantahala National Forest surrounds Highlands. You can enjoy it on foot or by car (see the *Attractions* section for scenic routes). If you're interested in hiking, contact the District Ranger, U.S. Forest Service, District 2010, Flat Mountain Road, Highlands, N.C. 28741 (828-526-3765).

Ski Scaly, seven miles south of Highlands on N.C. 106, is the state's southernmost ski area. It has four slopes and a vertical drop of 225 feet. The lodge offers cafeteria meals. Rental equipment and instruction are available. For information, contact Ski Scaly, Box 339, Scaly Mountain, N.C. 28775 (828-526-3737).

Accommodations

The number of accommodations in and around Highlands is increasing—a result of the current building boom. For many people part of the fun of staying here is spending the night in an old-fashioned lodging. Ask about off-season rates.

High Hampton Inn & Country Club. *Expensive/Deluxe*. Eleven miles east of Highlands, just south of Cashiers on N.C. 107 (828-743-2411 or 800-334-2551). This warm, family-oriented resort has a rustic style it has preserved since it was built in 1932. The exterior is covered with chestnut-bark shingles; inside, the inn has log banisters in the stairwells and natural-wood paneling on the walls and ceilings. The enormous lobby has four stone fireplaces around a central chimney and baskets of magazines and jigsaw puzzles for guests to relax over. The inn's 235 rooms have private baths but no televisions or telephones; guests come here to get away from it all. Meals are served buffet-style in the large dining room, with waitresses filling beverage requests. It sounds casual, but men are expected to wear coats and ties for dinner. The inn has an 18-hole golf course, outdoor tennis courts, a lake with a sand beach, and rental canoes, sailboats, and fishing boats. If you like walking, you'll find lovely trails. There are planned activities for children and teens and a long list of special seminars, golf and fishing schools, and art workshops. The inn is open from April to Thanksgiving. Long stays receive discounts. The rates include three meals.

Fairfield Sapphire Valley. *Moderate/Expensive*. On U.S. 64 (828-743-3441). This top-rated resort offers a range of activities year-round. Set on green, forested slopes, it looks like an attractive housing development with rows of townhouses behind stands of trees. The lodgings range from luxurious hotel rooms to efficiency rooms with kitchens to one-, two-, and three-bedroom condos with separate living areas. All are comfortably furnished and attractively decorated and have splendid views of the surrounding mountains. The kitchens are fully stocked; if you don't cook, the restaurant is open for lunch and dinner. Recreation facilities in the bracing air (you're 3,400 feet up) include an 18-hole championship golf course, an outdoor pool, tennis courts, a lakeside beach, and a health club. You can also go horseback riding and rent bicycles, canoes, paddleboats, and fishing boats. In addition, a variety of activities—seasonal golf clinics, children's game days, weekly family bingo—are offered in the community room. There are also four ski slopes with a 425-foot vertical drop; equipment rentals are available.

Skyline Lodge. *Moderate/Expensive*. Flat Mountain Road (828-526-2121). This lodge has 50 guest rooms and several two- and three-bedroom cabins located on 50 private acres. A wide variety of recreational facilities is offered, including a sauna, a steam room, a swimming pool, and tennis courts. Hiking trails located on the resort grounds lead to a 45-foot waterfall. A full-service restaurant is open on the weekends in season. The rooms are available May through the first weekend of November, while the cabins remain open year-round.

Mountain High Motel. *Moderate/Expensive*. Second and Main Streets (828-526-2790). This property combines country decor with urban amenities. There's a huge stone fireplace in the lobby, as well as a golden chandelier. The motel offers cozy rooms, some with small balconies; the deluxe rooms have four-poster beds, fireplaces, and Jacuzzis. Golf packages are available.

Oakmont Lodge. *Inexpensive/Moderate*. N.C. 107 just north of U.S. 64 in Cashiers (828-743-2298). Oakmont Lodge is a very interesting strip motel on eight acres of land. Antique farm equipment—plows, harrows, buckboards, and grindstones—is displayed on the surrounding property. There's plenty of room for the kids to run. The 20 pine-paneled rooms are comfortably, though somewhat rustically, furnished. The lodge's three apartments, complete with kitchen, sleep six. The restaurant is open for lunch and dinner.

Inns and Bed-and-Breakfast Guest Houses

4½ Street Inn. *Expensive*. On 4½ Street between Chestnut and Hickory Streets (828-526-4464). This inn has 10 guest rooms with private baths. Guests receive a gourmet breakfast, afternoon refreshments, and home-baked cookies. The rooms include morning papers and fluffy robes, while outdoors there's a hot tub and a sun deck. Even though guests are only five blocks from the heart of town, they'll never know it while relaxing on the back porch. Bikes are even provided for guests who wish to explore town.

Highlands Inn. *Moderate*. Main Street (828-526-9380). A three-story white frame hotel that extends half a block, the Highlands Inn has dominated Main Street since it opened in 1880. It attracts a loyal crowd of guests. Rocking chairs sit on the flagstone veranda, and flags flap from the second-floor railing. The hotel is open from April through November. Guests can dine at the inn's Kelsey Place Restaurant, which serves all three meals with the exception of lunch on Sunday and Monday and dinner on Monday and Tuesday. An extended continental breakfast is included in the room rate.

Old Edwards Inn. *Moderate*. Main Street (828-526-9319 or 888-526-9319). Old Edwards Inn is directly across the street from Highlands Inn but has a completely different ambiance. Offering "21 good rooms for ladies and gentlemen," it feels elegantly country, if you can imagine that. A moose head hangs in the reading room, for example, and there's dark wainscoting in the hallways. But the rooms are light, with hand stenciling on the walls and pretty coverlets on antique pencil-post and canopy beds. A continental breakfast is included. The Central House Restaurant, in the same building, is open to guests for all meals. The inn is open year-round.

Restaurants

Highlands isn't bursting with restaurants, though there are several. And keep in mind that Macon County's liquor laws are complicated. Brown-bagging is permitted in almost every restaurant, and some within the town limits do serve wine. Call ahead to check on your chosen restaurant's policy.

Peoletti's. *Expensive.* Main Street (828-526-4906). This is the Italian entry in Highlands. It offers lasagna with spinach and sausage and manicotti with ricotta and herbs for lunch. Even more elaborate choices are available for dinner: veal scaloppine piccata, chicken with prosciutto and mozzarella, and battered trout. The restaurant is open for dinner Monday through Saturday.

Nick's. *Moderate/Expensive.* N.C. 28 at Satulah Road (828-526-2706). This is where you'll find the locals. It's a casual place with calico curtains and bright copper pots. The lunch menu features steak, club, and fish sandwiches; dinner offerings include lobster crepes, lamb chops, steak, and shrimp. Nick's is open for lunch and dinner Thursday through Tuesday.

Central House Restaurant. *Moderate/Expensive.* Main Street (828-526-9319). Part of Old Edwards Inn, Central House echoes the country theme. Soups, salads, and sandwiches make up most of the lunch offerings. Seafood entrées are the specialty for dinner—snapper, blackened catfish, and crab-stuffed North Carolina trout—though chicken and steak are listed as well. Breakfast is available to guests of the inn only, but lunch and dinner are served daily. The restaurant is closed from New Year's Day to Valentine's Day.

Lakeside Restaurant. *Moderate/Expensive.* Smallwood Avenue overlooking Lake Harris (828-526-9419). This place, which bills itself as "a casual restaurant with serious cuisine," comes highly recommended by local residents. Fresh seafood is available, along with beef, veal, lamb, chicken, and pasta dishes. Between June and October, Lakeside serves dinner from Monday through Saturday and lunch daily. During April, May, and November, the restaurant is closed Sunday and Monday. Reservations are strongly recommended for dinner.

Franklin

Franklin calls itself the "Jewel of the Southeast," partly because of its setting in Nantahala National Forest and partly because it is the center of a thriving gem-mining industry.

In the latter part of the 19th century, a state geologic survey revealed a high occurrence of corundum—the rock that yields crystals containing rubies and sapphires—in the Cowee Valley, just north of Franklin. Several commercial mining companies dug exploratory mines (one under the auspices of Tiffany & Company of New York) hoping to find a steady local source of gems. Rubies were found in all the gravel beds, but not in quantities sufficient to support the expensive mining operations.

Commercial mining ended around the turn of the century, but the Cowee Valley has continued to yield hundreds of rubies, sapphires, and other gemstones, producing a bonanza of tourism and almost $30 million in annual revenues for the town of Franklin. The predominant industry in this town is the business of accommodating visitors who want to find gemstones. There are several gem shops that will sell you raw stones or cut and mount those you find. Outside town, you can visit the beautiful Nantahala National Forest and Nantahala Gorge, which offer many recreational options.

Franklin has one significant historic relic. At the bottom of the hill on U.S. 64 Business is a large, grass-covered mound—all that remains of an 18th-century Cherokee village called Nikwasi. Many archaeologists have asked permission to excavate it, but in the end, Franklin officials always decide against it. It's best to leave some things just as they are.

ACCESS:
Franklin is located at the busy crossroads of U.S. 64, U.S. 23/411, and N.C. 28.

The Macon County Airport has a 3,800-by-60-foot lighted runway. For information, call 828-524-5529.

VISITOR INFORMATION:
Contact the Franklin Area Chamber of Commerce, 425 Porter Street, Franklin, N.C. 28734 (828-524-3161 or 888-510-GEMS).

The *Franklin Press* is a twice-weekly newspaper. The *Macon County News* is published weekly.

Attractions

According to an Indian legend, rubies appeared in the Cowee Valley because the beautiful daughter of a tribal chief fell in love with the son of her father's archenemy. She met him in secret. Enraged when he discovered they were meeting, her father ordered that the lovers be put to death on the spot. Because their love was great and true, the blood of the Indian maiden and her brave ran together into the earth and hardened into precious stones.

When you go mining for rubies and crystals, you pay for three or four buckets of rock and soil from the mine (there may also be an entrance fee at some of the mines). Then, sitting at the edge of the flume line (a trough with gently flowing water), you rinse the rocks a quarter of a bucket at a time, breaking up chunks of mud and looking for raw stones—which bear little resemblance to transparent cut stones. Some mines enrich the dirt with gravel known to contain some stones, and if you're taking children, it's a good idea to choose one of these "salted" mines, where you'll have a better chance of finding gems.

What's the likelihood of finding a large gem-quality ruby? Almost nil. But you can have a lot of fun finding small, pretty stones that make nice jewelry.

The gem mines, totaling well over a dozen, are located five to nine miles from downtown Franklin on U.S. 441 and N.C. 28. They are listed and described in a folder available from the chamber of commerce. The mines are open daily from roughly 8 A.M. to 5 P.M. from April through October.

Museums

Franklin Gem and Mineral Museum, on Phillips Street just off West Main Street, displays a range of mineral specimens, fossils, and Indian artifacts, including a room of North Carolina samples, one of specimens from other states, and one of rocks that glow under fluorescent light. The mineral museum, established and maintained by volunteers of the Gem and Mineral Society of Franklin, is in the old city jail, a small brick structure built in the 1850s and used until 1972; upstairs, you can see "the slammer." The museum is open Monday through Saturday from 10 A.M. to 4 P.M. and Sunday from 1 to 4 P.M. from May through October. Admission is free. For information, call 828-369-7831.

The **Scottish Tartans Museum and Heritage Center**, at 95 East Main Street, celebrates the Scottish heritage of the North Carolina mountains. Displays document the evolution of the kilt and the influence of the Scots on Appalachian and Cherokee culture. Visitors with Scottish ancestry can find their family tartan in the Tartan Room. The gift shop includes items from Scotland and handmade Appalachian crafts. The museum is open Monday through Saturday from 10 A.M. to 5 P.M. and Sunday from 1 to 5 P.M. Admission is $2 for adults and $1 for students and seniors. For information, call 828-524-7472.

Ruby City Gems & Minerals, at 130 East Main Street, isn't strictly a museum. It's a lapidary shop that sells raw and cut gemstones, lapidary equipment and supplies, and mineral samples such as geodes and amethyst crystals. The museum, located on a lower level, offers a professional display of hundreds of mineral samples—including a sapphire specimen weighing 382 pounds—in well-lighted glass cases. The shop is open Monday through Saturday from 9 A.M. to 5 P.M. from April 1 through December 31. For information, call 828-524-3967.

Special Shopping

MACO Crafts, Inc., located three miles south of Franklin at 2846 Georgia Highway (U.S. 441), is one of the largest craft cooperatives in the Appalachian Mountains. About 250 members create a vast array of decorative and utilitarian items for sale here. You'll find pottery, baskets, embroidered aprons, stained glass, candleholders, wreaths, many kinds of dolls, and Christmas decorations. Quilts are for sale here, including some exquisite creations by master quilters which can cost up to $1,800. The lower level displays a large selection of fabrics and quilting supplies. The shop is open Monday through Saturday from 9 A.M. to 5:30 P.M. and Sunday from 1 to 5:30 P.M. from May to November; it is open Monday through Saturday from 10 A.M. to 5 P.M. and Sunday from 1 to 5 P.M. from November to May. For information, call 828-524-7878.

Recreation

Rafting in the Nantahala Gorge, about 20 miles north of Franklin, will appeal to those who like thrills and outdoor excitement. Several companies offer guided raft trips down the Nantahala River, which features class II and class III rapids. Safety equipment is issued, and the guide tells you everything you need to do, so it's fun even for those with no rafting experience. The trips last about four hours and don't require any special clothing, though you'll probably want to get into dry clothes afterward. Children weighing less than 60 pounds aren't allowed to go. Raft trips operate from April through October. Rates range from $20 to $40 per person. For a complete list of the companies that operate on U.S. 19 between Bryson City and Andrews, call 828-524-3161.

You can also make reservations to see the Nantahala Gorge or the nearby Tuckasegee River by rail. Several different options are available for these excursions. The Nantahala Gorge trip, which includes crossing Fontana Lake on a trestle which is 791 feet long and 179 feet high, departs and returns to Bryson City. This 4½-hour trip can include a seat in the club car—which has a table between seats—a box lunch, or lunch at a restaurant during the hour layover at the gorge. For more variation, you can ride the train to the gorge, take a raft trip on the river, and return by bus. The Tuckasegee River excursion departs and returns to Dillsboro. This three-hour trip travels along the river and through the 836-foot-long Cowee Tunnel. Again, you can choose club-car seating, a box lunch, or lunch at the Jarrett House or another Dillsboro restaurant. For a schedule and the costs of various options, call 800-872-4681, extension 5.

Seasonal Events

Macon County Gemboree, a semiannual gem and mineral show, takes place in late July and mid-October. Specimens are on display and for sale. For information, call 828-524-3161.

Side Trips

Wayah Bald (pronounced Why-a) is a massive stone outcrop in Nantahala National Forest at an elevation of more than a mile. Its baldness is a dramatic contrast to the lush forestland surrounding it. You can see Wayah Bald from downtown Franklin, but the trip to experience it up close takes about an hour. You can park close to the summit, then walk about a quarter-mile on a paved trail to the top for a spectacular view. Take U.S. 64 West to S.R. 1310, then turn right on S.R. 69. This two-lane road takes you deep into the forest, where you'll see wildflowers and rhododendron and streams playing down hillsides.

Dillsboro, about 20 miles north of Franklin on U.S. 441 through a beautiful mountain valley, is a lovely little town on a thickly wooded hillside. It features several antique shops. In a two-block area, you'll find stores offering furnishings, crafts, toys, and gifts. Most of the shops offer a map published by the Dillsboro Merchants Association.

To see a lot of craft items in a short time, go to Dogwood Crafters, on Webster Street, a craft cooperative carrying the work of many different artisans. Riverwood Shops, across the railroad tracks on River Road, consists of nine shops in four old houses; these shops feature wares of professional quality—hammered pewter, leatherwork, weavings, and more. The Old School, an antiques mall, is on the west side of the highway before you get to Dillsboro. In this renovated elementary school, a number of dealers display different specialties. The presentation in this spacious setting is very pleasing—it's fun to browse around.

You can stay overnight at the **Squire Watkins Inn**. *Moderate.* Just off U.S. 441 South (828-586-5244). Shielded by a thick stand of trees, this three-story Victorian house is beautifully restored and furnished. The large, airy rooms have private baths and antique beds spread with quilts. Breakfast is served in the dining room on a lace tablecloth under a beautiful chandelier. Weekly rates are available for the inn's two cottages. No credit cards are accepted.

For a terrific meal, stop at **The Jarrett House**. *Inexpensive/ Moderate.* Main Street (828-586-0265). A regional landmark since it opened as a hotel in 1882, this three-story white frame building has verandas with fancy ironwork railings on all three floors. Famous for its family-style meals, the restaurant features fried chicken, baked and country ham, and mountain trout. Each meal comes with bowls of vegetables, slaw, stewed apples, and hot biscuits—you keep wishing you'd never fill up. And try the vinegar pie. Personal and out-of-state checks are accepted, but credit cards are not. The restaurant is open daily for lunch and dinner.

For more information about attractions in Dillsboro, call the Jackson County Chamber of Commerce at 800-962-1911.

John C. Campbell Folk School, about 60 miles west of Franklin in Brasstown, is a folk crafts school that was founded in 1925 to preserve and teach traditional Appalachian crafts and to provide economic opportunity for Depression-era farm families by selling their high-quality woodcarvings. The week-long courses, offered all year, include pottery, weaving, basketry, woodcarving, bookbinding,

Appalachian dancing, and newer crafts such as jewelry making and kaleidoscope making. Students come back year after year and often sign up for several courses at a time. The craft shop sells a variety of pottery, weavings, decorative ironwork, split-oak baskets, and beautiful works done by some of the original Brasstown carvers. It is open Monday through Saturday from 8 A.M. to 5 P.M. and Sunday from 1 to 5 P.M. For information, call 828-837-2775.

Accommodations

Although there are a number of places to stay in Franklin, you won't find much diversity.

Country Inntown. *Inexpensive/Moderate*. 277 East Main Street (828-524-4451 or 800-233-7555). This well-managed 50-room motel is at the bottom of the Main Street hill, very close to the Nikwasi Indian mound. It's always full in July during the Macon County Gemboree because of its spacious rooms and good location. It has an outdoor pool, but you have to cross the street to reach a restaurant. Rates are slightly more in October during the foliage season.

Inns and Bed-and-Breakfast Guest Houses

Buttonwood Inn. *Moderate*. 50 Admiral Drive, just off U.S. 441 South (828-369-8985). Buttonwood Inn is set back under trees overlooking the Franklin Golf Course, so it's quiet. Built as a summer cottage in the 1920s, the inn has four guest rooms with polished wood floors. Old quilts decorate the house throughout. A full breakfast is served in the dining room. No credit cards are accepted.

Heritage Inn. *Inexpensive/Moderate*. 43 Heritage Hollow Drive (828-524-4150). This inn is located in Heritage Hollow, a quaint country village within the town of Franklin. Each of the six bedrooms has its own entrance, porch, and private bath. A fully furnished one-bedroom apartment is also available but is usually rented out to those staying three or more nights. A full breakfast is served in the dining room. Two of the rooms have kitchenettes. The inn is open year-round. Traveler's checks, personal checks, and some credit cards are accepted.

Summit Inn. *Inexpensive*. 210 East Rogers Street (828-524-2006). As its name implies Summit Inn offers a view—over the city to the Great Smoky Mountains and Wayah Bald. The lobby of this rambling, 1898-vintage house is filled with antiques. Each of the 13 guest rooms is decorated differently—in one, there's a crazy quilt on an iron bed, wicker chairs, braided rugs, and an old Underwood typewriter. Eight of the rooms have private baths; the others share baths. Limited service is available in the off-season. No credit cards are accepted.

Restaurants

Summit Inn. *Moderate*. 210 East Rogers Street (828-524-2006). Summit Inn serves five-course dinners on Friday and Saturday evenings only, so reservations are a must. Dinner is generous, with the chef serving up such local specialties as trout. You may find a different main course on the menu each weekend, depending on what the chef feels like preparing. No credit cards are accepted.

The Frog and Owl Kitchen. *Moderate*. 46 East Main Street (828-349-4112). This mountain bistro has been serving up gourmet delights for over 28 years. The name comes from things near and dear to the owner in her youth—from her high-school nickname (Froggy) and from the luck that always seemed to follow her sightings of owls after she moved to the mountains at 17 to open her first restaurant. Her luck seems to have continued with this unique little restaurant, which also features a wine shop and deli. Fresh Atlantic salmon and Long Island duckling breast with Roquefort sauce are among the specialties here. Lunch is served Monday through Saturday and dinner Friday and Saturday. Select credit cards are accepted.

The Great Smoky Mountains

As you leave the Blue Ridge Mountains heading west from Asheville, another natural wonder looms ahead—the Great Smoky Mountains. They get their name from the persistent haze that veils the rounded summits.

Cherokee legend says the haze originated at a time when the Cherokees had been smoking the peace pipe with enemies. Though the meeting continued for seven days, they all continued to quarrel. Annoyed, the Great Spirit turned the men into grayish white flowers called Indian pipes and made the smoke hang over the mountains to remind men that they should live together in peace. The scientific explanation is that the haze results from an excess of oxygen and humidity created by the thick forestation, which mixes with a microscopic mist of rosin-scented organic compounds called terpenes.

The Smokies boast some of the most rugged terrain in the eastern United States and are a naturalist's paradise. More than 1,000 varieties of flowering plants and hundreds of species of mosses and trees have been identified here. The Smokies contain the largest stand of old-growth hardwoods in North America.

Fortunately, much of this magnificent natural area has been incorporated into the national-park system to ensure that its wild beauty will be preserved forever. Unfortunately, visitors will find that some of the tawdriest kind of tourist development has intruded. Nevertheless, the westernmost mountains are considered by many to be the most beautiful part of North Carolina.

Great Smoky Mountains National Park

More people visit this park than any other in our national-park system—nearly 10 million visitors per year. Compare that to over 5 million in the Grand Canyon, nearly 4 million in Yosemite, and around 3 million in Yellowstone.

The park comprises more than a half-million acres along 70 miles of the North Carolina–Tennessee border, encompassing some of the oldest mountains on earth. They include 16 peaks more than 6,000 feet high, with only one transmountain road cutting through them. Between the entrances at Cherokee, North Carolina, and Gatlinburg, Tennessee, Newfound Gap Road twists and turns, revealing one spectacular view after another. At the height of the fall color season, the road is so crowded it can take twice as long to make the crossing as it does during the other seasons.

Legislation to establish the park was enacted in 1926, but raising the money to buy the property was difficult, and the purchase itself was complex. In the designated area, 85 percent of the property was owned by 18 timber companies; the rest was owned in tiny parcels by nearly 6,000 homesteaders. State appropriations and individual contributions totaled $5 million—exactly half the amount required. John D. Rockefeller, Jr., matched the amount to acquire all the land, and the park opened to the public in 1934.

In addition to verdant natural beauty, the park preserves more than 75 historic structures—log cabins, barns, mills, and stables of homesteading families who settled in the mountains in the 19th century. In the valley called Cades Cove, a display of historic structures including several cabins, a church, and a mill has been preserved. You can drive the 11-mile one-way loop road around the settlements and adjacent pastures or stop at the bookstore and stroll among the buildings. After dark, the kids can discover the fun of an old-fashioned hayride.

There are many ways to see the park. If you have time for only a brief look, you can drive Newfound Gap Road, but you'll miss much of the park. A smaller road leads up to Clingmans Dome, the highest peak in the park, at 6,634 feet; for the best possible view of the Smokies, walk a half-mile up to the observation tower.

Lacing the park are more than 800 miles of trails of varying degrees of difficulty that you can travel on foot or on horseback. For some, back-country camping offers the best of the mountains. However you choose to explore it, Great Smoky Mountains National Park will make a lasting impression on you.

The busiest months are June, July, August, and October, when the campgrounds are full and the roads crowded. You'll enjoy your trip on Newfound Gap Road more if you can avoid making it on a summer weekend.

Even in summer, it can get quite cool, so remember to bring a jacket. Rain gear isn't a bad idea either, since the park gets 50 to 80 inches of rain annually. One other caveat: Bears are wild animals and can be very dangerous. If you see one, enjoy watching it from a distance.

ACCESS:

Great Smoky Mountains National Park is 50 miles west of Asheville on U.S. 19. The North Carolina entrance is at the town of Cherokee.

VISITOR INFORMATION:

There are three visitor centers that offer maps, guidebooks, museum displays, weather and road information, schedules of park activities including ranger-guided walks and talks, and calendars of special events. The centers are open daily except Christmas.

Sugarlands is two miles south of Gatlinburg, Tennessee, at park headquarters. During the summer, it presents a 20-minute film highlighting what to see and do in the park. For information, contact Great Smoky Mountains National Park, 107 Park Headquarters Road, Gatlinburg, Tenn. 37738 (423-436-1200).

Oconaluftee, two miles north of Cherokee, is the southern entrance to the park. A short walk away is the Mountain Farm Museum which is made up of an assemblage of buildings found at the turn of the century. Corn is ground every day at the water-powered Mingus Mill, located a half-mile north of the farmstead.

Cades Cove is on the Tennessee side of the park in the area of a re-created pioneer mill community, which includes water-powered Cable Mill. Rangers offer 30-minute guided walking tours of the mill area daily during the summer.

An information-packed tabloid, *Smokies Guide*, is the official newspaper of the park. You can pick it up at any visitor center.

In case of emergency, call park headquarters at 423-436-1230.

Recreation

For **hiking**, there's an almost endless variety of trails. For easy, self-guided nature trails, consider the following:

> Spruce Fir Trail (0.5 mile) from Clingmans Dome Road
> Cades Cove Trail (0.3 mile) from Cable Mill Junction
> Smokemont Trail (0.7 mile) from Smokemont Campground
> Elkmont Trail (0.7 mile) from Elkmont Campground
> Cove Hardwoods Trail (0.7 mile) from Chimney Tops Picnic Area

Noah "Bud" Ogle Trail (0.7 mile) from Cherokee Orchard Road
Cosby Trail (1 mile) from Cosby Campground
Sugarlands Trail (1 mile) from Sugarlands Visitor Center
Balsam Mountain Trail (0.7 mile) from Balsam Mountain
    Campground
Laurel Falls Trail (2.5 miles) from Fighting Creek Gap
Alum Cave Bluffs Trail (5 miles) from Alum Cave Bluffs trailhead

If you're a serious hiker, you'll need serious maps. Maps and publications are available at the visitor centers. *The Smokies Hiking Map and Guide* provides an up-to-date hiking map with topographical lines and current back-country campsites. Another reliable source is *Hiking Trails of the Smokies,* which describes every hike in the park.

The Appalachian Trail zigzags for 70 miles through the park on the crests of the mountains between Davenport Gap, near the eastern boundary, and Fontana Dam, in the southwest. All back-country **camping** is free but requires a permit, which can be obtained at any ranger station or visitor center. In addition, if you plan to camp in the shelters along the Appalachian Trail, reservations are required. They can be made by calling the back-country office (open Monday through Friday from 8 A.M. to 6 P.M.) at 423-436-1231.

There are also 10 developed campgrounds with water but without showers or trailer hookups. Camping costs between $10 and $15. Reservations for Cades Cove, Elkmont, and Smokemont Campgrounds can be made by calling Biospherics at 800-365-CAMP. The campsites close in November and reopen in mid-March.

For **picnicking**, you have a choice of 10 areas with tables and fire grates at various locations in the park.

Horseback riding in the park is available from several concession stables. For addresses and telephone numbers, call 423-436-1200.

Fishing for brown and rainbow trout is popular in park streams all year long, but you must have either a North Carolina or a Tennessee license, both of which are honored throughout the park. Fishing for brook trout is prohibited, however. Check at any visitor center for regulations regarding size and catch limits.

Naturalist programs are offered by rangers from May to October at developed campgrounds and visitor centers. Some are talks only, some involve short walks, and some are geared especially for children. Topics include wildflowers, hardwood trees, animal habitats, and pioneer life. There are also sunset and twilight walks.

Park regulations prohibit littering, defacing natural features, picking flowers, digging up plants, feeding wildlife, and letting pets run loose.

Accommodations

Only one facility offers accommodations inside the park.

LeConte Lodge. *Inexpensive.* On top of Mount LeConte (423-429-5704). This lodge is accessible only by a half-day hike. The premises are definitely rustic and the meals decidedly plain. Reservations are required. The lodge is open from late March through late November.

Cherokee

The town of Cherokee is named for the Cherokee Indians, one of the Five Civilized Nations of Muskogean-speaking people. They were the first Indians to have a written language, created by Sequoyah in 1821. At one time, they were an extremely powerful nation, controlling a territory of 135,000 square miles ranging from the Ohio River southward into northern Georgia and Alabama.

As white settlers moved into the mountains, the Cherokees were pushed farther and farther westward, as the settlers' craving for land seemed insatiable. The Cherokees gave up large portions of their land in several treaties, but these agreements were continually broken by the settlers. Soon, the United States government decided that the only way to meet the needs of a growing country was to remove all the eastern Indians to designated areas west of the Mississippi River. In 1835, the federal government pressured a few Cherokees to sign the Treaty of New Echota, which ceded all their land to the government in exchange for resettlement.

Many refused to move, and in one of the most ignominious episodes of American history, the Cherokees were forced into an overland emigration to Oklahoma. About 4,000 Cherokees died on the 1838 march, which has since been called the "Trail of Tears." The several hundred who remained in the mountains were finally granted the legal right to remain in their homeland in 1866. The town of Cherokee, population 600, is now the largest community in the Qualla Boundary, part of almost 56,000 acres of reservation land held in trust for the eastern Cherokees. About 8,200 members of the Eastern Band of Cherokee Indians reside in communities throughout the Qualla Boundary.

In this town, you'll find a few very interesting attractions dedicated to preserving the Cherokee heritage—the Museum of the Cherokee Indian, Oconaluftee Indian Village, Qualla Arts and Crafts Mutual, and the outdoor drama *Unto These Hills*. Apart from that, you'll find an exploitation of place and people. Virtually everything has a pseudo-Indian theme, and most enterprises have nothing to do with the Cherokees: Papoose Motel, Tee Pee Restaurant, Totem Pole Gifts. For better or for worse, gambling has arrived in Cherokee—most recently in the form of a large, neon-emblazoned casino—promising only an increase in this type of development.

The town is crowded with stereotypical souvenir shops and bizarre attractions. In one place, for example, you can pay a quarter to watch a chicken put a ball through a little basketball hoop.

If you respect Native Americans, stop in Cherokee to see the authentic Cherokee Indian offerings, then continue on to Great Smoky Mountains National Park.

ACCESS:
Cherokee is located 48 miles west of Asheville at the intersection of U.S. 19 and U.S. 441. Immediately north of Cherokee is the southern entrance to Great Smoky Mountains National Park.

VISITOR INFORMATION:
Contact Cherokee Travel and Promotion, Box 465, Cherokee, N.C. 28719 (828-497-9195 or 800-438-1601). The visitor center is on the west side of the street where U.S. 19 and U.S. 441 merge.

The weekly newspaper is the *Cherokee One Feather*.

Attractions

Museum of the Cherokee Indian, on U.S. 441 North, is a stone building that traces the history of the Cherokees, honors outstanding individuals, and exhibits examples of traditional arts and crafts. Newly renovated in 1998, the museum offers an intensive look into the history of the Cherokees. Artifacts and relics are presented in real-life settings of the time period. A seven-minute, three screen, multi-sensory animated creation story explains who the Cherokees are and why their tribe was important. In the display halls, you can see maps of the Trail of Tears, newspaper accounts of the emigration, and handmade tools, baskets, and beadwork. One display features Sequoyah's syllabary, and you can listen to a number of audio samplings of the language. The gift shop carries books and souvenirs. The museum is open daily from 9 A.M. to 5 P.M. from September to May and from 9 A.M. until 8 P.M. from June through August. Admission is $6 for adults and $4 for children ages six to 12; children under six are admitted free. For information, call 828-497-3481.

Oconaluftee Indian Village, located on Drama Road a half-mile north of U.S. 441, is a re-creation of a Cherokee village of 250 years ago, set on a lovely, sylvan hillside. You can watch Cherokees working in their lean-to shelters creating tools, equipment, and decorations like those used two centuries ago. Their other activities include carving weapons and cooking utensils, grinding corn, cooking, finger weaving, making baskets and beadwork, and burning out dugout canoes. One-hour tours leave every 10 minutes, but you may linger and ask questions or take pictures if you like. An interesting highlight is the seven-sided council house. Surrounding the village is a beautiful botanical garden with paths that lead up and around mossy rocks where water trickles slowly; trees and shrubs have identifying signs. There are flower and vegetable gardens as well. The village is open daily from 9 A.M. to 5:30 P.M. from mid-May through October. Admission is $10 for adults and $5 for children ages six through 13;

Oconaluftee Indian Village at Cherokee
Photograph by Clay Nolen
Courtesy of N.C. Travel
and Tourism Division

children under six are admitted free. For information, call 828-497-2315.

Special Shopping

Qualla Arts and Crafts Mutual, Inc., on U.S. 441 North, is the most successful Indian-owned and -operated craft cooperative in the United States. You'll find handmade Cherokee baskets, beadwork, pottery, woodcarvings, masks, and dolls. Another room displays crafts made by Indians of other tribes. The cooperative is open daily from 8 A.M. to 6 P.M. during the spring and fall, until 8 P.M. in the summer, and from 8 A.M. until 4:30 P.M. in the winter. For information, call 828-497-3103.

Recreation

Fishing is a good bet here, because streams and ponds on the reservation are stocked twice weekly and you don't need a state license. You do, however, need a tribal fishing permit, which costs $5 a day; these are available at convenience stores, campground offices, and other locations. For more information, contact the Fish and Game Management Enterprise at 828-497-5201.

Seasonal Events

Unto These Hills, by Kermit Hunter, is the most popular outdoor drama in the state. The words and music tell the story of the forced emigration of the Cherokee people. It's performed in the 2,800-seat Mountainside Theater on U.S. 441 North every night except Sunday from mid-June to late August. Shows begin at 8:45 P.M. until the end of July, when they begin at 8:30 P.M. Reserved seats are $14, regular admission for adults is $11, and children between six and 13 are $5. For tickets, contact Mountainside Theater, P.O. Box 398, Cherokee, N.C. 28719 (828-497-2111).

Side Trips

Located about 50 miles west of Cherokee on N.C. 28 North, **Fontana Village** is a resort community developed from the housing units of the construction workers who built Fontana Dam in 1941.

The dam is the highest in the eastern United States and the largest facility of the Tennessee Valley Authority. When the dam was completed in 1945, the housing development was sold to private owners, who turned it into a family resort village. The mountains that reach down to the very edge of beautiful Lake Fontana make a magnificent setting for an extended family vacation. The village has an inn with 94 rooms, some with fireplaces, and 250 rustic cottages equipped with kitchens. A restaurant, a buffet house, and a village cafe all serve meals if you choose not to cook. Recreational activities are many and varied—miniature golf, swimming, boating, fishing, hiking, horseback riding, archery, and badminton. A playground, craft classes, and other organized activities are available for children. The village is open year-round. Contact Fontana Village, Fontana Dam, N.C. 28733 (828-498-2211 or 800-849-2258).

Joyce Kilmer Memorial Forest is one of the few remnants of virgin forest left on the East Coast. The forest is left completely to nature's control; no plants or trees, living or dead, may be cut or removed. As a result, the forest contains magnificent examples of more than 100 species of trees, many of them over 300 years old. A two-mile recreation trail loops through the forest and there are over 60 additional miles of hiking trails in the forest and the adjoining 14,000-acre Slickrock Wilderness Area. To reach the forest, take U.S. 129 North from Robbinsville and follow the signs. For information, contact the Cheoah Ranger Station at 828-479-6431.

If you want to stay overnight in the area, try the **Snowbird Mountain Lodge**. *Expensive*. 275 Santeetlah Road (828-479-3433). This lodge is a rustic mountain inn built of chestnut logs and native stone. There is an excellent view of the Snowbird range from its flagstone terrace. All three meals are included with the room; breakfast and dinner are served in the dining hall, and a bag lunch is provided at midday.

Accommodations

Best Western Great Smokies Inn. *Moderate*. Acquoni Road off U.S. 19/441 (828-497-2020). This looks like a mountain lodge, with a stone exterior and pine paneling in the lobby. The 152 rooms aren't especially large or fancy but can fill the bill for a good night's rest. The inn has an outdoor pool and a restaurant that is open for all meals.

Comfort Inn. *Moderate*. U.S. 19 South (828-497-2411 or 800-228-5150). Another solid link in this chain of dependable, comfortable motels, the Comfort Inn offers 88 pleasantly decorated rooms, as well as an outdoor pool and a Jacuzzi. It is open from late March through late December.

Inns and Bed-and-Breakfast Guest Houses

Hemlock Inn. *Expensive/Deluxe*. Off U.S. 19 east of Bryson City (828-488-2885). Hemlock Inn is a lovely one-level building on a Smoky Mountain hilltop. Here, you can sit in a porch rocker and gaze across an open meadow to another range of mountains, and all you'll hear is the songs of the birds. The unpretentious inn offers 21 clean rooms and four cottages furnished with country-style furniture. You can enjoy fires in the hearth of the big family room. The meals served in the dining room at breakfast and dinner include home-baked bread and homemade desserts.

Fryemont Inn. *Moderate*. Fryemont Road, Bryson City (828-488-2159). The Fryemont, an old-fashioned country inn built by timber baron Amos Frye, opened in 1923. The hardwood floors gleam in front of the fieldstone hearth in the lobby. The 44 chestnut-paneled rooms, some with four-poster beds, are furnished simply; you'll notice the hand-hewn window frames and special touches such as the basket with herbal bath granules in the bathroom. The inn has a tennis court and a swimming pool, and there's a bandstand in the dining room for weekend entertainment. The inn is open from April through October.

Randolph House. *Inexpensive/Moderate*. Fryemont Road, Bryson City (828-488-3472). Randolph House, the 1895 mansion that timber magnate Amos Frye built for himself, shares a parking lot with Fryemont Inn. The seven cozy guest rooms are furnished with antiques, some going back to the 1850s. The sitting room has a number of overstuffed chairs where guests can enjoy whiling away the quiet evenings after dinner. Gourmet dining is the norm here—trout, flounder, prime rib, and stuffed Cornish game hen are on the menu, as well as homemade desserts. Breakfast and dinner are included in the room rate. The inn is open from mid-April through October.

Restaurants

The Chestnut Tree. *Inexpensive/Moderate*. In the Holiday Inn Cherokee on U.S. 19 South (828-497-9181). This is about the fanciest restaurant you'll find in Cherokee. It features mountain trout, steak, and chicken, as well as a good selection of sandwiches for lunch. It is open for breakfast and dinner Monday through Saturday and for all three meals on Sunday.

Grandma's Pancake and Steak. *Inexpensive*. U.S. 19/441 (828-497-9801). Grandma's is an ultracasual family restaurant where you can get great country breakfasts any time of the day and steak, shrimp, and chicken entrées for lunch and dinner. The restaurant is open for breakfast and lunch Monday through Thursday and for all three meals Friday, Saturday, and Sunday.

Tee Pee Restaurant. *Inexpensive*. U.S. 441 North (828-497-5141). Though the selection here is standard, the food is a cut above most of the places in Cherokee. Mountain trout is the specialty of the house. Buffets are offered for each meal, but only at certain times; diners can order off the menu at any time. Open daily for breakfast, lunch, and dinner.

Maggie Valley

Named for its first postmaster's daughter, Maggie Valley is a resort community at the foot of the Balsam Mountains, whose peaks reach up to 6,000 feet. It's four miles from the Blue Ridge Parkway and 16 miles from Cherokee and the entrance to Great Smoky Mountains National Park.

Cradled between steep mountain slopes, the town is a strip three miles long. Its permanent population of about 200 all seems to be involved in the tourist trade. Along Main Street, there are motels one after another and souvenir shops that sell trinkets not made in the area.

The big attractions in Maggie Valley are Cataloochee Ski Area, a theme park called Ghost Town in the Sky, and the Stompin' Ground, a rustic performance hall where regional cloggers and musicians dance and sing.

ACCESS:
Maggie Valley is on U.S. 19 about 30 miles west of Asheville.

VISITOR INFORMATION:
Contact the Maggie Valley Chamber of Commerce, P.O. Box 87, Maggie Val-
ley, N.C. 28751 (828-926-1686). The chamber is located on the south side of Main Street, which is also U.S. 19.

The Waynesville newspaper, the *Enterprise Mountaineer*, produces a tabloid of regional activities and adver-tising called *Adventure in the Smokies.*

Attractions

Ghost Town in the Sky, on U.S. 19 at the west end of town, is a facsimile of an Old West town. Visitors take the chairlift or incline tram to the top of the mountain, where the town includes a general store, dancing girls in the Silver Dollar Saloon, and an occasional bank robbery or gunfight in the street. There are 20 carnival-type rides and live shows by musicians and Indian dancers. This attraction draws thousands of tourists—its advertising brochure pictures people crammed shoulder to shoulder in the street. It is open daily from May through October. Admission is $18.95 for adults and $13.95 for children ages three to nine; children under three are admitted free. For information, call 828-926-1140.

Cultural Offerings

Stompin' Ground, on U.S. 19, has a wooden stage where you can see professional clogging teams do their lively, noisy dancing to Appalachian music provided by fiddlers, guitar strummers, and banjo pickers. It's happy family entertainment. The Stompin' Ground is open from May through October and offers country bluegrass clogging, line dancing, and waltzing at 8 P.M. The audience is often encouraged to participate in the festivities. There is an admission charge. For information, call 828-926-1288.

Recreation

Cataloochee Ski Area was the first ski area established in North Carolina. Built in 1961, it was so successful that it spawned a new state industry. The lodge and restaurant have a friendly atmosphere; families are welcome. There are nine slopes with a vertical drop of 740 feet. Ski instruction and equipment rental are available. For informa-tion, contact Cataloochee Ski Area, 1080 Ski Lodge Road, Maggie Valley, N.C. 28751 (828-926-0285 or 800-768-0285).

Seasonal Events

Folkmoot USA is a 10-day cultural event in July that features traditional dance groups from all over the world performing in several western North Carolina cities. Maggie Valley hosts performances at the Stompin' Ground. For information, call 828-926-1686.

Moonlight Race is a nighttime eight-kilometer footrace on the last weekend in August. For information, call 828-926-1686.

Accommodations

Maggie Valley Resort and Country Club. *Expensive/Deluxe.* A half-mile from the intersection of U.S. 19 and U.S. 276 (828-926-1616 or 800-438-3861). Located in a lush setting with a mountain backdrop, Maggie Valley Resort offers 64 luxurious rooms, 11 private villas, a golf course, tennis courts, and an outdoor pool. Breakfast and lunch are included in the room rate and are served in the resort's restaurant, which has an entire wall of windows looking out on the mountains. Golf privileges are also included in the rate.

Jonathan Creek Inn and Villas. *Moderate/Expensive.* 4324 Soco Road (828-926-1232 or 800-577-7812). This inn has unfinished wood on the exterior and 42 very comfortable rooms with back doors that open onto Jonathan Creek. All rooms have refrigerators and coffee makers, and some feature whirlpools, hot tubs, fireplaces, and wet bars. The three villas are an option for even more privacy. An indoor pool is available to all guests. You won't want to spend all of your time indoors, though, as the grounds of the inn are gorgeous. There are several garden areas, hammocks, a picnic area, and even a gazebo for guests to enjoy.

Best Western Mountainbrook Inn. *Inexpensive/Moderate.* 3811 Soco Road (828-926-3962 or 800-752-6230). This 50-room motel is located in the center of Maggie Valley. The rooms feature a microwave and a refrigerator. A pool and a hot tub are also available.

Comfort Inn. *Inexpensive/Moderate.* Soco Road (828-926-9106 or 800-228-5150). This inn is deluxe by budget-hotel standards. The 67 rooms, some with Jacuzzis, are large. Continental breakfast is included.

Inns and Bed-and-Breakfast Guest Houses

The Cataloochee Ranch. *Deluxe.* Off U.S. 19 near the entrance to Ghost Town in the Sky (828-926-1401 or 800-868-1401). Located atop a mountain overlooking Maggie Valley, this is a special place with spectacular eye-level views of the mountaintops. You'll enjoy attentive service in a rustic but well-appointed lodge. There are 22 units (in seven cabins and two lodges) with pine paneling and quilts on the beds. Horseback riding is the prime activity here, but hiking trails and trout fishing are also available. Rocking on the porch or sitting before the fireplace in the lodge are popular as well. Hefty country-style breakfasts and dinners are served from April through November and are included in the room rate.

The Laurels. *Moderate.* Carley Road off N.C. 209 in Lake Junaluska (828-456-7186). This small inn has three guest rooms, one with a private bath. The house is decorated with antiques, many of them made locally. The refinished heartpine floors provide an air of elegance. A full breakfast is offered daily.

Smokey Shadows Lodge. *Inexpensive/Moderate.* 1.5 miles up the mountain off U.S. 19, by the ski area (828-926-0001). This primitive-style lodge has 12 chestnut-paneled rooms and ceilings of unpeeled log beams. A separate cabin sleeps six. A long porch extends across the back of the building and offers a view of another mountain peak. Meals, not included in the room rate, are country gourmet—you'll not go hungry here. The lodge is open year-round.

Restaurants

Maggie Valley Resort and Country Club. *Moderate/Expensive.* A half-mile west of the intersection of U.S. 276 and U.S. 19 (828-926-1616). This is as upscale as you'll find in Maggie Valley, and it's nice indeed. The restaurant has a sweeping view of the mountains; one whole wall is a window. It serves regional specialties such as mountain trout and well-prepared standard fare such as prime rib, New York strip steak, and chicken. The restaurant is open daily for breakfast and dinner. The pub located in the club is open for lunch. Reservations are necessary for dinner.

J. Arthur's Restaurant. *Inexpensive/Moderate.* Soco Road (828-926-1817). J. Arthur's welcomes families in its big, rambling, ranchlike building. Prime rib and steak are the specialties, but there are some surprises such as a Gorgonzola cheese salad. Kids will find a range of hamburgers and sandwiches to their liking. The restaurant is open for dinner daily in the summer and Wednesday through Saturday in the winter.

Waynesville

Waynesville is a pleasant little town. It doesn't have a manufactured attraction like Ghost Town in the Sky to put it on the map, but it enjoys the spillover from the popular spots in the area. There are many people who enjoy coming to Waynesville just to experience a small, quiet mountain town that has a drugstore with a soda fountain.

Among the charms of Waynesville are its many street festivals in the summer. You can enjoy a variety of entertainments at these outdoor celebrations, from parades to dance exhibitions to food to crafts. This may be a place you'll visit to get away from the crowds of Cherokee or Maggie Valley, but end up staying longer than you expect.

ACCESS:
Waynesville is located at the intersection of U.S. 74 and U.S. 276.

VISITOR INFORMATION:
Contact the Greater Haywood County Chamber of Commerce, 107 Woodland Drive, P.O. Drawer 600, Waynesville, N.C. 28786 (828-456-3021 or 800-334-9036).

The *Enterprise Mountaineer* is published three times a week. It produces a tabloid of regional activities and advertising called *Adventure in the Smokies.*

Attractions

Downtown is about two blocks of low-rise buildings that haven't suffered the indignity of renewal. However, the downtown area has revitalized itself over the last few years. Visitors will find a nice selection of gift shops and art galleries, as well as a bakery, restaurants, craft studios, and an assortment of other stores.

Museum of North Carolina Handicrafts, at 307 Shelton Street, houses a collection of pottery, porcelain, baskets, woodcarvings, and turned bowls in a historic house with a two-tiered porch and chimneys of handmade brick. The museum has a gift shop that features a variety of crafts. The hours are seasonal, so call before you visit. Admission is charged. For information, call 828-452-1551.

Seasonal Events

Smoky Mountain Fall Days, held during the months of September and October, feature a different activity and festival nearly every day in the towns of Waynesville, Maggie Valley, Canton, and Clyde.

Festivities include the Smoky Mountain Folk Festival, the High Country Quilt Show, and the Church Street Arts and Crafts Show. For information, call 828-926-7538 or 800-334-9036, or look them up on the Web at http://www.smokeymountains.net\html\fall.

Folkmoot USA, held during July, is a 10-day festival of international dancing with guest groups from all over the world. Many performances are held in Waynesville. For information, call 828-452-2997.

Side Trips

See *Great Smoky Mountains National Park*
See *The Blue Ridge Parkway*
Dillsboro—See *Franklin: Side Trips*

Accommodations

Waynesville Country Club Inn. *Expensive*. Country Club Road (828-452-2258). This is the town's most elegant lodging. Densely wooded mountains rise behind the three-story fieldstone inn, which was built in the 1920s and is centered around a 27-hole golf course. The inn has 92 luxurious guest rooms and a villa. It also has tennis courts and a heated outdoor pool. The wood-paneled dining room is open for all three meals. In-season rates include breakfast and dinner; rates are lower off-season.

Oak Park Inn. *Inexpensive*. 314 South Main Street (828-456-5328). This brick-faced strip motel is angled away from the street so you don't hear traffic. It has 41 pleasant rooms, some with kitchens.

Inns and Bed-and-Breakfast Guest Houses

The Swag. *Deluxe*. Hemphill Road off N.C. 276 (828-926-0430). The Swag has earned a reputation as one of the mountains' most exclusive inns. Located on top of a private mountain, the rustic inn is made of hand-hewn logs taken from original Appalachian structures, including a century-old church. Visitors can take advantage of the private entrance to Great Smoky Mountains National Park, use the indoor racquetball court, take a swim in the private spring-fed pond, or just relax in a hammock on the Swag's secluded 250 acres. Be sure to ask about the special programs offered throughout the summer. The Swag is open from May through mid-November.

Balsam Mountain Inn. *Expensive*. A half-mile from the intersection of U.S. 23/74 and the Blue Ridge Parkway (828-456-9498). Opened in 1908 to serve the highest railway depot east of the Rockies, this restored National Historic Place has beautiful mountain views from its two-tiered porch. The 50 rooms have private baths, and suites are available. Guests enjoy the 2,000-volume library, the card and puzzle room, and the spacious lobby with two fireplaces, wicker furniture, and Oriental rugs. There are telephones in the rooms, but there isn't one TV in the entire inn. The room rates include a full country breakfast. The inn's restaurant features breakfast and dinner Monday through Saturday; all three meals are offered on Sunday.

The Yellow House. *Expensive/Deluxe.* 89 Oakview Drive, off Plott Creek Road at Oakview (800-563-1236 or http://www.bbonline.com/n.c./yellowhouse/). This inn is pure starlight and moon dust in the mountains. Each of the six guest rooms has a private bath, a fireplace, and a wet bar or refrigerator. When not nestled away in their individually decorated rooms, guests can enjoy one of the balconies, the veranda, or the library. Outdoors on the inn's 2½ acres is a lily pond with a footbridge. A gourmet breakfast is served on the veranda, in the dining room, or in your bedroom. A 50 percent deposit is required for a reservation, and children under 12 are not allowed. A two-night stay is required on weekends, holidays, and during the month of October.

Ten Oaks. *Moderate*. 224 Love Lane (828-452-4373). This charming bed-and-breakfast has two guest rooms and two suites, each with its own sitting area, fireplace, and private bath. The large front porch is perfect for rocking and taking in the mountain views. Ten Oaks is open year round. Rates include breakfast and an afternoon refreshment. MasterCard and Visa are accepted.

The Snuggery. *Moderate*. 419 North Main Street (828-456-3660, 800-409-4776, or http://www.snuggery.com). This bed-and-breakfast is located only a few blocks from the downtown area, making it a pleasant place to stay during the city's festivals and fairs. Some rooms have private baths. Rates include a full breakfast. For an extra charge, the Snuggery will pack an excellent picnic lunch to take along on your journeys through the mountains.

Restaurants

Lomo's Bakery and Cafe/Lomo Grill. *Moderate/Expensive.* 44 Church Street (828-452-5222). Located in downtown Waynesville, this restaurant has received sparkling reviews for its unique Italian and Mediterranean cuisine. The interior has a distinctly Mediterranean feel, and the service is impeccable. Lunch and dinner are served downstairs in the bakery Monday through Saturday, and dinner is offered upstairs Wednesday through Saturday.

Bogart's. *Inexpensive/Moderate.* 303 South Main Street (828-452-1313). This casual restaurant and tavern gets lively at night. The rustic interior is highlighted by stained-glass windows. There's a good selection of burgers and sandwiches, plus entrées of rainbow trout, stir-fried chicken, veal Parmesan, and sirloin tips. Lunch and dinner are served daily.

Mast Candy Barrel. *Inexpensive.* 55 North Main Street (828-452-0075). Though not a true restaurant, this place will more than satisfy your sweet tooth. The old-fashioned soda fountain draws customers in not only for a refreshing cold drink but also for a sense of nostalgia. You'll feel like a kid again, enjoying floats and delving into the candy bins.

Appendix

The following pages contain a collection of key facts and phone numbers that should help answer travel queries and make it easier to plan a North Carolina vacation.

State Agencies

North Carolina Division of Travel and Tourism
301 North Wilmington Street
Raleigh, N.C. 27601
(919-733-4171 or 800-VISIT NC)

This should be your first contact for further information about North Carolina. The tourism office provides state maps and several useful publications. It publishes a full-color booklet (over 150 pages) listing accommodations, campgrounds, events occurring around the state, and state parks and historic sites. The booklet also contains a free map. If you stop by the Raleigh office, you can pick up free brochures for many attractions statewide.

Coastal Management Division
(information about regional-beach access facilities)
2728 Capitol Boulevard
Raleigh, N.C. 27687
(919-733-2293)

Historic Sites Section
North Carolina Division of
Archives and History
532 North Wilmington Street
Raleigh, N.C. 27604
(919-733-7862)

North Carolina Aquariums
417 North Blount Street
Raleigh, N.C. 27601
(919-733-2290)

North Carolina Department of Transportation
1 South Wilmington Street
Raleigh, N.C. 27601
(919-733-2520)

North Carolina Division of Forest Resources
512 North Salisbury Street
Raleigh, N.C. 27604
(919-733-2162)

North Carolina Division of Parks and Recreation
512 North Salisbury Street
Raleigh, N.C. 27604
(919-733-4181)

North Carolina Wildlife Commission
512 North Salisbury Street
Raleigh, N.C. 27604
(919-733-7291)

General Sources

Blue Ridge Parkway
Superintendent
400 BB&T Building
Asheville, N.C. 28801
(828-271-4779)

**Cape Hatteras
National Seashore**
Superintendent
Route 1, Box 675
Manteo, N.C. 27954
(252-473-2113)

**Cape Lookout
National Seashore**
Superintendent
131 Charles Street
Harkers Island, N.C. 28531
(252-728-2250)

Cherokee Visitors Center
P.O. Box 460
Main Street
Cherokee, N.C. 28719
(828-497-9195 or 800-438-1601)

**Great Smoky
Mountains National Park**
Superintendent
107 Park Headquarters Road
Gatlinburg, Tenn. 37738
(423-436-5615 or 423-436-1200)

**National Forests
in North Carolina**
Superintendent
160 Zillicoa Street
Asheville, N.C. 28802
(828-257-4200)

**North Carolina
Bed-and-Breakfast
and Inns Association**
P.O. Box 1077
Asheville, N.C. 28802
(800-849-5392)
www.bbonline.com/nc/ncbbi

**North Carolina Campground
Owners Association**
1418 Aversboro Road
Garner, N.C. 27529
(919-779-5709)

**North Carolina
High Country Host**
(covering areas listed in the High
Country section)
1700 Blowing Rock Road
Boone, N.C. 28607
(828-264-1299 or 800-438-7500)

**North Carolina
Hotel and Motel Association**
P.O. Box 30457
Raleigh, N.C. 27622
(919-786-9730)

**North Carolina
Ski Areas Association**
P.O. Box 106
Blowing Rock, N.C. 28605
(828-295-7828)

**Smoky Mountain
Host of North Carolina**
4437 Georgia Road
Franklin, N.C. 28734
(800-432-HOST)

**Travel Council
of North Carolina**
4101 Lake Boone Trail
Suite 201
Raleigh, N.C. 27607
(919-787-5181, ext. 242)

North Carolina Welcome Centers

I-77 South
P.O. Box 410724
Charlotte, N.C. 28241-0724
(704-588-2660)

I-77 North
P.O. Box 1066
Dobson, N.C. 27017
(336-320-2181)

I-85 South
P.O. Box 830
Kings Mountain, N.C. 28086
(704-937-7861)

I-85 North
P.O. Box 156
Norlina, N.C. 27563
(252-456-3236)

I-95 South
P.O. Box 518
Rowland, N.C. 28383
(910-422-8314)

I-95 North
P.O. Box 52
Roanoke Rapids, N.C. 27870
(252-537-9836)

I-26
P.O. Box 249
Columbus, N.C. 28722
(828-894-2120)

I-40 West
P.O. Box 809
Waynesville, N.C. 28786
(828-627-6206)

State Historic Sites

Alamance Battleground
5803 N.C. 62 South
Burlington, N.C. 27215
(336-227-4785)

Aycock Birthplace
P.O. Box 207
Fremont, N.C. 27830
(919-242-5581)

Historic Bath
P.O. Box 148
Bath, N.C. 27808
(252-923-3971)

Bennett Place
4409 Bennett Memorial Road
Durham, N.C. 27705
(919-383-4345)

Bentonville Battleground
5466 Harper House Road
Four Oaks, N.C. 27524
(910-594-0789)

Brunswick Town
8884 St. Philips Road SE
Winnabow, N.C. 28479
(910-371-6613)

CSS *Neuse*
P.O. Box 3043
Kinston, N.C. 28502
(919-522-2091)

Charlotte Hawkins Brown
  Memorial
P.O. Box B
Sedalia, N.C. 27342
(336-449-6515)

Duke Homestead
2828 Duke Homestead Road
Durham, N.C. 27705
(919-477-5498)

Historic Edenton
P.O. Box 474
Edenton, N.C. 27932
(252-482-2637)

Elizabeth II
1 Festival Park
Manteo, N.C. 27954
(252-475-1500)

Fort Dobbs
438 Fort Dobbs Road
Statesville, N.C. 28625
(704-873-5866)

Fort Fisher
P.O. Box 169
Kure Beach, N.C. 28449
(910-458-5538)

Historic Halifax
P.O. Box 406
Halifax, N.C. 27839
(252-583-7191)

Horn Creek Living History Farm
320 Hauser Road
Pinnacle, N.C. 27043
(336-325-2298)

House in the Horseshoe
324 Alston House Road
Sanford, N.C. 27330
(910-947-2051)

North Carolina Transportation
   Museum
P.O. Box 165
Spencer, N.C. 28159
(704-636-2889)

North Carolina State Capitol
1 East Edenton Street
Raleigh, N.C. 27601-2807
(919-733-4994)

Polk Memorial
P.O. Box 475
Pineville, N.C. 28134
(704-889-7145)

Reed Gold Mine
9621 Reed Mine Road
Stanfield, N.C. 28163
(704-721-4653)

Somerset Place
2572 Lake Shore Road
Creswell, N.C. 27928
(252-797-4560)

Historic Stagville
P.O. Box 71217
Durham, N.C. 27722
(919-620-0120)

Thomas Wolfe Memorial
52 North Market Street
Asheville, N.C. 28802
(828-253-8304)

Town Creek Indian Mound
509 Town Creek Mound Road
Mount Gilead, N.C. 27306
(910-439-6802)

Tryon Palace
610 Pollock Street
New Bern, N.C. 28562
(252-514-4900)

Vance Birthplace
911 Reems Creek Road
Weaverville, N.C. 28787
(828-645-6706)

Outdoor Recreation

Most of these natural areas are mentioned under their locations in the guidebook. The index will tell you exactly where. This is a quick-reference telephone listing.

National Recreational Areas

Blue Ridge Parkway
(828-271-4779)

Great Smoky Mountains
National Park
(423-436-1200)

Nanatahala National Forest
(828-257-4200)

Pisgah National Forest
(828-877-3265)

Uwharrie National Forest
(910-576-6391)

Cape Hatteras National Seashore
(252-473-2113)

Cape Lookout National Seashore
(252-728-2250)

Croatan National Forest
(252-638-5628)

State Parks and Recreational Areas

Boone's Cave
(Lexington)
(704-982-4402)

Carolina Beach
(910-458-8206)

Cliffs of the Neuse
(Goldsboro)
(919-778-6234)

Crowders Mountain
(Gastonia)
(704-853-5375)

Duke Power
(Statesville)
(704-528-6350)

Eno River
(Durham)
(919-383-1686)

Falls Lake
(Raleigh)
(919-676-1027)

Fort Fisher
(Wilmington)
(910-458-8206)

Fort Macon
(Atlantic Beach)
(252-726-3775)

Goose Creek
(Washington)
(252-923-2191)

Hammocks Beach
(Swansboro)
(910-326-4881)

Hanging Rock
(Danbury)
(336-593-8480)

Jockey's Ridge
(Nags Head)
(252-441-7132)

Jones Lake
(Elizabethtown)
(910-588-4550)

Jordan Lake
(Durham)
(919-362-0586)

Kerr Lake
(Henderson)
(252-438-7791)

Lake James
(Marion)
(828-652-5047)

Lake Waccamaw
(910-646-4748)

Lumber River
(Fairmont)
(910-628-9844)

Medoc Mountain
(Hollister)
(252-445-2280)

Merchants Millpond
(Gatesville)
(252-357-1191)

Morrow Mountain
(Albemarle)
(704-982-4402)

Mount Jefferson
(Jefferson)
(910-246-9653)

Mount Mitchell
(Burnsville)
(828-675-4611)

New River
(Jefferson)
(336-982-2587)

Pettigrew
(Creswell)
(252-797-4475)

Pilot Mountain
(Winston-Salem)
(336-325-2355)

Raven Rock
(Lillington)
(910-893-4888)

Singletary Lake
(Elizabethtown)
(910-669-2928)

South Mountains
(Morganton)
(828-433-4772)

Stone Mountain
(Roaring Gap)
(336-957-8185)

Theodore Roosevelt
(Atlantic Beach)
(252-726-3775)

Waynesborough
(Goldsboro)
(919-731-5680)

Weymouth Woods
(Southern Pines)
(910-692-2167)

William B. Umstead
(Raleigh)
(919-571-4170)

Fishing and Hunting

You can get a fishing or hunting permit from any license agent, of which there are many. Look for them at hardware or sporting-goods stores or K-mart stores. Some licenses expire June 30, while others expire one year from their date of purchase.

For further information, contact the Wildlife Resources Commission, 512 North Salisbury Street, Raleigh, NC 27611 (919-733-7291).

Resident fishing license—$20
   daily permit—$5
   trout license—$10
Nonresident fishing license—$30
   daily permit—$10
   three-day permit—$15
Saltwater recreational fishing does
not require a license.

Resident sportsman license—$40
   hunting license—$15
   big-game permit—$10
   trapping license—$25
Nonresident sportsman
   license—$40
   six-day hunting license—$25
   big-game permit—$40

Bicycling

To help cyclists find safe and interesting places to ride, the Bicycle Program of the North Carolina Department of Transportation has identified primary and secondary roads that are relatively safe for cycling because of low traffic volume and good roadway conditions. Various routes encompassing over 3,000 miles have been mapped, and others will be available in the future.

Sample routes:

Mountains to Sea—700 miles from Murphy to Manteo
Piedmont Spur—200-miles east to west route
Carolina Connection—200-mile north-south route
Ports of Call—300 miles in the coastal area
Cape Fear Run—160 miles from Raleigh to the Cape Fear area
Ocracoke Option—175 miles from the Wilson area to the Cedar Island ferry
Southern Highlands—120 miles from the Blue Ridge Parkway to Lincolnton

Maps and tour routes are available for selected local areas.

To order one or more of these free guides, contact The Bicycle Program, NCDOT, P.O. Box 25201, Raleigh, N.C. 27611 (919-733-2804).

Aid for Handicapped Travelers

Access North Carolina is an excellent travel guide for disabled persons. Providing accessibility information for virtually every tourist attraction in the state, it evaluates parking lots, entrances, interior and exterior sites, water fountains, and restrooms. It also mentions special tours and access for blind and deaf persons.

It is available at no charge from the North Carolina Division of Travel and Tourism, 301 North Wilmington Street, Raleigh, N.C. 27601 (800-VISIT NC or 919-733-4171)

Hotel/Motel Toll-Free Numbers

These numbers may be called from anywhere in the continental United States. Consult your local telephone directory for regional listings.

Best Western International
(800-528-1234)

Comfort Inns
(800-228-5150)

Courtyard by Marriott
(800-321-2211)

Days Inn
(800-325-2525)

Econo Lodges of America
(800-446-6900)

Hampton Inn
(800-426-7866)

Hilton Hotel Corporation
(800-445-8667)

Holiday Inns, Inc.
(800-465-4329)

Howard Johnson
(800-446-4656)

Hyatt Corporation
(800-228-9000)

Marriott Hotels
(800-228-9290)

Quality Inns
(800-228-5151)

Radisson Hotel Corporation
(800-333-3333)

Ramada Inns
(800-228-2828)

Red Roof Inns
(800-843-7663)

Renaissance Hotels and Resorts
(800-468-3571)

Sheraton Hotels and Inns
(800-325-3535)

Car Rental Toll-Free Numbers

Avis Reservations Center
(800-831-2847)

Budget Rent-A-Car
(800-527-0700)

Dollar Rent-A-Car
(800-421-6868)

Hertz Corporation
(800-654-3131)

National Car Rental
(800-227-7368)

Thrifty Car Rental
(800-367-2277)

U-Haul Equipment Rental
(800-468-4285)

North Carolina State Ferries

Reservations are recommended on the toll ferries along the Outer Banks. Schedules are shown below. For more information or reservations on the North Carolina ferry system, call the numbers listed below or 800-BY FERRY.

Southport	Fort Fisher	Ocracoke	Swan Quarter
March 25 - November 17 Departure Times		**Year-Round Departure Times**	
5:30 A.M.	6:15 A.M.	6:30 A.M.	*7:00 A.M.
7:00	7:45	12:30 P.M.	9:30 A.M.
8:30	–		
9:15	9:15	*4:00 P.M.	4:00 P.M.

Crossing - 2½ Hours
Capacity - 28 cars
Fare - One Way

Pedestrian	$1.00
Bicycle Rider	$2.00
Motorcycle	$10.00
Vehicle and/or combination less than 20'	$10.00
Vehicle and/or combination 20' to 40'	$20.00
Vehicle and/or combination up to 55'	$30.00

Southport / Fort Fisher March 25 - November 17 Departure Times (continued):

Southport	Fort Fisher
10:00	10:00
10:45	10:45
11:30	11:30
12:15 P.M.	12:15 P.M.
1:00	1:00
1:45	1:45
2:30	2:30
3:15	3:15
4:00	4:00
4:45	4:45
–	5:30
6:15	7:00
7:45	8:30

Ocracoke Terminal   252-928-3841
Swan Quarter Terminal   252-926-1111

November 18 - March 24 Departure Times

Southport	Fort Fisher
5:30 A.M.	6:15 A.M.
7:00	7:45
8:30	9:15
10:00	10:45
11:30	12:15 P.M.
1:00 P.M.	1:45
2:30	3:15
4:00	4:45

Crossing - 30 Minutes
Capacity - 38 cars
Fare - One Way

Pedestrian	$.50
Bicycle Rider	$1.00
Motorcycle	$3.00
Vehicle and/or combination less than 20'	$3.00
Vehicle and/or combination over 20'	$6.00

* Additional departures: Memorial Day thru Labor Day

370 Appendix

Hatteras	Ocracoke	Cedar Island	Ocracoke
May 1 - October 31 Departure Times		**May 20 - September 30 Departure Times**	
5:00 A.M.	5:00 A.M.	7:00 A.M.	7:00 A.M.
6:00	6:00	8:15	–
7:00	7:00	9:30	9:30
7:30	8:00	–	*10:00
8:00	8:30	–	10:45
8:30	9:00	Noon	Noon
9:00	9:30	1:00 P.M.	–
9:30	10:00	1:45	–
10:00	10:30	3:00	3:00 P.M.
10:30	11:00	–	4:30
11:00	11:30	6:00	6:00
11:30	Noon	8:30	8:30
Noon	12:30 P.M.	**April 8 - 21 May 6- May 19 October 1 - October 31 Departure Times**	
12:30 P.M.	1:00		
1:00	1:30		
1:30	2:00	7:00 A.M.	7:00 A.M.
2:00	2:30	9:30	9:30
2:30	3:00	Noon	Noon
3:00	3:30	3:00 P.M.	3:00 P.M.
3:30	4:00	6:00	6:00
4:00	4:30	8:30	8:30
4:30	5:00		
5:00	5:30	**November 1-April 7 April 22 - May 5 Departure Times**	
5:30	6:00		
6:00	6:30		
6:30	7:00		
7:00	8:00	7:00 A.M.	7:00 A.M.
8:00	9:00	10:00	10:00
9:00	10:00	1:00 P.M.	1:00 P.M.
10:00	11:00	4:00	4:00
11:00	Midnight		
Midnight	———	**Crossing - 2¼ Hours Capacity - 50 cars Fare - One Way Same as Ocracoke-Swan Quarter**	

November 1 - April 30 Departure Times

Leaves Hatteras and Ocracoke every hour from 5 A.M. to midnight

Crossing - 40 Minutes Capacity - 30 cars Fare - Free

Ocracoke Terminal   252-928-3841 Cedar Island Terminal   252-225-3551

Cherry Branch	Minnesott		Aurora	Bayview
Year-Round Departure Times			**Year-Round Departure Times**	
Ferries cross approx. every 20 minutes between 5:47 A.M. and 8:27 A.M.			6:15 A.M.	5:30 A.M.
			8:30	7:00
8:45 A.M.	8:45 A.M.		9:45	9:10
9:15	9:15		11:15	10:30
9:45	9:45		12:45 P.M.	Noon
10:15	10:15		2:15	1:30 P.M.
10:45	10:45		4:45	3:15
11:15	11:15		6:15	5:30
11:45	11:45		8:30	7:00
12:15 P.M.	12:15 P.M.		10:00	9:15
1:15	1:15		12:30 A.M.	11:00
1:45	1:45		**Crossing - 30 Minutes** **Capacity - 18 cars** **Fare - Free**	
2:15	2:15			
2:45	2:45			
			Currituck	**Knotts Island**
			Year-Round Departure Times	
Ferries cross approx. every 20 minutes between 3:15 P.M. and 5:59 P.M.			6:00 A.M.	7:00 A.M.
			9:00	10:00
6:45 P.M.	6:15 P.M.		11:00	Noon
7:45	7:15		1:00 P.M.	2:00 P.M.
8:45	8:15		3:30	4:30
9:45	9:15		5:30	6:30
10:45	10:15		**Crossing - 45 Minutes** **Capacity - 18 cars** **Fare - Free**	
11:45	11:15			
12:45 A.M.	12:15 A.M.			
	1:15			
Crossing - 20 Minutes **Capacity - 30 cars** **Fare - Free**				

Liquor

Laws regarding liquor sales vary greatly among counties through-out the state. In some counties, restaurant sales are forbidden, while package sales are allowed. Some restaurants in dry counties are allowed to sell wine but not spirits; others have brown-bag licenses, and customers may bring their own liquor. In all the major cities, liquor by the drink is available. If you are traveling a considerable distance, you are almost certain to encounter a change of regulation.

If you want to be sure to have alcohol on your journey, you might want to take your own, but keep it locked in the trunk of your car; it is illegal for any person to possess an open container of beer, wine, or liquor in a moving vehicle on the highways of North Carolina.

The legal drinking age in the state is 21 for all alcoholic beverages. Package store sales and individual drinks in restaurants are available Monday through Saturday from 7 A.M. until 1 A.M. and Sunday from 1 P.M. to 1 A.M.

North Carolina Climatic Summary

Average Temperature (F)

	January	July
Asheville	40	73.5
Boone	35	70
Charlotte	41	78.5
Winston-Salem	38.5	77.5
Raleigh	41	79
Manteo	45.5	79
Wilmington	46.5	79

INDEX